THE **FITTINGNESS** OF THE **INCARNATION**

DAVID BRAINE

THE **FITTINGNESS** OF THE **INCARNATION**

ESSAYS IN ANALYTIC THOMISTIC PHILOSOPHY AND THEOLOGY

EDITED BY

BRANDON DAHM
DANIEL DE HAAN
ANDREW WILLARD JONES
TONY SCHMITZ

FOREWORD BY

THOMAS JOSEPH WHITE, OP

The Catholic University of America Press
Washington, D.C.

The paper used in this publication meets the minimum

requirements of American National Standards for

Information Science—Permanence of Paper

for Printed Library Materials, ANSI Z39.48-1992.

∞

Cataloging-in-Publication Data is available from the Library of Congress

ISBN (hardcover): 978-0-8132-3927-9

ISBN (eBook): 978-0-8132-3861-6

ISBN (paperback): 978-0-8132-3860-9

CONTENTS

FOREWORD

When David Braine was thirty-seven, he was in a serious car accident that left him paralyzed from the chest down for the rest of his life. Those who knew David could attest that his life was extraordinary, given what he accomplished humanly and believed and practiced spiritually in the wake of this life upheaval. He was a brilliant philosopher, with a tenaciously questioning mind. He was also a devout Catholic, who was both faithfully prayerful and attentive to contemporary ethical dilemmas. He pursued longstanding conversations with a wide network of fellow scholars and graduate students across a variety of disciplines, always questioning, coming to conclusions, and seeking to understand more, while being humane, funny, gentle, and kind.

David inherited from Ludwig Wittgenstein, and from Anglo-American philosophy more generally, a lifelong interest in the philosophy of language. Following Elizabeth Anscombe, he wed this interest to a deep engagement with Thomas Aquinas, read frequently in conversation with contemporary philosophy and the modern sciences. In many respects, his thought is marked by hylomorphism, the theoretical acknowledgment that the body and the soul are co-principles of human nature. Human persons are spiritual animals, such that the organic body and the senses play a role even in our distinctively human spiritual acts.

This claim has many consequences, and David's philosophical and theological writings were often marked by the exploration of such. His approach to metaphysics generally, and to philosophical knowledge of God in particular, was marked by the realization that human beings learn through their senses and seek to derive ultimate explanations in a gradual way, by moving from what is more proximate in our experience to what is more primal in itself. Knowledge of God is not given a priori but sought logically and inferentially by the considerations of the human condition and the nature of the world.

In his philosophy of language, David immersed himself in linguistic and grammatical theory, paleontology and evolutionary theory, and contemporary philosophy of mind. He argued that there is something irreducibly spiritual to the way that human animals communicate with one another, something that refers us ineluctably to the reality of the spiritual soul present in each human person. Likewise in his reflections on the Incarnation, which one finds important contributions to in this volume, a central concern is the reality of God's absolute revelation in the flesh. What does it mean ontologically to say that God has become human, and if God truly has done so, how is it that this revelation of God in our human condition can be of universal significance for the whole human race? These are associated concerns. How does the spiritual animal that is man conjecture over the sense of his life, and seek to discover its purpose progressively by the consideration of the folds of the cosmos, the layers of human historical development, and the nature of human reasoning and communication, all the while tending toward questions regarding God and his self-revelation in our bodily cosmos?

Of course, the most remarkable thing is that David himself made this voyage daily from his chair, illustrating in a wonderful way the old Aristotelian adage that "the mind in a certain way may become all things." That is to say, the intellect goes out through the body and the senses, even from within very serious constraints of the human condition. The mind doggedly seeks the truth about the world, its natural configurations, history of structures, possible origins, and potential horizons of purpose. From within the limitations of his own human condition, David studied and wrote about cosmology, human biological origins, metaphysics, the nature of the human person, the final end of man, and the mystery of God. In doing so, he reflected back to us from within his unique constraints, something of what is best and most noble in human beings.

Consequently, it is both happy and fitting that some of the most substantive final papers of David Braine are published in this volume. They are a window into his vivid life of trust, truth seeking, and humanness. We should be grateful to the editors, as we can also be to the author, whose prayers and philosophical friendship we still count upon, as we hope he now sees things from a yet higher and even more insightful perspective.

Fr. Thomas Joseph White, OP
Thomistic Institute, Angelicum, Rome
September 14, Feast of the Triumph of the Cross

INTRODUCTION

During his life, David Braine published three major books, about twenty articles, and a couple of smaller booklets, but these did not exhaust his projects. In his will, David directed his trustees to encourage the publication of two books, one on the Incarnation and one on the realism of St. Thomas, as well as articles on a variety of topics. The description of his books in his will is worth noting:

> First, a book on the Incarnation, its conformity with the human situation in the Universe, nature, condition and destiny, on behalf of the whole cosmos, the reasons for belief in it, how Nestorian tendencies undermine it, how the workings of providence are to be explained, the historicity of the Gospels, and the character and the Church as its current flowering on Earth: and second, a book on the Realism of St. Thomas, the empirical roots of the inductions underlying philosophical knowledge of the existence of God, the significance of the reality of time and the non-Platonic character of God's eternity, and how the basis of ethics he offers is realistic.

Unfortunately, at the time of David's death in 2017, the books had been more planned than written. Yet, the articles included in this book provide a glimpse of what would have been and reveal some of David's insights into those topics.

The two chapters of Part I of the book introduce David's life and major works. Chapter 1 is a biography written by David's long-time friend Deacon Tony Schmitz. We learn about David's education and intellectual development, his accident and how it changed his life, how he engaged in public life through his writing, and, from some wonderful vignettes contributed by friends and caretakers, his humor and friendship. Through learning his history and stories from friends, we truly get to know David as a human person. In Chapter 2, Daniel De Haan takes us on a tour through David's major works, his three monographs. David's books are large and dense, and De Haan helpfully points out not just their main ideas but emphasizes the insights that hopefully continue to contribute.

The two philosophical essays of part two exhibit David at work sketching an Aristotelian critical epistemology and a presentation of Aquinas's natural theology that can stand on its own metaphysical principles without appealing to the principle of sufficient reason. As with his three philosophical monographs, the strengths of Braine's studies are found in his profound insights, his distillation of captivating but problematic positions and his incisive criticisms of them. So, despite the somewhat circuitous prose and inaccurate or highly misleading ascriptions of positions to individuals—such as Gilson, Lonergan, Scotus, Avicenna, and others in these essays—there remain important lessons we need to learn from Braine.

The first essay, "Two Kinds of Critical Philosophy," complements and extends the views he delineated in his 1971 paper on "The Nature of Knowledge." Most of the work is dedicated to the destructive task of confuting the dominant form of critical philosophy that he associates with rationalism, empiricism, and transcendentalism. Braine delineates five "intimately inter-connected" epistemological preconceptions that are "at the root of the false kind of critical philosophy." He argues that they rest upon "arbitrary diktat" which lead to "crippling restrictions upon the possibility of argument" making knowledge and criticism of knowledge impossible. This is because these capricious *a priori* straightjackets result in gross misdescriptions of the logical procedures, reliance on others, integration of experience and understanding, and the abiding potential to entertain critical objections at any point that comprise our pursuit of knowledge.

The rest of this essay is directed toward the constructive task of articulating an Aristotelian critical philosophy, one which recognizes the central place of dialectic for establishing principles and knowledge itself. Indeed, Braine's critical philosophy of knowledge rests on the Aristotelian insight that the intellect by its very nature is open and free "to interrogate or raise objection to a proof at any point, not merely in regard to its premises and presuppositions, but even in regard to its principles of method." Knowledge cannot be privately secured by a lone intellect, for "if a claim to knowledge is actually true, then any such proof must itself be capable of standing up to examination, and not only the knower's own examination at a time when he judges that he has knowledge, but to public examination." Braine concludes with some of the most illuminating points of this essay by distinguishing the dominant but problematic conception of the *a priori* with a sense of the *a priori* central to his Aristotelian critical philosophy; a point that merits quotation.

> Philosophy is, I believe, very much concerned with the *a priori* or non-empirical, if by this is meant the categorial or structural statements presupposed in ordinary statements of particular experience. It is also, I believe, very much concerned with the *a priori* or nonempirical, if by this is meant that knowledge which proceeds from the understanding, and which is independent of all that empirical knowledge which it is merely accidental to human nature that man should possess. Indeed, it is perhaps the *a priori* or nonempirical in this latter sense which constitutes the province of philosophy. But it is, I believe, very little concerned with the almost useless notion of the *a priori* or nonempirical as being that knowledge which is entirely independent of any judgements of experience whatsoever.

Braine's second essay, "The Shape of Natural Theology Without the Principle of Sufficient Reason in St. Thomas Aquinas," commences with a dialectic inspired by Etienne Gilson's criticisms of Thomists who introduced the principle of sufficient reason to defend Aquinas's natural theology, criticisms which Braine endorses. In the first section, Braine defends the Thomist thesis that existence cannot be reduced to a second-order feature of propositions. This is an abbreviated and, in some respects, clearer account of his more detailed arguments in *Reality of Time and the Existence of God* and *Human Language and Understanding*. What distinguishes this essay from those works is his extended engagement with Aquinas's treatment of the logical and real senses of *esse* as well as the concreteness of the *actus essendi* presupposed by the concrete things whose natures ground the powers they exercise in everyday causal commerce with other concrete substances in nature. Braine gives an analytic philosophy tour through Aquinas's *De ente et essentia* argument for the composition of *esse* and *essentia* in all creatures, defends it at length, and contends it is the key to understanding why the existence of the universe is wholly contingent and why this contingency cannot be a mere brute fact. The crux of Aquinas's argument depends on "the principle of the priority of actuality to potentiality," a principle that Braine argues underwrites the demonstrative arguments for God's existence in Aquinas's Five Ways. The concluding section of this extended essay concentrates on explicating and defending Aquinas's first three ways, especially the first way. He draws on Aquinas's *Q.D. De Potentia Dei* and the *Summa Theologiae* to elucidate the reality of secondary causality of creatures that remain totally dependent on the primary causality of God.

In the essays of Part III, which would probably have been included in some form in his book on the Incarnation, Braine offers a penetrating apology for the truth of the real, unique, and efficacious Incarnation of the second person of the Trinity. His aim is to demonstrate how characteristically modern attempts at undermining Christianity's central doctrine are premised on a misunderstanding. They tend to approach the Incarnation as a cramped, limiting doctrine, a doctrine which, if taken literally and maximally, insults the complexity of humanity and indeed of the cosmos itself. Braine, however, articulates in his characteristic thoroughness how orthodox Christology and Trinitarian theology are expansive and not restrictive. He shows how the Incarnation is capable of overcoming objections rooted in appeals to religious pluralism, historicism, or linguistic and cultural relativism, by absorbing them into itself and surpassing them, even outwitting them at their own game. These essays might be read as an extended commentary of St. Paul's assertion that Christ "is the image of the invisible God, the firstborn of all creation, for in him all things were created, in heaven and on earth, visible and invisible." Christ is the savior of all people and all the universe not because of anything particularly special about Western Civilization or even, for that manner, about mankind himself, but because all peoples are always already bound up together in a cosmic drama that includes all of history and all of creation as much as it does the individual biographies of each and every person and their particular relationships with each other and with Christ. Attempts at "saving" peoples of other times and other places, of other cultures, of other faiths (indeed, Braine even speculates about members of other intelligent species) through minimizing or dodging the doctrine of the Incarnation are wholly unnecessary and misguided because all these people are already included in the very fittingness of the Incarnation itself. God became incarnate to save man as man. He took on all of human nature, in all its historical and cultural complexity, so that all humans may call out "Abba, Father."

In the first theological essay, "The Uniqueness of the Incarnation: Why God Once Became Man," Braine articulates a theory of the fittingness of the Incarnation that focuses on the Ascension as its consummation. The Son's human and yet eternal communion with the Father is the unlocking of the possibility of that communion for the rest of humanity. Braine does not understand this in an instrumental manner, however. Rather, because the Incarnation was intended within the original creation, there was built into man from the beginning the possibility of such an elevation of his nature. This possibility was realized in Christ. As Braine explains, "In Jesus there arrived a created capacity for love and knowledge which, while not equal to God's infinity, was somehow proportioned to it in such a way as to allow a perfect expression of his divine sonship in his humanity; and God could not will or bring about the Incarnation without willing and bringing this about." But once a human son of God had been constituted, "it could not be limited, for it is in the created nature or state of man as such that men are brothers in spiritual community with one another, so that to choose to become Incarnate, to become one man alongside others, could not but carry with it the opening of sonship of God to all."

In the next essay, "The Incarnation and Man's Salvation," Braine extends the line of thought presented in the previous essay. Here, he focuses on man's social nature and how the Incarnation works our atonement from within and not from without. He responds to theories of atonement that present Christ's life and death as somehow removing obstacles to salvation, as if the problem of the fall was a problem of an external, legal, or moral sort. Such a conception individualizes salvation and renders the Incarnation, ultimately, arbitrary and disconcerting. But all this is too limiting, too constraining. As Braine succinctly puts it: "Eternal life is more than just the failure to perish everlastingly." Rather, through the Incarnation God "meshes" with humanity as humanity, making possible the elevation of mankind into the life of God.

To understand the fittingness of the Incarnation, one simply must understand "that human beings have been created and constituted by God as social and communal beings." Human beings do not simply have a history; they are historical—in their nature. Their fall was historical and social. So, too, is their redemption. So, too, is the Pentecostal grace, "the spirit of sonship," that flows into the historical Church only after and only through the Incarnation and Ascension. It is through this "receiving of the Spirit of sonship, whereby, through community with the risen, now forever human, Jesus our Lord, we are able to love God uncontrolledly, uninhibitedly, and ultimately to know him directly as in vision."

A particular emphasis of the two first essays is the importance of a proper understanding of the Ascension. Too often, the Ascension is passed over as little more than a fitting conclusion to Christ's Resurrection. Indeed, we too often think of the Ascension as the end of the Incarnation. But, Braine insists, the Ascension is in fact a crucial aspect of the atonement the Incarnation brings about. In the Resurrection, humanity overcomes death; but it is in the Ascension that human nature is elevated into the life of God. Henceforth, Christ as human, as a properly embodied human, is the second person of the Trinity. All of human history, all of human sociality, all of human nature in its vast complexity is included now in the Divine life. As Braine remarks: "I take it that the significance of the Ascension or glorification of Jesus is that in it, Jesus's humanity attained a freedom from restriction appropriate to who he was, a capacity to participate not just in a divine manner, but in a human manner in all the gracious works of the Father." It was, Braine argues, the Ascension that allowed for the efficacy of Pentecost and so the birth of the Church. This is so because it was only through the completion of the "work" of the Incarnation in the Ascension "that human beings can become in a full sense sons and daughters of God. The Holy Spirit is the Spirit of sonship whereby we are made able alongside Jesus, to pray 'Abba, Father'."

In his third essay on the Incarnation, "An Integral Doctrine of the Incarnation Against Dupuis's Religious Pluralism," Braine ostensibly responds to Jacques Dupuis's formulations in favor of religious pluralism. Really, however, he offers a rival understanding of religious pluralism that emerges from within a robust understanding of the historical nature of man. Braine offers a "thick" understanding of inculturation. He concedes that much of modern Christianity's approach to non-Western cultures and religions has been narrow, even bigoted. But this is no justification for collapsing Christianity and so the Incarnation into some generic understanding of "religion." Rather, the Incarnation must be expanded; Christ must be understood in his full "humanness." And the Church must abandon "divine right, absolutist" pretensions and reinsert itself into history.

Braine presents a survey of the historical formation of Incarnational and Trinitarian orthodoxy, of the most fundamental mysteries of the faith, in order to drive the point home. Christ was historical. He entered into a prepared people, into a thick, historical culture. He did this because "he wants human beings to be saved *as human beings,* that is in their intellect and thinking and in their imagination and arts, in their dancing and singing, in their music, art, and architecture, all these being brought together in their expression of love in worship and liturgy." In an analogous way, the Church must enter other cultures, including their religious traditions.

Braine seeks to preserve the dignity and otherness of non-Western cultures even while asserting that the only way to do this is to not merely retain but to double down on the uniqueness and efficaciousness, on the profound fittingness, of the Incarnation. Such an approach is in sharp contrast to attempts such as that of Dupuis which seek religious and cultural reconciliation through a reduction to sameness, normally a sameness rooted in the abandonment of the external for the internal, the abandonment of the bodily for the mental, of the ecclesial for the individualistic. Such a move is the mirror image of Western chauvinism. And it is unnecessary. As Braine convincingly demonstrates, premises of the inculturation "problem" by including them within its profound fittingness.

We have concluded this collection of Braine's theological writings with a brief editorial reflection on why Braine, the philosopher, felt so compelled to delve into the most esoteric of theological mysteries. The suggestion is that his theological work was not an idiosyncratic consequence of his "personal" faith, nor yet some sort of side-show to his philosophical reflections. Rather, Braine's philosophical project always found its foundation in his wonder at being that was grounded ultimately on the analogical tension between the finite creation and the infinite creator, a tension that is at the heart of the incarnational mystery. In a sense, his philosophy was always "about" his theology. Also included in these final reflections is a reproduction of sections from a talk Braine delivered sometime before 2014 in which he explains why he was engaged in his theological project and makes certain preliminary arguments.

In his theological essays, Braine demonstrates a sensitivity to contemporary problems even while powering through them with his relentless and yet kind reasoning. Braine shows how Christ really is the solution, how the Incarnation really is the center of history, of our lives, and of all creation, and how that centrality does not threaten us, but frees us.

* * *

David Braine left directions in his will for two books. Instead of trying to construct these books from pieces here and there, we decided to collect only the best and most complete papers for this single volume. The papers included are Braine's writings and all are previously unpublished. As editors, we started by selecting the papers. Braine left a flash drive with thousands of files without indicating which papers were further along or most important to him. Moreover, most of the papers are found in multiple versions. In each case, we tried to find the most complete and polished version. In no case did the choice affect any major thesis or argument in the paper. Braine has a difficult writing style, and although we erred on the side of leaving the text unchanged, editing the incomplete papers was required. The papers included in this volume, in our judgment, are representative of Braine's thought and, we hope, are a few steps closer to what he intended them to be.

The Editors

PART I

LIFE AND WORKS

CHAPTER 1

BIOGRAPHY OF DAVID BRAINE (1940–2017)

ONE SUNDAY AFTERNOON

It all began with an invitation. Would I care to climb Bennachie that Sunday afternoon? The year must have been 1972 or 1973, not very long after Gail (my wife) and I had arrived in Aberdeen.

I enjoyed hill walking in those days, so I accepted his friendly invitation and we set off, after Mass that Sunday, hiking up the slopes of Bennachie (*Beinn Na Ciche* in Scottish Gaelic meaning the "hill of the breast.") This is an iconic hill range in the North-East of Scotland, nineteen miles north-west of Aberdeen. Made up of several peaks, the highest of which, Oxen Craig, is 1,732 feet high, well short of a Munro (3000 feet), or even a Corbett (2500 feet). The more prominent summit, appropriately named Mither Tap (Mother's Breast), affords an astonishingly splendid view of the surrounding area all the way west to the Grampian Mountains and east to the North Sea. David often clambered up those slopes of a weekend, usually with a single companion, student, or colleague.

By the time we reached the Mither Tap summit, I had discovered that we shared a love of philosophy—he an eagle,

I a sparrow; that, after reading Physics and History at Magdalen College, Oxford, he had studied under Gilbert Ryle, editor of the then prestigious journal *Mind*, doyen at that initial phase of the Oxford "linguistic philosophy," author of *The Concept of Mind* which I had enjoyed in my undergraduate days both for its style and for its demolition of the Cartesian myth of the separateness of mental and physical existences. Little could I then have guessed that in the years which were to follow I would come to publish David's booklet *Medical Ethics and Human Life* (Palladio Press, 1979 and 1983), and play some tiny role in the parturition of his philosophical trilogy:

(1) *The Reality of Time and the Existence of God* (Oxford: Clarendon Press, 1988). A philosophical project of proving God's existence beginning from the sheer existence of things, as shown in their temporality and metaphysical, as distinct from logical, contingency. Nothing in the world has the power to make the cosmos continue to exist; yet it does, and not merely instantaneously. In a review of the book the Jesuit philosopher Norris Clark observed: "The book is definitely not for amateurs. It works its way to its conclusions by an austere and intricately interlocking pattern of argumentation that requires the closest attention even from a professional philosopher." I was once told that even Elizabeth Anscombe struggled with the complex prose.

(2) *The Human Person: Animal and Spirit* (Notre Dame, IN: University of Notre Dame Press, 1992). A powerful non-dualistic account of the human person that addresses the question of what it is for the human being to be animal, animal that is spirit, the animal, and not simply the soul, being open to God; a philosophical accounting for the possibility of personal transcendence of biological death; and

(3) *Language and Human Understanding: The Roots of Creativity in Speech and Thought* (Washington, DC: The Catholic University Press, 2014). A unified account of speech and language that integrates linguistics, psychology, and philosophy. The fruit of fifty years' reflection on the structure and meaning of language, begun while studying for his B Phil under Gilbert Ryle, his first mentor in philosophy and sort of wise "philosophical uncle" when David transitioned from physics and history to academic philosophy in 1962.

By the time, we had returned to the car park at the foot of Bennachie late that Sunday afternoon, he had discovered from me the story behind my being deported as an editor, publisher, and journalist from what was then Southern Rhodesia, by the illegal white regime still in power there in 1970. For my part, I had also learned that David's instincts were at heart Aristotelian; that he had come late to the study of Thomas Aquinas; that metaphysics had priority over epistemology; that he had been received into full Communion with the Catholic Church by Fr. Michael Hollings in Oxford, where Elizabeth Anscombe[1] and Michael Dummett were the other main philosophical influences upon him; and that he was fiercely opposed to Duns Scotus on a number of questions including the latter's holding to a univocal conception of existence, the full implications of which error I began to understand only many years later. David hoped Scotus would never be declared a Doctor of the Church. That afternoon was the beginning of a friendship and a conversation that deepened over the years—particularly from 1977, the year of his accident, onwards—a forty-five-year long conversation that came to a most grace-filled and edifying, if distressful, end upon his death in Aberdeen Royal Infirmary on 17th February 2017.

PARENTS

David Dimond Conway Braine was born in Paignton, Devonshire, on the 2 September 1940. He was born a twin, but due to incompetence on the part of the doctor who had failed to notice that there were two babies, his twin sister died at birth, and David's mother nearly did so also. (In 1984, I found David, at the age of forty-four, investigating

1 For a recent and most illuminating exposition on Dominican influences on Anscombe from her first arrival at Oxford, see "The Influence of Victor White and the Blackfriars Dominicans on a Young Elizabeth Anscombe: An Essay accompanying the Republication of G. E. M. Anscombe's "'I Am Sadly Theoretical: It Is the Effect of Being at Oxford' (1938)" by John Bergman, New Blackfriars 102, no. 1101 (September 2021): 706–23. "There are some striking features of the roles Victor White and Donald McKinnon played in Anscombe's life as an undergraduate.... These two Thomists, while teaching her Aquinas and Plato, also shared her Catholic social and political commitments, and undoubtedly helped to confirm her in the Catholicity of her minority viewpoint on the morality of the war."

closely the phenomenon of human monozygotic twinning. As a good Aristotelian, he studied closely the current edition of *Gray's Anatomy* and the most up to date research on human embryology. I had recently been invited by my bishop to serve as a member of the Catholic Bishops' Joint Committee on Bioethics and our first major task was to make our submission to the Government Committee of Inquiry into Human Fertilization and Embryology—the 1984 Warnock Committee and Report. It was a huge help to have David's reflections on the human *neo-conceptus* as a person and on the problem of monozygotic twinning. (Also useful was Elizabeth Anscombe's lecture *Were You a Zygote?* given to the Royal Institute of Philosophy, London, that same year.)

David's mother was Edith Mary Harrison Smith, a mathematics teacher, born in Birmingham and brought up there. (David's student lodgers found her an imposing figure, a formidable matriarch, free with forthrightly expressed opinions.) She met her husband, David's father, when they were both students at Birmingham University.

He was Charles Dimond Conway Braine a chartered civil engineer and a Fellow of the Institute of Civil Engineers, born in South Africa and, like his father, a founder of the South African Institution of Civil Engineering. They were the first to make dirty water drinkable. He did this in Southern Africa, Palestine-Israel, and Malaysia, among other places.

SIBLINGS

David was their fifth child, if we include his twin sister who died at birth, as we ought to.

His eldest sibling, Martin, was 14 years older than David. Born in Kuala Lumpur on June 3, 1926, Martin Dimond Stewart Braine studied mechanical engineering in 1946 at the University of Birmingham, following his parents. He subsequently attended the University of London (B.S. in psychology), where he attended lectures by Jean Piaget, which influenced his later research on the development of logical reasoning. Martin continued his education at New York University gaining his doctorate in psychology under the supervision of Elsa Robinson. He worked in Washington, D.C. at Walter Reed

National Military Medical Centre. After an interval of about fifteen months in Israel (leaving shortly before the Six-Day War) he joined the Department of Psychology at the University of Santa Barbara at the end of 1967. Awarded a Guggenheim Fellowship, Martin transferred to New York University in 1971 where he remained until he predeceased his brother, dying of cancer on April 6, 1996.

Martin married Lila Ghent (Rosenzveig) in 1960. She, the same age as her husband, was born in 1926, in Montreal, Quebec, to Amelia and Josef Rosenzveig, who had both, separately, emigrated from Romania on account of the pogroms in that country at the time. Lila was the first person in her family to attend college and her degrees came from McGill University in Montreal, culminating in a doctorate in psychology in 1951. With her first husband, Emmanuel Ghent, she moved to New York City where she worked in New York Hospital. After marrying Martin, she lived successively in Washington D.C., Jerusalem, and Santa Barbara, moving back to New York in 1971. After several years teaching at New York University, she became head of the Psychology Department at Barnard College, Columbia University. Over time, her interests shifted from perception, especially children's perception, to a larger focus on developmental psychology. She was one of the founders of the Women's Studies Program at Barnard College and its first chair in 1977–78. Apart from her academic occupations, Lila was politically active in feminist movements and struggles for racial and economic justice. In retirement, she was active with Jews for Racial and Economic Justice, and Jewish Voices for Peace. She attended her last demonstration within a month of her death at Roosevelt Hospital on January 19, 2015.

Martin and Lila's children, Jonathan (1961) and Naomi (1964), are David's only nephew and niece. Naomi is a Professor of Sociology at Brooklyn College in New York City "whose professional work is deeply informed and shaped by a long history as a social justice activist." Her professional work focuses on collective action and public health, with a particular focus on HIV/AIDS. She and David spent quite some time discussing HIV as a societal phenomenon, including the intersections of the political and the ethical. David's nephew Jonathan is an astrophysicist at the *Observatoire Aquitain des Sciences de l'Univers* in the University of Bordeaux, interested in the evolution of galaxies and, thus, in the formation of stars, the origin of the elements. He is the author of the first detections of dense (molecular) gas in dwarf tidal galaxies and in the outer zones of spiral galaxies. Both Jonathan and Naomi were able to visit David in the Hugh Dependency Unit at Aberdeen Royal Infirmary the week or so before David died.

As we shall shortly have occasion to observe, although they were rarely able to visit each other, living so far from one another, David shared a number of fields of interest with Martin and his family: cosmology, human biological origins, psychology, linguistics, a passion for social, racial, and economic justice. David always manifested a real affection and respect for the Jewish religion and people.

It was when David was well on in developing his thought on the subject of his last book and had actually started drafting the first few chapters of the massive tome which became *Language and Human Understanding: The Roots of Creativity in Speech and Thought* that a conversation with Martin, his psycholinguist brother, alerted David "to key difficulties." These discussions, David wrote in his *Introduction and Overview* to the book, "quickly disabused me of the idea that I had only philosophers to satisfy. Although we found ourselves grappling with closely related problems and agreed in some of the ideas key to their solution, such as that of 'predicate,' nonetheless we found that we used much common vocabulary with quite different presumptions, springing from the gulf between our respective backgrounds of argument and concern. The differences in our assumptions were as startling as the lack of overlap in our reading. How foreign the approaches of philosophers, linguists, and psycholinguists could seem to one another was thrust before my eyes in a particularly vivid way. Thus, I had to avoid the behavior of the proverbial ostrich speaking only to the like-minded or to philosophers alone, and grapple with theoretical linguistics at a much deeper level, taking account of functionalist as well as Chomskyan approaches to grammar. Also, I had to consider the relationship between linguistics and neuroscience." And it was Lila who pointed David toward the work of the psychologist J. J. Gibson.

David is survived by two sisters, both older than he.

Barbara Mary Dimond, was born ten years before him, in 1930. She studied for her B. Com at Birmingham beginning in 1949, gained her Tennis Blue there, and became an economist at the University of Birmingham where she met her husband David Chivers Smith, who after demobilization from the army, also graduated as a B Com. He went on to work in marketing for a number of leading Midlands firms including Antler Suitcases, BSA Ltd and J B Brooks, retiring in 1991. He died in 2018. Barbara was appointed Director of the Centre for Urban and Regional Studies. In 1994 she was awarded an OBE for services to the Wages Councils and chairing Industrial Tribunals. She wrote the history of the British motorcycle industry as well as *A Hundred Years of Business Studies in Birmingham* to celebrate the University's centenary. She also served as Chair of the West Midlands Study Association. They had no children.

Christine Ella Dimond, the younger of his surviving sisters, was born in 1934. After "an eleven-and-a-half-week courtship" she married Peter Marsh in 1959. Peter had been born in 1926 in a small town called Limbe in what was then the British Protectorate of Nyasaland, now Malawi. At the age of eight, he had to make a three-day journey to attend St George's College, run by Jesuits, in what was then Salisbury, the capital of Southern Rhodesia, now Harare in Zimbabwe. At the age of eighteen, he was sent to the University of Cape Town to study engineering in the footsteps of both his father and his grandfather. He volunteered for the South African Army as soon as he could. Demobbed in 1945, he returned to Cape Town University to complete his degree in civil engineering. His first post was with the Nyasaland Railway Company, but he soon realized there was little future in small-time Limbe and Blantyre. Once again, he set out for the more cosmopolitan neighboring Southern Rhodesia where he joined a civil engineering firm in Salisbury. "He hated it, and after a last Christmas in Nyasaland, he received out of the blue a letter asking if he would like to join East African Railways and Harbours." He joined the company in 1950 as Assistant Engineer, "retiring as Acting Chief Engineer in 1977 following three hearts attacks. Peter died in exile in Devon in January 2011."

When Christine and Peter had set out for Nairobi, Kenya in 1959, Christine worked for the Royal Commonwealth Society "living in a tent" for almost a year. They subsequently moved to Tanzania where she worked with disabled local children, with the Brownies and with

Corona Worldwide. She now lives in Taunton, North Somerset, and has served for many years as the International President of the charity *Corona Worldwide*, having served time as Chair and then President of the Tiverton and Honiton Conservative Association, as well as Chair of the Western Area Farming and Environmental Council. *Corona Worldwide* helps families to live in countries other than their own and then settle them back home, principally in Commonwealth countries. "Sadly, we also had no children."

Christine has most kindly furnished me with some snippets of information about David's childhood. She writes: "David was always highly intelligent, and he could read before I could. He read anything and everything. He loved comics to the horror of his parents but by six it was any book from comic to H. G. Wells."

I myself recall once being told by David himself that in childhood he devoured the Encyclopaedia Britannica—the eleventh edition, 1933, I think; and that he once wrote a history of the world (or was it a history of the universe?) when scarcely into his teens.

Christine continues: "David went to an odd prep school in Sutton Coldfield, run by an ex-Etonian who quickly realized he was clever and pushed him academically, so he gained a state scholarship to St John's, Leatherhead in Surrey (1953 – 1958). At school he played rugby and cricket, but after school he enjoyed walking, climbing, skiing and was also interested in birds and wildlife, which was encouraged by his aunt Joyce, a real birder. He went up to Oxford as a keen Anglican. It was whilst there that he became a Catholic."

PHYSICS AT MAGDALEN COLLEGE

David excelled at St John's. In the summer of 1955, he passed GCE 'O' level (equivalent to a High School diploma in the U.S.) in nine subjects—in English Language, English Literature, French, Latin, Divinity, Elementary Maths (89%), Additional Maths (85%), Physics (92 %), and Chemistry (90%). Two years later, in July 1957, still aged 16, he took 'A' level in Mathematics (Group IV) and 'A' and 'S' papers in Physics and Chemistry. In September 1957, Mr. Peacocke, the head of the Science Department in the school, wrote to the Senior Tutor at Magdalen College, Oxford: "I am writing a testimonial on behalf of D.D.C. Braine, who will be taking the Scholarship examination for

Magdalen in March 1958. David Braine is a boy of remarkable ability. He obtained a Scholarship to the school on entry in September 1953. He took his 'A' levels in Chemistry, Physics, and Mathematics for the first time last July ... he got Distinctions in Chemistry and Physics. He was only 17 on 2nd September this year. Apart from his scientific ability, he is a remarkably versatile boy and is very well read as is shown by alpha minus on the General paper. He is secretary of the school Scientific Society and is also a member of the Historical Society and takes his full part in school activities..."

In view of David's future first monograph, it is interesting to note the following observations that Peacocke added in a supplementary, supportive, letter the following year, on February 6th, 1958:

> He is industrious as well as being intelligent and masters new ideas with rapidity.... He read a paper to the Scientific Society last term on "Time" which was notable for its clarity and depth. Most of the questions at the end came from members of the staff, who were present. He is no narrow specialist. He belongs to seven other school societies including the Historical Society to which he recently read a paper entitled "Science and History," the Musical Society, and the Debating Society.

David's headmaster wrote endorsing the recommendation of the head of the science department in support of David's application for admission to Magdalen:

> I have no doubt he will win an Open Scholarship. He is broad-minded and eager to acquire knowledge over a wide range of subjects, both his general and specialist knowledge is well above average. In character he is absolutely reliable, very serious and conscientious in matters of conduct, where he has the highest principles. He is certainly suited to a University education, and I should expect him to obtain First Class Honours.... One of the ablest boys we have had at St John's during my period as Headmaster. He is a boy of high ideals and a becoming modesty.

On 27 March, 1958, David received notification informing him that Magdalen had elected him to a Demyship (a specific type of scholarship peculiar to Magdalen College—Oscar Wilde, Lewis

Gielgud, Lord Denning and T. E. Lawrence were famous recipients) on his performance in the Natural Science Scholarship Examination. David wrote to Geoffrey Warnock, who was now his Senior Tutor at Magdalen, saying that he expected to take up residence in October:

> "The subject I propose to read is Physics. Although I hope, later, to be ordained, and have seriously considered reading other subjects such as History or Theology. I am certainly now decided to read Physics."

HISTORY OR THEOLOGY?

On 28 May, 1959, in his third term of his first year at Oxford, and just in advance of his taking Honour Moderations in Natural Science, David wrote to change Honours School:

> "Dear Mr. Adams,
>
> I am proposing to change Honours School at the end of this term—a change from Physics to History. Before this is finally settled, I would be very grateful for an opportunity to discuss the possibility of reading theology."

Sensing urgency, Adams agreed to talk this over with David early the next morning, which was a Saturday, at 9:00 am. Evidently, the option of reading theology was cast aside—at least for the time being—and it was agreed that he should take the complete three years to sit his finals in history, rather than attempting to do so in just two.

David wrote to Warnock on 7 June:

> I hereby apply to the Tutorial Board for permission to read in the Final Honours School of Modern History in the coming academic years. I have been advised that it would be unwise for me to seek admission to the Second Public Examination in this school until Trinity Term, 1962 that is the twelfth term after my matriculation. . . . I would be very grateful to you if you would put this application before the Tutorial Board at its next meeting this term.

Warnock agreed to do so, and David was granted leave to read for the Final Honour School of Modern History beginning the following term. To take another three years at Magdalen involved much further correspondence with the Awards Branch of the Ministry of Education, which eventually approved this change for the purposes of his State Scholarship. Warnock gave very helpful support in this matter. (David's father, in process of withdrawing from a partnership and striking out on his own, was not at the time of David's going up to Oxford in a position to fund his son's undergraduate studies. And, in fact, he died during his son's second year at Oxford.)

Early in January 1961, David was at home when he wrote to his tutor about being awarded an Exhibition. (At Oxford, students who perform at a demonstrably first-class level in one year, often but not necessarily the first year, may be awarded an "Exhibition." Exhibitioners who then perform at first-class level in a subsequent year will be promoted to a scholarship.) This particular bursary amounted to £5 p.a. for one year) and would reduce the level of his Demyship emoluments accordingly, though not necessarily his State grant:

> Dear Mr. Warnock,
>
> I have recently been informed that the Haberdashers' Company have elected me to the Culverwell's Exhibition for 1961. I understand that before receiving the amount of this quite unexpected Exhibition, I need to send a certificate of residence at Magdalen. I should be grateful if you would have such a certificate sent to me.
>
> My father's impending death may delay my return to college for a day or two this term, but I would be grateful for an opportunity fairly soon during the term to discuss with you how the Ministry of Education will compute the amount of my grant. Doubtless they will take a long time to work it out as the factors involved will be complex.
>
> I want to take this opportunity for thanking you again for your efforts on my behalf in securing the Ministry grant for a fourth year. This now assumes much greater importance. Thank you.

The following month, on 17 February, the Secretary of the General Advisory Council of Training for the Ministry, Church House at Westminster, wrote to Mr. Adams seeking a reference for David, who had applied to this Council as a candidate for Ordination:

(1) In considering a man as a possible candidate for ordination we should look first for evidence of the reality of his own faith in God. His convictions, if sincere, will find expression (a) in worship, (b) in serious regard for God's law in the ordering of his own moral life. . . .

(2) Not every enthusiastic communicant and good-living man, however, is a suitable candidate for Holy Orders. That vocation normally presupposes certain special aptitudes. These may perhaps be listed under the following headings. (a) Intelligence. It should be recognized that the service of the Church today requires in her ministry an average of intellectual ability equal to that of e.g., doctors or solicitors. . . . (b) Promise of pastoral capacity and power of leadership. . . .

(3) In all this, regard should be had to potentiality than to (sic) actuality. A candidate's ideas and desires at this stage are often largely unformulated.

Adams responded:

Thank you for your enquiry about Mr. D.D.C. Braine.

Mr. Braine came up with a Demyship in Natural Science and changed over to History after taking a Second in Science Moderations. There is no doubt that he is very able (and well aware of it!). He has a wide-ranging mind and gives vigorous expression to it.

Mr. Braine is active in the various religious societies and groups, and regular in his attendance at the College Chapel. It has been his intention to seek ordination since before he came up, and there has been no wavering in this. He is perhaps lacking in a sense of humor and inclined to be intellectually aggressive, but the latter is a defect not uncommon at his age. I can see no obstacle to his having a very successful career in the Church.

In the same month David wrote, through the Senior Tutor, to apply to the Travel Committee for a grant toward the cost of a Summer Vacation course at Besançon in France:

"I ask this because I wish to offer the French Revolution as a Special Subject in the School of Modern History. If I am to do this, it will be necessary to gain a greater command of the French language."

His budgets were detailed but modest.

PHILOSOPHY WITH RYLE

There was no further correspondence in respect of Anglican ordination. But on 9 June he appealed, again through Warnock, to the Tutorial Board to remain in residence in Oxford the next year:

> "My precise plans have yet to be worked out with Professor Gilbert Ryle with whom I communicated briefly at the end of Hilary. I saw no reason for raising the matter further before my Finals and trust to clarify matters shortly after Finals, that is after 13th June. My purpose is to study philosophy."

Just over a week later, he wrote to the Senior Tutor again:

> This letter follows an earlier one a week ago and our conversation this morning and should make more precise my plans for next year which leads me to apply to the Tutorial Board for permission to remain in residence.
>
> I have up to the present read natural science for Honour Mods and modern history for Final Honour Schools which I took this year. I plan to study philosophy next year. To do this profitably I need not only reading but some experience of philosophical writing, and criticism in this. As a beginner, I would be helped by tuition which would also reveal how well-fitted I was for the work. The position of Oxford from the point of view of philosophical teaching, and my experience of methods of study here make it obvious that if it is at all possible, I should do my study here.
>
> I need to spend the time until the end of Hilary or Trinity term next year (1963) doing groundwork previous to turning to particular research. I have discussed the matter with Professor Ryle and, in accordance with his suggestions, the best plan seems to be tuition until that time to be followed, if I prove up to it, by research as a Probation B Litt student. The matter now lies with the College, as I apply for permission to remain in residence next year and secondly seek tuition if this is possible.
>
> In case the question is raised, I will remark that I plan to support myself next year, though I would naturally be glad if other means could be found. I can also support myself for further years, though with more difficulty, but would hope that, if my work makes proceeding with research worthwhile as I hope, then financial

> assistance might be found from public authorities. I mentioned this for purposes of reference.
>
> I would be very grateful to you for putting this application to the Tutorial Board and hope very much that permission be given.

The Tutorial Board turned down David's application to remain in residence—at least until such time as the Faculty Board should admit him to the status of Probationer student for the degree of B Litt in Philosophy—and the Ministry of Education did not accept as eligible for an additional maintenance grant his period of residence after his Final examination when revising for his viva. Intrepid and undeterred, David changed tack by changing degree course, from B Litt to BPhil. (The Oxford BPhil is regarded as a very demanding graduate degree, well-known and respected in the philosophical world. Involving two years of seminars and a research thesis, it was designed to be a preparation for teaching philosophy at university level.) Once again making application to the Senior Tutor of the College, David wrote in the following terms:

> Dear Sir,
>
> I am putting forward an application for permission to take the Examination for the Degree of Bachelor of Philosophy in Trinity 1965 and to be placed on the Register of Bachelor of Philosophy Students in Michaelmas 1963. I understand that I need the permission of the Tutorial Board of Magdalen to do this. I also will need permission to return to the status of Resident Member of the College in this coming Michaelmas 1963. I hereby apply for these permissions.
>
> This term I have been working in philosophy with Mr. Warnock as Tutor, and it is on his advice that I am proceeding now to apply to do the BPhil in Philosophy, according to the hope that I had at the beginning of the (academic) year in moving on from work in History to philosophical work. I am in the course of making an application for a State Studentship.

The College granted permission to return into residence, but the Ministry of Education did not select him for the award of a State Studentship. He appealed to the College for financial help either by way of a grant or at least a loan, adding:

> If it be asked what I want to do the BPhil for, the answer is that it seems to me worthwhile to do this work, and I want to open the possibility of going into University teaching in it, and to continue study of it. (You referred the other day to the possibility of my going into a seminary which I have mentioned in the past, but over the course of this year I have become less clear than before about this, I could almost say *even* than before.)

The College offered him a loan of £100, without interest.

David did confide to me that he had occasionally wondered whether he might be called to become a Dominican friar. Certainly not a Jesuit. I no longer have a record of exactly during which year he was received into full Communion with the Catholic Church, though I do remember clearly that he always made a point of commemorating the day, 29 June, the Solemnity of St. Peter and St. Paul, and also the day of his first Communion, which for some reason were distinct. It certainly happened in his Oxford years, while Fr. Michael Hollings was incumbent at the Old Palace, the Oxford University Catholic Chaplaincy, just off St. Aldgate's. David also looked up to, and received counsel from, Fr. Jock Dalrymple (senior), Michael's cousin. Before his conversion from Anglicanism, as well as after it, he often attended St. Nicholas Orthodox Church on Ferry Road in Marston, Oxford. Unusually, this parish served both the Russian Orthodox and the Greek Orthodox communities in Oxford, or at least did so in that era.

After Oxford, David maintained friendships with contemporaries, such as Nicholas de Lange, a Reform rabbi who studied with Ignaz Maybaum, a disciple of Franz Rosenzweig. De Lange went on to become a fellow of Wolfson College in Cambridge and Professor of Hebrew and Jewish Studies at Cambridge. He is the author of many books on Judaism, amongst them, *Origen and the Jews: Studies in Jewish-Christian Relations in Third-Century Palestine* (CUP) and an article, "Jesus and Auschwitz" (New Blackfriars). David also kept up with Anthony Bloom (Metropolitan Anthony of Sourozh), another prolific author.

The philosophers Gilbert Ryle, J. L. Ackrill, and Geoffrey Warnock all wrote references ("very satisfactory member of the college," "hard-working" "responsible" "respectable," "perfectly satisfactory," "virtuous") in support of David's application for a State Studentship for which he was selected at the end of June 1964, but not without further computational complications.

His next letter to Warnock, dated 15 October 1965, was in fact sent from King's College in Old Aberdeen. Directly upon completing his BPhil, David had been offered his first academic post as Lecturer in 1965 in what was then the Department of Logic at the University of Aberdeen, one of Scotland's ancient universities, founded by Pope Alexander VI in 1495 at the request of the great Scottish Renaissance figure, Bishop Elphinstone.

> "Dear Mr. Warnock
>
> I write to thank you for taking the trouble you did in writing to the Department of Education and Science on my behalf and am glad that the trouble was not fruitless. I regard the outcome as eminently satisfactory ... I send you my warm best wishes. I am happy to say that I am well settled in now, and things in Aberdeen seem very satisfactory for me."

And his final letter to Warnock, as far as I know, was written on 19 December 1966:

> "Dear Mr Warnock,
>
> I enclose a cheque in order to complete the repayment of the loan the College made me in 1963."

LIVELY BEGINNINGS IN ABERDEEN

From his first arrival, David, like many incomers, continued to live in Aberdeen for the rest of his life.

Apart from his teaching and tutorial commitments, David launched himself with gusto into a range of other activities. Very early on after his settling in Aberdeen, David became involved in the Aberdeen World Poverty Association, soon finding himself its chairman. He invited a recently arrived (1967) colleague in the Department of Moral Philosophy, Nigel Dower, to join him as Secretary. They engaged in their campaigning work energetically and remained a dynamic duo as the Aberdeen World Poverty Association turned into the Aberdeen World Development Association. (Dower attributes his own subsequent research interests and academic involvement in global ethics, the philosophy of development, environment, and international relations, and spells of teaching philosophy in Zimbabwe and Malawi to his friendship with David in their early years together in Aberdeen.)

Their collaboration continued as office holders in the Aberdeen United Nations Association, "fostering the goals of maintaining peace, security and disarmament." David sided with Elizabeth Anscombe rather than with Wittgenstein in his attitude to the Bomb.

When in 1956 it was proposed that Oxford University should honor Harry Truman, the former U.S. President, who had ordered the dropping of atom bombs on Hiroshima and Nagasaki, with a degree, Anscombe publicly opposed the proposal. She made her case for refusing to confer an honorary degree on Truman to the University members in the ancient house of Congregation. After rising and asking permission to speak in English, her powerful and courageous speech did not receive even the compliment of opposition. Apart from the support of her friend Phillipa Foot, her speech was greeted with silence. Only four dons said "*non placet.*" This episode drove her to give the course of lectures that became the difficult but hugely important book *Intention.* David, though still a schoolboy at the time, was astonished at the Oxford dons' utter imperturbability, which today seems extraordinary. The objection to the proposal of the degree was after all on the grounds of a government's targeting and killing innocent civilians or noncombatants.

Subsequent discussions with David persuaded me of the immorality not only of the use of nuclear weapons but also of their very possession on these same grounds. If deliberate direct killing of noncombatants is wrong, to threaten to do so must also be wrong. To threaten this involves a conditional intention to use the weapons in given circumstances.

Anscombe's mentor, Wittgenstein, had a rather different reaction to the atomic bomb. In his *Ludwig Wittgenstein: The Duty of Genius*, Ray Monk writes "In a curious sense he [Wittgenstein] even welcomed the bomb" and he quotes Wittgenstein as saying:

> The hysterical fear over the atom bomb now being experienced, or at any rate expressed, by the public almost suggests that at last something really salutary has been invented. The fright at least gives the impression of a really effective bitter medicine. I can't help thinking: if this didn't have something good about it the philistines wouldn't be making an outcry. But perhaps this too is a childish idea. Because really all I can mean is that the bomb offers a prospect of the end, the destruction, of an evil,—our disgusting soapy water science ... there is nothing good or desirable about scientific knowledge and that mankind, in seeking it, is falling into a trap.[2]

It was in the course of conversations about the possibility of exceptionless norms or categorical prohibitions that the idea emerged of writing and publishing under my Palladio Press imprint David's first short book or booklet (forty-nine pages). *Medical Ethics and Human Life* was released in 1979, with a second edition in 1983 which was reprinted by Wipf and Stock in 2018. I had been impressed by a paper, *The Rational Case against Abortion,* David read to the Aberdeen Circle of the Newman Association. (In this paper, which he read again to a medical students' society, he considered, in as analytical a way as possible, deliberately avoiding emotion, what seems to be the primary question raised by the large-scale practice of abortion. No appeal was made to revelation or religious premises.)

In *Medical Ethics and Human Life,* David was concerned to offer a Christian explanation to non-Christians as well as articulating a Christian appeal to fellow Christians. One chapter is devoted to answering objections appealing to consequences. So often situations are misdescribed.

> If the man is allowed to die, normal treatments being continued but not expected to prevent death, no man is responsible for his death or for its time, but it is the disease, or nature, or God, that is to be blamed, whereas if euthanasia is administered in form of pill or injection, those whose action and consent to action is involved are responsible, not the disease, nature, or God. To pretend that man is responsible whichever happens is to assume

2 Ray Monk, *Ludwig Wittgenstein: The Duty of Genius* (New York: Penguin, 1990), 485.

> an omni-responsibility in man which he does not have. To ignore the distinction between events following on my action, resulting from concomitant circumstances for which I am not responsible, and, by contrast, things directly intended, as means or ends, in the action itself, is to elevate man to the situation of God. Even the pagan world before Christ could have seen such a pretense, of being responsible for what in fact nature is responsible for, as an example of *hubris* or overweening pride.... The Christian must support the pagan in rejecting this pose or role of omni-competence or omni-responsibility. (*Medical Ethics and Human Life*, 22)

It was the growing threat of legislation admitting euthanasia that launched David into a passionate lifelong defense of all innocent (meaning not actively harming) human life, whether unborn, newborn, handicapped, learning-disabled, elderly, or enfeebled, or noncombatant in war. The practice of any pruning of the human race called for a new urgency to the application of the principle of respect for life as a gift. "Against this tendency every human being needs to make a stand in the name of humanity itself." Each new attempt to legalize euthanasia provoked him into a flurry of well-argued letters addressed to members of both the House of Commons and the House of Lords. Other conflicts also evoked campaigning letters and late-night phone calls to government ministers from him. During various conflicts in Syria and Iraq, he vigorously championed the Kurds.

David was gregarious, loved barbecues and parties, particularly at Easter and Christmas. He spent generous portions of his time socializing with students, and when appointed a warden of Hillhead Halls of Student Residence, he took his pastoral responsibilities seriously. He himself speculated that he may never have got down to writing his three monographs were it not that his spinal injury now restricted his multifarious activities and socializing, thus pinning him down more to his desk.

HIS ACCIDENT IN 1977

One March afternoon in 1977, David together with two student companions, set off driving down south on what is now the A90 to attend the presbyteral ordination of a seminarian who had attended some of David's philosophy classes. Just as they approached the City of Perth, David agreed to hand over the driving to one of his companions. On pulling out of the layby the car was smashed into, headlong, by a huge on-coming heavy goods vehicle. The students survived with relatively minor scratches and bruises. David sustained a major spinal injury that rendered him paraplegic (paralyzed from the chest down) for the rest of his days. He was taken to the closest hospital at Bridge of Earn, where his condition was assessed. David was in his prime at the age of thirty-six.

The following morning, I received a call asking me to bring him some clothes, toiletries and reading matter. I found him prostrate, between two flat boards. One had to sit on the floor at his head to converse with him.

After further assessment over the next week or so, it was decided to send David to Stoke Mandeville Hospital in Buckinghamshire, one of the largest specialist spinal units in the world. The pioneering rehabilitation work carried out there by the famous German-expatriate Sir Ludwig Guttmann was widely admired. He believed that sport was a major method of therapy for injured military personnel, helping them build up physical strength and self-respect. David, as with all patients there, was pushed to the limits of what he was capable of by the regime initiated by Guttmann, whose work had led to the development of the Stoke Mandeville Paraplegic Games, precursors of the Paralympic Games.

When Gail and I drove down to visit David at Stoke Mandeville, we found David appreciative of the spartan and demanding regime there. The other beds in his ward were all occupied by young men who had suffered motorcycle accidents. Above their beds, I recall, were pinned up posters of their beloved but dangerous machines.

We never, then or subsequently, spoke of the detail of the horrific accident. But he did, when occasion called for it, himself speak of the consequences of it.

WHY NOT ME?

Let us suspend our narrative for a moment. Once, on the occasion of yet another attempt to legalize euthanasia, I invited him to write an article on the subject for our diocesan magazine, *Light of the North.* He wrote:

> Men and women have lost any appreciation of how, compared with life in God which is the fruit of the life of discipleship, the suffering each person undergoes pales into relative insignificance. Yet, it is only a living faith that can help us keep a firm grasp of this—this living faith is not a matter of a sense of consolation or reassurance, but of God's love for us in helping us hold fast to hope in him in the midst of much suffering.

Referring to his own experience he continued:

> I had never thought about my death until the time of my motor accident. At that time people said: "Aren't you angry with God?" to which my answer was "No," and "Don't you ask: 'Why me?'," when I felt "Why not me?"—American contemporaries had died or suffered injury in Vietnam, and I had a reputation as a dangerous driver—it surprised people that I was a passenger and not the driver in the accident!
>
> Some people have their main difficulties at the beginning—for me, although I had some initial setbacks, for the most part difficulties have arisen in later stages.
>
> Initially, I had the prospect of being able to drive freely with hand controls indefinitely and of continuing in my existing job right up to retirement. I have been helped by a multiplicity of willing student and staff helpers, faithful through all my most difficult times. . . .
>
> We none of us have our life under our control, neither our health nor our family, nor our jobs, nor our mental faculties, nor the lead up to and conditions of our death. Certainly, I do not have my life under my control, to know of future years.

David also asked himself what preparation had he had for any of what happened to him? Well, for five years whilst a student at Oxford, he had a week as a helper in Lourdes in the summer. He now recalled:

> I realized that what made Lourdes a religious place was this spirit of acceptance and the message from the sick to the healthy that God is more important than health, and also that faithfulness, service of others, unstinted generosity in giving and willingness to receive help are all more important than health itself. I had at that time, not the least conception that this message might one day apply to me.

> For me, suicide, whether physician-assisted or not, and "voluntary euthanasia" are kinds of "cop-out" from the human condition, a declaration of dissociation from those who went before us in two world wars, as well as present wars if the cause is just, and from all those who went before us. It is also a cop-out from any sharing of the situation of people in poorer countries. It is a piece of individualism—an opting out from sharing the life and lot of the rest of humanity.
>
> And nobody should close off what possibilities there are before them, what they can give to others or what others in ways they don't realize may learn from them. . . .
>
> Life is a gift. We must not close off its possibilities. Some of the disabled and terminally ill have produced their most valued work in the period of their disability and sometimes long illness—in my case, I published almost nothing until two major books and many articles from 1988 onwards, long after my accident in 1977.[3] Life has unexpected possibilities in directions one would never have conceived of. Many have found fulfillment in outgoing social and care activity, which they had never conceived of.

This spirit of acceptance, by no means easily reached, I myself witnessed in the 80s when David was persuaded to come to a healing service at Aberdeen's St. Mary's Cathedral one evening. It was led by a Fr. Rookey, whose healing ministry had brought an end to suffering for many. I stood next to David in his wheelchair as Fr. Rookey proceeded along the line laying hands on people seeking healing. When the priest came to David, whom I introduced, he said: David, stand up! David raised his eyes to Fr. Rookey and responded: "Father, I shall stand at the resurrection on the last day!"

Once Gail and I took him in his wheelchair to an outstanding performance of *The Nutcracker Suite* by the Bolshoi Ballet at His Majesty's Theatre in Aberdeen. I noted tears trickling down the cheeks of both David and Gail. He was marveling at the beautiful, strong and graceful movements of the dancers, fluid and free, and she was thinking how such free movement was now denied him, once so strong and active.

3 He had yet, at that point, to write his third tome, *Language and Human Understanding: The Roots of Creativity in Speech and Thought.*

RETURN TO ABERDEEN

But we have got ahead of ourselves. Let us revert to our narrative, back-tracking to the point when David returned to Aberdeen from Stoke Mandeville.

He was, in due course, transported back by ambulance to Aberdeen and reinstalled in the flat he had been occupying as warden to the students in the Hillhead Halls of Residence. Stoke Mandeville had taught him to retain as much independence for as long as was possible. At that stage he continued to be able to propel himself in his wheelchair, even up and down curbs. He learned to drive a specially adapted vehicle to go swimming and otherwise get about. But even then, there was always a need for a companion for these outings as well as for dressing and undressing when rising and retiring at night. I, with a gradually expanding team of others, was able to help with this in the period he remained in the hall of residence. (Later, David had to abandon driving himself, and our sons, Karl or Julian, would drive him in his vehicle to Sunday Mass at the cathedral or elsewhere in the city.)

With funds received in compensation for the accident, David was able to purchase a pair of slightly dilapidated adjoining houses at the top of the High Street (104 – 106) in Old Aberdeen, next to the handsome former town hall of the "auld toun." These now paired houses, accessed through a pend called Greenlaw Court, were once the family home of Bishop Ian Begg, the Episcopalian bishop of the Diocese of Aberdeen and Orkney.

Aberdeen architect Oliver Humphries was commissioned to join the houses together, adapting them to the needs of a wheelchair-bound paraplegic. Decorous Palladian dormer windows were restored. The first-floor drawing room on the High Street side was an elegant and spacious space with a balcony that looks out over a fine courtyard, at the far end of which an arched gateway opens out onto a lawned garden that hosted many a summer barbecue for students and friends. This room is where David delivered his Gifford Investigations in the 80s and was thus christened the Gifford Lounge. Here David also hosted the often-lively *Communio Study Circle* meetings initiated by Francesca Murphy and myself.

In his will, David bequeathed this heritable property to a Catholic community, if such could be found by me and fellow executors, that "bound to the Roman Catholic Church, dedicated to the purpose of the study both of the Roman Catholic faith and matters related to it and also to studies arising from the thought, faith, and religious life of St. Thomas (Aquinas) and St. John of the Cross. If it is possible this Community should endeavor to provide mutual benefit to Aberdeen University and the Students thereof."

Happily, with the assistance of Bishop Hugh Gilbert OSB, such a community has been found and, after some necessary restoration and alterations of the house, a small community of the Apostolic Sisters of St. John, founded in France in 1984, were installed in September 2020. The house is now called St. Peter's Priory, in line with David's expressed wish, and the sisters work closely with the Catholic Chaplaincy to the University.

From the time David moved into Greenlaw Court, he supported and was supported by cohorts of student lodgers. He had a predilection for medical students, most of whom received a copy of *Medical Ethics and Human Life*. His influence, particularly on medics, was hugely beneficial. It was a happy arrangement and, with but rare exceptions, a happy house. Some of the residents became his amanuenses, taking dictation for his various book projects, articles, and memoranda to Westminster, bishops, and even to the Holy See. While there always remained a need for daily professional nursing care, teams of helpers at bedtime became established, as at Hillhead Hall of residence, some of these helpers being residents of the house and some colleagues and other friends.

Following the merging of the Departments of Logic and Moral Philosophy, David was awarded a Gifford Fellowship from 1982 to 1988. It was during this period that David delivered what he called his "Gifford Investigations." The first series was the origin of *The Reality of Time and the Existence of God*, the first book in his trilogy; the second series he presented in 1984 from which came his second monograph, *The Human Person: Animal and Spirit*, and the central ideas of his third book on language and understanding were developed in 1990, until they culminated in the publication of *Language and Human Understanding: The Roots of Creativity in Speech and Thought.* David took medical retirement in 1989, becoming Honorary Lecturer from 1989 to 2002. From that year till his death in 2017 David remained an Honorary Research Fellow.

The Preface to *The Reality of Time and the Existence of God* recorded the names of over two dozen residents and others who has been involved as scribes and helpers: "There is no substitute for the determination and devotion of friends." The preparation of his second work extended from 1984 into 1992 and "perhaps sixty people have helped me as the work passed through different transformations in the extraordinary system of help which has supported me in the exigencies, physical and psychological, arising out of my spinal injury."

When *The Human Person: Animal and Spirit* was published in 1992, four years after his first work, I offered to host a book launch at Blackwell's University Bookshop, conveniently sited just across the road from Greenlaw Court. How many people would he like to invite? The answer came the following morning: eight typed pages of names of proposed guests! First on the list was the Bishop of Aberdeen, Mario Conti (subsequently translated to the archbishopric of Glasgow in 2002), who regularly used to celebrate Mass in David's study, followed by the university principal, and then over two hundred colleagues, philosophers and divines, his doctors and nurses, the army of secretaries and helpers, as well as friends from afar such as Elizabeth Anscombe and Peter Geach who regretted they could not make the journey from Cambridge. More than a hundred did accept the invitation, somewhat overwhelming the Blackwell's staff. Nor were they accustomed to a seven-page speech explaining why there could be no short cuts in the argument of the book:

> Principal, my Lord bishop, all of you who have come from a distance to be here, and all who have been here as colleagues . . . and all who have helped me in so many ways. . . .
>
> Philosophy is in some ways like mathematics, an invalid argument is no better than no argument at all, and again and again both in in my first book about time and God and in this book, I have had to return, again and again, to root out argument which would not wash—at every stage seeming to myself to be my own most severe critic. I do not understand how solid work in areas such as these is to be accomplished in shorter time. It is a pity although also a providence of heaven to have had a sort of medical sabbatical to make it possible. . . .
>
> This second book presents something in a way less plain—the nature of what it is to be a human being. For we are cleft in

two by a divide culturally and inside each of us.... In this field philosophy is the underservant of truth—here in a matter affecting every human being. Now it is easy to produce easy theories. There is an easy theology—the human being as two independent entities, body and soul interacting—at death the soul going on and the body perishing, but then what point does the physical world and the body have for the human being? What point the imagination? What point a "resurrection" of the body? What point to the physical expression of friendship or love? What community between the human being and the animals let alone with the rest of nature? This theology found in Descartes and in some strains of Indian understanding reduces the body to the status of something external, little more than a token or symbol. But what needs to be recognized at this stage is that the body is a part of us, integral and internal to the expression of our nature and life....

What I show in this book is that although it may be awkward for theology, awkward for psychology, awkward for the ambitions of computer science, a sore thumb even in biology and medicine, the basic project of reducing the human being or other higher animals to their parts is demonstrably impossible—neither perception nor intentional action, sensation or emotion can be treated in this way as if the mental was in the soul or brain and outer bodily goings-on merely its external causes or effects. Rather, Aristotle was right that the body could not be understood as an aggregate of causally interacting parts, but rather its parts and their behavior are only intelligible in relation to the living thing as a whole....

But then if the human being is a unity like the other animals, the body being integral to its nature, how does it differ from the other animals? Not in consciousness—this he shares with the other higher animals. But mostly in language—not in the less structured communication patterns seen in other animals, but in the structures observed in linguistic and semantic theory, seen in literature and seen in the unfolding forms of science and mathematics....

In this way I open out and legitimate the vision of the human being in community with his environment, at once a biological being and a spiritual one, so we are both at once in our care and stewardship of creation, both at once in our roles of relationships and community with other human beings and both at once in our openness to the God who remains the furnace energizing the existence of life of all things, and to whom, because of our reflective, intellectual or spiritual nature, we can be starkly bare. I thank you for your presence here to join me in this celebration.

QUESTIONS CONCERNING THE REBIRTH OF JEWISH EXPRESSIONS OF FOLLOWING CHRIST

In the spring of the following year, 1993, Jaroslav Pelikan, then Sterling Professor of History at Yale University, came to deliver an outstanding set of the Gifford Lectures, entitled *Christianity and Classical Culture*, examining the Christian encounter with Hellenism. He mapped out the importance of the Cappadocian system of natural theology as it developed in relation to classical culture. The lectures eventuated in a book that traces broadly "the metamorphosis of natural theology from classical culture to apologetics to dogmatics in relation to the thought and writings" of the four Cappadocians: Gregory of Nazianzus, Basil of Caesarea, Gregory of Nyssa and Macrina, the sister of the latter two, who has been well described as among the first Church Mothers.

The subject greatly interested David. Alas, current health problems kept him housebound, preventing him from attending the lectures. Around this same time David was fairly exercised by another set of questions in respect of Christian Jews—considered as people who converted not so much convert from one religion to another, but rather, who like Mary and the Apostles, entered into the fullness of their own religion. Was the continuance of some degree of Jewish observance—by way of witness to fellow Jews that by becoming Catholic Jews they had not abandoned their Jewish identity—legitimate in today's circumstances, so different from the context in Paul's day? These remain real questions of identity for groups such as the Towards Jerusalem Council II (TJCII) initiative promoted by the late Mgr. Peter Hocken, or the Association of Hebrew Catholics, and elegantly reflected upon since then by the late Jewish Archbishop of Paris, Cardinal Jean-Marie Lustiger, who insisted his Jewish identity could not be erased by baptism.

In 1989 David wrote a *Memorandum on the Continuance of Jewish Observance amongst Jewish Christians* addressed to the Congregation of the Doctrine of the Faith for their consideration. It was an updated elaboration of a memorandum on the same subject submitted in October 1988 to the Dutch Cardinal Willebrands, then President of the Commission for Religious Relations with the Jews, following on an even earlier one to the Commission in 1986. Willebrands had visited Aberdeen to deliver the 1988 Hay of Seaton Memorial Lecture entitled *Modern Anti-Semitism*. David received acknowledgements of receipt but no response to either memorandum. He was well aware of the delicacy of these questions.

His memorandum (the second one dated 1989) began:

> "I have been reluctant to initiate any public debate in regard to the matters I first raised in a memorandum to the Commission in 1986, firstly because of the weight of the Church's earlier disciplinary tradition in regard to Jewish observance by Christian Jews, and secondly because of the sensitiveness of Jewish feeling in this area."

If a definitive positive ruling decided against greater freedom, it would offend Jews. Equally, if new, freer discipline came in, it would also offend Jews. "The question is of the truth."

Pelikan had been a consultant on Jewish-Christian relations at the time of the Second Vatican Council, and so I was dispatched to meet the genial Professor clutching a copy of the second memorandum together with an offprint of David's recently published article on *The Inner Jewishness of St. John's Gospel as the Clue to the Inner Jewishness of Jesus* (*Studien zum Neuen Testament und seiner Umwelt, Serie* A, *Band* 13, 101–57, 1988). A couple of days later Pelikan responded graciously, but negatively, in a hand-written letter:

> Thank you for sending me your article on St John, and (as of this morning) your memorandum to the Holy See on the problem of continuing adherence to kosher laws etc., by Jews who become Christian.
>
> As Tony Schmitz told you, I do have a deep interest in Jewish-Christian relations, above all a historical concern about "de-Judaization" in its relation to "Hellenization of Christianity," but no less a theological concern about (to use your term) the "irrevocable" covenant with Israel. I was on the mailing list for the successive drafts of the Council decree and made some suggestions. I continue to be active on the subject, and in the autumn, I am giving

> a keynote lecture entitled "*Hebraica veritas*" for a conference sponsored by the Institute for Advanced Study in Israel on Jewish-Christian relations in the Middle Ages. (The conference is being held at Wolfenbüttel—shades of Lessing!)
>
> For all these reasons I do find myself sharing your apprehensions about the impact of your proposals on the Jewish community. They are by no means convinced by Christian protestations of accepting—at long last—the permanence of the covenant with Israel. And until they are more convinced, it will simply play into the wrong hands to reopen the question of the discipline of ritual observance by Jewish Christians. What we need to face, it seems to me, is the question of the secularized or even assimilated Jew who suddenly begins to think again about the reality of God and revelation. Before wanting such a person to consider Christian truth claims, I want him or her (and nowadays it's a "her" more often than not) to straighten out the relation to the Jewish tradition. Only then will it be time to talk about the coming of Messiah—for which, after all, both Jews *and* Christians have waited for a long time.
>
> Again, my thanks for sharing with me your thoughtful essays. I'm sorry they came in my final days here (I return tomorrow morning), so that we couldn't get together personally. But I do hope we can stay in touch. (My card is enclosed.)

They did manage to hold a phone conversation before Pelikan returned to Yale.

There the matter rested, apart from a short last shot. I proposed to David that one might consult the eminent Swiss theologian, von Balthasar, at the time a member of the International Theological Commission. It was agreed that I write to him in Basel enclosing David's (second) memorandum. By return, I received a one-line response from Basel: "I am with St Paul!" Which hardly answered the question. But good of him to respond so promptly.

In some ways the position of Catholic Jews is analogous to that of the Eastern Churches in union with Rome, occasionally awkward for both Orthodox and Catholics. David continued to take a keen interest in the work of the minority-view theses and reconstructions of three French scholars on the question of early Hebrew Gospels—the philosopher, Hellenist and theologian, Claude Tresmontant

(*Le Christ hébreu*); his collaborator the philosopher and historian Jacqueline Génot-Bismuth (*Un Homme Nommé Salut: genèse d'une hérésie à Jérusalem*); and biblical scholar, founder of the journal *Revue de Qumran*, Abbé Jean Carmignac (*The Birth of the Synoptics*).

David continued to hold to the view, (also espoused by the *Association of Hebrew Catholics*, but somewhat different from the opinions of other *Messianic Jewish* groups), that it may be legitimate to continue some Jewish Sabbath or other customs, by way of witness to fellow non-Christian Jews indicating that becoming Christian did not involve repudiating one's Jewish identity and heritage. Nevertheless, it was wise to await Rome's approval before seeking, say, a Hebraic Rite, as distinct from the Roman Rite in Hebrew, as already practiced in Israel.

RESSOURCEMENT THEOLOGY

David came late to von Balthasar and respected him, although not uncritically, occasionally expressing himself somewhat fiercely against certain of his theses (particularly *Urkenosis* within the Blessed Trinity). It was probably Daniélou who first introduced him to the theology of early Jewish Christianity. But it was the teacher of both these giants, Henri de Lubac, whom David admired and respected most. He came to de Lubac's defense in the 2007/8 symposium in *Nova et Vetera* on Lawrence Feingold's massive *Natural Desire to See God According to St. Thomas and His Interpreters.* In his article "The Debate between Henri de Lubac and His Critics," David opened:

> Those that seem most exact in their refutation of Henri de Lubac all appear to be open to reply out of the texts of de Lubac himself, especially when fortified by considerations drawn from Étienne Gilson's *Being and Some Philosophers*. Yet the work of Feingold himself, a work of such quality that it ought to be made more readily accessible, is open to no such easy reply. However, neither de Lubac nor his critics, not even Feingold, show awareness of some of the key background problems underlying their debate; and it is with a consideration of these problems that I shall begin.[4]

4 "The Debate between Henri de Lubac and His Critics," *Nova et Vetera* (English edition) 6, no. 3 (2008): 543–90.

Gilson and the other Swiss theologian, Cardinal Charles Journet were men he esteemed most highly. The work of the Belgian Jesuit Émile Mersch he also found congenial and commended to others.

FINAL LARGE PROJECT

In his final year David set his heart on completing a projected book on the Incarnation. Various sections and outlines were drafted, including a (completed) essay on *The Uniqueness of the Incarnation: Why it is impossible for God to be incarnate more than once.* But during the last months of his illness, it was a great struggle to concentrate and remain focused on the project, however much he wanted to work on it. In his Deed of Settlement (or Will), he directed myself and fellow trustees, among other things, "to organize, edit, distribute, and publish my papers and other academic materials." A David Braine website is at the time of writing being established.[5]

More specifically he desired the editing and publication of

> my two current collections of texts being restructured into: first, a book on the Incarnation, its conformity with the human situation in the Universe, nature, condition and destiny, on behalf of the whole cosmos, the reasons for belief in it, how Nestorian tendencies undermine it, how the workings of providence are to be explained, the historicity of the Gospels, and the character ... of the Church as its current flowering on Earth: and second, a book on the Realism of St. Thomas, the empirical roots of the inductions underlying philosophical knowledge of the existence of God, the significance of the reality of time and the non-Platonic character of God's eternity, and how the basis of ethics he offers is realistic.

It has not proved possible to publish two collections of papers, but this book combines as far as practicable David's two desiderata. My fellow editors have in my opinion understood well David's insights, and as David's literary executor I am most grateful to them.

5 This website is https://www.davidbraine.com/

THE GREENLAW COURT HEROES

This story would be woefully incomplete without a tribute to the generations of residents who supported David in the last thirty years. Alas a complete record of them has not been kept as far as I know. We have already alluded to the preface of his first book, where he named over two dozen scribes and helpers. Over sixty such were involved in the dictation of his second. The opening of each academic year brought fresh residents into the house as those who had graduated departed. Summers could be a problem. The worst challenge to the support system came one summer when all the student residents departed for the vacation. Two young Dominican friars from Blackfriars in Oxford—David Jones and Anthony Fisher—came to the rescue. The former is now Director of the Anscombe Bioethics Centre in Oxford and Professor of Bioethics at St. Mary's University in Twickenham. The latter is now the ninth Archbishop of Sydney in Australia.

The last cohort of students who were resident during David's final illness faithfully and affectionately accompanied him through those last months, including keeping vigil at his bedside, day and night, first in the High Dependency Unit and then in the Respiratory Medicine Ward at Aberdeen Royal Infirmary. David had a horror of admission to ordinary hospitals, other than specialized spinal units, having suffered several times over the years from lack of experience and skill in dealing with paraplegics. Knowing his views, these students were particularly vigilant, guarding against the officious or premature application of any *Do Not Resuscitate* regime when he suffered respiratory arrest on several occasions. In fact, there was some medical incompetence at his death—to do with the treatment related to pressure sores—just as there had been medical incompetence at his birth when he lost his twin sister. On behalf of his family and with the encouragement of one of the consultants, I lodged a complaint with the Grampian NHS Trust, demanding to see the medical records for the duration of his stay in hospital. After a second letter of complaint an apology was received nine months after his death, with the happy outcome that in future a different bowel regime will be afforded cases like his. It took a further twelve months to receive his medical records.

Martin O'Donnell, together with Conor McAvoy, Tom Crespo, Nelly Bogilova and Claire Organ were the ones who were there with me for this last days. Let their voices speak for the many who came before them. Martin writes:

> I think David's faith, sense of humor, and zest for life were his shining attributes which made being a part of students' lives so easy for him, as well as his love of bringing people together for food, particularly at Easter and Christmas parties. I know I am one of many individuals who feel lucky to have met David and was helped massively by him to grow as a person—as well as as a student. I was also lucky enough to be part of David's only trip out of the UK following his accident. This was to Lourdes and included a road trip to Barcelona and Montserrat, as well as visiting his family around Brussels. All of which included tours around cities and cathedrals. This was "an excursion for the ages," and a pilgrimage for David. On top of being a religious trip, David also visited family he had not seen for many years, including his brother's widow who would pass away not long after our trip.

Claire Organ, David's last secretary, guardian of the cheque book, and a sort of nonresident "housemother," writes:

> I do have very fond memories of "wine time"—when it used to hit 9:00 p.m. and the bottle of red wine, a plate of olives and rye bread would come out and (although I could not drink alcohol as I was driving) we would then discuss all sorts of topics—economics, world issues, politics, etc. But what I enjoyed the most was when David would enlighten me about the Father Brown mysteries and we would watch an old film, or he would go into great depth about Tolkien, and we would read a passage together from *The Lord of the Rings* trilogy or some of Christopher Tolkien's work about his father. We had many fruitful discussions about Tolkien's works—not only *Lord of the Rings*—but also his Monsters and Beowulf—I loved that! And when the Pluscarden Monastery CDs went in we would sit and just listen to the monks singing. That's why I love going to Pluscarden now—it just reminds me of our evenings together, especially when he got a wee bitty tiddly and he would sing to me as I was putting him to bed—oh it was fantastic! He did not sing very well, and neither do I, but it was funny. We would warble away at all sorts of songs.

I also loved our beach walks—no matter the weather—especially when a group of us (Andrew, Pele, Colm, and Ed) would all venture down to the sands and have a picnic in the rain or wind.

The curries he ate—and I had to make—were an endeavor! Not too much chili but enough to blow your head off!

My favorite quote and I think it's one many of us have adopted was "HAPPY TIMES!" We always sign off our emails with that now.

I remember once I was stopping over and David banging on his bedroom ceiling at 3:00 a.m. so I could come down and pick up a book that had fallen on the floor! And his constant need to understand and process information in order to educate us—as well as his brilliant way of educating medical students sent down from the GP practice. Oh, that was funny!

I miss the way his glasses would not sit straight on his face—and me having to stand in front of him holding a huge tome, trying to read it out loud to him upside down, with my Brummie accent. He would always try and get me to pronounce something correctly. And the one I love is that I could not for the life of me spell "convenience." So, he said: "Right, it's spelled like 'convent,' only when you get to the 't,' stop, and put an 'i' there. Remember 'i' before 'e,' and then carry on." And I was like "Eh?!" But you know what? I can spell it now—every time I have to, I remember David and his really odd explanation. HAPPY TIMES!

Ray Landells, now a GP in Dorset, married with four children, writes:

I first met David at the Aberdeen University Catholic Chaplaincy at the bottom of the stairs where he sat in his wheelchair listening to Mass being celebrated in the lounge on the floor above on Sunday evenings. He had the firmest handshake I have ever known! After doing all his weights to build upper body strength since being in a wheelchair ... he had a grip as strong as his character.

I moved into David's home at Greenlaw Court before my second year at University. The agreement being that in return for lodgings I was available to "work" for David, typing on the computer in his study whilst he dictated many long sentences and vocabulary that was unfamiliar to me (a non-philosopher, words such as "isomorphism"). The unique set up there (helping with secretarial/administrative and personal care) appealed to me immediately and I lived at Greenlaw from 2004 to 2008, which felt like home, whilst a medical student.

We would break for food, medications, a "pus"' (to correct his position in the chair). He enjoyed the occasional glass of Côte du Rhône, with a large slice of stilton on bread. Bedtime routine was making his night-time peppermint tea and glasses of water whilst he did weights and then got hoisted onto the bed for personal care and then we recited Night Prayer together on many occasions. I enjoyed sitting in his vacant wheelchair during this time and having good conversation at bedtime. There were sometimes many long pauses in his thought and speech, but this taught me patience and a respect for David's wisdom.

It didn't take long to consider David as a close friend or even a member of the family. And like any family member he could be difficult at times—obstinate and determined to get his own way, understandably, after being wheelchair-bound for nearly forty years. He knew better than anyone how things should be done concerning his care—but we were open to any suggestions and improvisation. Every hour sitting next to David and typing on the keyboard felt purposeful and the daily routine of making cups of coffee, meals, and so on, was rewarding and affiliating, knowing how many decades he had lived in that house and all the many people who had stayed and gone over the years.... I think he enjoyed the youthfulness around him for most of the time! David was a remarkable individual. With all the obstacles he overcame, living to seventy-six, he is an inspiration to us all. Thank you, David, for having us, befriending, advising, supporting and inspiring us to persist despite adversity and overcome our hurdles.

Conor McAvoy writes:

I will never be able to thank David for all he did for me and so many students who shared his home. In the last couple of months of his life people came from all over the world to thank him, but David's humility refused to acknowledge he had done anything extraordinary. I remember once getting a phone call over Christmas saying he had given my bedroom keys to a stranger who had turned up at the house after Mass one evening. I was sceptical that this was a good idea, but David insisted this was the Year of Mercy and,

> unless I had any jewels hidden in the room, there wouldn't be a problem. In his homily at David's requiem Deacon Tony reminded us of an occasion when David said that he would stand upright before the Lord on the last day. That thought will always bring me great comfort.

Many similar tributes from former residents and friends appeared on the Greenlaw Court Facebook page after he died early in the morning on 17 February, 2017. Someone remembered David saying: "Life is only the orchestra tuning up to play the main concert to follow." A friend abroad wrote: "For so keen an intelligence enlightened by faith the face-to-face must be uniquely glorious."

Following his Requiem Mass, celebrated by Bishop Hugh Gilbert OSB at St. Mary's Cathedral on March 9th, David was buried, by permission of Abbot Anselm Atkinson OSB, in the monks' cemetery at Pluscarden Abbey, after being led there by the monks chanting the *In paradisum*.

St. Gregory the Great, the biographer of St. Benedict, wrote that the mark of greater people is that "in the pain of their own suffering, they do not lose sight of what might help other people; while they patiently bear the adversity that afflicts them, they still think to teach others what might be necessary; in this they are like certain great doctors who, they themselves struck, forget their own wounds in order to attend to others" (*Moralia in Job*, I, 3, 40). The inscription on the plain wooden cross at the head of his grave, among the places of rest of generations of monks buried and regularly prayed for there, reads:

David Braine
1940 to 2017
Philosopher
RIP

Deacon Tony Schmitz OSB Obl.
June 29th, 2021, Solemnity of St. Peter and St. Paul
Anniversary of David's reception into full Communion
with the Catholic Church

CHAPTER 2

BRAINE'S MAJOR WORKS

Daniel De Haan, editor

David Braine generated three large and difficult philosophical monographs on God, the human person, and human language. Alongside these three major monographs, David penned several articles, chapters, and shorter works touching on a range of issues from ethics to metaphysics, epistemology, psychology, and dogmatic theology. Many of these treat in detail aspects of Aquinas's philosophy and theology.[1] Braine's books do not make for easy reading, but those who have struggled through them have found these three studies to be littered with rewarding insights, many of which still merit greater attention and more systematic exposition. It seems fitting, therefore, to provide an overview of these three monographs and bring to his potential readers' attention the riches they might enjoy by patiently working through his unwieldy but profound studies.

Braine's first two books, *The Reality of Time and the Existence of God* (*RTEG*) and *The Human Person: Animal and Spirit* (*HPAS*) are both trailblazing adventures into relatively

1 Full bibliographical information for these studies can be found at the end of this volume.

uncharted territories. They leave for future settlers a path of deep insights and profound suggestions for future exploration. His third monograph, *Language and Human Understanding* is different in kind. It is more innovative than his two earlier works, and it also succeeds in establishing a systematic foundation for future inquiries. Indeed, one of the achievements of *LHU* is that it is among the essential points of departure for all future Thomist or like-minded enquiries in the philosophy of language.

THE REALITY OF TIME AND THE EXISTENCE OF GOD (1988)

In the aftermath of the demise of logical positivism and its declarations that philosophical talk about God was literally meaningless, there was a strong resurgence of work in philosophy of religion starting around the time of the 1955 publication *New Essays in Philosophical Theology*, edited by Antony Flew and Alasdair MacIntyre. In the decades that followed, Alvin Plantinga and Richard Swinburne became the formidable founders of analytic philosophy's distinctive approaches to philosophy of religion. Among their many contributions, Plantinga and others developed sophisticated defenses of the ontological argument for God's existence while Swinburne and others defended probabilistic and design arguments for God's existence. In a 1968 issue of *Mind*, Braine reviewed Charles Hartshorne's contribution to these debates, *Anselm's Discovery: A Re-examination of the Ontological Proof for God's existence*. Commenting on these wide-ranging Anglo-American debates in his review of Braine's *RTEG*, Swinburne points out:

> There is, however, an obvious gap: there has, despite the enormous influence of such arguments in the history of philosophical theology, been no modern articulation in the tradition of Anglo-American philosophy of a Thomist cosmological argument (of a kind set out in Aquinas' first four "ways"). David Braine's book plugs this gap. It is a long, sophisticated presentation of a Thomist cosmological argument, an interesting attempt and one well-grounded in sensitivity to the history of philosophy.[2]

2 Richard Swinburne, Review of *The Reality of Time and the Existence of God. The Project of Proving God's Existence* by David Braine, *The Journal of Theological Studies* 40, no. 1 (April 1989): 329—31, especially 329.

Swinburne aptly situates *RTEG* within those debates as a continuation of Thomist cosmological arguments. As Braine himself notes, "My argument is close to the prime mover argument of Aquinas (the 'First Way'), properly understood."[3] The aim of his argument is "To show that God exists from the sheer existence of things as this is exhibited in their temporality, in the real contingency of the future, the temporality whereby their continuance is not yet fixed or settled and whereby at an earlier time they might never have come to be."[4]

RTEG commences with four "investigations" on the philosophical notions crucial to the strategy of Braine's overall argument. The first investigation concerns the question of the reality of time. Braine surveys both philosophical and scientific issues concerning time and contends that no matter what theoretical physics establishes with respect to time, "it remains that, absolutely speaking, the continuance of things in existence is, if time is real, in need of explanation."[5] Central to *RTEG* is the question of "existential inertia," as more recent debates label it:[6] do beings that exist continue existing so long as their existence is not interfered with? Braine rejects the thesis that composite substances in time exhibit existential inertia,[7] arguing that the reality of time means "that at any juncture the future relative to that juncture has real contingency because it still simply does not exist and is in no way 'given.'"[8] Establishing the reality of time as a dramatic now with a distinctive directionality exhibited in causal relations plays an important role in Braine's argument for "the impotence of the temporal to ground existence and the need of such a ground which went with it."[9] Woven within his myriad discussions of time, we sometimes encounter intriguing suggestions about God's eternity,

3 See Braine, *RTEG*, 223–24 for discussion.

4 Braine, *RTEG*, 1.

5 Braine, *RTEG*, 15.

6 Cf. David Braine, "God, Being and Person," in *Analytical Thomism: Traditions in Dialogue*, ed. Craig Paterson and Matthew Pugh (Aldershot: Ashgate, 2006), 1–24; Edward Feser, "Existential Inertia and the Five Ways," *American Catholic Philosophical Quarterly* 85, no. 2 (2011): 237–67. Feser cites Braine's treatment of the "Mythology of inertia" on pp. 256, 261–62.

7 See Braine, *RTEG*, 14–15.

8 Braine, *RTEG*, 339.

9 Braine, *RTEG*, 342.

practical knowledge, freedom, and action in time, but Braine does not develop any of these points beyond a mere sketch.[10]

The second investigation addresses the nature of explanation and causation. Braine rejects the Humean consensus on causation common to analytic philosophy by arguing *against* mere regularity and *for* the primacy of causal powers. Explanations involving laws of nature are secondary abstract descriptions that characterize real aspects of causal agents, which are exercisers of active powers.[11] Reality and causation are closely intertwined for our grasp of what is real is bound up with causal relations in the world. In short, Braine endorses a version of the Eleatic Principle: we ascribe "reality" only to that which makes a causal difference. Explanation tracks causal relations, but whereas causal agency pertains to what occurs in reality, explanation is a "second-order concept, a concept which we use in describing or referring to our thought about the world."[12] Throughout *RTEG*, Braine espouses a critical realism which acknowledges the openness and limitations of what we finite human enquirers bring to our investigations, and that ultimately our explanations of reality cannot undermine the very reality and nature of the humans doing the enquiring. This is why a "Physicist's contemplative understanding of reality must include as an integral and cardinal part of itself an appreciation of those causal actions and relations which are also objects of knowledge and concern to the ordinary man."[13]

An overarching theme of Braine's work is the importance of a rigorous pursuit of rational enquiry that avoids and can critique the excesses of various Procrustean rationalisms. Neither explanation nor causation are one-size-fits-all notions. They are both polymorphic notions which we can only understand by appreciating the variety of their manifestations; causes exhibit "irreducibly different modes of causal agency."[14]

10 Braine, *RTEG*, 45; 130–35 ff.

11 Braine, *RTEG*, 78.

12 Braine, *RTEG*, 72.

13 Braine, *RTEG*, 71.

14 Braine, *RTEG*, 80.

> We know of the actual application of these concepts [of composition, positive existence, causal agency, actuality, potentiality] in respect of cases of secondary causality first, and from this know a posteriori of the coherence of the statements applying these concepts in these cases.... Then at a second stage we recognize that the conditions of this coherence include the operation of God's primary causality in causing the reliable continuance of the natures operative in secondary causality. What unites the different applications of the word "cause" is not a single univocally understood general proposition, but the understanding of a single analogically understood concept, an understanding realized in a variety of different types of application.[15]

His third and fourth investigations confront issues surrounding existence in logical theory and metaphysics respectively. Braine leaves us some hints that his discussion of existence in logical theory in Chapter IV is synthesizing the riches of twentieth century logical theory with Aquinas's Aristotelian sense of being as the truth of propositions or the fact of existence, while Chapter V presents a synthesis of analytic metaphysics with Aquinas's notion of the act of existence (*actus essendi*) as the fundamental sense of being.[16] Braine attacks some of the fundamental logical dogmas of analytic philosophy, "The favorite among these is that which is expressed in formal logic by the existential quantifier."[17] He argues at length that this dogma, first "ignores the presupposition of existence which arises whenever any quantifier whatsoever is used."[18] Second, it ignores tensing, and third, it ignores the "interrelations of general and singular statements, and the primitiveness of the existential presuppositions associated with statements which are 'singular.'"[19] Braine also introduces here several illuminating suggestions and ideas about "presupposition" that build on insights of P. Strawson, J. L. Austin, and others. His later work on pragmatics seems to flesh these out in more detail.

15 Braine, *RTEG*, 83.

16 Braine, *RTEG*, 104; 154–57.

17 Braine, *RTEG*, 86.

18 Braine, *RTEG*, 86. Braine argues that "existence is not a predicate, but presupposed to any predicate" *RTEG*, 144; see also *RTEG*, 147.

19 Braine, *RTEG*, 86.

In his metaphysical investigation of existence, he adumbrates the core meanings of "positive existence" as substances with existence, accidents, or enriching attributes of substances, and situations in which they manifest their causal powers.[20] He concludes that "to have real existence is to have the active power to 'efficiently cause' something, i.e., to act causally. It is not that active power is what real existence means, is, or consists in, but that the possession of it is sufficient criterion of real existence."[21] Braine draws on the insights of Étienne Gilson's interpretation of Aquinas on the metaphysics of *esse* in his creative amplification of Aquinas's arguments for the real distinction and composition of existence (*esse*) with the nature or essence it actualizes. "Existence is what gives actuality to properties, and so is explanatorily prior to or explanatorily presupposed by them and cannot flow from or be included amongst them without self-causation being involved."[22] "The continuance of the very stuff of the Universe, the fact that it goes on existing, is not self-explanatory. It is incoherent to say that the very stuff of the Universe continues to exist by its very nature since it has to continue to exist in order for this nature to exist or to be operative. Hence, nature presupposes existence."[23] And, "*for a thing to be caused in any respect requires a distinction between the subject and its existing, whether the latter is directly caused or presupposed in a change which is caused.*"[24]

On the basis of these investigations, Braine launches the many other topics and problems taken up in *RTEG*. These include epistemological issues concerning first-order and second-order enquiries, employing philosophy of language to show the incoherence of some metaphysical projects, responding to Kantian challenges to metaphysics, methods for avoiding anthropomorphism in our understanding of God's perfections,[25] understanding general principles, and a critique of the principle of sufficient reason. Braine also develops a novel account of personhood and why the First Cause

20 Braine, *RTEG*, 109, 149–57.
21 Braine, *RTEG*, 123.
22 Braine, *RTEG*, 125.
23 Braine, *RTEG*, 10.
24 Braine, *RTEG*, 145.
25 Braine, *RTEG*, 300.

must be personal, along with arguments for the indispensability of an *a posteriori* philosophy theology for any revealed theology.

Noteworthy among Braine's "Lessons of History" concerning "the structure of the causal argument to God's existence," is his own account of the classical distinction between primary and secondary causality.

> The positive existing of creaturely substances is the existing of things that cannot exist instantaneously but only through time, a time through which they exercise their characteristic activities and passions according to their natures. It cannot then be an existing which God maintains without their activities in exercise of their natures continuing, and their activities are in general theirs only, not His, i.e., not activities of which he is the subject. But his upholding does not causally depend on their activity but vice-versa.... And all the positive existing presupposed to their activities is His activity.[26]

While there are many insights scattered throughout *RTEG*, one of Braine's most trenchant disquisitions concerns the launching point of his own argument for God's existence, which is based not on the finitude or the contingency of substances but on their compositeness.[27] His perspicacious analysis of compositeness provides us with a metaphysical investigation that is of enduring philosophical value for the light it sheds both on his own arguments for the distinction between nature and the act of existence in all created substances, and for the way Braine employs this notion of compositeness to arrive at a cogent explanation of both the contingency and derivativeness of temporal substances as well as why their ultimate First Cause must be infinite, underivative, and incomposite.

A final noteworthy innovation in Braine's causal argument for God's existence comes out of this understanding of composite substances. Their causal relations within time and their complete derivativeness lead to the conclusion that, unlike in Aquinas's arguments for God's existence, there are no intermediaries even

26 Braine, *RTEG*, 136.
27 Braine, *RTEG*, 155–65.

within *per se* causal orders. This is because "only that which is such as to be incapable of having a cause, i.e., intrinsically underivative, can thus give or sustain existence. On this suggestion, only the intrinsically underivative can cause temporal continuance and there is no room for a regress even beyond one cause, no room for even one intermediate, let alone for an infinite regress in causes. The First Cause will be immediate to the continuing existing of temporal things as its direct cause."[28]

As a number of his reviewers noted, Braine's *RTEG* is an arduous work to get through. Yet it contains some trenchant criticisms and insights concerning how analytic philosophers do versus how they should understand the metaphysics of existence. Braine was one of the few analytic philosophers of his era sympathetic to Aquinas who attempted to develop and defend what has more recently been characterized as Analytic Existential Thomism.[29] There remains much more important work to be done on this front, and future enquiries would benefit significantly from reading Braine's *RTEG* and attempting to flesh out in more detail the brief but penetrating arguments he presents there.

THE HUMAN PERSON: ANIMAL AND SPIRIT (1992)

Overt references to the influence of Aquinas are peppered throughout *RTEG*, but *HPAS* exemplifies how a contemporary philosopher can reformulate for oneself the questions, distinctions, and arguments Aquinas pursued so as to arrive at one's own contemporary defense of a holistic philosophical anthropology. Braine does not, moreover, slavishly follow Aquinas. But, like Aquinas did in his own day, Braine draws upon the best insights and resources of his contemporaries in order to advance Aquinas's own arguments as well as engage new questions and objections which Aquinas could not have anticipated. The book is filled with apposite and perspicacious arguments drawn from Ludwig Wittgenstein, Gilbert Ryle, J. L. Austin, Elizabeth Anscombe, Gabriel Marcel, Maurice Merleau-Ponty, James Gibson, and Karol Wojtyła. By marshalling such a wide range of

28 Braine, *RTEG*, 343.

29 See Turner C. Nevitt, "How to be an Analytic Existential Thomist," *The Thomist* 82, no. 3 (2018): 321–52.

philosophical perspectives in the development of arguments for a Thomist anthropology, Braine demonstrates the perennial relevance of Aquinas's distinctive form of enquiry and its eminently defensible conclusions about what human persons are.

The first part of *HPAS* addresses our human animality and the second part concerns "how this animal can also be a spirit, a spiritual or intellectual being whose existence transcends the body." Braine follows this order because the "first need is to understand the human being's character as an animal living in the world, and it is only at a second stage that one can go on to understand what is special to human beings, what is involved in intellectuality and the capacity for reflection and choice."[30] It is this intellectual dimension of our animal life that reveals human animals are persons as well.

In Part I, Braine establishes his holistic philosophical anthropology by focusing on the psychophysical unity manifested in our shared animal capacities for perception, emotion, and action. He argues for the need and superiority of this holistic anthropology against the dominant positions of materialism and dualism by delineating the common and distinct deficiencies with both positions. Anticipating enactivist theories of perception, Braine articulates a holistic account of perception as inseparable from psychological behavior, which he amplifies in his rich treatments of sensation, emotion, and action. Significant is his non-dualistic doctrine of psychological or "mind-involving" statements intended to counter the fundamental mistakes in introspectionist doctrines (which unduly isolate psychological phenomena from physical phenomena) and behaviorist doctrines (which reduce psychological phenomena to "behavioral" phenomena conceived as mere physiological movements). Against these standard pictures of psychological attribution, Braine shows that when speaking about "human beings and the other higher animals" we actually employ "irreducibly hybrid facts and propositions—hybrid in that they straddle the mental and the physical, and irreducibly hybrid in that there is no analyzing them into separate mental and physical components together with coordinate relations."[31]

30 Braine, *HPAS*, xvii.
31 Braine, *HPAS*, 171.

To highlight the holistic psychophysical unity of human and other animal behavior Braine demonstrates the primacy of agent causation over event causation against the position of neo-Humeans like Donald Davidson. After correcting the errors concerning efficient causation generated by event causal theories that attempt to reduce agent causation to event causation, Braine turns to confute the contention that final causality is reducible to efficient causality. Against reductive mechanistic theories of teleology, Braine defends the irreducible nature of teleological explanations for understanding the reality of unified and purposeful causal agency of animal living.

Braine then brings together these investigations concerning the psychophysical unity of animal perception, emotion, and action at the level of both explanation and reality to articulate his first refutation of mechanistic physicalism. He argues that,

> mind-involving explanations positively exclude any more basic mechanical or physical explanation of the phenomena concerned—and that this is true not just at the level of the 'phenomenon,' the level of experience and of description tailored to experience, but at the level of fundamental explanation and reality. It is not the involvement of teleology alone, but the involvement of mind-involving concepts which enables us to demonstrate that these explanations are basic, and thus to demonstrate that physicalism is false.[32]

Braine's refutation of materialism is accomplished "not by resorting to dualism" but "by drawing on the consequences of what it is to be an animal with consciousness, drawing not upon something peculiar to human beings, but something they share with the higher animals."[33]

Braine brings Part I to a close with a chapter that sets out in detail five major characteristics shared by humans and other animals in virtue of their common psychophysical nature. He concludes that what "human beings share with the animals, viz., perception, sensation, emotion, and intentional action, suffice to reveal—firstly at the level of description and secondly at the level of explanation—that neither

32 Braine, *HPAS*, 249.
33 Braine, *HPAS*, 339.

human beings nor the higher animals can be regarded as mechanisms (not even a kind of mechanism labelled 'biological')."[34]

In Part II, Braine shifts to what is specific to human persons and is that in virtue of which they are incarnated *spirits*, as revealed in the creative understanding manifested in human language. Here we see the germ of Braine's innovative account of language sketched for the first time, which would later develop into the full-fledged systematic account articulated in *HUL*. We find, among many noteworthy discussions, the introduction of his version of the distinction between *langue* and *parole*, the integral role of pragmatics within semantics, what distinguishes thinking in the medium of words from imagery, and such strokes of genius as his explication of the intentionality and teleological unity of thinking (to oneself or aloud) in the medium of words, wherein "the earlier part of the expression of the thought carries a meaning-towards-the-whole within which the rest unfolds."[35] Braine explains for us how,

> the teleology for the more extended thought whereby the whole of it is embraced or comes within the context and direction [is] set by its *arche* or beginning in the mind—so that whatever comes later comes as part of the same tree, an element in the unfolding of the same course of thinking, so that in this way the unity of the thought remains, a unity stronger than that of the unity of the expression of thought. Within what is presented as the expression of thought there is always liable to be that which is adventitious, and there may be a revolution in the direction or sense so that the supposed unity of the expression is no longer a true unity of meaning or thought, but a unity only in some sociological sense.[36]

Human linguistic understanding and expression reveals another irreducible hybrid or psychosomatic unity, but one that surprisingly also discloses the disembodied transcendence of human intellectual capacities due to the essentially informal, flexible, self-reflexive, and unrestricted expressiveness of human language. This account of

34 Braine, *HPAS*, 339.
35 Braine, *HPAS*, 443.
36 Braine, *HPAS*, 445.

human linguistic understanding provides the backbone for Braine's second refutation of mechanistic physicalism in his four arguments which aim to conclude that linguistic understanding and thinking have no bodily organ.

Braine argues that the psychophysical unity of human animality is not self-enclosed within the physical order but is open to intellectual transcendence.[37] While he rejects the causal closure of the physical, he also rejects substance dualism in favor of a distinctively Aristotelian form of holism, a holism that does not preclude the human transcendence of the body. Braine presents this holistic or "'unistic' conception of the human being as a psychosomatic unity"[38] by integrating a concrete phenomenological approach with a more abstract Aristotelian ontological explanation. He employs these together to address Aquinas's query of how it is "possible for the human soul to be both a form and a concrete individual thing [*hoc aliquid*]."[39] Like Aquinas, Braine resolves the query by concluding it is possible for the soul to be both form of the body and to exist of itself for "the existence of the subject is primarily correlative with activity as such, and the character of this existence is set by the character of the activities. If some of the activities, especially ones most nodal to life, transcend the body, then existence and life transcend the body. This way of presenting the matter embodies the kernel of the view of Aquinas."[40] Accordingly, "*it is the existence of the body and of its parts, not that of the soul, which is dependent and incomplete in its nature by itself.*"[41]

The book concludes with two explanations for how human beings transcend the body. The first explanation articulates a phenomenological understanding of the human soul's transcendence, which identifies the soul or subjectivity of phenomenological experiences with the explanatory soul as both substantial form of the body and as per se subsisting.

37 Braine, *HPAS*, 348–50.
38 Braine, *HPAS*, 480.
39 Braine, *HPAS*, 481.
40 Braine, *HPAS*, 538.
41 Braine, *HPAS*, 525.

> Once the human soul, considered as the subject of understanding, perception, imagination, memory and emotion, i.e., considered phenomenologically, has been granted to have reality in its own right, and not merely phenomenological status, there is a compulsion to regard this soul as what gives the body the kind of life (nature understood in terms of and realized in behavior) and thereby the kind of unity which it has, giving unity, nature, and function to the parts of the body. That is, there is a compulsion to identify the human soul, understood phenomenologically, with the human soul as understood in the way Aristotle understood the form of the human body.[42]

The second explanation makes the case for how the human person transcends the body without drawing upon a phenomenological or ontological concept of soul. "When a human being comes to be, we have the coming to be of a focalized subject of a nature to have operations which are not bodily, and thus the coming to be of a being whose *esse* transcends the body. This being persists through life and does not cease at death."[43] Braine argues that classical arguments for the transcendence of the soul are, if not dispensable,[44] at least depend upon those for the transcendence of the human being as such. "Now, if it is legitimate to talk of the phenomenological soul at all, then one will certainly say these things of the soul and its *esse* will indeed be none other than that of the human being as such. But in speaking of its transcendence in *esse*, one will say nothing which one has not said in speaking of the transcendence of the human person."[45]

The concluding section of *HPAS* meditates on the significance of death in light of the understanding of the human person defended in Braine's extended disquisition on the question of the Psalmist and the epigraph of the book: what are human beings … ? "From the standpoint of philosophy, the datum is that, because of the way human linguistic understanding and thought transcend the material, death is

42 Braine, *HPAS*, 525–26.
43 Braine, *HPAS*, 540.
44 Braine, *HPAS*, 527.
45 Braine, *HPAS*, 542.

not a closure of life or hope, but only a closure of knowledge of and control over what is to come."[46]

Braine's *HPAS* received different reviews from a number of prominent philosophers. In his critical review, E. J. Lowe rightly drew attention to Braine's strong denouncements and his inaccurate portrayals of the positions of some of his interlocutors. James Ross praised it as an "extraordinary book, in scope, in passionate convictions argued intensely, and in its replacement of both dualist and materialist views.... In subject-matter, scope and length, it is a constructive alternative to Rorty's *Philosophy and the Mirror of Nature*, not supposing that philosophy needs a new occupation, but providing us with new answers in continuity and transformation of the old."[47] But he also cautiously observed that the "reader has to adjust to the fact that, though thoroughly familiar with recent philosophy, Braine is deeply disenchanted with most of it, regarding it, as I do too, as enshrining a tissue of unexamined obvious falsehoods."[48] It is a testament to Braine's wide-ranging philosophical competences that no one else has since attempted to articulate a constructive Thomist philosophical anthropology of the same magnitude since Braine's *The Human Person: Animal and Spirit*.

Future Thomistic enquiries in philosophical anthropology still need to learn many lessons from this work as they seek to re-ask Aquinas's and Braine's questions for themselves and to articulate still more contemporary and systematic accounts of the psychological and ontological facets of human persons. Besides Braine's extraordinarily novel approach to language, Thomists need to appreciate his incisive criticisms of all forms of physicalism and dualism and his noteworthy insistence on the psychophysical unity of human acts of perception, emotion, imagination, understanding, and intentionally acting without giving up the metaphysical theses, similar to Aquinas's, that linguistic understanding reveals the subsistence and transcendence of the human person.

46 Braine, *HPAS*, 544.

47 James Ross, Review of David Braine, *The Human Person*, *The Philosophical Quarterly* 44, no. 177 (1994): 536–38, especially 536.

48 Ross, Review of David Braine, 537.

LANGUAGE AND HUMAN UNDERSTANDING: THE ROOTS OF CREATIVITY IN SPEECH AND THOUGHT (2014)

Braine's *magnum opus* on language comes in just under eight hundred pages; it truly defies summation. He notes, "This book has been over twenty-one years in the writing, the fruit of fifty years' preoccupation with language."[49] As with his two earlier monographs, he traced some of the "central ideas of the book" to the Gifford Investigations he presented as Gifford Fellow of the University of Aberdeen in 1985.[50] Readers of his earlier *The Human Person*, will not be surprised to see the crucial role language plays in Braine's anthropology.

> A right account of language is, I believe, the key to a right account of the nature of human understanding and thought, and thereby the key to a right understanding of human nature as a whole. Yet the whole theory of language is in considerable disorder, and my aim must therefore be first to seek to remedy this. This will take me into the heart of current debates in linguistics, philosophy, and psychology, and lead me to undertake an extended study of grammar. The effect will be to show how language exhibits the ultimate freedom of the human intellect and will from conformity with mechanically applicable rules and from limitations set by neurology. The brain plays a key role in the normal functioning of the human mind but does not determine or shape linguistic understanding and thinking in the medium of words, as this develops through adaptation to and learning within a social external environment of other speakers and hearers, all within a setting of natural things.[51]

LHU is divided into three major parts. The first part lays the groundwork and commences with the dynamic *expression* of meaning of words. Braine develops upon his earlier work's account of the meaning of words at the level of language-possession (*langue*) and at the level of language-use (*parole*). His detailed explication of

49 Braine, *LHU*, xiii.
50 Braine, *LHU*, xiv.
51 Braine, *LHU*, 1.

this distinction ingeniously integrates and linguistically amplifies Aquinas's scholastic distinction between the intellect's acquisition of *intelligible species* as first acts or *habitus* and their deployment in intellectual understanding and its expressive formation in concepts (*concepta*) as second acts or *operationes*. "The *langue*-understanding of a word comes to birth in the act of our first understanding of its exercise in *parole*, each kind of understanding ranking as a *hexis*."[52]

> Entities at the rank of the sentence or utterance (whether propositions, questions, commands, or whatever) require to be understood and defined primarily at the level of *parole* or language-use, whereas entities at the rank of word, morpheme, or lexeme have to be understood and defined at the level of language-possession, or *langue*, as well as that of language-use, or *parole*. Since the meaning of sentences has to be understood by reference to the meaning of their words and other lexical factors, the problems of understanding the relationships between sentence and word, sentence-meaning and word-meaning, and of understanding the relationships between *langue* and *parole*, language-possession and language-use, are inseparable.[53]

As we learn a language, we come to acquire linguistic understanding of words' *langue*-meanings through our linguistic understanding of their myriad expressions in *parole*-meanings. Words can be expressive of single or multiple focuses of meaning, such as we might find listed separately in a dictionary. But even single focuses of *langue*-meaning can generate an indefinite number of discourse-significances or *parole*-meanings in speech and writing,[54] demonstrating how language enables us to make an "infinite use of finite means"—Braine's favorite refrain from Von Humboldt. Sentences, then, are "linguistic deliverances formed in the act of speech or writing, a lexical factor [or word] gaining what sense or discourse-significance it has as a functional constituent in the act of speech or composition."[55] Braine argues that pragmatics is integral to semantics. This is revealed in the ways the

52 Braine, *LHU*, 375n18.
53 Braine, *LHU*, 81.
54 Braine, *LHU*, 94.
55 Braine, *LHU*, 91.

words of *langue* and the indefinite purposes for which we employ them in speech give expression to their potential manifold meanings from one context to another. But it this is also manifested in the inherent informality, flexibility, and analogically extended use of words in linguistic operations. It is these features and not the exaggerated emphasis on endless recursive iteration of linguistic operations that displays what is extraordinary about linguistic understanding.

> It is this which enables us to communicate intelligibly, even when we are dealing with unanticipated kinds of situation or raising fresh problems and dealing with them in unprecedented ways.[56]

> A word's particular meaning is typically actualized in a multiplicity of different kinds of way, not reducible to any one mechanically applicable rule, obedience to which is formally decidable. Accordingly, we cannot define a language or speech system as a definite or enumerable totality.[57]

On the basis of the peculiar integrated flexibility exhibited by linguistic understanding, Braine argues for an indivisible *capacity* for linguistic understanding which seems to be distinctive of human beings. He explores at length the evolutionary history of *Homo sapiens* and explains why the discontinuity of the emergence of an indivisible language capacity is not in conflict with the biological continuity of humans with their evolutionary ancestors.[58]

This theme of the biological and psychological continuity shared among humans and other animals is developed at greater length in Part II. Braine draws upon the work of James Gibson and others to articulate the ways in which the psychological and biological capacities of animals are dynamically geared towards their environments and the myriad affordances that are exigent and relevant to their survival and flourishing.

> Gibson's environment-geared or "ecological" model of visual perception makes the cognitive aspect of perception inseparable from the gearing of our motor activity to the natural environment, a

56 Braine, *LHU*, 105.
57 Braine, *LHU*, 186.
58 Braine, *LHU*, 233–42.

> model intelligible only in the context of an Aristotelian conception of human unity and function. Gibson's way of thinking about perception provides a model for how we should think about the human use of speech—speech being adapted not just to the natural environment in general, but to the social environment of a community of people speaking the same language. Within this social environment it will be the norm for hearer and speaker to understand the same by what the speaker has said. This norm determines how we describe and assess deficiencies in speech and its understanding.[59]

It is on the basis of this continuity that Braine goes on to explore the development of the distinctive and holistically conceived multi-modular psychological and biological capacities required for humans to learn and use language. He discusses at length the variety of environmental, developmental, and social constraints which "semantics and pragmatics set upon the human organism, tuning the various parts of the brain so that they fulfill their roles in our use of language according to its general functional semantic structure."[60]

Braine then turns to the nature of linguistic understanding itself as exhibited within our awareness of our acts of linguistic understanding in communication. He draws upon his holistic anthropology from *HPAS* and expands its critique of behaviorism, introspectionism, and representationalism and articulates an even fuller account of the features of teleology and intentional action that are integral to linguistic understanding. Braine incisively sums up his own view in contrast with those he rejects in the following extended quotation.

> [A]ny view whatsoever that proposes that the only way thoughts are realized ontologically is in brain states or processes will be open to the objection that there can be no isomorphism between thoughts and brain states or processes—for the same reasons that there can be no isomorphism between thoughts and states in the world. For speech and thought do not portray the world, but purport to report or describe features of it. Statements are not pictures, even if they

59 Braine, *LHU*, 295.
60 Braine, *LHU*, 361–62.

> sometimes enable us to form pictures. In making a statement or forming a judgment, human beings (although within the world as psychophysical unities) in speech or thought as it were makes a cut, dividing between truth and falsity—by saying that P, excluding whatever is incompatible with it—but portrays nothing. In this, they exercise an act of mastery, not just the mastery of bringing deliberations to conclusions, but being able to do this without having their thinking limited to proceeding along tramlines set by supposed internal limitations set by language, whether stemming from the speech customs of their society or from their neurophysiological make-up.
>
> Grammar at least imposes no such limitations. For, as part three will indicate, the only constraints reflected by syntax are those set by pragmatics and general logic, with these constraints shaping the role of other language-users in learning to speak and molding the parts played by brain processing in the learning and use of language—the processing which allows us, even as we speak, to adopt appropriate vocabulary, inflections, word order, and morphology with such rapidity.[61]

Part III's extraordinarily ambitious project, which nearly spans the same length as the first two parts, is aptly titled "Rewriting the Philosophy of Grammar and Restoring Unity to the Theory of Language." Braine joins the ranks of those linguistic theorists fundamentally opposed to Chomsky and his disciples whose linguistic theorizing prioritize syntax and are moved to argue for innate universal grammar. For Braine, our human form of life, as in many other animals, is embedded within a lived environment, one that for humans is also socially structured as well. Contrary to Chomsky, Braine argues that the grammatical, logical, and other ways languages are structured are not autonomous from the pragmatics of human interactions and living within common environs. Accordingly, it is not innate neural modules that are the generative and determinative of the "universal grammatical or conceptual structures" of language; rather it is "semantics, as reflecting understanding, and pragmatics, as reflecting the structures of human communication, which alone set

61 Braine, *LHU*, 396.

universal limits to "grammatical structure" in any of the ways that this has been commonly understood."[62]

Braine's linguistic theory draws on the lived contexts in which humans make *utterances* that are *expressive* of what humans mean to communicate. "The basis of every grammar lies in the structures of topic, subject, and predicate together with affirmation, negation, and interrogation—all of which have pragmatic aspects, albeit of different kinds. These structures arise in the same ways in connection with every subject-matter, abstract as well as concrete."[63]

Braine zooms in on the ways utterances are integrated through the *verbal* form of predicates, which *say* something about a subject or topic. He surveys the extensive literature on how children learn languages by imitation and singles out Michael Tomasello's psycholinguistic work in particular for detailing "the connection between the key role of verbs and the role played by pragmatics or the context of human interaction in which they are learned."[64] Children learn not only to imitate the actions of others (e.g., spinning a top), but also to imitate the verbal announcement of one's action, like saying "I spin (it)" or some similar "primitive sentential form, a form within which the content-introducing element is the verb, setting the framework for the whole utterance."[65] So while nouns are often learned by ostension, "verbs are learned in being used as verbs, not by first naming an action, which would be by means of a noun, and then using this noun as a verb."[66] The generative basis for verbs and nouns is therefore not incidental for Braine. He elaborates upon the "distinction between referring or 'naming' expressions and saying or 'verbal' expressions" where sayings are fundamental because of their "overarching functional role."[67]

In connection with these topics Braine addresses at length important grammatical and logical issues concerning "general logic," sentences, clauses, names, sense, reference, affirmation, negation, force, cognates, morphology, lexicons, syntax, parameters, and

62 Braine, *LHU*, 766.
63 Braine, *LHU*, 400.
64 Braine, *LHU*, 437.
65 Braine, *LHU*, 438.
66 Braine, *LHU*, 439.
67 Braine, *LHU*, 528.

many other grammatical, logical, and philosophical factors relevant to the ways *langue* is employed in *parole* to comprise the pragmatics of semantics. Throughout his confrontation of these issues, we find appreciative discussions and critiques of such formidable thinkers as Chomsky, Frege, Wittgenstein, Ryle, Austin, Strawson, Davidson, Geach, Dummett, Grice, and many others.

In the final chapters Braine develops at length his account of grammaticalization and his arguments that

> discourse and sentence structure shape phrase structure, rather than phrase structure shaping sentence structure. By contrast, in Chomsky's minimalist approach, beginning with morphemes, in successive stages, ever larger phrasal groups are formed until sentential "phrases" are reached. In this bottom-up approach the properties of each lexical item as set within the lexicon determine the ways it can be joined ("Merge") with other items to form the successive complexes and determine how these can themselves be joined.... Chomsky has provided successively more sophisticated construction manuals for constructing sentences as static entities, but what we need instead is a grammar which models what is spoken as something live, not as something static. We are deceived through always looking at the written word on paper. Yet even in the act of reading and understanding we have something dynamic.[68]

Braine's systematic tour of language teaches us that language is most manifest in the activity of human speech. We first learn languages that are spoken in our early acts of imitating and then understanding the speech of others, then of ourselves. "Both language at the level of what is learned, *langue*, and language at the level of use, "speech" [*parole*], are public things appreciated by a community of people using the same language. Thus, speech and *langue* are both by nature public and shared. What belongs to the individual is the understanding of speech and knowledge of *langue* and the capacity for these." Yet all these abilities "are grounded in a more general understanding or intellectual capacity"[69] that transforms mere animal signaling into conceptualized meaningful linguistic expressions. It is here that

68 Braine, *LHU*, 705.
69 Braine, *LHU*, 745.

Braine uncovers the extraordinary "roots of our ability to express an infinite range of thought with a finite vocabulary."[70] Braine concludes by returning to the arguments of *HPAS*, now with an even deeper more profound reflection on the transcendent nature of linguistic understanding.

> What acts, or is exercised in activity, exists; and therefore, since both the understanding exercised in judgment and speech and the command of view exhibited in judgment transcend the body, human existence must also transcend the body. Yet these activities are at the same time, of their very nature, expressed through speech and coordinated with the use of the imagination, both involving the brain and how its activity is organized.... This makes speech activities uniquely important for the appreciation of the special nature of human beings. Here the character of the activity of thought seen in speech exhibits us as having an existence which transcends the body, so that when any new human being comes into existence, a new root of initiative, a new author of thought and action, is operative in the world—even while such thought requires the body for its characteristically human growth and expression.[71]

Braine's *LHU* lays a firm foundation for Thomist enquiries concerning the inextricable place of language in human life, and he also draws attention to crucial characteristic of rational animals that are frequently omitted by Thomists, namely, our essential sociality and the ways in which we develop within a human ecological context, including the social scaffolding that developmentally enables the exercise of our rational powers. These and other topics addressed in Braine's *LHU* provide valuable resources for contemporary Thomist investigations on human evolution and related questions. Similarly, recent Thomist studies on Aquinas's and broadly neo-Aristotelian arguments for the immateriality of the intellect will benefit from a careful study and more systematic exposition of Braine's own important contributions to arguments for the immateriality of the intellect both in *HPAS* and in *LHU*. Finally, despite a resurgence of interest in Aquinas's

70 Braine, *LHU*, 746.
71 Braine, *LHU*, 753.

metaphysics of existence and the analogy of being, few Thomist studies have engaged at length the relevant issues the analogy of being kicks up within philosophy of language. Any sophisticated contemporary Thomistic account of how we can meaningfully and truthfully talk about God and engage in the enquiries of natural theology will find indispensable arguments and expositions on the indefinite flexibility and creative potential of linguistic meaning and human understanding in Braine's *HLU*.

Given the extraordinarily broad expanse of topics taken up in each of these monographs, this brief surview of Braine's three monographs has inevitably left out many other points of interest and reasons for engaging these books. The aim is to encourage others to read Braine's work by providing an orientation into these challenging studies and highlighting some of the more impressive treasures that he unearthed that still require more careful and systematic philosophical excavation and refinement.

BIBLIOGRAPHY:

WORKS OF DAVID BRAINE

"Explanation and Modality." Bachelor's thesis, Oxford University, 1965.

"Infinite Sets." Paper presented to the Interdisciplinary Seminar on the History and Philosophy of Science, University of Aberdeen, Aberdeen, 1968.

Review of *Anselm's Discovery: A Re-Examination of the Ontological Proof for God's Existence*, by Charles Hartshorne. *Mind* 77, no. 307 (1968): 447–50.

"The Nature of Knowledge." *Proceedings of the Aristotelian Society* 72, no. 1 (1972): 41–63.

"Two Kinds of Critical Philosophy." Paper presented to Société Belge de Logique et de Philosophie des Sciences, Brussels, 1972.

Coauthor Michael Clark. "Varieties of Necessity." *Proceedings of the Aristotelian Society, Supplementary Volume* 46 (1972): 139–87.

"Observations on the Trinity: A Response to Professor Lochman." *Theology* 78, no. 658 (1975): 184–90.

"Truth and Definiteness." Paper presented at the University of St. Andrews, St. Andrews, 1976.

"Why Abortion?" In *Light and the Darkness.* Mowbray: Unity Press, 1981.

Prayer: Living with God, booklet. Aberdeen, Gilcom South Church, 1982.

Medical Ethics and Human Life. 2nd Edition, booklet. Aberdeen: Palladio Press, 1983. (1st edition, Palladio Press, 1979) Reprint, Eugene, OR: Wipf and Stock, 2019.

"The Place of the Virgin Mary in Dogmatics." *Scottish Journal of Theology* 37, no. 2 (1984): 145–62.

Coeditor Harry Lesser, eds. *Ethics, Technology, and Medicine.* Avebury Series in Philosophy. Aldershot: Gower Publishing Company, 1988.

"Human Animality: Its Relevance to the Shape of Ethics." In *Ethics, Technology, and Medicine*, edited by David Braine and Harry Lesser, Avebury Series in Philosophy, 6–30. Aldershot: Gower Publishing Company, 1988.

"Human Life: Its Secular Sacrosanctness." In *Ethics, Technology, and Medicine*, edited by David Braine and Harry Lesser, Avebury Series in Philosophy, 54–63. Aldershot: Gower Publishing Company, 1988.

"The Inner Jewishness of St. John's Gospel as the Clue to the Inner Jewishness of Jesus." *Studien Zum Neuen Testament Und Seiner Umwelt* 13, Series A (1988): 101–57.

The Reality of Time and the Existence of God: The Project of Proving God's Existence. Oxford: Clarendon Press, 1988.

The Human Person: Animal and Spirit. Notre Dame: University of Notre Dame Press, 1992. Reprints, London: Gerald Duckworth and Co., 1993; Notre Dame: University of Notre Dame Press, 1994; Eugene, OR: Wipf and Stock, 2018.

"God, Eternity and Time—An Essay in Review of Alan G. Padgett, *God, Eternity and the Nature of Time*," *The Evangelical Quarterly* 66, no. 4 (1994): 337–44.

"The Human and the Inhuman in Medicine: Review of Issues Concerning Reproductive Technology." In *Moral Truth and Moral Tradition: Essays in Honor of Peter Geach and Elizabeth Anscombe*, edited by Luke Gormally, 226–39. Dublin: Four Courts Press, 1994.

"Reply to Cockburn." *Religious Studies* 30, no. 3 (1994): 353–60.

"A National Wealth Service." Review of *Medicine, Money, and Morals,* by Mark A. Rodwin. *Times Higher Education Supplement,* no. 1141 (1994): 22.

Review of *From Existence to God,* by Barry Miller. *New Blackfriars* 75, no. 881 (1994): 228–30.

"What Makes a Christology into a Christian Theology?" *New Blackfriars* 77, no. 905 (1996): 288–302.

"Cosmological Arguments." In *Philosophy of Religion: A Guide to the Subject,* edited by Brian Davies, 42–54. Washington, DC: Georgetown University Press; London: Cassell and Co., 1998.

"The Relationship Between Philosophy and Cultures." Reflection on *Fides et Ratio,* by Pope John Paul II, no. 14. *L'Osservatore Romano,* Weekly English Edition (1999): 5–6.

Review of *Redirecting Philosophy: Reflections on the Nature of Knowledge from Plato to Lonergan,* by Hugo A. Meynell. *International Philosophical Quarterly* 40, no. 4 (2000): 521–23.

"The Active and Potential Intellects: Aquinas as a Philosopher in His Own Right." In *Mind, Metaphysics, and Value in the Thomist and Analytical Traditions,* edited by John Haldane, 18–35. Notre Dame, IN: University of Notre Dame Press, 2002.

"Aquinas, God and Being." In *Analytical Thomism: Traditions in Dialogue,* edited by Craig Paterson and Matthew S. Pugh, 1–24. Aldershot: Ashgate Publishing, 2006. Reprint, Abingdon: Routledge, 2016.

Review of *Aquinas on Being,* by Anthony Kenny. *British Journal for the History of Philosophy* 14, no. 2 (2006): 346–49.

"The Debate Between Henri de Lubac and His Critics." *Nova et Vetera* (English edition) 6, no. 3 (2008): 543–90.

"The Church's Teaching on the Virgin Mary." *Nova et Vetera* (English edition) 7 (2009): 877–970.

End of Life Assistance (Scotland) Bill ELA298 [Internet]. 2010. https://archive.parliament.scot/s3/committees/endLifeAsstBill/evidence/ELA298.pdf

Review of *The Trinitarian Theology of Saint Thomas Aquinas,* by Giles Emery. *Scottish Journal of Theology* 64, no. 1 (2011): 120–24.

"Life and Human Life: Their Nature and Emergence—The Singularity of Human Life." In *The Missing Link: A Symposium on Darwin's Framework for a Creation-Evolution Solution*, edited by Roy Abraham Varghese, 132–60. Lanham, MD: University Press of America, 2012.

Language and Human Understanding: The Roots of Creativity in Speech and Thought. Washington DC: The Catholic University of America Press, 2014.

BIBLIOGRAPHY:

REVIEWS OF DAVID BRAINE'S WORKS

(listed in ascending chronological order)

Lesser, Harry. Review of *Medical Ethics and Human Life*, by David Braine. *Journal of Medical Ethics* 10, no. 3 (1984): 162–63.

Quin, Philip L. Review of *The Reality of Time and the Existence of God: The Project of Proving God's Existence*, by David Braine. *The Review of Metaphysics* 42, no. 2 (1988): 378–79.

Helm, Paul. Review of *The Reality of Time and the Existence of God: The Project of Proving God's Existence*, by David Braine. *Philosophical Books* 30, no. 3 (1989): 185–86.

Swinburne, Richard. Review of *The Reality of Time and the Existence of God: The Project of Proving God's Existence*, by David Braine. *The Journal of Theological Studies* 40, no. 1 (1989): 329–31.

Wilder, Alfred. Review of *The Reality of Time and the Existence of God: The Project of Proving God's Existence*, by David Braine. *Angelicum* 66, no. 1/2 (1989): 361–65.

Bergum, Vangie. Review of *Ethics, Technology, and Medicine*, edited by David Braine and Harry Lesser. *Philosophy in Review* 10, no. 10 (1990): 394–96.

Clarke, W. Norris. Review of *The Reality of Time and the Existence of God: The Project of Proving God's Existence*, by David Braine. *International Philosophical Quarterly* 30, no. 1 (1990): 109–11.

Goodwin, George L. Review of *The Reality of Time and the Existence of God: The Project of Proving God's Existence*, by David Braine. *The Journal of Religion* 70, no. 4 (1990): 656–57.

Hasker, William. Review of *The Reality of Time and the Existence of God: The Project of Proving God's Existence*, by David Braine. *International Studies in Philosophy* 23, no. 3 (1991): 98.

Stump, Eleonore. Review of *The Reality of Time and the Existence of God: The Project of Proving God's Existence*, by David Braine. *The Philosophical Review* 100, no. 4 (1991): 657–60.

Martin, Christopher. Review of *The Reality of Time and the Existence of God: The Project of Proving God's Existence*, by David Braine. *New Blackfriars* 73, no. 860 (1992): 289–91.

Kerr, Fergus. Review of *The Human Person: Animal and Spirit*, by David Braine. *New Blackfriars* 74, no. 873 (1993): 333–37.

Urban, P. Linwood. Review of *The Human Person: Animal and Spirit*, by David Braine. *Choice* 30, no. 11 (1993): 1783–1784.

Schlesinger, George N. Review of *The Reality of Time and the Existence of God: The Project of Proving God's Existence*, by David Braine. *Noûs* 27, no. 4 (1993): 548–50.

Baldner, Steven. Review of *The Human Person: Animal and Spirit*, by David Braine. *Philosophy in Review* 14, no. 6 (1994): 381–83.

Champlin, T. S. Review of *The Human Person: Animal and Spirit*, by David Braine. *Philosophical Book* 35, no. 2 (1994): 119–21.

Clarke, W. Norris. Review of *The Human Person: Animal and Spirit*, by David Braine. *International Philosophical Quarterly* 34, no. 3 (1994): 376–78.

Cockburn, David. "Braine on the Mind." Review of *The Human Person: Animal and Spirit*, by David Braine. *Religious Studies* 30, no. 3 (1994): 343–51.

Crosson, Frederick J. Review of *The Human Person: Animal and Spirit*, by David Braine. *American Catholic Philosophical Quarterly* 68, no. 2 (1994): 233–36.

Lowe, E. J. Review of *The Human Person: Animal and Spirit*, by David Braine. *Philosophy* 69, no. 268 (1994): 244–46.

Ross, James F. Review of *The Human Person: Animal and Spirit*, by David Braine. *The Philosophical Quarterly* 44, no. 177 (1994): 536–38.

Blosser, Philip. Review of *The Human Person: Animal and Spirit*, by David Braine. *The Thomist: A Speculative Quarterly Review* 59, no. 2 (1995): 341–45.

Harrington, Thomas. Review of *The Human Person: Animal and Spirit*, by David Braine. *Revue Philosophique de La France et de l'Étranger* 185, no. 4 (1995): 516–19.

Burrell, David. "David Braine's Project: The Human Person." *Faith and Philosophy: Journal of the Society of Christian Philosophers* 13, no. 2 (1996): 163–78.

Deschepper, Jean-Pierre. Review of *The Human Person: Animal and Spirit*, by David Braine. *Revue Philosophique de Louvain* 95, no. 3 (1997): 564–65.

Brower, Jeffrey. Review of *Mind, Metaphysics, and Value in the Thomistic and Analytical Traditions*, edited by John Haldane. *Notre Dame Philosophical Reviews*, 2003.

Barnes, Gordon. Review of *Mind, Metaphysics, and Value in the Thomistic and Analytical Traditions*, edited by John Haldane. *Faith and Philosophy: Journal of the Society of Christian Philosophers* 21, no. 1 (2004): 110–16.

Goldberg, Nathaniel. Review of *Language and Human Understanding: The Roots of Creativity in Speech and Thought*, by David Braine. *The Review of Metaphysics* 68, no. 1 (2014): 158–59.

PART II

PHILOSOPHICAL PAPERS

CHAPTER 3

TWO KINDS OF CRITICAL PHILOSOPHY[1]

Société Belge de Logique et de Philosophie des Sciences

GREETING

You have done me undeserved honor in inviting me to speak to you, and for this I thank you most unreservedly.

To express the ideas which I wished to present to you, at the time when I chose the title "Two Kinds of Critical Philosophy," required a much longer paper than I ever anticipated. This larger paper I here present to you in writing. I thank you for giving me this incentive to force myself to put these ideas on paper. Whatever there is here which, through misjudgment, or overconfidence, or ignorance, or haste in writing, requires correction, I ask it of your kindness to correct, either at the meeting or by writing to me.

1 The title of this paper is Braine's, and it was written to be delivered at the noted meeting in 1972. We found no record that it was presented again or ever published. In this paper there were endnotes without clear indications of where they belonged. Based on the content, indications in the text, and the order of notes, we did our best to locate their intended home and made them footnotes. If we added anything beyond completing the citation, we indicate it by square brackets and "Editor's note."

In my lecture on 18th November, I shall concentrate on parts I and III only.

The key sections will be Part I, sections 2, 4, 5 and 8, and Part III, sections 1, 3, 4 and 5.

David Braine, Logic Department, University of Aberdeen, November, 1972.

INTRODUCTORY REMARKS

This paper arises out of the paper on the Nature of Knowledge which I gave to the Aristotelian Society in London, in November, 1971, almost exactly one year ago.[2] I do not want today to reproduce the detailed and sometimes intricate arguments which made up that paper. Rather, I wish to explain the wider context within which those arguments ought to be seen, the larger strategy within which they play a key role.

Modern philosophy has, I believe, been dominated by certain almost universal tendencies or preconceptions. I shall identify and describe five of these, five tendencies or preconceptions which, as it seems to me, have largely determined the shape, equally, (a) of the rationalism of Descartes, (b) of the empiricism of Hume and his followers, and (c) of the transcendental philosophy of Kant and Husserl—so much so, that it is possible to regard these philosophies as merely modifications or developments within a single constant framework. Each of these three traditions—rationalist, empiricist, and transcendentalist—is in its way critical, concerned not just with what is true, but with the procedures for deciding what is true, and with the source and extent of their validity, and concerned with this with a view to eradicating false claims to theoretical knowledge.

This, then, is the first of my two "kinds of critical philosophy," the kind which has grown up within the framework determined by these five preconceptions or tendencies. I shall call it the Cartesian kind, after its initiator. (You will observe that I am using the word "critical" in a very informal sense, and not with any special reference to Kant).

And, up against this Cartesian kind of critical philosophy, represented in the empiricists and in Kant, I see the possibility

2 David Braine, "The Nature of Knowledge," *Proceedings of the Aristotelian Society* 72 (1971): 41–63.

of another, quite different, kind, which for convenience I will call Aristotelian, a kind which arises by means of the rejection of these five misguided tendencies and preconceptions, to which I have referred, and which therefore falls outside the framework within which we have been accustomed to think.

Accordingly, my primary task in this paper is to describe these tendencies and preconceptions to you, and to make it plain to you, both that it is possible to reject them, and that it is necessary to reject them. And here, the heart of the matter is this, that, instead of regarding epistemological questions as prior to all others, we should regard them as parasitic upon the others, so that there is an interdependence. In effect, we learn whether or not our cognitional procedures are sound, not prior to their exercise or use, but by means of their exercise. In this sense, we must reject what I shall call the transcendentalist preconception (I.4). However, underlying everything I say, you will discover also a second center of anxiety, namely proof by argument. In effect, I regard the Cartesian and transcendentalist approach as ultimately destructive of all proof by argument, or sayable justification, and therefore destructive of the possibility of appeal to "reason." And I wish to show how, by contrast, the Aristotelian approach restores the possibility of argument and the usefulness of resort to rational discussion. By this means, I mean to show that the Aristotelian approach, far from representing the end of criticism, on the contrary, is required in order to make genuine criticism possible.

PART I. THE CARTESIAN AND TRANSCENDENTALIST FRAMEWORK DESCRIBED

I.1. THE RESTRICTION OF ARGUMENT.

What, then, are these five—closely inter-related—tendencies or preconceptions?

I place first the tendency to place systematic restrictions upon the use of argument, and the kinds of argument used.

This tendency appears in three ways. Firstly, in the exclusion of dialectical argument, in the Aristotelian sense: that is, exclusion of argument which is (a) non-deductive, (b) informal, in the sense that it does not seem possible to give formal representation to that on which the force or cogency of the argument seems to depend, and (c) liable to appeal to precritical judgment in support of its premises, and of the steps by which it proceeds—the exclusion, that is, of the sort of argument of which the Aristotelian corpus is full, of which Aristotle explicitly approves (*Nicomachean Ethics*, 1145b 2–7, *Physics*, 211a7–11, *Topics*, 101a35-b4. cf. 100a22-b26), and which in the *Topics* he calls dialectical. In a sense, the very first movement of thought in modern philosophy, the Cartesian method of doubt, amounted precisely to this: a refusal to admit dialectical argument in this sense into his philosophy, because of its reliance upon pre-critical judgment.

This tendency to restrict argument appears in a second way in what I call the Humean standardization of argument, the preconception that, except for certain special and peculiar exceptions, legitimate argument is restricted to two kinds, the deductive kind, and an inductive kind, induction being understood here in a narrowly Humean sense. And the peculiar importance of this, both in the empiricist tradition and in Kant, has been that it has excluded any *a posteriori* argument from actual experience except of a narrowly inductive kind.

And then, lastly, the tendency to restrict argument appears in a third way in every recurring presumption that, if what we say in justification of our judgments or claims to knowledge is to be of any use, i.e., if the argument or logos or reasons we offer are to have any force, then this justification or argument must make appeal only to independent or prior knowledge, or independently justified judgments. This is the preconception that all effectual argument or valid justification is inferential, i.e., revealing the thing known as capable of being known by means of inference, i.e., by reasoning from independent or prior knowledge, (or revealing the judgement involved as capable of being reached by means of inference from other independently justified judgments)—a preconception I discussed in my paper, "Nature of Knowledge," and which still appears in some contemporary writing, e.g., in Ayer and Quinton.[3] It is, in its very nature, a hierarchical preconception, involving the notion, in Frege's words (*Grundlagen* § 3), that the "ultimate ground" upon which the justification of a judgment rests is to be found by "discovering

3 Braine, "Nature of Knowledge," 51–54.

its proof," and "following it up right back to the primitive truths":[4] the notion, that is, that there are primitive truths known without possibility of support from reasoning, intuitively or by non-discursive reflection, and that these serve as the foundations for all the rest of our knowledge, which is built up by means of inference from them.

I.2. INTUITION AS EXCLUSIVE OF ARGUMENT: COHERENCE THEORY

I.2.1 I come now to the second tendency to which I wish to refer, closely associated with the first. This is the tendency to suppose that intuitive or non-inferential judgment is in its very nature unreasoned and undiscursive, neither needing support from rational argument and discussion, nor in typical cases capable of such support: the tendency to suppose that, because within any finite course of argument there must be some things which are not actually argued for but merely assumed, and because there are many things we know without actually using argument as a means of knowledge, it is therefore natural that there should be cases of knowledge in which argument in support of the claim to knowledge is, not only not actual, but also not possible.[5] And some people suppose that this way of thinking is to be found even in Aristotle, when he speaks of *nous*; but here they are deceived; it is indeed essential to his view that intuition or insight (*nous*) should be exclusive of demonstration and the possibility of demonstration, but this does not mean for him that it is exclusive of all argument whatsoever—nor, for that matter, that prior experience is irrelevant to it. On the contrary, it is his normal practice to offer what he regards as legitimate dialectical (i.e.,

4 [Editor's Note: Gottlob Frege, *The Foundations of Arithmetic*, trans. J. L. Austin, 2nd rev. ed. (New York: Harper and Brothers, 1960) § 3, pp. 3–4.]

5 In a longer paper, I would have discussed how it is necessary to regard intuition as discursive, (a) if we are to explain the possibility of error in its operations, (b) if we are to explain the role of reflection prior to some intuitive judgments. The view that the non-inferential judgments of the understanding are undiscursive and therefore free of error has led to the peculiar view that all a priori knowledge is certain—since this is supposed to be founded on non-inferential judgments, e.g., (a) as to simple consequences of the meanings of words, and (b) as to the validity of the steps within inferences.

non-demonstrative) argument for the judgments of intuition or *nous*, i.e., for the primary indemonstrable principles within each science: and this dialectical argument can quite legitimately proceed a posteriori, making mention of the experience from which the intuition or insight arose, justifying what is prior in itself or in nature by reference to what is prior in knowledge, or more evident, to us.

In regard to this preconception that non-inferential or intuitive judgment is normally incapable of support by argument, for the present, let it suffice to say that I think it fundamentally misguided, and largely the result of the unnatural exclusion of dialectical argument. For, as I said in my London paper, (50f.):

> If a person is to class as having knowledge, then it appears quite essential that, if he were to claim it, his claim should be capable of surviving his own examination, i.e., that it should be possible for him to reflect in a rational way upon his position without ceasing to think that he knows. And, for this to be possible, it seems indispensable that there should be something or other which it would in principle be possible for him to say (at least to himself) which would justify him, if he were to consider the question in thinking or judging that he knew that P. Accordingly, my view is that, wherever there is a legitimate claim to knowledge, there must always be something or other, of some sort, which could validly be said in support of it—i.e., in a very wide sense of these words, some sayable "reason" or "argument" (*logos*) in favour of the claim to know, adequate to serve as a "justification" for it.

I.2.2 Let me clarify the point here. I am not representing actual argument as the universal means to knowledge, but the possibility of argument as a universal condition of knowledge. Except in the case of inferential judgments, argument is never the means of knowledge. The basic means of knowledge are not argument, but experience of the actual, and the exercise of the understanding. If we consider the whole system of the judgments which a person makes, the arguments which he can use constitute a set of relations internal to this system, relating its members to each other: hence, argument cannot be the means whereby the person knows that the system as a whole has any correspondence to reality. Clearly, then, this system of judgments, as a whole, can only be grounded in reality by means of some judgments being known to be true, not purely by means of argument, but in some non-inferential or partly intuitive way.

But it does not at all follow that this system of judgments is grounded in reality by means of various individual non-inferential judgments, each being separately (taken in isolation from the others) known to be true, independently of its relation to the others—nor that some of these individual judgments are known purely empirically, or some purely a priori.

This does not follow, because we can, on the contrary, say that the system is grounded, not by means of individual judgments taken individually, but only by means of a whole set, or whole sets, of judgments, taken as a structured whole (or wholes), (i.e., taken with the arguments interrelating its members), being all together known to be true. None of the members of such a set need be without the possibility of authentication (as knowledge) by means of argument appealing or referring to the rest of the set, but none will be known by means of such argument: i.e., none will be purely inferential, each will contribute some evidentness to the whole, but none will be certain except in virtue of its relation to the whole.[6]

I.3. THE RELATION OF EXPERIENCE AND UNDERSTANDING: THE A PRIORI

Moreover, it would be natural to say that the knowledge that such a set of judgements (taken as a whole) is true is gained, not by experience of the actual alone, nor by the exercise of the understanding alone,

6 This is not in any way a Coherence theory of truth. On the contrary, I would insist that truth in the use of "factual" is distinct from (e.g.) some "evaluator" propositions, still belongs to propositions individually and consists in a correspondence between their senses and the facts. (Of course, the same sentence may carry different senses on different occasions, and, in order to determine in what sense it is to be understood on a particular occasion, we may well have to consider the relations it is understood to have with other statements, or the applications of a whole system of which it is part. But a different sense makes a different proposition and a different judgment). It could perhaps be called a Coherence theory of Knowledge: not in the sense that a judgment of coherence gives knowledge, for it does not, but in the sense that no judgement can be verified individually; no claim to knowledge authenticated individually independently of its relationships to other judgments or claims to knowledge.

but always by the two working together—with the result that, within such a set, because of the dependence of each judgment upon the whole set, no individual judgment will be "purely a priori," and none "purely empirical." And we could surmise that even the most basic of so-called a priori truths (with one class of exception) were included within such sets of interdependent, non-inferential, judgments. In effect, understanding and experience are, both of them, faculties whose exercise is in judgments, and (with one exception) there is no need to suppose one of them to be exercised in one set of judgments and the other in another—both could be exercised in all.[7]

I say with one exception, because it seems evident that we must make some exception for formally universal principles, such as the principle that formal contradictions are false, that the substitution of purely nominal *definiens* for *definiendum* preserves truth, and that the union of two disjoint pairs is a four, and for the tautologies which result from their application. We must make this exception because it seems mad to say that experience of the application of these principles in connection with concrete subject-matter is relevant to the justification of their application in connection with abstract subject-matter—e.g., that experience of counting beads is relevant to counting truth-functions or counting numbers. Presumably, then, these judgements are the work of the understanding alone (it may involve empirical concepts). In effect, Kant proposed an asymmetry: he recognized that experience of the actual has no judgments purely its own, but always depends on the understanding; but, by contrast, he mistakenly refused to accept that in a parallel way the understanding has no judgments purely its own (except mere tautologies).

7 This view is in certain respects similar to that of Quine in parts 5 and 6 of W. V. O. Quine, "Two Dogmas of Empiricism," *The Philosophical Review* 60 (1951): 20–43, but it does not involve (i) his conventionalism, (ii) his misuse of the term "analytic" to mean something like "purely a priori," (iii) his implicit acceptance of key elements in a representationist or idealist account of perception, or (iv) his implicit rejection of the notion of proposition or statement as something with invariant sense in favor of some quasi-sociological notion of "statement"—features of that article which appear to me open to the gravest objection.

I.4. THE TRANSCENDENTALIST PRECONCEPTION THAT EPISTEMOLOGY IS PRIOR

The importance of this preconception that a priori truths (and especially those which are pure in the Kantian sense of not containing any merely empirical concepts) are purely a priori in this sense of being known independently of all empirical judgments and incapable of support by means of any argument appealing to them, that is, incapable of support by means of any dialectical a posteriori argument, derives largely from its connection with the next of my five tendencies and preconceptions.

This is the preconception that epistemological or second-order knowledge is necessarily prior, epistemologically although not psychologically or genetically, to non-epistemological or first-order knowledge. The assumption is that, in respect to any sufficiently general category or class of question, i.e., in respect to any sufficiently wide field within which knowledge might be claimed, any first-order knowledge from inside the field is necessarily dependent upon and posterior to second-order knowledge as to the legitimacy of relying upon the various methods and procedures by means of which it is thought that questions within this class can be answered and first-order knowledge within the field obtained.

From this it immediately follows that, in the case where the first-order knowledge under consideration is our ordinary empirical knowledge of the actual, all this knowledge is dependent upon and posterior to the second-order knowledge contained in epistemology, i.e., the second-order knowledge, for instance, which tells us that it is legitimate to rely upon perception, or memory, or the methods of induction. And from this it seems to follow quite simply and directly that all this second-order or epistemological knowledge is purely a priori in the sense of being known independently of any judgments of experience of the actual, and incapable of being supported by reference to experience of the actual in any way at all, because any such appeal would supposedly involve circularity. And in this way, we are robbed of any possibility of lending a posteriori support to a priori truths by argument appealing to our knowledge of actuality. The notion of a mutual interdependence of a priori truths and judgments about the actual is thus quite excluded.

And, in a parallel way, in the case where the first-order knowledge under consideration is knowledge in the field of morals (e.g., as to what life or actions are worthwhile or good or right or worthless or bad or wrong), we find ourselves debarred by some philosophers from any possibility of appealing, either to the examination of those individual cases where the moral judgments to be made seems to be clear and undisputed (so-called "moral perceptions"), or to any agreed and seemingly evident general principle from within the field, in order to authenticate some suggested method of deciding some particular moral question. Rather, the questions as to whether and how any moral question is to be decided have to be resolved, as it were, outside morals—not just non-empirically, but in a sense amorally. Again, the notion of a mutual interdependence between first-order and second-order judgements, the first-order depending in one way upon the second-order ones, but again the second-order ones depending in other ways upon the first-order, so that neither is without qualification posterior to the other, is assumed to be quite excluded.

This way of thinking, whereby the second-order principles upon which first-order knowledge depends are thought to be authenticated, never in any way through the understanding's actually exercising these principles in order to get first-order knowledge, but always by means of the understanding's withdrawing into itself, as it were, and ignoring all first-order judgments as either irrelevant or not to be relied upon, (unless it be for the single first-order judgment: I exist, as the subject of my perceptions or *pensees*), appears first in modern philosophy in Descartes, and persists in Kant, the empiricists, and Husserl.[8] One could call the preconception underlying this way of thinking transcendentalist, inasmuch as it involves that the basic principles, upon which a form of knowledge or experience, in the sense of not being knowable from experience or knowledge belonging to that form or type.

8 But even this is not clear. Perhaps we are using the word "understanding" equivocally here, inasmuch as no understanding of any "nature," no understanding in regard to any subject-matter, and, in a certain sense, no understanding (as we say) "of anything," is involved in these judgments. Of course, "understanding the meanings of words" may be involved, but it seems quite certain in any case that the sense of the word "understanding" is not univocal as between "understanding the nature of something" and "understanding the meaning of a word."

I.5. THE EVIDENTIALIST PRECONCEPTION

Fifthly, and finally, amongst these tendencies and preconceptions which have shaped my first kind of critical philosophy, the Cartesian, there is another, underlying or reinforcing all the rest, and this is the preconception which I shall call evidentialist—the preconception, I mean, that every condition upon which a person's knowledge depends must lie within the review of the knower's own mind and open to his inspection, so that the validity of the reasons for thinking that the condition is satisfied will be evident to him.

This is the preconception which I discussed at considerable length in my London paper ("Nature of Knowledge," §1), and which I thought ("Nature of Knowledge," §6) to underlie the position taken up recently by Professor Ayer in *Problem of Knowledge*, as well as the classical positions of Descartes, Hume and Kant. In that paper, I described it as the preconception that any justification for a claim to knowledge, to be adequate, must be what I called unconditional. That is, every condition or presupposition of the knowledge must have been examined and discovered to be free from mistake, or examined to discover its probability and relied upon no further than this probability allows. And the soundness of a person's grounds for thinking that he has knowledge depends solely upon the relation between him as subject and his present mental contents, to the sense of what he could make present to his consciousness.

(I was tempted to describe this preconception as introspectionist or mentalist because it makes the soundness of a person's grounds in this way depend solely upon what he can discover by an introspective examination of the contents of his mind).

I.6. A CONFUSION ABOUT NECESSITY AND CAUSALITY

These, then, are the five tendencies or preconceptions, each of a purely epistemological character, to which I referred as being at the root of the false kind of critical philosophy which I called Cartesian. They are, I believe, intimately interconnected, in the sense that acceptance of any one of them leads, I believe, naturally or necessarily to the acceptance of all the others.

They have, of course, been historically associated with other tendencies or preconceptions of a metaphysical, rather than an epistemological kind; for instance, a tendency to atomism, either an atomism of objects, leading to the denial of the reality of certain relations, or an atomism of propositions or facts, leading to the belief that the only conceptual or a priori necessities are tautologies. But, of these accidentally associated metaphysical preconceptions, there is only one which requires to be mentioned now.

This is the preconception that the notion of one fact or object making the occurrence of another fact or object necessary or non-accidental must be explained in terms of the notion that the occurrence of the second can be inferred or known with necessity or probability from the occurrence of the first, an inference which will depend upon some knowledge of general laws: a preconception which arises from confusing a physical or quasi-physical sense of the word "necessary" with an epistemic or inferential sense, i.e., confusing causal determination with implication.[9] And, as a result of this false preconception, causal connection, instead of being regarded as a real relation *in rebus*, and therefore as a relation between things as they are, and not merely as they appear, has been regarded as merely consisting in a conformity to law: with the result that an idealist view of causal connection, whereby causal connections obtain between facts and objects only as they appear, has seemed possible—since the appearances are required only to conform to law, not to have real relations with one another.

I.7. THE RESULTING MISDESCRIPTION OF EXPERIENCE

It is, of course, evident that this whole system of tendencies and preconceptions has also been associated with something else, namely the tendency to atomize our knowledge, by experience, of particular fact. And doubtless this is one of the main reasons underlying the restriction of all argument from experience to mere induction. And perhaps the main importance of much modern Anglo-Saxon writing

9 My paper, "Varieties of Necessity," *Proceedings of the Aristotelian Society, Supplementary Volumes* 46 (1972): 139–87 was designed to remedy this confusion.

in philosophy will prove to lie in the way in which they have revealed the viciousness of this tendency, (a) in showing that experience involves the knowledge of things as being in some real connections (the Wittgensteinian demonstration of the necessity of conceding the existence of a priori or conceptual connections, or connections to deny which would involve a different language-game or form of life, of a nonanalytic kind, especially in the philosophy of mind, and in relation to the connection of mind with action, has this consequence), and (b) in establishing the necessity of a realist account of perception, against the believer in sense-data, be he phenomenalist or representationist, and be he dualist or central-state materialist, i.e., in establishing that it is not possible to describe human conscious experience in perception in such a way as to remove the implication of relatedness to existing objects, i.e., not possible to regard the objects of perception as having a merely intentional character, (and showing the so-called argument from illusion to be simply invalid).[10]

However, I have not given this tendency to atomize and idealize experience any separate mention, (i) because it seems in a sense well-known, or at least much documented, (ii) because it is largely a mere result of the other tendencies and preconceptions which I have mentioned, and (iii) because I wish to avoid mere palliatives—i.e., to avoid the attempt to keep the redescription of experience to a minimum in the hope of being able to leave the rest of the Cartesian framework unaffected.

I.8. THE HIERARCHY OF KNOWLEDGE WHICH RESULTS FROM EVIDENTIALISM

I have already remarked upon how the evidentialist preconception—the preconception, that is, that a person's having knowledge depends, not just upon the validity of the reasons he might have for thinking the various conditions of his knowledge to be satisfied, but upon this

10 The prejudice that any such realist view must be naive and involve the conception that correct perceptual judgments result from the incorrigible exercise of an infallible faculty, is entirely baseless, and arises from the preconceptions described earlier, especially the fifth or evidentialist, and the second or intuitionistic ones.

validity's being in each case evident to him—leads to a search for what I called "unconditional justifications."

But the further observation which I want to make now is this. The only ways of getting unconditional justifications are by means of:

> (a) appeal to premises which are supposedly themselves unconditionally and infallibly known: e.g., the naive idealist supposes that we have an unconditional knowledge of our own mental states, the naive realist claims this in regard to perceptual facts about material things, the moral intuitionist in regard to moral truths, and perhaps some phenomenologists in regard to essential truths—all this is supposed to be the work of undiscursive intuition.
>
> (b) appeal to transcendental principles declaring acceptance of various other sorts of premises (not themselves unconditionally known) to be legitimate: these transcendental principles (declaring, for instance, that it is legitimate to rely upon memory, or perception, in judgments as to what is probable) being themselves unconditionally known.
>
> (c) reliance upon principles of inference for drawing inferences from the premises introduced under (a) and (b): this reliance being justified, either (i) by the supposed fact of a principle's being in itself self-evidently or intuitively valid and in this way unconditionally known to be valid, or else (ii) by means of appeal to some unconditionally known transcendental principles declaring such reliance to be justified (e.g., declaring it legitimate to rely upon inductive procedures in judgements as to what is probable).

Thus, the search for unconditional justifications, first, forces one into a hierarchical view of knowledge (see above), whereby knowledge is conceived to rest upon foundations, and then, secondly, forces one to regard these foundations as being capable of being provided only by means of some mixture of (i) naive exercises of intuition, and (ii) exercises of intuition coupled with reliance upon (difficult to prove) transcendental principles.

And, all this, whose effects are so patent both in Kant and in the empiricist tradition, simply stems from the misguided evidentialist preconception, introduced by Descartes.

PART II: THE DESTRUCTION OF ARGUMENT IN THE CARTESIAN AND TRANSCENDENTALIST SYSTEM

This, then, is the framework which has determined the shape of the first of my two kinds of critical philosophy, the kind which, for convenience, I have labelled "Cartesian," but which I find represented equally in Descartes, in the empiricists, and in Kant.

Let me now begin to indicate to you why I consider this whole system of tendencies and preconceptions, and with it this whole tradition in criticism, so highly objectionable.

The first and most fundamental root of my objection to this Cartesian system is that I believe it involves such crippling restrictions upon the possibility of argument and makes both knowledge itself and any genuine or discriminating criticism of knowledge impossible. For, I believe that these restrictions lead inevitably to a dependence upon undefended philosophical dogma, or arbitrary diktat, in the resolution of philosophical disputes. Where natural modes of argument have been destroyed, it turns out either that no argument is possible at all, or that peculiar new philosophical modes of argument, whose credentials turn out, upon examination, to be spurious, have to be resorted to.

Secondly, I believe that these tendencies and preconceptions have generated a gross misdescription of the procedures which we actually use in getting knowledge from experience and drawing so-called "inductive" conclusions from experience. So gross is this misdescription that it has instituted an almost complete divorce between philosophical proofs and justifications for claims to knowledge and the natural or scientific proofs of the same claims. And it appears to me that the critique or analysis of natural argument, not only in science, but also in morals, which has been prevalent since Hume, is founded upon just such misdescription.

Thirdly, this critique of natural argument has been associated with a systematic confusion in regard to the very character of "Logic," as the study or science of argument, itself—a confusion which shows itself in the almost complete identification of what I believe Husserl called "truth-logic" and "consequence-logic," two things which must be sharply distinguished. And this is a confusion which the Cartesian system in its very nature is bound to generate.

Let me now explain and substantiate each of these three points in turn in sections II.1, II.2, and II.3, respectively.

II.1. THE ULTIMATE DEPENDENCE OF BOTH KNOWLEDGE AND CRITICISM UPON DOGMA IN SYSTEMS OF THE CARTESIAN TYPE

What I had in mind in my first point was this.

II.1.1 There do exist, I believe, critical arguments, of a powerful kind, against the possibility of certain kinds of objective knowledge, e.g., in morals or of natural theology. Now, it happens to be my opinion that, upon examination, it turns out, in the cases of morals and of natural theology, that none of these powerful arguments is actually efficacious and probative, and that each can be rebutted. But many would disagree with me here, and it still remains that these arguments have a very considerable force, a force which derives from their appropriateness or appositeness to the area of discourse. I have in mind, for instance, arguments which draw upon an analysis of cases of actual moral disagreement, the arguments of Kant's Antinomies, and arguments to the effect that teleological arguments for God's existence of an omnipotent, all-perfect, uncreated, Creator *ex nihilo* must always fail. These arguments, whether or not they are satisfactory, are at least "scientific" in the sense of not being alien to the subject or science under consideration.[11]

Now, it is precisely here that my objection comes in—because, as it appears to me, wherever, within these traditions, we come upon any actual proposal, in regard to some class of popularly made claim to objective knowledge, that this class of claim is false, there we will find (upon thorough examination) that the principal argument justifying this proposal ultimately turns upon the acceptance of some general critical principle, which has to be accepted as mere dogma, incapable of support by argument, and, indeed, which itself forbids any justification being offered for it. And it appears too that any method of criticism which in this way depends upon dogma, or the arbitrary diktat of the philosopher, ought to be recognized as valueless: each new type of application of such a method of criticism involves, in a sense, a *petitio principii*.

11 I have in mind here the arguments relating to (i) the implications of the Indeterminacy Principle in physics, (ii) free-will, (iii) the intelligibility of "pure chance," and (iv) the question whether God is his own cause or reason.

II.1.2 The force of this objection is particularly apparent in the case of the empiricists.

Thus, it is a commonplace that the logical positivists supported their position upon the principle that all meaningful claims to knowledge are either analytic or else capable of empirical verification, and that this principle is itself (if they are right) neither analytic nor empirical, and therefore is itself indefensible—except by procedures (e.g., of philosophical or intuitive induction) which it itself declares to be outlawed. And it will be found that, wherever in Hume or the empiricist tradition some class of claim to knowledge has been rejected (e.g., in Professor Hare's arguments against the possibility of moral knowledge), the situation is essentially the same. Moreover, the *petitio principii* is peculiarly obvious here. That the proof of a moral proposition is not to be achieved by means of any trivial logical transformations of those sorts which arise in every subject-matter (e.g., the one exemplified in the substitution of "x is young and x is a dog" for "x is a puppy"), or the procedures exemplified in mathematics, or by the procedures exemplified in physics, biology, and history, or by any combination of these, may conceivably be evident. But to make the dogmatic or unsupported statement that no other types of probative argument are possible except these, and then to give this as one's principal reason for supposing that no moral argument is probative, is simply to beg the question. That is to say, if some person says that moral argument is sometimes probative without being either "deductive" (in the narrow empiricist sense) or "inductive" (in that broad sense which allows this word to cover all knowledge in natural science and history), and that this statement that "All probative argument is either deductive or inductive" is simply false, then merely to repeat this very statement dogmatically or unsupported is not to produce any argument whatsoever against him. There do indeed exist many perhaps weighty arguments of a less general kind, against moral objectivism, (e.g., arguments from the apparent existence of moral antinomies: arguments of this sort can be drawn from Sartre, and also from the anthropologists who make it appear that opposite moral judgments may each of them be perfectly well-founded, each in the different value system associated with a different culture), but this entirely general empiricistic critical argument is mere *petitio principii* and perfectly empty.

Now, I do not say that the fact that such general critical principles as "All probative argument is either deductive or inductive" always outlaw their own defense, is the only thing wrong with these principles. On the contrary, even if (*per impossibile*) they had not outlawed their own defense, they would still have been indefensible—for I believe that the appearance of plausibility in these principles depends wholly upon the maintenance of a studied ambiguity in such terms as "analytic" and "empirical," and upon an abstention from too close an examination of the actual procedures of our thought, and the actual variety in modes of knowledge and argument—either of which would have revealed the gross-ness and enormity of the oversimplification involved in these principles. But, nonetheless the fact that they do outlaw their own defense does add an extra dimension of ridiculousness to the resting of a critical method upon them.

II.1.3 However, it requires to be recognized, what is much less commonplace and obvious, that the same type of reliance upon indefensible dogma recurs, in a much more subtle way, in Kant. It happens like this.

(i) The restriction of objective knowledge to objects of possible experience (to the exclusion of morals and religion) is grounded upon the view that the conformity between the objects of our knowledge and the a priori concepts and principles which apply to them can only be explained by supposing that it is our faculty of knowledge which itself generates, determines or limits, the objects of knowledge.

(ii) This view is, in turn, grounded upon the twin assumptions, (a) that a priori or non-intuitional concepts are independent of experience, an assumption which seems to be false, inasmuch as, although these concepts are not concepts of inner or outer intuition, it nonetheless remains true that they are acquired and understood only through and by means of their exercise in judgments of intuition, or in judgments depending on intuition (on the Wittgensteinian view that the identification of concepts depends upon some agreement in judgments in which they are exercised), and (b) that the a priori principles relating to these a priori or non-intuitional concepts are pure in the sense of being known independently of all judgments of experience.

(iii) My argument in the Appendix (Part IV) of this paper suggests that the strategically more important of these two assumptions, namely (b), is actually false. However, all that matters for my present argument is this, that in Kant's own thought, this assumption, (b), is itself grounded upon another prior assumption, namely the assumption that the only way in which experience could become relevant to a proposition asserting strict necessity would be by means of presupposing some principle known independently of all judgements of experience.

(iv) But this prior assumption is itself just a development of the Humean view that, unless some a priori principle known independently of experience (such as "Every event has a cause") could be appealed to, the only argument capable of being drawn from experience is merely a blind Humean induction.

Thus, surprisingly and astonishingly, it turns out that the whole positivistic or critical element in Kant's main strategy, the element which consists in limiting objective knowledge to appearances, ultimately depends upon a reliance, at one key point, upon the empiricist dogma (a dogma which elsewhere Kant would not perhaps accept without qualification) that all probative argument is either deductive or inductive—i.e., upon an application of this dogma in one very wide case. And the validity of this application of this dogma will not be an analytic proposition; nor, since it is presupposed in the transcendental deduction, does it seem that it is proved by the transcendental deduction.

II.1.4 This, then, is part of what I had in mind when I implied that the Cartesian or transcendental system had the effect of making the resolution of philosophical debates, and especially the answering of highly disputed epistemological questions as to the extent of objective knowledge, dependent upon dogma or diktat, and therefore (in a sense) arbitrary—and that it thereby also made a genuine critique of knowledge impossible.

This dependence of criticism upon mere fiat, or mere unsupported declarations on the part of philosophers, appears in its starkest form in the case of what Professor Ayer has called the method of descriptive analysis. This method allows one to describe each group of procedures within human thought, and to reject some on the ground that they generate logical inconsistency; but, as to the remainder, some will be accepted and some rejected, but there will be no reason or justification for accepting some rather than others, since there will be no proof and no refutation of any of them.

II.1.5 But I said, not only that the Cartesian system made the criticism of knowledge depend on dogma, but also that it made knowledge itself depend upon dogma, and therefore impossible.

This is, I believe, the automatic result of making knowledge into a hierarchical system, in which some foundational propositions, including some contingent empirical facts and some necessary a priori laws, are known by pure intuition or without possibility of proof by argument, and everything else is known by means of inference from these empirical facts or according to these a priori laws (as laws of inference). Equally, it also, I believe, results automatically from the exclusion of a posteriori argument for a priori principles, or for second-order epistemological principles, that some of them should be incapable of proof of any ordinary sort, because neither provable from prior principles, nor provable a posteriori.

As I remarked earlier (I.7), and as Mr. Quinton has observed (*British Analytical Philosophy*, eds. Williams and Montefiore),[12] it seems possible to adopt some palliative measures, and institute some limited modifications within the Cartesian system, in order to make objective empirical judgments depend for being known upon coherence authenticating intuition. But no such modification can be achieved in the case of the a priori laws upon which the whole hierarchical system depends (including any laws governing these procedures whereby coherence authenticates intuition). And this is where resort to dogma seems vicious, both because these laws do not always seem evident, and because it is upon them (rather than upon the empirical facts) that philosophical disputes actually turn.

II.1.6 There have been, of course, various methods suggested whereby these foundations of the hierarchy of knowledge might be, as it were,

12 Bernard Williams and Alan Montefiore, eds., *British Analytical Philosophy* (London: Routledge, 1966).

underpinned. The method of descriptive analysis as presented by Professor Ayer, we have already dismissed (descriptive analysis as it occurs in Wittgenstein is a totally different matter, for there it seems to have some transcendental significance, in a quasi-Kantian way). Descartes' system for underpinning the foundations, depending as it does upon the precepts that every clear and distinct idea is true, and upon certain disputed arguments for God's existence, has never seemed coercive. What remains to be considered is therefore only the so-called transcendental or quasi-Kantian method for underpinning the foundations.

In regard to this last point, let me make the precautionary remark that it is vital to distinguish for what purpose an argument of the so-called transcendental sort is being put forward. There appear to me to be two main possibilities:

(a) The purpose of putting transcendental argument forward may be in order to provide a proof, whether "objective" or "subjective," for certain kinds of claims to knowledge. In this case, I believe it to represent an illegitimate attempt to supply a purely second-order or meta-theoretical justification, in a place where what is required is a justification which draws at least in part upon first-order considerations. I will substantiate my claim that this is illegitimate later (Part III). What I am anxious at this juncture to point out is that it does not follow from this that all use of transcendental argument is illegitimate, because (on the contrary) it very often has a different role, which I shall now indicate.

(b) Transcendental argument is very often put forward, not in order to prove claims to knowledge, or under-pin the foundations of knowledge, but as a kind of buttress, merely in order to refute certain specious or false types of objection to proofs of claims to knowledge, i.e., to provide a properly second-order refutation (drawing only indirectly upon first-order knowledge) of methods or types of objection which are of such a kind that to rely upon them involves some incoherence at the second-order level. This use of transcendental argument, far from being directed towards the proving of claims to knowledge, on the contrary, presupposes that both knowledge and an adequate non-transcendental proof of the claim to knowledge exist already, (i.e., that the knowledge already exists, not merely as natural disposition, but as already objectively validated), and is solely concerned to refute certain "contentious" or "eristic" (in the Aristotelean sense) objections to claims to knowledge. And there are many examples of this more modest use of transcendental argument amongst contemporary Anglo-Saxon writers, for instance, in the writings of Strawson, and in many expositions of Wittgensteinian ideas.

The question next arises as to which of these two kinds of use of transcendental argument is involved in Kant's main strategy. And here the answer unfortunately seems to be the first, the illegitimate kind: for he does seem to regard the reasonableness of relying on these a priori principles upon which he thinks that we do rely, in extending our empirical knowledge, as dependent on our recognition that this knowledge relates only to objects as appearances, i.e., to objects in so far as they are formed by the mind. Knowledge as natural disposition precedes this recognition, but knowledge as science depends upon it.

And, indeed, it is only by means of a use of transcendental argument of this first and illegitimate kind that one could hope in any way at all to alleviate the problem of the foundations of our a priori knowledge, while remaining within the framework set by the five tendencies or preconceptions which I named. For, what these a priori propositions need is not a mere rebuttal of objections to them, but some reason for thinking them true, i.e., proof, whether "objective" or "subjective." (They need this because some of them are in some dispute.)

Perhaps I should add that I not only regard the Kantian use of transcendental argument as illegitimate, but also as being inefficacious and ill-conceived even within its own terms. I make these remarks, not to prove or justify my anti-Kantian standpoint (that would take another paper, perhaps of greater length), but solely to indicate the character of some of the objections which it seems to me require to be made: e.g.,

(a) transcendental arguments prove, upon examination, to be too weak for their purpose: e.g., the coherence of experience which is necessary for an objective temporal order to exist, presupposes some conformity to law, but much less than the complete physical determinism which Kant imagines, and less in fact even than that order which we actually discover in experience,

(b) it is plain that which (of various possible intuitions) intuitions actually present themselves to us, and which laws they actually determine, is not determined solely by the mind (even if the fact that they will determine some laws or other is determined by mind), and it is not plain that to outlaw the demand for explanation of these things (by making causal relations obtain only between appearances) is legitimate, and

(c) there is a fundamental incoherence (I would contend) in the very notion of a "knowledge of causal relations between objects, as appearances," since causal efficacy seems to be a criterion not merely of objectivity, but of reality or actuality as distinct from mere appearance (even objective appearance), an incoherence which was hidden from Kant because of his explanation of causality in terms of conformity to law.

To sum up this part of my argument: in Descartes, in Kant, and in the method of "descriptive analysis," we find various new types of non-standard, or "dialectical," argument, which these philosophers have put forward in substitution for the old quasi-a-posteriori Aristotelian type of dialectical argument which they have outlawed; and what I have argued is that these new forms of argument are inadequate to this purpose of lending support to the "foundations" of the rest of knowledge, and that their credentials here are very poor, (and indeed much less good than the credentials of the older and more natural a posteriori argument which they supplanted).

II.1.7 There is, then, in my view, no valid means of escape, within the Cartesian system of tendencies and preconceptions, from the hierarchical situation in which some foundational propositions have to be accepted as the basis for the rest of knowledge, even though no reason at all can be given for accepting them.

It is perhaps paradoxical that, while the orthodox amongst Catholics at least insist that the acceptance of the dogmas of religion can be in some sense justified to reason, and rank fideism as a heresy, we in philosophy should (by contrast) find ourselves seemingly driven back to a dependence upon dogmas or foundational a priori principles, whether for proof, or for criticism, which are not merely not actually supported by argument, but also (if the Cartesian preconceptions are accepted) incapable of such support, and therefore literally indefensible. And it has been my main aim in this paper to show how philosophers can escape from this fideistic (or as the English might call it, "fundamentalist") predicament.

II.2. THE MISDESCRIPTION OF INDUCTION: THE ILLEGITIMACY OF "NON-CONSTRUCTIVE SUMMATION"

I come now to my second main objection to this "Cartesian" tradition in criticism, as represented in the empiricists and in Kant, namely that their critique of natural argument, which has led to the twin conclusions, (a) that the extraction of general principles or laws from experience depends upon reliance upon a priori principles of a sort known (if known at all) entirely independently of judgments of experience of the actual and therefore upon principles which are not provable in any standard or non-transcendental way and (b) that all standard argument is either deductive or inductive, is founded upon a misdescription of naturally occurring argument. What we find is not a constructive approach such as would allow us to locate actual examples of places in natural argumentation at which the argument would break down unless appeal were made to some purely a priori principle, but rather some highly dubious non-constructive argument purporting to show that such places must exist somewhere or other, even if we cannot locate where. And an almost exactly parallel situation arises where the critique of morals is concerned.

II.2.1 In order to make it plain what it is that I have in mind here, let me begin by considering a possible example of natural argument, and the complexity which it exhibits.

> (i) We dissect numerous rabbits and discover that in all these the appendix is disproportionately large relative to the size of the rabbit, by comparison with the human case. We then infer, let us suppose, that all rabbits have large appendixes. However, contrary to what some say, we make no reliance upon any general principle of induction here. On the contrary, we rely perhaps (I oversimplify here: but will correct the oversimplification later) upon

a much more limited inductive principle, namely the principle that morphological features tend to be constant within the same biological species—i.e., the principle that inductive procedures are reliable in this carefully delimited area, similarities being in respect of morphological feature, and application being limited to biological species. And it is noteworthy that in performing the induction here we are already presupposing whatever is involved in the possession and application of two theoretical conceptions, the conception of morphological feature, and the conception of biological species.

(ii) The question may next be raised, what put us into the position of knowing that morphological features (unlike colors) tend to be constant within the same species? To this, a partial reply will say: the use of certain inductive procedures (although not "the general principle of induction in an unrestricted form and without the assistance of any theoretical conceptions"). But this is not enough, one cannot learn this by induction unless one knows what biological species and morphological features are, so as to be able to apply these concepts: but what experiences or processes of thought put us into possession of this knowledge, and selected these theoretical conceptions for this prominence?

(iii) I have grossly over-simplified the whole course of reasoning—for it is well-known that morphological features tend to subserve some purpose, indispensable to the life or to the satisfactory life of the species possessing them: and the inductive knowledge of this general tendency, not to mere correlation, but to causal or explanatory connection, would fortify any confidence in constancy in morphological features within the same species.

(iv) Further, more determinate knowledge of the actual function of the appendix in the life of those rabbits which I had examined would justify much greater confidence in a generalization, at least to rabbits with the same diet or habitat, than the inductions mentioned. And in another case, e.g., the proposition "All mammals have at least one kidney," such theoretical knowledge of the function of the organ, would be determinative of the certainty of the proposition, and the role of induction would be less, or at a different level.

II.2.2 What, you may ask, has been my purpose in presenting you with this example, much simpler than most, of so-called "inductive" argument or proof? Well! mainly this: to indicate how difficult it is, in considering any actual examples, to find any evidence of reliance upon inductive procedures of the purely Humean sort, i.e., procedures in which the principle of induction is relied upon in an entirely unrestricted form and without the support and guidance of any prior theoretical presumptions (e.g., presumptions as to constancy in morphology within species, or as to the explanatory or functional role of certain types of morphological feature in the life of organisms)—and to make it apparent how difficult it is, in any actual proof of a scientific proposition, to find any evidence of reliance, either upon any completely general principle, or upon any principle which is incapable of support by further argument.

Indeed, the appearance is that uninstructed or blind induction of the Humean sort is simply non-existent in the procedures for justifying claims to knowledge or even probability. (Even the unfortunate inference from "All observed swans are white" to "All swans are white" depended for what limited cogency or plausibility it had upon some such presumptions as that colour is preserved within races, and that sufficient observations had been made to exclude the likelihood of there being unobserved races). And without the support and guidance of theoretical presumptions (which are never completely universal in their relevance, but always related to some particular subject-matter or type of subject-matter, inductive procedures might have some methodological use, in looking for things which one might later seek either to explain or prove but have precisely zero justificatory or probative force.

Thus, the reason why the validity of force of blind uninstructed induction cannot be proved is not primarily because any proof of it would involve circularity. Indeed, it is not plain beyond question that such circularity, in which the conclusion aimed at in a proof or argument is somehow relied upon or presupposed in the proof or argument itself, but not as a premise, is necessarily always vicious. (*Prima facie*, it appears that the coherence of the results of relying upon memory and perception cooperatively lends some support to the proposition that memory is to be relied upon). The primary reason why such proof of the validity or force of blind uninstructed induction is impossible is that such induction has no validity or force, and that the inductive argument relied upon to prove it would itself have no force because it was blind or unsupported by any prior theoretical presumption.

But it might reasonably be objected, surely there do exist some completely universal theoretical presumptions upon which such a proof could be grounded? Not, perhaps, the principle that "Every event has a cause" (which seems to result from a rash generalization of the Aristotelian principle that every substance which begins to exist has causes); nor, perhaps the principle that every state of affairs has a sufficient reason for its obtaining; for there appear to be scientific or quasi-empirical reasons as well as philosophical ones, for supposing that both these principles are actually false, and in any case not at all evident, although useful methodologically. But, rather, such more modest principles as "Order or regularity tends to have explanation," and "Exceptions to regularities tend to have explanation," principles which appear to be completely universal—and, indeed, even formally universal, inasmuch as they seem to underly our reliance upon Humean induction even in mathematics, e.g., in judging Fermat's Principle probable, or hoping to find a proof for it. However, I believe this appearance of universality is deceptive, because the notion of "explanation" is analogous, not univocal: the sense in which a proof of Pythagoras' Theorem "explains" the fact of its truth is not utterly unrelated linguistically to the sense in which the Kinetic Theory of cases "explains" Boyle's Law, and to the sense in which mention of the causes of an event "explains" the event; but it still remains that we have here three different senses of the word "explain," not one. Accordingly, "Order or regularity tends to have explanation" is not a universal theoretical presumption, but rather represents the form or character which certain types of theoretical presumption, when they arise, exemplify.

II.2.3 However, the custom of philosophers within the Cartesian tradition has been to dispense with any too close examination of the forms which empirical argumentation actually takes in practice, and to omit any consideration of the difficulties I have mentioned. Instead, since the time of Hume, they have tended to adopt an entirely a priori approach of roughly the following, high-handed and nonconstructive, kind.

In effect, the empiricists have said this: "Whatever the argument which intervenes between the ultimate data or premises and the empirical law or principle of necessity which represents the conclusion of the reasoning, and however complex this argument may be, it remains true that ultimately it can only draw upon a certain class of ultimate-datum-statements, namely statements of observed particular empirical fact; from these, no law-like statements, and no general theoretical presumptions, follow deductively; therefore, a blind induction, uninstructed by any theoretical presumption, must have been relied upon at some stage in order to reach the empirical law-like conclusion; therefore, any proof of a law-like empirical conclusion must involve reliance upon the principle of induction in its unrestricted form, i.e., upon a principle not provable either deductively or inductively, and therefore not provable at all.

Meantime, in the Kantian tradition, the above argument has been, in effect, slightly varied, in order to allow that the faculty of knowledge, or intellect itself, might supply, not only the principle of induction, but also some theoretical presumptions justifying and guiding its application: but these theoretical presumptions, just as much as the principle of induction, appear to be incapable of deductive proof, and incapable of a Humean-type of inductive proof; and, accordingly, it is concluded that they are not merely a priori in the sense of being supplied by the understanding, but purely a priori, in the sense of being known independently of any judgments of experience of the actual and incapable of any kind of a posteriori proof—because it is assumed that all allowable a posteriori proof is inductive.

Moreover, it is worth noting, in passing, that in the case of moral argument these philosophers have adopted an exactly similar method of approach, in effect saying this: "Whatever the intervening argument between the empirical data and the moral conclusion, it remains true that it can only draw upon a certain class of datum-statements, viz., statements of empirical fact; from these no moral conclusion follows either deductively or inductively; therefore, any proof of a moral conclusion must have involved reliance, at some stage or other, upon some moral assumption, itself not provable either deductively or inductively, and therefore not provable at all or at least not 'objectively' provable."

II.2.4 In regard to all these arguments, the following preliminary objections require to be made.

(a) They assume that the only standard, or intra-scientific or non-transcendental, procedures for effectual or probative argument, are either deductive in a strict sense, or inductive in a strict sense. This assumption is neither proven, nor at all obvious or evident, nor (indeed), upon a review of the variety of human argument, very plausible.

(b) They assume that the "ultimate data," upon which a person could legitimately be relying for his knowledge, have been correctly identified. This might be questioned in certain obvious ways, e.g., (i) the empiricist assumption that the ultimate empirical data are atomic, unrelated phenomena, as rejected even by the Kantians, and (ii) the supposition that a person might understand a moral question, deliberate about it at all, while being in complete ignorance of all moral truths, so as to be unable to take any moral truths as a datum, seems mistaken. But this assumption needs to be questioned in another way, as follows.

(c) They assume that there is an enumerable and potentially identifiable totality which comprises all the data relevant to the consideration of the satisfactoriness or probative force of the reasoning which leads up to a conclusion: that is, all the data, meaning both empirical and theoretical or a priori, and including, under the heading of theoretical or a priori, all the principles stating the validity of the methods of argument or modes of inference utilized in the reasoning. But this assumption presents difficulties.

(i) The empirical "data" tend to have presuppositions of an a priori or quasi-a priori kind, as Kant recognized, and it is difficult to be sure one has enumerated all these presuppositions (yet, if the "empirical data" count as knowledge, these presuppositions on which they depend have an equal or better title to be so counted, and an equal or better title to be counted amongst available data).

(ii) The "theoretical data" seem (perhaps deceptively) to be capable of a great variety of different kinds of a posteriori support, (appeal to this has not at this stage of the critic's argument been proved to be illegitimate), and it is very difficult to draw any limit to the "data" which might be relevant here.

(iii) It does not seem obvious that the "principles of method" relied upon in empirical argumentation are enumerable, or that "induction" constitutes an enumerable set of kinds of procedure, let alone a single species of procedure.

(iv) It has been demonstrated (by Goedel) that, even where undoubtedly deductive methods are concerned, these methods are not enumerable.

Accordingly, it is not only obscure as to whether all the "data" have ben correctly identified—this is the question raised by observations (a) and (b) above—but it is also very obscure as to whether it even makes sense to speak of "all the relevant data" at all. And I shall later give reason to suppose that there simply is no such totality, as "all the data relevant to the consideration of the question of the efficacy of a proof as a proof (i.e., its demonstrativeness of probative force)."

I call this process, whereby it is considered legitimate to speak of all the data, and all the reasoning, relevant to the consideration of the satisfactoriness or efficacy of the proof of a certain conclusion, and to conceive the whole completed chain of pieces of reasoning as constituting one single extended argument or proof, despite the fact that most or all of the data, and most of the reasoning, is unidentified and unidentifiable, a process of Non-Constructive Summation. It can be "justified," as I shall now show, only by means of resort to quite unprovable postulates.

II.2.5 In a sense, the basic trouble with this type of critical approach, exemplified above all in the empiricists, is precisely this non-constructivity.

Presented with an actual piece of reasoning, the critic assumes that the premises and principles of this piece of reasoning must either be counted as amongst the ultimate data, or else must be supported by some other actual pieces of reasoning—whereas, as I shall indicate later, all that human knowledge requires is that such ancillary pieces of reasoning should be possible, not actual. Then, having postulated a completed chain of such pieces of actual reasoning (most of them fictitious, since all that knowledge requires is that at each stage of an argument the premises and principles involved in that stage should be capable of support by further argument, i.e., that at each stage some argument should be actualizable, not that a whole chain should be completable, i.e., carried right back to starting points which count as data because no argument is possible in support of them, or the completed chain actualizable as a whole), the critic then postulates that the whole chain can be summated or treated as a single argument, whose strength is wholly dependent upon the evidentness of the things which have been assumed as data, at the various stages of the argument.

Because the approach is in this way non-constructive, proceeding by postulation, not by study of actual argument, and because (for good or ill) such completed chains of reasoning do not have any actual psychological or historical existence, we have no idea as to what all these postulated prior stages in the reasoning look like so as to be able actually to examine (i) what data they rely upon, (ii) whether they draw upon purely a priori principles, incapable of a posteriori support, (iii) whether it is legitimate to add them together. (This last question, (iii), is the question of the legitimacy of the Cut: i.e., if X,Y,Z imply P, and P,Q,R, imply S, then we would normally say that X,Y,Z,Q,R, imply S, independently of P?).

As a result of this inability to examine these postulated chains of reasoning (because of their fictitious character), the only way our critic can reach any conclusion about them at all is by means of postulates. Accordingly, he postulates (1) that, in any such chain of pieces of reasoning, each separate stage will be either deductive or inductive. Then he either mistakenly infers from this, or postulates, (2) that any two such stages can be coalesced, or added together and treated as one, (i.e., that the Cut is always legitimate). Lastly, because he wrongly thinks that such chains can be completed and must be actualizable in completion, and because he infers from (2) that circularity within a chain will always be vicious, he goes on to lay down (3) that these chains must always be finite. Naturally enough, once these postulates are granted, everything else the critic wants follows—and, in particular, from (2) and (3) it at once follows that a completed chain can be taken as a single whole and treated as one argument, from various data to the determined conclusion.

II.2.6 But to proceed in this way, by the multiplication of unprovable postulates, and in a way in which, once these have been accepted, is so completely free from the possibility either of being confirmed, or of being corrected, by reference to a consideration of actual arguments, appears to me quite worthless, and to provide no sound basis for the criticism of anything. The most apt descriptions of it are precisely Aristotle's: it is alien to science, and merely contentious or eristic.[13]

The ultimate data upon which all knowledge is supposed to be founded do not seem to be identifiable. The postulated completed chains of reasoning whereby we get from them to the starting points of our ordinary day-to-day arguments appear to have no psychological or historical existence. And, if we work backwards from our conclusions then, while we readily arrive at points where further argument seems unnecessary, we nonetheless never appear to arrive at any point where argument is clearly absolutely impossible (or so I judge from reflecting about actual examples).

Thus, the non-constructivity of this type of critical approach is apparent, not only in its method, but also in its results. In connection with any well-established truth, it purports to prove the existence of three things: (a) a completed set of the data relevant to its proof, (b) completed chains of reasoning leading back to these, and (c) points where argument is impossible, i.e., where individual data can be identified. But it gives us no means of producing, in connection with any ordinary case, verifiable examples of any of these three kinds of thing, not even the third.

II.3. THE CONFUSION OF "TRUTH-LOGIC" WITH "CONSEQUENCE-LOGIC"

Thirdly, I said that the Cartesian approach led to a confusion between what I believe Husserl called truth-logic and consequence-logic, or

13 Cf. Aristotle, *De Gen. et Cor.*, 316a5-14; *Physics*, 184b25-185a19, 186a4—9, 187a12. Aristotle's view is that merely eristic, or contentious, and unscientific arguments against a "scientific" thesis can be refuted, but that only "scientific," or in the case of physical questions, "physical" ones require to be so: the word "dialectical" in these passages implies "contentious" or "eristic," whereas in *Topics*, I. 1—2, it does not imply this, but, on the contrary, excludes this.

(as I prefer to call them) between a Logic of Knowledge and a Logic of Analysis: i.e., a confusion in regard to the very nature of the science of argument itself.

II.3.1 In order to see what I have in mind, let us consider an example of what we can conveniently call the deductive representation of an argument. In common cases, the process of arriving at knowledge of a conclusion is like this.

Firstly, there are some signs, grounds, or data, which we take as premises.

Secondly, there are what I shall call analytic or logical principles of procedure in argument, principles of the sort which apply equally in every subject-matter, whose application is a purely formal matter, not involving reliance upon any synthetic knowledge from within the subject-matter, and statements exemplifying whose application are merely analytic or empty of any content in regard to the subject-matter concerned.

Thirdly, there are often principles of procedure in argument of a different, non-analytic, kind: whose application is not a matter of formal rule, and statements exemplifying whose application are synthetic. For instance, the application of the principle of induction is never merely formal: it always presupposes other non-analytic principles from within the subject-matter, (a) as to what counts as a real similarity, and (b) as to the extent to which the regularity observed is significant, i.e., justifies a firm inference. And the statements exemplifying its application, i.e., conditional statements in which the premises appear in the antecedents and the conclusion appears as the consequent of a conditional, are synthetic.

And, fourthly and finally, there are what I will call presuppositions of normality. For instance, if I am reasoning about some particular nontrivial action done by some person I do not know. I use it as a principle of argument that, when a person does some non-trivial action, he has some motive; but, in applying this principle to this particular man, I presuppose that he is rational and not insane. This is what I call a presupposition of normality: it is not a principle of argument, because it relates to the particular; and it is not like a premise stating a piece of evidence or sign of the truth of the conclusion, because, although I have good reason for assuming it, it nonetheless remains the case that it could easily be false without my knowing this, and I am not required to check it before assuming it. Now, in the deductive representation of this inference here involved, what happens is (in effect) this, that, with the exception of the analytic or logical principles, and any merely nominal definitions, all these things are grouped together indifferently as premises. That is, the ordinary premises stating pieces of evidence or evidential data, the non-analytic principles of argument, the principles presupposed in the application of these (e.g., as to what counts as a real similarity, and what degree of regularity is significant), and presuppositions of normality, are all grouped together without discrimination as premises. And the conclusion is represented as if it were arrived at by means of inference from these premises, the logical principles serving as rules of inference.[14]

II.3.2 We are now in a position, with the help of this example, to see rather more clearly the nature of the difference between, on the one hand, Logic as a study of the logical relations between propositions, what we might call Analytical Logic, or Logic of Analysis, or Logic of Formal Validity, and, on the other hand, Logic as the study of the role of argument or discourse in the acquisition of knowledge of truth, what we might call Epistemological Logic, or Logic of Knowledge, or Logic of Demonstrativeness.[15]

From the point of view of Logic as concerned with the logical relations between propositions, the deductive representation of an argument is all that one requires in order to study it, and one needs to

14 Of course, I oversimplify here: but the point is that, if there are any differences between the different types of proposition or rule relied upon in an argument, these differences are relevant to the deductive representation of the argument only in so far as they are formal differences, i.e., differences in the ways in which our formal rules of inference require us to handle them. Differences in epistemological status are as such irrelevant.

15 This is, I think, the distinction Husserl had in view when he spoke of consequence-logic and truth-logic: but I think the phrase "truth-logic" is misleading, inasmuch as, for good or ill, consequence-logic is commonly presented as being concerned precisely with connections between the truth-values as syntactically related propositions, and Husserl's "truth-logic" is concerned with knowledge or probability of truth, rather than truth tout court.

make no discrimination between the different types of proposition and rule relied upon in argument, except for purely formal discriminations, such as the one between premise and analytic law of inference. For example, from the point of view of this Logic of Analysis, the distinctions between evidential premises, non-analytic principles, and presuppositions of normality, are not as such of any relevance at all.

By contrast, from the point of view of a Logic of Knowledge, concerned with the efficacy of the argument in establishing or showing or demonstrating the truth or probability of its conclusion, these distinctions are, of course, of capital importance. Any such Logic of Knowledge will be concerned, not only with the identification of the premises, but with their role in the argument, and the canons governing the propriety of relying upon them, and these are quite different for the different types of premise I mentioned. From the point of view of the Logic of Knowledge, then, the deductive representation of an argument, inasmuch as it makes no discrimination between the different kinds of premise, far from being a perspicuous representation of what the evidential force or demonstrativeness or cogency of the argument depends upon, is (on the contrary) liable to be grossly misleading.

We can now see one of the chief parts of the evil in what I called the evidentialist preconception about knowledge, the preconception which required that everything upon which a person's knowledge depends should be within the review of the knower's own mind, the preconception (that is) that the only sufficient or adequate justification for a claim to knowledge is one which is unconditional or free from any unchecked presuppositions—namely that it abolishes the epistemological relevance of those distinctions between different types of premise which I mentioned, and thereby makes the Logic of Knowledge merely a trivial extension of the Logic of Analysis.

II.3.3 The importance of this question of the differences in status of the different things which the Analytical Logician counts as premises appears also in another way, and one which is relevant to the Summation discussed in my last section, and to the question of when circularity is vicious. For, differences in the character of premises make a difference to the legitimacy of adding arguments together, i.e., to the legitimacy of the Cut: that is, if X,Y,Z imply P, and P,Q,R imply

S, then we can say that X,Y,Z,Q,R implies S? Yes, if P is a mere premise and not a principle of method in argument in the second argument—and in this case, if S and X are identical, we will have a case of vicious circularity, or *petitio principii*. No, if P is a principle of method in argument in the second argument—and, in this case, perhaps, if S and X are identical, there will still be no vicious circularity.

PART III: THE RESTORATION OF ARGUMENT

III.1. THE BASIS FOR A REJECTION OF CARTESIANISM: A SUMMARY OF MY LONDON PAPER

Such, then, are the evils which appear to me to flow from this Cartesian system of tendencies and preconceptions: misdescription of the procedures of our thought, resort to spurious new types of justification, and dependence upon unsupported dogma. But how are we to escape from these evils? and how are we to make the rejection of these tendencies and preconceptions even intelligible? This was the question to which I addressed myself in my London paper on the "Nature of Knowledge." And the answer which I have there, still appears to me to be in its essentials correct. Let me therefore very briefly summarize the argument of that paper. In that London paper, in effect, I attacked the Cartesian and transcendentalist system on three fronts.

In the first place, I attempted (in §§2–3) to demonstrate that the transcendentalist preconception that second-order epistemological knowledge about a field was necessarily prior to and independent of any first-order knowledge from within the field, far from being obviously true, proved upon examination to be highly counterintuitive. The discussion was intricate, but, in effect the basis of my argument was this, that in normal cases we prove "P is proved" by means of proving "P," not vice-versa, and in general the soundness of an argument (or of any other procedure for getting knowledge) was recognized in the act of exercising it in getting knowledge, and not prior to or independently of such exercise. And though an already established procedure could be authenticated or even established as more certain, this was only by comparing the results of using it and examining the coherence of these results—or else by examining whether they cohered with the results of using other already established procedures. Hence, always, the only way of assessing the soundness of procedures was by means of their exercise, or with the help of exercising other prima facie established procedures.[16]

In the second place, it seemed to me that the Cartesian scheme—both in its tendency to suppose that any genuine justification must be concerned to state the grounds of some inference, and also in its evidentialist presumption that the soundness of my grounds for claiming knowledge must depend solely upon things immediately present to my consciousness, such as judgments, beliefs, memories, experiences and any other intuitions there may be—was wedded to a conception of knowledge as being something like "justified true belief," the justifiedness being supposed to arise from this relationship of me to the contents of my mind. And I therefore proceeded, by many arguments (§2, §4.2, §5.3, §5.4 all subserved this purpose), to show that this explanation of the nature of knowledge was unacceptable, and (§4.2) that as a result the conception that argument or justification was limited to the case of knowledge by inference was baseless.

And then, in the third place, I proposed a new definition of knowledge, as being (in effect) the satisfactory end-position to be sought after when our faculties are exercised in regard to a question of truth or falsity, or (as I put it) an "intellectually satisfactory intellectual position in regard to a fact." And I indicated the many advantages that this account had, even merely as a definition (§5.3, §5.4, cf. §4.2). But my main concern was to point out that this account of the nature of knowledge

16 Although the meta-theory or methodology of a science can generate new procedures for arriving at new truth within the science (as the proof of Goedel's Incompleteness Theorem, and the proofs of the usefulness first of Cepheid variables, and then of the red-shift of nebulae, for estimating astronomical distance, in their different ways exhibit), it cannot do this without assuming the reliability of some of the procedures already accepted within the science or theory whose methodology or metatheory it is: e.g., if I am to conclude to the truth of (n) (Fn) in the Geodelian way, then I need to assume not only the consistency of the theory which allows me to prove F(1), F(2), F(3), etc., but also its demonstrativeness, i.e., the truth of its axioms, and the validity of its inferences, because I need to know that each of F(1), F(2), etc. can be demonstrated to be true. And, in general, a metatheory can never prove the demonstrativeness of any of the procedures within a theory, except by means of assuming the demonstrativeness of some of these procedures or of some other equivalent or more powerful ones.

removed from us any compulsion to accept either the evidentialist or the transcendentalist preconceptions [these had been described, without these names, (a) in §1 and the beginning of §6, and (b) in §3].

It appears to me that this quasi-Aristotelian account of "knowing that P" as "being in an intellectually satisfactory position in regard to the fact that P," gave knowledge a situational character, whereby it was quite intelligible that the soundness of the knower's grounds might depend upon things not within the knower's immediate review (or which he had not in fact reviewed), contrary to the evidentialist demand for an unconditional knowledge whose every condition or presupposition had been reviewed and checked upon by the knower. This dependence on things not reviewed or checked upon might make the knower's position less than ideal but did not make it unsatisfactory. Moreover, the soundness of the knower's grounds could not only depend upon things outside his review; it could even be confirmed by a consideration by other people of such things, so that (as we say) his grounds might be sounder than he knew. And it was perfectly natural that the satisfactoriness of his situation should depend upon a wide variety of facts within the field of knowledge concerned, and that these facts should be appealed to in a posteriori argument to show that his situation was in fact satisfactory, i.e., that he did have knowledge—quite contrary to what the transcendentalist assumes.

III.2. THE RESULTING "ARISTOTELIAN" POSITION: ITS "REALIST" AND "QUASI-VERIFICATIONIST" CHARACTER

These, then, were the reasons which I gave for rejecting these last two preconceptions, the transcendentalist and the evidentialist.

And my second kind of critical philosophy, the one which I am calling (for lack of any better name) "Aristotelian," is the one which results as it were automatically or naturally, simply from the rejection of these two preconceptions, and of the false restrictions upon argument which result from them.

III.2.1 The "Aristotelian" approach which I wish to recommend is therefore "realist" in at least one sense of this highly ambiguous word.

It is realist in admitting the legitimacy of bringing a posteriori argument, drawing upon first-order knowledge from within a field, to bear upon second-order or epistemological questions about the procedures to be adopted in order to get knowledge from within a field; and in regarding reliance upon at least some argument of this kind as indispensable, so that, for instance, at least some knowledge of the real is a precondition of any epistemology, and at least some knowledge in morals a precondition of any genuine "metaethics."[17]

The objection has been made to me that such a dependence of epistemological conclusions upon a resort to first-order precritical or pre-systematic judgment or knowledge puts one in a position in which one would not, for instance, be able to criticize the beliefs of the Azandi tribe about witches. But this objection involves two false suppositions. (1) It supposes that I think that, within each restricted species of judgment, (so that these judgments which exhibit the peculiar Azandi beliefs about witches, etc., constitute a "species"), some must be accepted uncritically. But this is not true. And any species, or genus, of judgment must survive the test, not only of consistency with other accepted judgments, but also of freedom from arbitrariness: e.g., if the decision between the truth of the Azandi beliefs and the truth of European beliefs were rationally arbitrary, then we would have to say that neither constituted knowledge. (2) It supposes that this species of judgment amongst the Azandi, and the associated "conceptual structures," are, as it were, rationally isolable, or independent of those judgments on which Azandi and Europeans agree, so that argument to disprove the Azandi beliefs is impossible; but I do not believe this, and it appears to me that the problem is, not the non-existence of appropriate argument, but the absence of motivation for an Azandi (granted his beliefs) to pay it requisite attention.[18]

17 This is in accord with the views of some recent Anglo-Saxon writers: e.g., (i) the view that the province of ethics cannot be defined merely formally, and that it is not a sufficient definition of a "moral" rule that it is a universal prescription for action, but that what makes a "moral" rule into a moral rule (rather than, for instance, just a law of etiquette) is some special connection (of an ill-understood kind) with human happiness and harm; (ii) the view that it is a criterion of the acquisition of a moral concept (or of a moral word's having been understood) that there should be agreement in certain moral judgments involving this concept.

18 [This Aristotelian position will also be realist in two other senses: firstly, in the sense that it rejects the evidentialist preconception, and therefore

III.2.2 This sort of realism has its importance within every area of philosophy. But within epistemology itself its importance is paramount, and for this reason: that it restores to us the possibility of argument and of proof by argument—indispensable tools for which, as both history and logic show, there is no substitute. And it achieves this merely by removing those unnatural and false restrictions upon argument which it has revealed as being baseless.

Yet, what requires to be noted is this, that in the very act of restoring argument, and with it the possibility of knowledge, it at the very same time restores to us the possibility of the criticism of knowledge.

If proof by argument is never possible, then the absence of such proof will appear no great matter amongst men, and criticism will be determined only by arbitrary diktat, or by the limits of what our "animal nature" (Hume) will allow us to doubt. But, on the other hand, if we can insist that argument of an appropriate and adequate kind must always be possible, (a) in proof or justification of any legitimate claim to knowledge, and (b), in the case of any true claim to knowledge, in rebuttal of objections to the argument proving or justifying the claim, then criticism will be restored—for, in that case, the absence of argument or the possibility of argument will be significant of an absence of knowledge. Now, my Aristotelian restoration of argument makes this insistence, which nature demands, possible—and thereby restores a genuine criticism, free from any arbitrariness.

You will notice that I have mentioned to you two things, (a) argument in proof of claims to knowledge, and (b) argument in rebuttal of objections to supposed proofs of claims to knowledge. Both are necessary if knowledge is to exist.

The first requirement, that any legitimate claim to knowledge must be capable of surviving the knower's own examination and must

---

regards any merely psychological or introspectionist account of the intellectual conditions of knowledge as impossible; i.e., what makes it legitimate to rely upon something as a ground is never something merely "mental"; this involves the rejection of idealism. Secondly, in the sense that there will no longer be any adequate reason for refusing to consider causal efficacy as a criterion of reality (in the case of objects) or of actuality (in the case of facts), and therefore no reason to deny the possibility of knowledge of things as they are, as well as of how they appear.]

therefore be capable of adequate support by argument, at least by the knower himself, is one to which I referred earlier (when discussing intuition). The position I take up here is quasi-verificationist: where there is knowledge, there must be a means of verification, that is, "appropriate and adequate argument" in support of the claim to knowledge. In this sense, the main epistemological mistake of the verificationists of the Vienna Circle was not their requirement that every kind of proposition in regard to which knowledge was possible should have a method of verification, but their narrow conception of "verification," and their restriction of types of method of verification in effect to two, quasi-mathematical and crudely empirical.[19] Before proceeding to consideration of my second requirement, I deal with two of the more obvious objections to this quasi-verificationist position: a priori knowledge of conceptual truths and intuitive knowledge of one's inner states.

(1) A priori knowledge of conceptual truths need create no difficulty. Consider the case of the man who knows a priori that fear involves the thought of danger or of something unwanted. How could he prove his claim to know this? Many answers suggest themselves. One would say this: (a) a person does not have fear, if for him to call his emotion "fear" would be to violate the criteria for the proper use of the word "fear," (b) it is a criterion of whether the word "fear" has been understood that a person understands that fear involves the thought of danger or of something unwanted. Then further questions might be asked, as to how he knew (a) and (b). But these could, in turn, be answered. And so on. This argument does not express the means of knowledge, which would be by imagining a case of fear, and performing an intuitive induction, and not by any such a posteriori argument as is involved in (b). But what is required is not an expression of the means of knowledge, but a proof or test or authentication of a claim to knowledge. To prove a piece of metal is not to make it, and to prove a will is not to make it—and similarly with non-inferential knowledge.

(2) Intuitive knowledge of one's own opinions and intentions creates no difficulty. Consider the following example. Suppose that

19 I owe this way of viewing the situation to Mr. Michael Dummett, and it was indeed one of the original seeds from which the thoughts of this paper have grown.

we have before us a person who knows that he believes that porridge is good food. Now, I am not saying that, from no premises at all, this man can prove to himself the truth of the judgment "I believe that porridge is a good food." No! what I say is merely this. The claim to know that he believes that porridge is a good food must be capable of surviving the man's own examination. Suppose, then, that he does examine the claim. He will say to himself "I think that I know that I believe that porridge is a good food, but do I really know this?" He can then argue to himself that it is part of the nature of opinions or beliefs that, if a person thinks that he knows that he has a certain opinion, then he does indeed know that he has this opinion: and much argument could be offered in favor of this essential truth. And then, from this essential or conceptual truth, together with the given premise "I think that I know that I believe that porridge is a good food," the man can correctly infer "I know that I believe that porridge is a good food."

III.3. THE CRITICISM OF THE PROCEDURES FOR OBTAINING KNOWLEDGE

My first requirement was that for a claim to knowledge to be legitimate, then the claim itself must be capable of standing up to the knower's own examination of it, so that the knower himself must have proof available to him. My second requirement is this, that if a claim to knowledge is actually true, then any such proof must itself be capable of standing up to examination, and not only the knower's own examination at a time when he judges that he has knowledge, but to public examination. That is to say that everything on which the efficacy of the proof as proof depends, the truth of its premises, the correctness of its presuppositions, and the soundness of the principles according to which it proceeds, all these must be open to review: not indeed that they need all be provable, but in the sense that objections to them can be adequately rebutted.

Notice that the question here is not that of legitimacy of the claim to knowledge, of the justifiedness of the knower's thinking that he had knowledge, nor of the justifiedness of the knower's thinking his "proof" of his claim to knowledge to be adequate; all this will indeed be required, but only because his "proof" must be capable of standing up to his own examination of its efficacy or satisfactoriness as a proof of the truth of his claim to knowledge, i.e., as a justification of his own judgment that he has knowledge. But the question at issue is not that of legitimacy of the claim to knowledge, but of its truth; and not of the knower's justifiedness in thinking his proof adequate, but of the actual efficacy or satisfactoriness of his proof as proof; for the truth of the claim to knowledge depends, not just on the possibility of the man's justifiedly thinking the premises, the presuppositions, and the method of some proof available to him, to be sound, but upon these things being actually sound.

It follows from this that there is no restriction, either in the raising of objections to the premises, presuppositions, or method, of some proof of a claim to knowledge, or in the rebuttal of these objections, upon the considerations or data to which appeal is made. Just as an objector can bring forward new observational or empirical data in order to impugn the premises, presuppositions, or method, of some proof of a claim to knowledge, in order to show the claim to be ill-founded, so also a defender of this claim can bring forward new observational or empirical data in defense of these premises, presuppositions, or method. Of course, if the knower examines the credentials of the proof of his claim to knowledge at the very time of making it, then he can only appeal to data within his reach at that time. But further or later consideration or review of his claim is always possible, both to himself and to others, and this can draw upon considerations or data not accessible to the knower at the time when he first possessed the knowledge.

Nor are the new data necessarily all of a straightforwardly empirical kind. There can also be new theoretical data or considerations, relevant both in attack and defense of claims to knowledge, new in the sense that it would be historically or biographically inept to supposed to have been accessible to the knower at the inception of his knowledge.

What I am saying then is this. The intellect is free to interrogate or raise objection to a proof at any point, not merely in regard to its premises and presuppositions, but even in regard to its principles of method. But, when objections or queries have thus been raised, in regard to the proof of a claim to knowledge, there are no restrictions upon the considerations or data to which the intellect may appeal in defense of this proof. As the intellect is free to appeal to any new considerations or data in impugning a proof, so also it is able to appeal to new considerations in defense of it. The Evidentialist preconception that the defender of the proof of a claim to knowledge may appeal only to data accessible to the knower at the time of his knowledge represents a restriction which is entirely without warrant, and *ultra vires*.

You may understand my position better if I compare it with some of the things said by Karl Popper. He has insisted that all our conclusions, at least in science, are always open to re-examination. And, if one allows for the possibility of bringing new theoretical considerations to bear, as well as new empirical ones, and of re-examining the truth of a conclusion by means of a reexamination of an existing proof, then I think that, indeed, in a sense, this is universally true, and not only within the empirical sciences.

But my present thesis is a different one, but closely related to his, it is that all our proofs, and procedures of proof, are in a valid sense, always open to reexamination.

I say, "in a sense" and "in a valid sense," because I do not think that "reexaminability" implies "corrigibility" or "falsifiability." It seems to me quite common for the reexamination of a proof to confirm its satisfactoriness, and to do this in such a way as to confirm the certainty of its conclusion. Even within the empirical sciences, this happens: e.g., it appears to me that a re-examination of our reasons for accepting that the planets go round the sun rather than the earth, that the blood circulates from the arteries to the veins in a single circulatory system, or that there has been evolution amongst the vertebrates, reveal these things as certain; and it seems to me foolhardy to maintain that these theses remain corrigible in anything of the same sense that any particular theory about gravitational or quantum phenomena remains corrigible.

And, in any case, I do not know even the beginnings of a satisfactory account of the meaning of "can" in "can be falsified" or "can be corrected." Certainly, it is neither logical consistency, nor physical possibility, which is concerned. And any account must take account of the fact, that what is actually true, whether or not we know it, is in a certain obvious sense incapable of being shown to be false.

III.4. THE RESTORATION OF TRUTH-LOGIC, OR A LOGIC OF KNOWLEDGE

Firstly, then, knowledge depends for its existence on the possibility of satisfactory or efficacious proof of the claim to possess it (and public knowledge upon public accessible proof), and, further, secondly, the existence of satisfactory proof depends upon the possibility of some review of the question of its satisfactoriness, and of rebutting any objections raised against it.

I am now in a position to state a further key point. We must now recognize that the possibility of reviewing the satisfactoriness of a proof as a proof is absolutely dependent upon the existence of *unused available and relevant data*, i.e., upon the existence of considerations (perhaps observational, perhaps theoretical, in character) which were not actually used in the proof, i.e., to rebut objections to the premises, presuppositions, and principles of method, relied upon in the proof.

Accordingly, both knowledge and proof depend upon the existence, alongside any proof of knowledge, of unused data relevant to the consideration of the question of the force or efficacy of the proof as a proof. And, because these unused data are not internal to the proof, they do not need to be all of them present in any sense to the mind of the knower; to require this in every case is just the Evidentialist mistake. The only thing which can be required universally is this, that they should have a situational availability: i.e., an availability such that, if an objection is raised, then the situation of the knower, or of the persons considering his claim to knowledge, is such as to allow them, perhaps with the help of further theoretical reflection, perhaps with the help of further observation, perhaps by a combination of the two, to bring these unused data, these considerations not appealed to in the proof itself, to bear upon the question of the force or efficacy of the proof as a proof.

We can now see the full extent of the viciousness of that Non-Constructive Summation, which I discussed earlier, which supposed that one could gather together, within one totality, all the available data in any way relevant to the consideration of the efficacy of the proof of a claim to knowledge as a proof, i.e., to the consideration of the extent to which this proof established or demonstrated the truth of the claim to knowledge (e.g., all the available relevant observational or empirical data, and, if any purely theoretical or a priori data existed, these as well). I speak of this as vicious, because clearly, if this totality exists, i.e., if the available and relevant data constitute a finite or definite set, then the strongest conceivable proof or justification for a claim to knowledge will be one which utilizes the whole of it, i.e., all the available data; and this proof, the strongest possible one, will be incapable of review, because there will be no relevant available unused data (whether observational or theoretical) to which one could make appeal in order to rebut objections to the proof. This is vicious, because as we have seen, the very possibility of knowledge, or of proof, depends upon the existence, alongside any proof however strong, of unused available data relevant to the considerations of the efficacy of the proof as proof.[20]

We are also now in a position to understand better what is wrong in the confusion of Truth-Logic or a Logic of Knowledge with the Logic of Formal Validity or Consequence-Logic. For, what is true of proofs is true also, in the corresponding way, of methods of proof.

The point here is this. Formal validity is a merely internal property of a method of proof, independent of any relation to any data not explicitly stated or used in the proof itself—whereas, by contrast, the strength of a method of proof, or its tendency to contribute to knowledge, or to establish conclusions, is not a property merely internal to it, but a property determined by its relation to those considerations (whether they be theoretical or observational, a priori or empirical) by reference to which we decide what its strength or demonstrative force is. That is, the strength or demonstrative force of the method of proof is a property determined by the relation between the proof and those considerations which we have to weigh in our

20 This appears to be the basis or justification of J. L. Austin's method of refuting the argument from illusion for an idealist or representationist view of perception (*Sense and Sensibilia*). There are, of course, other arguments for this view of perception which need to be dealt with, and of which (unfortunately) Austin neglected to take adequate note. But this argument, from illusion, depends entirely upon the Evidentialist assumption, and is, therefore, I believe, entirely without force; and for the most part it is well dealt with by Austin.

deliberations as to the soundness of all the principles upon which the method of the proof depends. And, whereas in the case of formal or merely analytic methods of proof, the pattern of these deliberations as to their soundness takes on relatively restricted forms, the situation with methods of proof in general is, I believe, quite different—the methods for authenticating them are very various, according to the different types of principle involved, (and also the different types of presupposition of normality which a method of proof is liable to permit one to accept without any check upon them).

We could add this remark: the ultimate cause of the impotence of the method of descriptive analysis for the purposes of justifying anything is precisely this, that *ex hypothesi* it describes only the internal properties of the methods and procedures which it considers, and these, in isolation, because merely internal, can justify nothing.

III.5. CONCLUSION

Neither a proof, nor a set of intuitive judgments, nor a proof grounded upon a set of intuitive judgments, is, (we ought to recognize), of any use by itself for founding any piece of human knowledge.

Human knowledge is made possible, not by any finite set of finite processes of proof or analysis, drawing upon some finite collection of intuitive or non-inferential data of fact or probability, but by the coexistence, both of finite processes of proof, and of exercises of intuitive or non-inferential judgment, with a nonfinite set of procedures for discovering and utilizing considerations or data relevant to the examination of the satisfactoriness of a proof, or the soundness of a judgment.

There is no point in any proof, whether in supposedly intuitively known premises, or seemingly evident principles of reasoning, in which the proof is exempt from question. The intellect is inventive in raising queries and objections at, as it were, unexpected points. At some points of course, the structure will be secure, and all objections unreal or factious: but this will reveal itself, not in their being dismissed without examination, but in the possibility of examining them and finding them to be unreal. For the intellect is inventive, not only in finding grounds for query or objection or doubt, but also in finding ways of rebutting particular objections and types of objection.

When I speak of the data available and relevant to the examination of the credentials of a proof as not constituting a "finite or definite set," and of the checking procedures for discovering and utilizing such data as constituting a "nonfinite" set, I do not mean that these data or these procedures are more numerous than any finite collection. What I mean is that there is no rule whereby they could be enumerated, either so as to bring them into one-to-one correspondence with some finite collection, or so as to bring them into one-to-one correspondence with the natural numbers, so that in this sense they are non-enumerable; and that this is not because of their large number, but (analogously to the definitions of real numbers, as the Richard paradox shows) because they are "nonfinite" in the sense of being not definite in number.

In Goedel's Incompleteness result, we have, it appears, a metamathematical demonstration, within one limited field of human inquiry, of the impossibility of regarding either theoretical data, or procedures of proof, as being definite in number or enumerable. But, in this paper, I have tried to give philosophical reasons for thinking that this result needs to be generalised to apply to every area of human inquiry.

And it is this non-enumerability of procedures for discovering and utilizing theoretical and observational data, i.e., this freedom or capacity of the intellect both to interrogate nature and to interrogate itself at unexpected points, and to deal with these interrogations in unexpected ways, which (I believe) makes it possible for man, unlike a Turing machine, to review all his judgments and procedures; and which thereby (I have contended) makes possible both proof or argument and the criticism of proof or argument, and thereby also makes possible both knowledge and the criticism of knowledge; and which provides man with that natural protection which he has, both against skepticism, and against systematic error.[21]

21 But still exceedingly various, and not rule bound. Cf., inter alia, George Kreisel, at the end of Section 6, of "Hilbert's Programme," reprinted in Benacerraf and Putnam, ed., *Readings in Philosophy of Mathematics* 2nd ed. (Cambridge: Cambridge University Press, 1983).

APPENDIX[22]
PART IV: THE NOTION OF A PRIORI OR ESSENTIAL TRUTH

What I have said so far absolutely requires some clarification of the notion of a priori truth. Firstly, it requires to be shown that the knowledge which proceeds a priori from the understanding of concepts (or from the appreciation of "essences," or from reflection upon what is involved in the meanings of the words we use and the "language-games" of which they are part), is not totally independent, as knowledge, of all judgments of experience—except in the case of vacuous analytic statements (i.e., formally universal principles, and the tautologies which are their instances). All synthetic a priori knowledge is impure, in the sense of being in a certain special and limited way, dependent upon judgments of experience of the actual—so that between a priori and empirical knowledge there is an inevitable interdependence.

Secondly, it requires to be realized that the notion of "a priori truth" is often used by philosophers for purposes which have nothing to do with "total independence of experience." These ambiguities need to be resolved.

Thirdly, it requires to be shown that the Kantian and empiricist notion of a priori truth, as a thing known entirely independently of all empirical judgments, is perfectly useless, because of the absence of any satisfactory criterion for its application—i.e., of any criterion which would (a) give us confidence in our judgment in disputed cases, or (b) show us how to deal with propositions to whose truth both theoretical or a priori considerations and also observational considerations seem relevant (a type of proposition whose existence is excluded in the Cartesian kind of critical philosophy).

This last point seems to be of vital importance, because one of the most peculiar effects of the Cartesian and transcendentalist system is that it seems to make it difficult or impossible for two types of consideration, the one theoretical or a priori, and the other observational or empirical, to be relevant to the truth of the same proposition—despite the fact that this happens everywhere in science.

22 [Editor's note: David calls this an appendix because it couldn't be included in the talk, but he clearly considers it an important part of the paper. We leave it here as both "appendix" and "Part IV" as David had it.]

The system of preconceptions and tendencies which I labelled "Cartesian" has made it appear that arguments are in short supply. The truth is that arguments with some force are in abundant supply. The real problem is not the lack of appropriate arguments, i.e., arguments with some force, but lies in describing the process of weighing up disparate kinds of argument, all of which have some force.

IV.1. THE SENSE IN WHICH A PRIORI KNOWLEDGE DEPENDS UPON EXPERIENCE

IV.1.1 Of course, both Kant and the empiricists concede that a priori knowledge is in some cases impure in the sense that it involves empirical concepts. But then they insist, that, once the concepts are given, this suffices to determine the truth of the propositions. To understand the concepts involved in a proposition, that is, the meanings of the linguistic expressions used in it, this may depend upon experience—but all the rest of the work, and in particular the work of judging whether the proposition is true or false, is the work of the understanding—for, although the understanding may draw upon concepts or ideas drawn from experience, it does not draw upon any judgments from experience—or so they tell us.[23]

Against this, I say this, that an a priori judgment in which something is judged as being seen to be intrinsically necessary, may presuppose the coherence, or the applicability, of the concepts employed in it, and that these things can in normal cases only be known by means of actual experience of the actual.

IV.1.2 For instance, we have the concept of fear, and this is a concept which involves, not just a conjunction of thoughts relating to possible danger, feelings described as feelings of fear, and desires to avoid the danger or wishes that the danger be not there or cease, but the occurrence in typical cases of a necessary or non-accidental connection *in rebus* between these thoughts, feelings, and desires. And the

23 Against this, there is also a Wittgensteinian type of argument, which seems sound, although I have not used it, that appreciation of meanings or grasp of concepts depends upon some agreement in judgments accepted as true—so that concepts and judgments are inseparable.

proposition that fear does involve such non-accidental connections is at the same time, a priori, in the sense that the understanding sees it as necessary from its very concepts, and synthetic, in that what is intended is not a mere stipulation that nothing should be called fear unless there exists these non-accidental connections in association with it, but a phenomenological description having relevance to some actual phenomena, a conceptual statement carrying synthetic implications in regard to these phenomena. And, so understood, it presupposes the coherence of the concepts involved.

But many philosophers have held that the existence of necessary or non-accidental connections *in rebus* is conceptually impossible or inconceivable, and from this it would follow that the concept of fear is incoherent. At this point, we must, of course, distinguish between the arguments which these philosophers use and the conclusions they reach. The understanding can, I believe, readily show their arguments to be unsound, but, although it thus shows their conclusion to be non-proven, it cannot, I believe, show it to be false. And, it is, I believe, only experience that shows this: experience shows that the concept of fear does have application, i.e., that fear is actual; and from this, it follows that fear is a conceptually possible thing (or "conceivable"), i.e., that the concept of fear is a coherent concept.

IV.1.3 Or, a second example. The informal, or ordinary pre-axiomatic or pre-mathematical concepts of straightness and parallelism, are, I believe, idealizations governing the description of the visual field, as known to perception, and governing all operations of visual imagination. And I believe that Kant was correct in thinking that acceptance of the propositions of Euclidean geometry as conceptually necessary or a priori truths about empirical space is a necessary consequence of the unrestricted use of these concepts. It appears to me clearly an error to suppose that the ordinary concept of straight line survives in non-Euclidean treatments of physical space.

The ordinary pre-mathematical concept of straight line does not envisage a straight line as existing in isolation, but within a context of other lines, including straight lines, from some of which it diverges, towards some of which it converges, to some of which it is skew, and to some of which it is parallel; and it is only in the degree that lines are parallel, by eye or in imagination, they can be compared as to straightness, and such comparison is envisaged to be possible, even in the very concept of straight line. Accordingly, the notion that no parallel lines exist, so that for instance no two always-equidistant lines could both be straight, a notion involved in the hyperbolic geometry relied on in General Relativity, involves a setting aside of the pre-mathematical concept of straight line.

It is a mistake to speak as if what happened in Relativity theory was that the pre-mathematical concept of "straight line" continued to have application, while the concept of "parallel straight lines" ceased to have application. Rather, what happened was that both these concepts were denied unrestricted and exact application (of course, both concepts retain some quite indispensable inexact or restricted application, the one we give them in ordinary life). And, the fact that it is just a mistake to suppose that the one concept remained in use, while the other was sacrificed, as if these pre-mathematical concepts were independent of each other, is made vividly apparent by the way in which popularizers of Relativity theory feel compelled to speak of "straight lines being curved."[24] What we have here is the phenomenon of closely related uses of the same word, and of modifications in its meaning and in the implications which it carries (the purpose of describing a "straight line" as "curved" in these popularizations is merely to indicate that certain of the normal implications of the use of the word "straight" have been abandoned). The mathematical definition of "straight," in terms of "shortest," does not express the meaning which the word "straight" has in its pre-mathematical use.[25] Kant and Hume both made this plain, when they remarked that this definition was not an identity but explained a quality in terms of a quantity. Rather, the function of the definition is not to express

24 The remarks of Paul Bernays seem apposite here: "To claim that metric geometry has an evidence restricted to the laws common to Euclidean and to Bolyai-Lobachevskian geometry, an exact metrical evidence which yet would not guarantee the existence of a perfect square, seems to me rather artificial." Paul Bernays, "On Platonism in Mathematics," 265 in *Philosophy of Mathematics*, ed. Benacerraf and Putnam, 258–71.

25 More accurately, I have in mind here the possibility of two lines in the same plane, one of them straight, and the other the locus of a point moving always at a fixed distance from the first line.

the meaning of the word "straight," but to state a criterion for the application of the word "straight." And, in non-Euclidean geometries, what persists is not the meaning of the word, but only this criterion of its application.

Accordingly, what we have here is a case in which the understanding, in making an a priori judgment from concepts, and, in particular, in making an a priori judgment from these ordinary pre-mathematical concepts, to the effect that the propositions of Euclidean geometry (taken in their standard physical interpretation) have a necessity which is from these concepts, has presupposed that these concepts have exact and unrestricted application, i.e., that they can be used affirmatively without qualification or reservation. And, what has happened since the time of Kant is that a highly complex blend of reasoning and experience has made it seem that this presupposition, of unrestricted and exact applicability, is actually false.

IV.1.4 And this is how it is, I believe, with all non-analytic a priori judgments, that is, all non-tautologous a priori judgments which bear upon particular subject-matters (i.e., which are not formally universal). All of them, whether they contain ideas or concepts derived from experience or not, depend upon or presuppose judgments based in experience as to the coherence or applicability of these concepts.

Moreover, it is important to note that this is even true where it is such concepts as material body, or rational animal, which are concerned. Consider the concept of rational animal, the concept, that is, of a person with a body who gets knowledge with the help of animal senses, clearly, a concept of central and strategic importance in any epistemology. Now, evidently, we do in fact have knowledge that this concept is a coherent concept, i.e., that the supposition of the existence of a rational animal involves no conceptual impossibility, because, after all, we know that such beings are actual, and what is actual must be free from any kind of impossibility. But what is important to realize is that this knowledge does not have any other source. It is not, for instance, because I am confident that the dualist account of man's nature leads to no conceptual impossibilities, or because I am confident that some materialist account of man's nature leads to no conceptual impossibilities, or because I have some other account which I can see to be free from these, that I know that a rational animal is a possible being—but only because I know him to be actual. Accordingly, the synthetic a priori truths which express what is intrinsic to a rational animal, will all presuppose the judgment drawn from experience of the actual, that a rational animal exists.

This judgment, drawn from experience of the actual, that some rational animal has actual existence, is not, of course, in any ordinary sense, "empirical knowledge" meaning, not just "knowledge drawn from experience," but "knowledge drawn from experience, of a sort which it is accidental that a man should have."

IV.1.5 Evidently enough, there is hierarchy amongst synthetic a priori truths. The concepts which give rise to them fall into mutually interdependent groups, each group generating a different set of conceptual or "essential" or a priori truths. And between these groups of concepts, or sets of truths, there seem to be three different types of hierarchy. First, logical hierarchy: thus, color-concepts presuppose spatial concepts, since each visible is (either intentionally or actually) situated two-dimensionally within a three-dimensional field; and perhaps the group of concepts including matter and space, and the group of concepts including person, each presuppose a more fundamental group including substance and cause. Secondly, epistemological hierarchy: in effect, on the Cartesian view, every group of concepts will epistemologically presuppose the group of concepts which includes immaterial substance and *cogito*; while for Kant, Professor Strawson and Aquinas, it will, in effect, be a group of concepts which includes rational animal which is privileged in this way. Thirdly, causal or explanatory hierarchy amongst the facts stated by the a priori truths: e.g., to the theist, general facts about persons must appear to have some sort of explanatory priority over general facts about bodily things, inasmuch as the concept of person in some way applies to God as well as to human beings.

But there is no need to introduce new concepts of the "a priori" to mark any of these gradations. And to attempt to mark any of them by means of the notion of "being known independently of experience" is merely to sow confusion.

IV.2. AMBIGUITIES IN THE NOTION OF EMPIRICAL JUDGMENT

What we need to realize is that what philosophers are in fact in practice usually concerned with when they talk about the a priori, and contrast the a priori with empirical judgments, normally has little or nothing at all to do with being "completely independent of all judgments of experience of the actual."

Thus, for instance, when philosophers contrast a priori statements with others, what they very often have in view is the contrast between, on the one hand, various ordinary statements of particular fact, and, on the other hand, principles which are regarded as belonging to the structure of thought, or conceptual scheme, or categorial framework, or form of life, which these ordinary statements are thought to presuppose. And both the phenomenological description of fear, and the geometrical propositions which I considered, were examples of a priori statements in this sense.

But what I have said should make two things plain. Firstly, although this distinction is of the utmost importance and usefulness, it would be better to find some other name for these categorial statements or presuppositions, other than the term "a priori." This is because the term "a priori" seems to imply both necessity and truth, and these categorial statements may in some cases be actually false, or incoherent, or (as some philosophers like to say) meaningless, and therefore not true, and certainly not necessary. The confusion among some English writers which has allowed them to classify some such statements as necessary, even while questioning their truth or acceptability, appears to me highly vicious.

Secondly, although these categorial or structural statements are indeed presupposed in judgments of experience, it does not at all follow from this that they are known independently of all judgements of experience. Certainly, the possibility of an experience of a certain type, and the conditions of that possibility, are prior in the order of reality to the actuality of such experience. But this does not make them prior in the order of knowledge. Kant appears to take the possibility of experience of the human sort, and that is for him the possibility of an objective knowledge for beings with sensible, but not intellectual intuition, as prior in knowledge to all actual experience. But this seems to me just a mistake. To be logically presupposed does not at all imply to be independently known. Nor is it at all plausible that we know of the real possibility of experience of this human sort, or of objective empirical knowledge without intellectual intuition, except by means and in the act of knowing it to be actual.

The origin of this mistake appears to me to lie in two confusions. One is the confusion which I have already mentioned, between (a) categorial or structural statements presupposed in judgments of experience, and (b) so-called a priori statements known independently of all judgments of experience. The second is no less important. It is the confusion between knowledge which is entirely independent of all judgements of experience, and knowledge which depends only upon that knowledge from experience, which man could not fail to have without failing to function as man, or which it is part of human nature that man should have. And, when one examines what philosophers say, one finds that it is very often this latter which they are really concerned with when they talk about a priori knowledge. That is, when they insist that this or that knowledge is a priori or necessary or nonempirical, very often what they really mean is that it does not depend upon experience, or knowledge from experience, of the sort which it is merely contingent or accidental that men should have, and which they could conceivably not have had. For instance, there are some categorial frameworks, or structures of thought, of whose actual applicability and therefore coherence, it is impossible for man functioning as man to not know—and what Kant calls "pure" a priori knowledge would all be of this sort, not merely a presupposition within some categorial or conceptual framework or other, but a presupposition within some framework knowledge of whose validity or applicability was indispensable to any functioning of man as a being capable of knowledge by experience. And there are other structures of thought, e.g., that relating to fear, of which we can say that, although they are not indispensable to any functioning of man whatsoever, nonetheless they are still natural to man, in the sense that experience shows that men are capable of having experiences to which these structures of thought cannot be refused application.

Philosophy is, I believe, very much concerned with the a priori or nonempirical, if by this is meant the categorial or structural statements presupposed in ordinary statements of particular experience. It is also, I believe, very much concerned with the a priori or nonempirical, if by this is meant that knowledge which proceeds from the understanding, and which is independent of all that empirical knowledge which it is merely accidental to human nature that man should possess. Indeed, it is perhaps the a priori or nonempirical in this latter sense which constitutes the province of philosophy.

But it is, I believe, very little concerned with the almost useless notion of the a priori or nonempirical as being that knowledge which is entirely independent of any judgements of experience whatsoever.

IV.3. (A) THE USELESSNESS OF "THE IMAGINABILITY OF ALTERNATIVES" AS A CRITERION OF WHETHER OR NOT A PROPOSITION IS TRUE A PRIORI, (B) THE DIFFICULTIES PRESENTED BY PROPOSITIONS TO WHOSE TRUTH BOTH THEORETICAL AND OBSERVATIONAL CONSIDERATIONS ARE SEPARATELY RELEVANT.

[Editor's Note: We did not find any text that completed this section in David's papers.]

CHAPTER 4

THE SHAPE OF NATURAL THEOLOGY WITHOUT THE PRINCIPLE OF SUFFICIENT REASON IN ST. THOMAS AQUINAS[1]

THE QUESTIONS POSED BY ÉTIENNE GILSON

Reginald Garrigou-Lagrange, known for his large influence on how St. Thomas was taught in the period 1915–1950, seems to have regarded St. Thomas's Five Ways as having each taken some empirical statement such as that we experience that things move, together with what he saw as two general self-evident principles. These two principles were the law of noncontradiction and the principle of sufficient reason (sometimes referred to as the law of causality).

Étienne Gilson regarded this approach to the interpretation of St. Thomas as fundamentally misguided in its reliance upon the principle of sufficient reason or so-called law of causality.

1 The title of the essay is Braine's. The earliest record of the paper we have is 2008, and he continued revisions at least until 2012. It appears that Braine was preparing it for publication, but we can't find evidence that it has been published or that it was ever presented.

He came to regard this view as having been injected into modern Thomism by the mid-19th century neo-Thomist, Sanseverino, whose approach he criticized in "*Les Principes et les Causes*" in *Revue Thomiste* 1952.

In Gilson's view, in his natural theology St. Thomas never *assumed* any general principle of causality or any comparable view such as that being as such is intelligible. Even if these principles might turn out to be deducible after having proved God's existence, they could not be assumed beforehand.

Instead, he thought that what St. Thomas was concerned with was causal action, and the fact that contingent things needed a causal agent to give them existence, even to maintain them in existence. He expressed this in terms of the need of such a causal agent as a condition of existence and spoke of a causal agent having the effect as "causation," contrasting this causation with "causality" such as is referred to when those who discuss Hume and Kant speak of a general principle of causality.

St. Thomas would indeed admit that in a certain sense there is a sufficient reason for every contingent fact, but only as a consequence of accepting God's existence, not as something one could assume in proving his existence. And the sense in which there is a sufficient reason for every contingent fact was not that there is a sufficient reason in the sense of something which might provide a ground for knowledge, but that there is a sufficient reason in the sense of a motive for God as governor of the world to bring it about or permit it to occur. For in St. Thomas's understanding, God does nothing except for some reason which makes it good—and permits no evil except in view of the good he will be able to bring out of it. (See the reply to the first objection in *Summa Theologiae,* I, q. 2, art. 3, and *Summa Theologiae,* I, q. 116, art. 1, art. 3, and art. 4, ad 2.)

In Gilson's attitude, he was I believe absolutely right. However, in the 1950s he came to think that this even meant regarding St. Thomas's doctrine of the real distinction of *essentia* and *esse*, essence and the act or actuality of being (*actus essendi*), in creatures, as theologically optional. He was thus led into the paradoxical position of supposing that, on the one hand, this was the primary insight which St. Thomas had to contribute to natural theology, and, on the other hand, it was not something integral to Christian understanding, and not to be treated as such in Catholic theology or in a Christian philosophy. In this way, in late age, he felt obliged to allow a theological pluralism, in which St. Thomas's approach and that of Duns Scotus were both to be considered as options. In drawing this further conclusion, he was I believe profoundly mistaken, sacrificing one of St. Thomas's main insights because of the misuse made of the idea of the real distinction of *essentia* and *esse* in creatures by those to whose *a priori* reliance upon principles of causality he opposed.

These are the matters upon which I wish to shed light in this paper, firstly in Sections 1 and 2 examining the way we should speak of being or existence and essence, looking at the problems first in their logical and then in their metaphysical aspects, secondly in Section 3 examining attempts at a proof of the existence of God through reliance on the principle of sufficient reason in some form, and thirdly in Sections 4 to 6 examining how St. Thomas himself sought a proof of the existence of God as first efficient cause. All the 'Five Ways' of proving God's existence which he proposes are of this kind, e.g., the First Way turns out, as I shall show, to be an argument to God as the first efficient cause of each individual case of a thing's being moved or altered, a kind of event of whose occurrence is known by the senses.

SECTION 1: EXISTENCE OR BEING (*ESSE*) AND ESSENCE

(a) THE LOGICAL ASPECTS OF STATEMENTS ASCRIBING BEING OR EXISTENCE: MODERN AND MEDIEVAL PERSPECTIVES

We can distinguish two general types of position in the history of philosophy in thinking about the logic of statements ascribing being or existence.

These types of position arise out of different responses to the following problem. On the face of it, if I say of something, say A, that A exists, I am predicating "exists" of A, or in other ways of speaking predicating existence of A or attributing existence to A. However, if it happens that A does not exist, it would appear that there is nothing that I can be attributing existence to, and that I am predicating existence of nothing.

The first and more natural response is to suggest that we have to distinguish between two types of significant predicate. One is of the kind which satisfies the criteria for application within a system of modern classical logic (or of any older logical system equivalent to some fragment of modern logic), i.e., what we might call a "logical predicate" or "attributive predicate" inasmuch as, in a generalized sense of the words, one-place predicates can be considered to attribute "properties" and many-place predicates to attribute "relations." And the other is of a kind which we could naturally describe as a "non-attributive predicate."

Traditional logic distinguished three kinds of statement, firstly singular statements of the kind "Socrates is mortal," and secondly, two kinds of general statement, the one universal, typified by "Every human being is mortal," and the other particular (because implying that something applied at least to part of the general class being spoken of), typified by "Some human beings are mortal," the latter also being called "existential" because it can be paraphrased as "There are human beings who are mortal."

And modern systems of symbolic logic recognize the same three-fold distinction and have devised ways of symbolizing each in different ways. Within this setting, "... is mortal" is a one place attributive predicate, and in all the statements the existence of human beings, as the domain, subject-matter or class about which generalization is being made, is presupposed. If it is suggested that we re-express "Every human being is mortal" as if it meant "Everything, if it is a human being, is mortal," or more accurately as if it meant "Everything is such that it is not the case both that it is a human and that it is not mortal," we presuppose the existence of "things" (a rather problematic presupposition in as much as the discovery of the logical paradoxes has shown that it produces contradictions as well as being rather stupid to try to generalize about everything at once, or to take "everything" as the subject-matter of some science or systematic study). In the meantime, the singular statement "Socrates is mortal" involves the additional presupposition that Socrates exists, and this is described as a presupposition because it is a condition of the truth both of the affirmation "Socrates is mortal" and of its negation "Socrates is not mortal," and to deny the proposition "Socrates is mortal" is taken to be the same or equivalent to asserting its negation "Socrates is not mortal."

According to this approach, both traditional and modern logic compel us to accept that there is a distinction between logical or attributive predicates and non-attributive predicates. Any statement of the existence of a general classes taken as one's subject-matter for enquiry, any generalization and any statement of the existence of a particular individual within such a class, are then examples of the significant predication of a non-attributive predicate.

The second response to the original problem is to say that in the existential statement 'X exists' we are indeed predicating something but not about X, but about something else of a seemingly more abstract kind, e.g., according to Duns Scotus, we are attributing existence to something called an essence, or, according to Frege, we are making a statement about a concept. Thus, according to Frege, when we make statements about things we are saying the things fall under certain first-level concepts, e.g., the concept horse, but if we say that horses exist we are, in his view, making a statement about this first level concept, applying existence as a second level concept, in effect to say that the concept horse has at least one instantiation or application. This view allowed him to say that to state that horses do not exist is to say that there are no horses, no objects to which the concept horse applies, and is equivalent to ascribing the number zero to the set of all horses. According to the terminology suggested in these rival accounts of existence, originating in the logical theories of Frege or, much earlier, Duns Scotus following Avicenna, existence is a genuinely attributive predicate, but used to ascribe being or existence, not to singular things or individuals, but either to concepts (Frege) or to essences (Duns Scotus says that being is an "accident" of an essence).

Many people think that they are taking up the Fregean view when they say that there is no existence other than that expressed by the existential quantifier. They speak as if the only use of the verb "to exist" with which they had to deal was the one exemplified in such statements as "Tame tigers exist." I transmute "Tame tigers exist" into "There exist tigers which are tame" or "Some tigers are tame," and if pressed, transmute this into "There are things which are such that they were tigers and they are tame"—that is, in symbolic terms, I say: $(\exists x)$ ((x is a tiger) and (x is tame)). The view is that, by using the existential quantifier, or asserting existence, I here ascribe a second-level attribute to the concept "tame tiger."

However, in the first transmutation, I presuppose the existence of tigers, and in the second I presuppose the existence of "things."

However, logicians are well aware that if you try to generalize about every "thing" of any kind at the same time, and apply the laws of classical logic you will get one of the logical paradoxes. Therefore, this theory about "there being no existence other than that expressed by the existential quantifier" cannot be right, since in any use of quantifiers in either classical or intuitionistic logic, it is presupposed that one is talking about a non-empty domain, that is every quantifier has to range over a domain of things which is not empty, and this kind of presupposition cannot be paraphrased in terms of the existential quantifier. This fits with the Aristotelian and medieval precept that any science presupposes the existence of its subject matter. [Beyond this, in classical logic, considering only "attributive predicates," the same presumption is involved when ~(∀x)(Fx) is treated as equivalent to (∃x)(~Fx),[2] that is, intuitively "Not everything is F" is equivalent to "There exists something which is not F," i.e., "Something is not F."]

Moreover, we can make no sense of either of the statements "Some tiger is tame" and "Something is such that it is a tiger and it is tame,"[3] unless these imply in the first case, given that a is a tiger, that a is tame, and in the second case, given that a is a thing, that a is a tiger and that a is tame. Likewise, we can make no sense of the statements "Every tiger is tame" and "Everything is such that it is not the case both that it is a tiger and that it is not tame" (commonly over simplified as "Everything is such that, if it were a tiger, it would be tame'), unless we can infer, respectively, of any arbitrarily chosen tiger, x, that x is tame, and, of any arbitrarily chosen thing, x, that it is not the case both that x is a tiger and that x is not tame.[4]

2 The exceptions in intuitionistic logic arise when the way of establishing ~(∀x)(Fx) provide no means of identifying anything which would make (∃x)(~Fx) true, cases conspicuous when the ranges of significance of predicates and the ranges of quantifiers extend over infinite sets.

3 That is, in the symbolism of modern logic, respectively ($\exists_{\text{tigers}}$x) (x is tame)) and (∃x) ((x is a tiger) and (x is tame)).

4 That is, in symbolic terms, unless we can infer from ($\forall_{\text{tigers}}$x) (x is tame) to (x is tame) and, from (∀x) (~ ((x is a tiger) and ~ (x is tame))) to (~ ((x is a tiger) and ~ (x is tame))), since in the symbolism of predicate logic, given a predicate F(...), roughly speaking, F(...) means that, given anything in the domain of the relevant quantifier in the context concerned, the predicate F(...) will apply to it, we have not understood the symbolism.

In sum, we can make no sense of universal statements such as "Every tiger is tame," or $(\forall x)(Tx)$ where the domain of the quantifier is tigers, unless they imply that any arbitrarily chosen tiger x is tame, and we can make no sense of particular statements such as "Some tiger is tame" or $(\exists x)(Tx)$ where the domain of the quantifier is tigers, unless they are implied by any singular statement "a is tame" where "a" is the name of a particular tiger.

We have here discovered a second way in which the view that there is no existence other than that expressed by the existential quantifier cannot be right. For we have discovered a second type of presupposition which cannot be stated in the symbolism of the quantifiers or by using any "attributive predicate," namely the presupposition of the existence of particular individual things within the area over which generalization is made, i.e., of the non-emptiness of the range of the quantifier in use.

Therefore, Quine had a double reason for saying that to be (i.e., for him, to exist) was to be the value of a bound variable, that is that, for the purposes of the application of modern logic expressed in the symbolism of the quantifiers, any name is presupposed to denote something which exists, and it has to exist within the domain of the quantifier concerned, no quantifier being presumed to range over just everything. He did not espouse the view that there is no existence other than that expressed by the existential quantifier.

(b) TWO SENSES OF THE WORD *ESSE* ACCORDING TO ST. THOMAS

In *Summa Theologiae* I, q. 3, art. 4, ad 2,[5] St. Thomas tells us that the word *esse* (*esse* being the infinitive of the verb "be") may signify two different types of thing. Firstly, the *esse* of X may signify X's *actus essendi* or act of being. Secondly, the *esse* of X may "signify the composition of the proposition which the mind discovers, conjoining a predicate to the subject." He goes on to say that in the first sense God's *esse* (*actus essendi*) is as unknown to us as his essence, whereas we know that this proposition, when we say, "God is" is true, since we know this from his effects. From this and other texts, it seems that, in the second meaning, *esse* or being consists in being the subject of true

5 Cf. *Summa Theologiae* I, q. 48, art. 2, ad 2.

propositions and corresponds to Quine's conception that to be is to be the value of a bound variable.

In this second meaning, for instance, blindness may be taken to have *esse* in two ways. What is most important for Aquinas is the way blindness has *esse* inasmuch as the proposition "Blindness exists" is true in the sense that there are animals which are blind, that is there are things of a kind to whose nature it belongs that they should be sighted but which cannot see, so that blindness is a privation they suffer. This is important because he does not wish to say that evils such as blindness are fictitious or as have merely abstract existence, since they have being in the sense that they are truly attributed to substances, but thinks that, although they are privations not mere negations, it is wrong to regard them as having positive existence. Blindness consists in the absence of something just as a hole in an object with a surface consists in the absence of something in the place where the hole is.

Of course, blindness also has *esse* in another way inasmuch as the proposition "Blindness is a privation" is true: taken in this second way, blindness is being spoken of as a mental object or "object of mind," and in this way inasmuch as the propositions "Four is an even number" and "Four is a perfect square" are true, the number four and other positive whole integers exist; in this second way, being is equivalent to being the value of a bound variable but a variable ranging over this or that kind of mental subject of predication. The numbers are not amongst the things which he is thinking about when he recognizes that objects of intellect (intelligible or thinkable) and objects of desire are not as such actual or existent.[6] In Descartes's inherited terminology such objects have only "objective reality," not subjects of predication with "formal reality," to which we might today apply an extensional logic.

However, it remains *esse* in its first meaning, as *actus essendi*, which is of chief interest to us in this paper. Both Duns Scotus and Suárez rejected the idea that *esse* had any such separate meaning, insisting that there was no other *esse* than the *esse commune* predicated of everything which exists.

6 *Commentary on Metaphysics IX* [Theta], *Lectio* 3, 1805 – 1806, in respect of what he lists as 758 in the translation of Aristotle he is using.

(c) THE SIGNIFICANCE OF ST. THOMAS'S DISTINCTION BETWEEN *ESSE* (AS *ACTUS ESSENDI*) AND *ESSENTIA* WITHIN METAPHYSICS

When Aristotle considers what the word "being" (*ousia*) was most appropriately applied to, he struggled as to whether it was matter that was fundamental in reality, the natures or essences of things (their formal causes) or the things and types of thing which exercised active power. In these considerations, he was confused by the appearance that the things and types of thing which exercised active power which we experience all seem to be composed of a nature together with matter. He ended up in a situation of oscillation in which sometimes by beings (*ousiai*) he meant natures or essences and sometimes he meant the things and types of thing which exercised active power. Augustine, when he speaks of God's *essentia*, is embroiled in the corresponding ambiguity with the corresponding Latin noun.

This left room for considering essences as if they had a certain reality in their own right in such a way that existence was something that might or might not be added to them. This way of thinking is often thought of as Platonic, because it reminds one of the picture of God as a *demi-ourgos* or Demiurge looking at a world of possible things and choosing which of them to give existence to and which not to give existence to. It is a way of thinking which becomes explicit in Avicenna, and which was perpetuated, first through Duns Scotus and his disciples, and then through Molina and Suárez, to be inherited by Leibniz, Voltaire, Hume and Kant along with many modern Anglo-Saxon thinkers. This approach appeared to guarantee the contingency of the world either in the sense of its dependence upon God, or in the sense of its existence being an arbitrary fact, but left the possibility that the existence of the world is necessary, until it had been established that the creator created freely.

It may be noted that in developing his approach in which existence or actuality is thought of as an accident or attributive predicate of essences, *possibilia*, or possible worlds, Duns Scotus laid the philosophical basis for the later development of characteristically modern forms of modal logic and metatheoretical thinking.[7] However,

7 See Simo Knuuttila, "Being Qua Being in Thomas Aquinas and John Duns Scotus," *The Logic of Being: Historical Studies*, ed. Simo Knuuttila and

in the same act he abandoned Russell's robust sense of reality, St. Thomas's sharing his logic with Frege, both rejecting the idea of existence or actuality as an attributive predicate, and St. Thomas insisting that primary reality and subjecthood belongs to concrete things, not to essences or possibles. The firmness and clarity of the concrete realism of St. Thomas is even more unmistakable than that of Russell.

In contrast to Duns Scotus, St. Thomas's approach creates a revolutionary clarity by making it unmistakable that the primary subjects of *esse*, in the sense of *actus essendi*, are the things which exercise active power.

For he holds that it is solely to substances, *substantiae*, as what Aristotle describes in the *Categories* as primarily and chiefly what are called *ousiai*, defined as the logical subjects which are neither predicated of nor present in a subject, that we should primarily ascribe *esse*, choosing to use the word *esse* instead of the word *essentia* so that it is our use of the word *esse* which guides our use of the words *ens* and *essentia*, not vice versa.[8] In giving this conceptual primacy to *esse* rather than *essentia*, St. Thomas escapes the accusations of Platonism so often levied against the Church Fathers, including Augustine, especially when they spoke of God's eternity, as if they had confused the atemporality whereby God possesses and enjoys his whole life all in one act without temporal division with the kind of timelessness possessed by the natural numbers. He is also in a better position to explain the unity of the Trinity according to Christian belief, explaining that the three Persons of the one God each exist by the

---

Jaakko Hintikka (Dordrecht: Reidel, 1986), 201–22, especially 209–11. Also, pp. 211–13 consider some fourteenth century developments and the importance of Suárez, as following this approach, although not the notoriety given to it by Molina, as well as how Leibniz made some compromises bringing him less distant from St. Thomas. See also *Reforging the Great Chain of Being*, ed. Simo Knuuttila (Dordrecht: Reidel, 1981), 217–34, which in earlier articles had shown the unimportance of unrealized essences for St. Thomas (pp. 163–207, 208–17).

8 In *De Ente et Essentia*, St. Thomas is clear that it is our use of the words *ens* and *esse* which determines our use of the word *essentia*, and in all later works it is clear that he considers that it is our use of the word *esse* which determines our application of the noun *ens*.

same *actus essendi*, so that there is only one *esse*, one *actus essendi*, in God, and therefore only one *ens* or being—whereas, if we say that the three Persons are one because they share the same essence or nature, it no more explains God's unity than to say that Plato, Socrates and Phaedo are one because they share the same essence or nature. If we have the unity of God's *esse* as already established, we may then perhaps be in a position to explain the real unity of God's essence.

Moreover, in speaking of these *substantiae*, spoken of in some contexts as *subsistentiae* in order to circumvent some of the ambiguities of the Latin word *substantia*, as subjects of *esse*, he is considering them as alone exercising an *actus essendi* or act of being in an unqualified sense. Amongst the things we experience, it is these subjects which are pivots of the whole system of the categories, the subjects of action and passion, and thereby also the subjects of the states, qualities, shapes and sizes we ascribe to concrete things. Whenever we assent to a true affirmative statement about some particular thing which exercises active power, we presuppose that it has an *esse*, *actus essendi* or act of being in an unqualified sense, and such an act of being is an actuality or *actus* (St. Thomas's rendering of Aristotle's word *energeia*). The *esse* which is presupposed to any affirmative statement about an existing substance is a positive actuality.

Other things apart from substances which have some kind of positive existence, such as the knowledge ascribed to creatures, have "*esse*" only in the derived sense that in virtue of possessing them (in the case of states) or performing them (in the case of actions) the *substantia* which possesses or performs them has super-added accidental *esse*—so wisdom has *esse* only in the sense that persons who are wise have such super-added accidental *esse* in virtue of being wise—the or an *actus essendi* of the wisdom is primarily an actualization of the potentiality of a person to be wise in his actually being wise, and only secondarily spoken of as the or an *actus essendi* of the wisdom itself.

Likewise, it is only *substantiae* which have *essentia* in an unqualified sense, while these other things with a positive existence have it only in a derived sense, e.g., as qualities, actions, passions or some other positive features of substances. By contrast, an attribute of substances such as blindness has no *essentia* as such, and, when asked "what is it?," we do not give a definition of an essence but only the meaning of the term used for it, explaining that to be blind is to lack sightedness in the case of a thing to whose nature it belongs to be sighted.[9]

In this primary use of the word *essentia* of substances, we have to make a distinction.

Firstly, we can mean the *essentia* of the natural kind to which the individual substance under consideration belongs, e.g., "man" or "animal," which is what is encapsulated in a definition, where, according to Aristotle, by "definition" we mean the definition of the essence, not just an explanation of the meaning of the name. How this distinction works can perhaps be most easily understood if I say that to say that an atom of the element copper is one which has 29 protons in its nucleus, this being fundamental to the explanation of its chemical and some physical properties, while the combination of a specification of atomic number and atomic weight helps explain radioactive-relevant properties. By contrast, today one might say that copper was the reddish brown metal most commonly used in electric wiring, in a first attempt to specify to an ordinary person what the word was used to talk about, i.e., the meaning of the name. Thus in the so-called "real" definition, one is trying to explain the nature shared by substances of a certain kind, their shared or 'universal' nature being what is considered to explain their shared fundamental properties.

However, secondly, we can consider the "essence" or "nature" of the individual substances as individuals, what is often called their "particularized essence," since it is this which plays a causal role in the behavior of the individual concerned, rather than anything abstract or universal. In St. Thomas's understanding, in the case of created things, each such particularized essence exists in two ways. In the first way, it exists in full actuality in the individual created thing concerned itself, the created thing, its *esse*, and its particularized *essentia* being co-constituted in God's act of giving being to the created thing, "the thing's *esse* being constituted according to the principles of its *essentia*" (*Commentary on the Metaphysics*, Gamma, 2, 1003b 22–33,

9 It is not relevant to the present discussion to discuss "intentional *esse*" in its relevance to light and to the means of knowledge or the existence of 'mental objects' such as the numbers and other objects which are treated as having essences which we define in mathematics.

in section 558 of *Lectio* 2). In the second way, the thing's particularized *essentia* exists in God's practical intellect in the manner in which what a person intends or chooses to make exists in his mind before it exists in reality. In order to explain these notions, one need not at this stage make any resort to the notions of potentiality and actuality.

Once one follows St. Thomas in acknowledging substances as the primary subjects of *esse* or existence, then realizing that in creatures in whose life there is an ordered succession of acts, as theologians have held to be true of angels as well as of human beings, and granting that some of the acts of angels are to be ascribed to particular times, for instance the particular visitations of Gabriel to deliver messages from God, St. Thomas's view leaves no room for the ideas expressed in a remarkable passage in Suárez's *Metaphysical Disputation* 21, section 2, 6. There Suárez says:

> God could reproduce the [same] angel by numerically the same action by which he had [initially] created him. For, as I have explained more fully elsewhere [*Metaphysical Disputation* 5, section 9, 5–6], it is no more difficult for him to bring about numerically the same action again than it is for him to bring about numerically the same effect again. However, as I noted above [*Metaphysical Disputation* 20, section 4, 13], he could also, if he so willed, use a different action to reproduce numerically the same effect.[10]

Suárez's thinking that such a reproduction of the same angel at different stages in the history of angels is possible is the result of his thinking of *esse* as primarily attributed to individualized essences, considered as possible realities, rather than to the created reality or substance itself. That an angel's *essentia* should be annihilated at one point in its life and brought out of annihilation at another, some period of what he refers to as "our time" having intervened, is, of course, in his view possible only by a miracle, but nonetheless in no way absolutely impossible. One can see in this that a second Duns Scotus, perhaps less cautious than the real Duns Scotus we know, was indeed alive in Suárez, with this possibility of a determinate angelic *essentia*, determinate even in

10 Francisco Suárez, *On Creation, Conservation, and Concurrence: Metaphysical Disputations 20–22*, trans. A. J. Freddoso (South Bend, IN: St. Augustine's Press, 2002), 124–25, cf. 74.

its individuality or *haeccitas*, jumping out of existence and back into it again at a later time or later phase of its life.

Before going further, one should register the way in which, in discussing the persons of the Trinity, St. Thomas distinguishes between what it is proper to say of a thing using concrete modes of speech and what it is proper to say of a thing using abstract modes of speech. Thus, he considers that it is perfectly proper to say that the Father begets the Son, and that here God begets God, but not proper to say that here deity begets deity which would involve that the essence of God begets the essence of God.[11] And, in general, acts are predicated of things using the concrete mode of speech. In sum, although God and his essence are not two distinct things, realities or actualities, nonetheless concrete terms for God and for the divine Persons are not freely intersubstitutable *salva veritate* with abstract ones. The same will apply, in St. Thomas's understanding, with angels: that is, even though there is in his view no real distinction between an angel and its essence, it is nonetheless the angel that acts, not its essence, so that, e.g., it is Gabriel that speaks to the virgin Mary, not the essence of Gabriel.

I spoke earlier of the created thing, its *esse*, and its particularized *essentia* being co-constituted in God's act of giving being to the created thing. However, there are vital distinctions to be made. Socrates's *esse*, being or existence is not an attribute, property or a relation attributed to Socrates, but something presupposed whenever we do predicate properties or relations of Socrates. By contrast, Socrates's *essentia* or essence is an attribute or property which we attribute to Socrates in the attributive predication "Socrates is a human being" and more generally when we attribute to him anything "essential" to him. This has to be put alongside what St. Thomas regards as the necessary "accidents" of Socrates in the technical logical sense in which the accidental is opposed to the essential, not to the necessary, such as the powers which belong to Socrates necessarily or by nature as a human being, such as the power to reason, judge and know, and the various sensitive powers, each attributed to Socrates in some attributive predication. Socrates's essence and powers are to be contrasted with the virtues and vices and other things of which St. Thomas would speak as habits (relatively longterm properties of Socrates) and along with these what he is at present doing or undergoing (among other non-longterm

11 *Summa Theologiae* I, q. 39, art. 5.

properties and relations of Socrates), all of which fall among Socrates's non-necessary accidents, but all are to be grouped together as each to be attributed to Socrates in an attributive predication, unlike Socrates himself and his existence or *esse*.

In the meantime, in a different way, anything else belonging to Socrates by his nature belongs to his composition—conspicuously his human soul and body, and within this body its various parts, (here there is a distinction to be made between his soul without which there would be no Socrates, and, for instance, his arm which while natural to him to have he may lose, e.g., in battle or in hospital, and even his whole body which he loses in death). Such is the structure envisaged by St. Thomas when he speaks of Socrates as a composite being.

(d) PLATONIC WAYS OF SPEAKING IN ST. THOMAS WHICH ARE MISLEADING AS TO HIS REAL MEANING

We are now in a position to consider what St. Thomas means when, in the *Summa Theologiae* I, q. 3, art. 4, he gives the following as a third reason for insisting that in God *esse* and *essentia* should be identical:

> Thirdly, because, just as that which has fire, but is not itself fire, is on fire by participation; so that which has *esse* but is not *esse*, is a *ens* by participation. But God is His own essence, as shown above (q. 3, art. 3) if, therefore, He is not His own existence He will be an *ens per participationem*, not *per essentiam*. He will not therefore be the first being—which is absurd. Therefore God is His own existence, and not merely His own essence.[12]

To understand this passage, the first thing one needs to understand is how he conceives the distinction between being something by participation and being something *per essentiam*.

When a creature is said to be wise or human, St. Thomas feels quite free to use Platonic metaphors and to express this by saying that it shares or participates in wisdom, humanity or human nature, and he feels free to adopt this way of speaking, not only with attributes such as wisdom and humanity, but also with a predicate such as *esse* which is not an attribute in the sense I explained earlier. Accordingly, creatures

12 *ST* I.3.4 mod. trans. English Dominican Fathers.

are said to participate in being (*esse*), and God is said to cause this being, communicating being to creatures, and this is expressed even in terms of pouring *esse* into creatures (*Summa Contra Gentiles*, I, 30), but not at all with the idea of natures as preexisting containers limiting how much *esse* can be poured into them. When he uses the metaphor of a container, saying "*Esse* stands in relation to other things, not as a container to what it contains, but as what is contained to a container" (*Summa Theologiae* I, 4, 1, reply to obj. 3), it is only to convey that "in speaking of the *esse* of a human being, or a horse, or whatever, *esse* itself is considered as something formal and contained, not as that which is capable of being," that is to make it clear that one is speaking of *esse* as a predicate, not as the subject of predication. We can see this in his sensitivity to the distinction between *esse* and *ens*.

In regard to this, *Lectio* II of his Commentary on Boethius's *De Hebdomadibus* is particularly instructive.[13] There he tells us that "just as we cannot say that *currere* itself runs, so we cannot say that *esse* itself is" while "just as we can say of that which runs or of the running thing (*currente*) that it runs inasmuch as it is the subject of running and itself participates in it, so we can say that a particular being (*ens* or *id quod est*) participates in being (*esse* or *actus essendi*)." He says further that *esse* itself "is participated in by other things, but does not itself participate in anything else," and in the next sentence makes it clear that when we say that an *ens* participates in *esse*, the *ens* is spoken of concretely while *esse*, spoken of as something participated in, is spoken of abstractly. The *esse* thus spoken of has no real existence as a Platonic form, but, as he explains in his reply to the second objection in *Summa Theologiae* I, q. 3, art. 4, has only the two functions, firstly of expressing the *actus essendi* of substances (either the *actus essendi* they have in virtue of their nature as substances, or the accidental *esse* they have in virtue of their positive properties, the *esse* which allows *esse* to be predicated of these positive properties in a secondary sense), and secondly of expressing eligibility to be a subject of predication, that is the *esse* which he describes in terms of merely "signifying the composition of a proposition [i.e., of a subject with a predicate]."

13 Anthony Kenny, *Aquinas on Being* (Oxford: Oxford University Press, 2005), 78–80, and John Wippel, "Metaphysics," in *Cambridge Companion to Aquinas*, ed. N. Kretzmann and E. Stump (Cambridge: Cambridge University Press, 1993), 85–127, particularly 94.

There is a serious question as to whether there is anything more to St. Thomas's sometimes seemingly Platonic ways of speaking than mere metaphor, as in the case I have just mentioned, in other places so as to make his position and argument depend upon such metaphors in these other places. The main place where this might seem to happen is in his way of speaking of the perfections, saying that God is *esse* itself, life itself, and wisdom itself, is *esse*, life, and wisdom *per essentiam* whereas creatures have *esse*, life, and wisdom *per participationem*.

However, if we examine his third argument for the identity of God's *esse* and *essentia* in *Summa Theologiae* I, q. 3, art.4, we find that he is here thinking along Aristotelian lines, not Platonic ones. What has courage, but is not courage, is courageous by participation, i.e., has "is courageous" predicated of it, but is not courageous in virtue of its essence, but by accident (*per accidens*, or in Aristotle's terms *kata sumbebekos*), or as he sometimes says *per alterum* that is, through something else added to his essence (in Aristotle's terms *kath'heteron*),[14] stands in contrast with what has an attribute, not by accident, but *per essentiam*, or in Aristotle's terms *kath'auto*.

In parallel with this, St. Thomas thinks that, if God had *esse*, but was not *esse*, he would have to be an *ens* by participation, and not *per essentiam*, [but by accident or in virtue of something else added to his essence (*per alterum* or *kath'heteron*) through an exterior agent,] so that he would not be the first being. I put part of the argument in square brackets because it is a part of St. Thomas's argument which he does not feel it necessary to express.

One can see from all this, how completely St. Thomas has purged his Platonic ways of speaking of what is called Platonism, so that there is nothing left to be ascribed to Plotinus.[15]

I have already registered the importance of the way in which, in discussing the persons of the Trinity, St. Thomas distinguishes between what it is proper to say of a thing using concrete modes of speech and what it is proper to say of a thing using abstract modes of

14 The equivalence of having an attribute by participation and having it *per alterum* (*kath'heteron*) is evident from the parallel argument in only the *QD de Potentia*, q. 3, art. 5, written only slightly earlier, in the third argument there presented (cf. the third argument presented *sed contra*, and the reply to the fifth objection in *QD de Potentia*, q. 7, art. 2).

15 Cf. n. 33 below with reference to von Balthasar.

speech. Acts are always predicated of things using the concrete mode of speech. As a result, even where there is no real distinction between a thing and his essence, concrete terms for the thing and its essence are not freely intersubstitutable *salva veritate* with abstract ones. Thus, as I remarked earlier, although, in his view, there is no real distinction between an angel and its essence, it is the angel that acts not its essence, so that, e.g., it is Gabriel that speaks to the virgin Mary, not the essence of Gabriel. Accordingly, when St. Thomas implies[16] that "the relation of a created thing's *esse* to the essence in it [its essence which is 'in it' in the sense of being 'part' of what it is 'composed of"] is comparable to the relation of actuality to potentiality," the essence concerned here is in not something which acts, since it is the created thing, not its essence, which acts and has the power to act.[17] It is in this way that, when St. Thomas thinks of a created thing's *esse* as something distinct from its *essentia*, the *essentia* is being thought of as something non-active (by analogy, spoken of as a passive potentiality).

SECTION 2: THE CONCEPTION OF THE EXISTENCE OF THE UNIVERSE AS ABSOLUTELY CONTINGENT

(a) WHAT IS IT FOR A CREATURE TO RECEIVE EXISTENCE?: THE CONCEPTION OF THINGS AS NEEDING A CAUSE OF BEING, NOT JUST A CAUSE OF COMING TO BE

In St. Thomas's conception what God causes is the existing of things in their natures, and this causing of things to be is exemplified as much in upholding things in existence as in creating them from nothing, the preserving of things in existence being just a continuation of the same

16 I say that this is what he implies in respect of every created thing, including angels, because it is what he denies of God, as well as being what fits with the contrast he makes between the way the essence of a thing is in it and the way accidents are in it.

17 St. Thomas describes such powers as in the essence as in their subject only in that the essence underlies them as their basis or ground, not in the sense that they are predicated of them. [Editor's Note: In this quotation Braine appears to be loosely translating what Aquinas says in *ST* I.3.4: "*Oportet igitur quod ipsum esse comparetur ad essentiam quae est aliud ab ipso, sicut actus ad potentiam.*"]

action as creating them *ab initio*—in this preserving of things, time is concreated.

Let us first explain this conception, today so unfamiliar, leaving consideration of its justification until later. This way of understanding matters appears most vividly when Aquinas discusses God's upholding of things in existence (*Summa Theologiae* I, q.104, art.1). There he tells us:

> Nor can the being of a thing continue after the action of the agent has ceased, if the agent is the cause of the effect not only in respect of becoming but also in respect of being. This is why hot water retains heat after the cessation of the fire's action, whereas the air does not continue to be lit up even for a moment when the Sun ceases to act upon it, because water is a matter susceptive of the fire's heat in the same way as it exists in the fire ... whereas the air is not of such a nature as to receive light in the same way as it exists in the Sun, which is the principle of light.

St. Thomas has no particular interest in God as causing things to come to be as such. The causing of things to come to be is commonly something natural. Thus, it is the potter who causes a pot to come to be. But in this process, the potter does nothing to give existence to the clay, nor to secure its continuance in existence and in its usual properties while being molded in his hands, while in the kiln to dry, and on the shelf waiting to be sold later. Of course, he may act to protect it from ceasing to be by natural causes, but he does not and cannot do anything to prevent it simply disappearing into nothing through no natural cause. This is unsurprising, since there is no particular risk of its simply disappearing into nothing, not from natural causes, any more than there is any particular risk of a rabbit simply coming into existence in our midst out of nothing, without any natural causes, material and efficient.

From St. Thomas's standpoint, causing things to continue to be presents the same difficulties as causing things to come into existence from nothing.

If things came into existence from nothing, modern thinkers might imagine that this might just happen without a cause, according to Hume's principle that nothing imaginable is absolutely impossible or the earlier rationalist principle that nothing conceivable is absolutely impossible. The Humean principle constitutes the empiricist version of the rationalist one, and is much less plausible since so many demonstrably impossible things are imaginable (in science fiction, I cannot only imagine a human being getting bestride a machine and travelling backwards in time in the manner described in H. G. Wells's *Time Machine*, so as to be in two different bodily states at the times of his conception and birth, or producing a long and contorted proof that there is only a finite number of prime numbers).

However, the original ground of this rationalist principle, in so far as it concerns real possibility, derived from its being inferred from the omnipotence of God who supposedly had the real power to accomplish any task the achieving of which did not involve anything involving a conceptual impossibility.[18] Against this background, these principles are as useless in establishing an agnostic view as in proving the existence of God.

Alternatively, a modern thinker might just suppose that things came into existence from nothing without a cause, and equally continue in existence without this having a cause, and he might just suppose that the onus of proof lies on the side of those who said a cause is needed and wait for them to offer some reason for saying a cause is required.

However, not unnaturally St. Thomas is free from these modern doubts, and assumes that for something to come into existence from nothing requires a cause.

We can now see the rationale of St. Thomas's standpoint, whereby the problem of causing things to come into existence from nothing is no greater that the cause of causing things to continue in existence. If the world had a beginning, God's creation of things out of nothing was the initiation of this action of causing the world to exist, and the upholding of things in existence is the continuance of the same action. But if the world had no beginning, its continuance would still need the exercise of the same power as the creation of things out of

18 God remains unrestricted in the power to accomplish anything genuinely conceptually possible, even though with his perfect intellect he will be aware of the conceptual impossibility of many things of whose conceptual impossibility human or other lesser intellects are unaware.

nothing, i.e., things would still need God's action in upholding them in existence. If his imaginative comparison of God's upholding the world in existence with the Sun's lighting up the air is appropriate, there is no less a difficulty in things continuing in existence without a cause than in their coming into existence from nothing without a cause, if there is a difficulty in either.

Accordingly, when St. Thomas speaks of God as the universal cause of being (having in view the being of substances, primarily the *actus essendi* which they have as substances, and only secondarily of the kind of being possessed by their positive accidental attributes), he is speaking of God in a way rejected by both Duns Scotus and Suárez. For Duns Scotus, any causing of coming to be is a causing of being, so that, when a volcano causes an island to come into existence or a potter causes a pot to come into existence, these would be causes of being.

(b) THERE IS NO ROOM FOR INTERMEDIATES IN THE GIVING OF EXISTENCE

In St. Thomas's conception, God alone possesses existence in his own right, and everything else derives its existence from him. He alone is so immediate to each thing as to be able to cause its being or uphold it in being. Either the existence of the world is a brute fact or its being is directly caused by God.

True, in order to show that God exists as first cause of the existence of substances and the universe within which substances exist, one has to show that the universe cannot have multiple causes but must come from one cause, and that it cannot be that this cause is itself caused by something else, and this by something else, and this by something else, and so on ad infinitum, unendingly, without there being any first cause. But once having realized that what has to be caused is not just coming to be, but being as such, seen as much in the continuance of the world, as in any supposed creation out of nothing at a beginning in time, then one is in a position to show that between what thus causes being as such cannot do it through intermediates of any kind. Therefore, since the one cause of the existence of substances and the universe within which substances exist is a cause of their being as such, there is no room for intermediates.

That there is no genuine possibility of intermediates between God and the world was argued by St. Thomas in *Summa Theologiae* I, q. 45, art. 5, and only a short time earlier with more extensive explanation in *QD. de Potentia*, q. 3, art. 4. God could create or to uphold things in being through a created deputy or minister, because the deputy or minister would not be acting on his own authority but relying upon God's authority, and, since what is required is a real power to produce an effect within nature, God's power and not just his authority would be involved so that God would have to be using him as an instrument, and St. Thomas argues that there can be no instrument in the giving of existence. When a man makes something using an instrument, his hands or the hammer are doing directly something which could not be done by the soul, mind or will of a human being by itself—the instruments under the control of the soul, mind or will can accomplish something which the latter could not accomplish by itself, and they can do this by working upon pre-existing materials, relying on the potentialities of preexisting things to be moved in the relevant ways, the hand of the potter in molding the clay or the hand of the blacksmith or joiner wielding the hammer, using it to get a nail into wood. But the task of creation is precisely one which can draw upon no preexisting materials with their preexisting potentialities. And an angel, that is a pure spirit, would be just as useless as an instrument as the potter or blacksmith.

Duns Scotus regards the fact that creatures are only finite things with finite nature as making the task of creating a creature out of nothing a merely finite one, requiring only a finite power.[19] But in St. Thomas's conception, the reason why God's power is required is not any infiniteness in the thing or nature created, but that to create something with *esse* where the alternative possibility is simply non-*esse*, that the thing does not exist and there is nothing corresponding to it

19 Suárez offers an argument that why only God is the universal cause of being is that it is only God who could create just any kind of being, whereas the power of a creature to create would be limited by the nature of the creature (Francisco Suárez, *Metaphysical Disputations 20—22*, Disputation 20, section 2, §§. 7 ff., §§. 23 – 39, pp. 28 ff., 38 – 51).

Nonetheless, in the end, Suárez does make the key concession that in order to create a being would have to exist *per essentia*, and nothing which possessed existence by participation would be able to create, *loc. cit*, §§ 40 – 42, cf. 1 – 6, pp. 51 – 52, cf. 25 – 28, although he does not regard St. Thomas's argument as demonstrative, §§ 43 – 44, p. 53.

in its place, that is so that it comes into existence "out of nothing," and continues to exist rather than simply disappearing into nothing, requires something which has *esse* in its own right. Moreover, the processes of making a pot or a metal or wooden artefact are processes which proceed in stages, and it is through envisaging such stages that we can understand the role of instruments, but there could not be any stages between the existence of something whether a particular substance or the universe as such and their non-existence with nothing corresponding to them preceding their coming to be out of nothing or following their disappearance into nothing—this is why St. Thomas thinks an infinite power is involved, not because the difficulties of the task are in some way indeterminate, but because of the absolute or instantaneous discontinuity between being and non-being.

For God to possess existence in his own right is for there to be no real distinction between God and his *esse* or *actus essendi*, in the strong sense that there is no room for him to have a cause of existence. There is only a formal distinction between God and his *esse* or *actus essendi* inasmuch as human modes of speaking and thinking compel us to speak and think in a way which imposes a distinction between a name and a propositional expression.

It is only in the case of creatures that St. Thomas supposes that there is a real distinction between a created thing X and its *actus essendi*, in the sense that there is room for created things to have a cause of existence.

For St. Thomas, the only compelling way in which we can show that in the case of creatures there is room for them to have a cause of existence is by showing that they actually have a cause of existence. And this is something which can only be shown *a posteriori*, if it can be shown at all. How either St. Thomas or Gilson conceive that it can be shown is something we have to consider later. But first let us mention how difficulties arise in any alternative position.

(c) DOES IT MAKE SENSE TO SAY THAT THE WORLD GOES ON "OF ITSELF," I.E., IN VIRTUE OF ITS OWN NATURE?

To say that nature goes on "of itself," by "existential inertia" as it were, is to confuse the retention of a property and the retention of existence, as if existence were a property. In the terms in which I explained the matter earlier, it is to neglect the distinction between predicates attributing properties or relations (that is, "predicates" in the sense relied on by logicians) and non-attributive predicates.[20]

The tendency to suppose that nature does goes on "of itself" arises from a mistaken analogy between things continuing in the same state of motion (or, more generally, for momentum to be conserved as Newton's principle expresses it), that is for a certain attributive predicate to continue to apply to them in virtue of their natures, and their continuing in existence. I say this because the same principle which St. Thomas insisted on in the case of God, that a thing's nature can never explain its existence, applies just as much to natural things and to the Universe as to God. For a thing to exercise its nature or essence requires the thing to exist, so that its existence cannot be an exercise of such a nature or essence. Accordingly, for the same reasons that God's nature cannot explain his existence, the nature of the universe at a particular time cannot explain its existence at later times—because having or exercising a nature presupposes the existence of the thing which has the nature. Presumably, the principle of the conservation of momentum obtains in virtue of the nature of matter or of matter/energy (or whatever the "substance" of the world consists of), but in that case its continuing to hold presupposes the continued existence of this matter or matter/energy (or whatever the "substance" of the world consists of).[21]

To restate the matter, if we assume the principle of special relativity to be valid, requires only limited readjustment. This principle has the consequence that there is no absolute simultaneity, no such thing as "the present over the whole universe" such as could be correctly and objectively agreed upon by all the participants in any

20 It is because, like Duns Scotus, he lacks this distinction that the problem of 'impressed impetus' gives rise to a difficulty for Suárez in his defense of the view that there is no formal distinction between the creation and conservation of being (Francisco Suárez, *Metaphysical Disputations 20–22*, Disputation 21, Section 3, § 23 [third difficulty mentioned]—§ 27, pp. 145 – 48).

21 Those who have followed Hoyle in not assuming the quantity of matter/energy to be constant, nonetheless presuppose that there is some such thing as the 'nature of things' which persists and governs the way in which this quantity changes—any other supposition takes such a theory as Hoyle's outside the range of scientific enquiry.

event at some juncture in space-time, if these are moving at different velocities relative to one another, as by the nature of the case is the typical situation when things interact. Each observer or participant in some event at some juncture in space-time must be *in some sense* "compresent" with other co-participants in that event, and it is this that allows us to speak of a juncture in space-time. We can then say that every co-participant in such an event will have a different vantage point from which to judge what is past relative to the juncture at which that co-participant is, but each will judge that the continued operation of things which are from this view-point contemporary according to their natures, presupposes the continued existence of the matter or matter/energy (or whatever the "substance" of the world consists of) considered to be contemporary with it from its view-point at that time in its own history. It will be noted that some notion of "compresence local to a juncture" is required for things to be co-participants in an event and this will be distinct from the notion of simultaneity.

The notion of simultaneity is a mathematically ideal notion of a cut within a period where a period is *a time over which continuous motion through a space takes place*, whereas the notion "being compresent" has to be understood rather in terms, not of times in the sense of periods, but of times in the sense of *times at which things co-participate in an event.*

It is a fundamental mistake in the history of thought to confuse the ideal notion of an "instant" as a dividing point in a period, analogous to a point as a dividing point in a line, with a "moment" in the sense of *the time at which an event takes place*. It is the second notion which is involved when we speak of the time at which one person hits another, or a person has the thought that the post has gone, or sees that something is moving—such moments are set in weak order with respect to instants, i.e., in regard to every moment there are some instants that are definitely before it and other instants which are definitely after it, but many instants of which there is no objective truth either in the statement that they are definitely before it or in the statement that they are definitely after it. What the special theory of relativity shows is that even physics needs to make a use at the microscopic level of the notion of moment which we have to employ in our macroscopic descriptions of human interactions, thoughts and perceptions.

(d) COULD THE EXISTENCE AND CONTINUANCE OF THE UNIVERSE BE JUST A "BRUTE FACT," REALLY CONTINGENT, NOT JUST LOGICALLY CONTINGENT, BUT WITHOUT A CAUSAL BACKGROUND?

Logically, it is possible for someone to *say* or *think* that nature goes on without a cause outside itself, but going on by what Norman Kretzmann calls "existential inertia,"[22] so that there is no need for it to be explained by there being a non-temporal upholder,[23] but to suppose this is just to give no explanation, not to give an alternative explanation. The situation is therefore that a person may indeed *say* or *think* that the existence of things and their continuance has no cause, but is just a brute fact, or as Russell expressed it in his debate with Frederick Copleston "the universe is just there, and that's all"—and that matter/energy does exist with the nature it has exhibited in what science discovers, and has now continued in existence for some 14 billion years, but its continuance in existence at any stage is just a brute fact just as much as its beginning to exist is on this view just a brute fact. To regard these things as just brute facts is at least to recognize that it is no use explaining either existence as such, coming into existence with nothing existing beforehand or continuing existence in terms of the nature of things, and to say and think that one can be satisfied with not offering or seeking after the possible

22 Norman Kretzmann, *The Metaphysics of Theism* (Oxford: Oxford University Press, 1997), 98, 101.

23 The reason why people find it so easy to think that nature just goes on of itself without this needing any explanation is that they have been taken in by a false analogy with what was involved in the change from Aristotelian to Newtonian ways of thinking in physics. In effect, Newton showed that, instead of following Aristotle in supposing that it is change of place which needs explanation, one could suppose that it is change in 'state of motion' which requires explanation, i.e., change in momentum. In his physics, it was momentum, not position, which was regularly conserved. However, momentum is just as much an attribute or predicate as position, and it is the explanation of the existence of that which has continued momentum or position which is at issue. People get confused because they think that Newton showed something more general, namely that it needs no explanation that things should go on in the state that they are: but momentum and existence are not logically the same kind of states or properties in the same sense.

nature of a cause. However, the possibility of saying or thinking such things does not affect the conclusion that here, *if* anything is to be able either to bring things into existence with nothing existing beforehand or to uphold things in existence, i.e., to cause their continuance, it has to be non-temporal.[24]

Now, it is true that philosophers can make very queer remarks about existence needing no more explanation than nonexistence, even when it is the existence of a universe whose nature is to reliably continue which is under consideration. But the common-sense view would seem to be that, the absence of something where there is or would be no reason to expect it invites no explanation (let alone the exercise of causal power). Thus, there is no reason to seek an explanation of nonexistence of the fictitious entities and people invented by novelists.

By contrast, the presence of something with positive existence of some kind whether or not there is reason to expect it to be present does invite explanation, even if the explanation is one we would antecedently expect. Continuing in real existence and not disappearing into nothing where we have no reason to anticipate such disappearance is a better candidate for needing explanation than continuing in nonexistence when we have no reason to anticipate the coming to be of something. It is the real existing of those things which have real existence which constitutes that which is positive in the existence of the Universe.

It is this of which I am asking whether it is just a brute fact, or whether it has to be the effect of the exercise of some causal power or powers.

To say that the universe is "just there and that's all," so that its existence and continuance are just brute facts and that is just how things are, and "that's all there is to be said about it," seems to be a response to the predicament that for a thing to lack a causal background where there is logical room for a causal background, is for these things to present themselves to us as facts which are paradoxically both really contingent, and yet at the same time metaphysically settled and necessary, somewhat as the past is settled and necessary. Part of

24 This is the argument of David Braine, *The Reality of Time and the Existence of God* (Oxford: Oxford University Press, 1988).

the problem is that they have been represented to us as outside the possible influence or control of any agent or other cause.

Yet, in order to make the distinction between real possibility and logical possibility, one would normally explain that for a thing to be really possible it had to be within the power of the natures at work in the world to bring its existence about or else already to be metaphysically settled and necessary, as the past is settled and necessary. By contrast, for something to be logically or conceptually possible all that is required is that there should be no incoherence in supposing it.

Therefore, the atheist and the agnostic are at a much more difficult situation in respect of explaining how it can be that the existence of things or the existence of the universe has a real, and not just a logical contingency, than the theist or the deist.

It is at this stage that we should consider how St. Thomas would justify his view that the existence and continuance of the universe have a real contingency because they are created by God. In considering this, we will discover why it is that he considers God alone to have the power to create, because he possesses existence as it were in his own right, whereas created things possess it in a different way, as something given to them, or which, as it were, they receive. How this is to be understood we will come to later.

SECTION 3: ATTEMPTS AT A PROOF OF THE EXISTENCE OF GOD THROUGH RELIANCE ON THE PRINCIPLE OF SUFFICIENT REASON

In seeking out how St. Thomas approaches the problems of why the existence and continuance of the universe should be considered to have a real contingency, of why the universe and the things of which it is composed need God as a cause of their existence and continuance, let me first identify a family of arguments of which he shows no trace.

(a) THE PRINCIPLE OF SUFFICIENT REASON IN ITS MODERN FORM, TYPIFIED IN LEIBNIZ

We need to distinguish two types of cosmological argument, distinguishing them according to whether (i) they rely upon the idea that everything of a certain sort requires a cause as a condition of its existence (meaning by "cause" an agent or agents with active power or powers adequate to cause the existence concerned), or whether (ii) they rely on Leibniz's principle of sufficient reason, "that every contingent truth or truth of fact must have a sufficient reason" (*Monadology* §36), or some equivalent requirement that every such matter of fact should have an explanation making it intelligible why it should be. Henceforth, I shall use the word "cause" when I mean an agent with active power which is cause of an effect, and the word 'reason' when I mean an explanation making it intelligible why some fact obtains.

In general, arguments of the second kind are unattractive because the principle of sufficient reason is questionable on three counts.

Firstly, it is unprovable. It serves admirably as a methodological principle, as Kant recognized, an ideal of reason. But there seems no *a priori* reason for us to suppose that "being is as such intelligible" (if there is a God, then presumably all things are intelligible to him, but in arguing for God's existence, we cannot use this to prove their intelligibility and go on to use this as part of our argument).

Secondly, the principle seems to be invalid within the sphere of explanation within modern physics. The received view of empirical scientists includes the Heisenberg indeterminacy principle, integral to quantum mechanics, as an established part of physical science. This principle as customarily understood implies that the principle of sufficient reason actually fails within physics, and not because of anything wrong with our physics. In received opinion (never accepted by Einstein), there are "why"-questions, seeking an explanatory reason for something, which naturally arise within our received modes of scientific description, but to which quantum theory requires that there be no answer, not because of a systematic defect in human capacities to discover or understand, but because of the absence of any ground for an answer *in rerum natura*. Furthermore, although human action is not called "accidental" (the meaning of this word is primarily both to exclude being the issue of intention and only secondarily to exclude having a unitary cause), it is commonly held that there is no cause *in rerum natura* which determines which of two motives will move us to action, that is no cause why we did A for the motive X instead of doing B for the motive Y, and that there is no reason why we did A rather than B beyond the motive X.

Thirdly, the way that the principle of sufficient reason brings the supposed regress of causes of contingent beings, or of reasons for their existence, to an end (i.e., in a being whose reason for existence lies in its own essence or nature) is unsatisfactory. What is relevant to a cosmological argument is the question of the explanation or cause, if any, of God's existence.[25] Here, Aquinas argues that God's essence (God's "nature," or, in later language, God's "real essence") cannot be the reason for God's existence. If God's nature or essence explained his existence (or its necessity), the two would have to be sufficiently distinct for one to be able to conceive God's existing as an exercise of this nature or essence. Yet something has to exist in order to exercise its nature, and so having a nature presupposes the existence of the thing having the nature, and therefore essence cannot explain existence ("existence cannot be derived from essence"). It is because of this that St. Thomas regards existence and essence in God as a single unitary actuality because it is only thus that neither can be prior to the other.

Accordingly, attempting a cosmological proof by means of the principle of sufficient reason seems a failure.

(b) THE COMPARABLE PRINCIPLE THAT BEING IS AS SUCH INTELLIGIBLE

In his book *Insight*, Bernard Lonergan purports to show that being is intrinsically completely intelligible, taking this to be a 'definition' of a second order kind. From this he infers that there must be a transcendent intelligence to which all being is as such intelligible.[26]

25 This is quite different from what is involved in Gaunilo, Aquinas, and Kant's objections to the ontological argument presented by Anselm. For this is a matter of our human modes of knowledge of God: and all the arguments are to the effect that from a nominal definition of God (i.e., what the word "God" means) we cannot deduce his existence and have nothing to do with explaining his existence.

26 In detail, he first tells us that being is all that is known together with all that remains to be known (Bernard Lonergan, *Insight: A Study of Human Understanding*, [London: Longmans, Green and Co., Ltd., 1957], 350), which might seem ambiguous as between saying that what is known or remains to be known is the case and offering a definition of being as what is to be known.

This "transcendent intelligence," by a little further argument he shows could only be God.

Earlier, Garrigou-Lagrange following in a long tradition of scholastic teaching held the same principle that being is as such intelligible but used this principle in a more indirect manner in expounding St. Thomas's proofs of God's existence.

We meet the same principle in other twentieth century authors, but only as something we must suppose as a norm or "transcendental condition" of rationality. And it seems true that neither Locke, nor Hume, nor Kant, nor anyone else has offered any adequate rational ground for restricting enquiry to the ill-defined field of the empirical.[27] The only grounds for restricting enquiries are either that they are nonsensical or as Aristotle would have expressed it 'unscientific' because alien to the subject matter being studied or kind of question being considered. Thus, to ask, "Is John six times more brave than David or only five times as brave?" is absurd as if such mind-involving states (including other virtues, desires, sureness of belief, and so forth) could have an exact measure on a continuous scale in the way physical properties typically do have such a measure because of some connection with spatial measurement. Or again, the way in which

---

However, he clearly means the second, explaining that it is a definition of a second order kind (pp. 350, 643). He goes on to offer what he regards as better formulations, namely, that being is what is to be known by intelligent grasp and reasonable affirmation (p. 445), and best that being is intrinsically intelligible (pp. 500, 552). From this (mentioned again pp. 499, 652, 655), he tells us that it follows that there is such a thing as what being is or complete intelligibility (pp. 643 – 45, 673) from which he says that it follows that there is a transcendent intelligence to which all being is as such intelligible (pp. 643, 672 – 73, 677, cf. 658).

27 We find such a principle proposed on this basis in Germain Grisez, *Beyond the New Theism* (South Bend, IN: University of Notre Dame Press, 1975), 67 – 82, with the most conveniently available criticisms of Locke, Hume, Kant et al. on pp. 94 – 228. The same presumption of the conditions of rational thought appears to have been made earlier in the works of Joseph Marechal (attacked by Gilson in Chapter 5 of Étienne Gilson, *Thomist Realism and the Critique of Knowledge* [San Francisco: Ignatius Press, 1986, trans. from the French of 1939], Emerich Coreth and Karl Rahner). All these figures before Grisez are discussed under the heading of "transcendental Thomists" in Eric Mascall, *The Openness of Being,* Chapters. 4 and 5 (London: Darton, Longman and Todd, 1971).

the Heisenberg indeterminacy principle has become built into the understanding of physical nature within modern physics gives reason to suppose it wrong to press certain physical enquiries too far.

(c) VON BALTHASAR'S APPROACH AND ITS PECULIAR BACKGROUND

The scatter in the thought of modern theologians in approaching these questions is exemplified by the case of Hans Urs von Balthasar.

When von Balthasar considers the principle that being is as such intelligible, he understands it is in a strong sense that is not just as something we have to suppose in order to justify our continuing enquiry, a "transcendental condition" of rational thinking, but as a categorical truth about reality. And he considers being intelligible in terms of there being an explanation or reason why something is the case, i.e., in terms of there being something satisfying the understanding rather than just providing knowledge. In particular, he wants to have an explanation of why there is something rather than nothing at all in existence. Indeed, yet more particularly he wants an explanation which is not just an explanation of the fact (which might leave it open that the ground of things' existence was dark in itself and something to be frightened at), but an explanation which reveals the ground of things as itself glorious or lovable in a way whose character transcends the glory and lovability of the phenomenal world.[28] But again there is no reason to think that such a principle is actually true, except in the sense that everything is intelligible in this way to God (God's *esse* being intelligible to God), but again evidently we cannot use this in a proof of God's existence, even though it will follow from his existence, once this is certain whether through philosophy or through faith.

The background of von Balthasar's raising the cosmological question in such a form, "Why is there anything at all and not simply nothing?," appears in his discussion of Heidegger, to whom he attributes this question.[29] For him, one has not raised any metaphysical

28 Von Balthasar, *The Glory of the Lord: A Theological Aesthetics* (San Francisco: Ignatius Press, 1991), V: 623–25.

29 Von Balthasar, *The Glory of the Lord*, V: 432, referring to the 5th edition of *Was ist Metaphysik?*, the 1949 revision of the 'Was ist Metaphysik?' of 1929, question until one has gone beyond any question posed in any particular science because each particular science always presupposes its subject matter as objectively given in some particular way.[30]

He goes on to argue that the phenomenal world contains an objective order not imposed by man, an order which we discover, preexisting natural scientific studies, not merely dependent on our construction. And he reckons that this objective orderedness we discover goes far beyond any orderedness anticipated before the development of modern science. But he considers that to make this the basis of metaphysics is to proceed by way of conjecture, and the imposition of some human interpretation (his thought here appears to have been deeply influenced by Kantian ideas), extrapolating so as to suppose that the order exhibited by phenomenally discovered being extends to being as such. He sees this as having the effect of making phenomenally discovered being in its order the object of wonder, instead of making being itself as such the object of wonder.[31] It appears that he is here rejecting any approach to proof of the existence to God analogous to St. Thomas's First Way if this is taken to be a proof of God on the basis of physics and cosmology (as if it were just an improved variant on that to be found in Aristotle's *Physics* VIII and *Metaphysics, Lambda*), instead requiring any philosophical approach to God to be rooted in metaphysics, not in physics or in any data provided by the senses.

In his view, the only explanation which reveals the ground of things as itself glorious or lovable in a way whose character transcends the glory and lovability of the phenomenal world is one which takes

---

revised after the radical change in Heidegger's thought commonly referred to as 'the turn' in which he moved towards a radical rejection of the whole tradition of western philosophy from Plato and Aristotle through the Scholastics (unfortunately all seen through the eyes of Suárez) to Kant, Fichte and Hegel, a rejection expressed in his resort to the Pre-Socratics, seen first in *Einführung in die Metaphysik*, delivered as a lecture in 1935, but only published in 1953.

30 Von Balthasar, *The Glory of the Lord*, V: 431, referring to the same 1949 edition of *Was ist Metaphysik?*, and representing Plato as the first to make it a particular science in *Platons Lehre von der Wahrheit, mit einem Brief über den Humanismus*, in its second (1947) edition combining a lecture on Plato's doctrine of truth (1930–31) revised in 1940 with the 'Letter on Humanism' of 1946.

31 Von Balthasar, *The Glory of the Lord*, V: 613–15.

one beyond that world, bringing one to the realization that existence is a gift, given by a free act of God, inviting one to think of being as a miracle.[32] As this freedom in the act of God is not in his view something which can be proved, it is unsurprising that he considers that metaphysics depends upon something given theologically *a priori* by revelation.

(d) THE DIFFERENCE BETWEEN THE NEED OF A CAUSE AS A CONDITION OF SOMETHING'S EXISTENCE AND THE REQUIREMENT OF AN EXPLANATION MAKING ITS EXISTENCE INTELLIGIBLE: GILSON AND BALTHASAR IN RELATION TO ARISTOTLE

It is striking that the question which von Balthasar raises is the question "Why is there anything at all and not simply nothing?" This is the very question which it has become customary to raise ever since the time of Kant, the question raised by some very non-Balthasarian Thomists such as Herbert McCabe, and seems to be framed within the framework against which one had thought that it was Balthasar's purpose to set aside, the framework set by Leibniz, Wolff and Kant. It is a "why?" question seeking an explanation making something intelligible, and not the causal question raised by Gilson or, in my view, by St. Thomas himself.

That is, Balthasar's presents God's action as the explanation of a fact, in particular the fact that there is something rather than nothing, the explanation of why the general proposition "There are things which exist, rather than nothing that exists" is true. By contrast, St. Thomas and Gilson's arguments to God present him, not as the explanation of the situation that some positive existential proposition is true, but primarily as the cause of the existence and continuance in existence of each singular individual of one the sorts of which we have experience so long as it has existence, as well as of its other perfections and having an end or purpose, its movements, and its being set within a context of other things. True, if we were to interpret St. Thomas's First Way simply in terms of some direct reliance upon

32 Von Balthasar, *The Glory of the Lord*, V: 625–27, consummating the argument of the whole section entitled "The Miracle of Being and the Fourfold Distinction."

Aristotle's *Physics* VIII and *Metaphysics, Lambda*, then it would concern a universe of things which includes animals and many other bodily things which come to be and pass away. Aristotle's argument is that the continuance of every other kind of body—involving change depends on the continuance of changes in spatial position and these on the reliability of the continuance of the physical universe, which for Aristotle and St. Thomas meant dependence on continued motion of the outermost sphere which is the primary thing to be moved.[33] And this impression that St. Thomas is concerned with the sustaining of a system consisting mostly or wholly of things which cannot be assumed to have a guarantee of perpetuity in themselves is confirmed by a consideration of his Second and Third Ways.

Yet, for Aristotle and St. Thomas, the principles on which the reproduction, growth and behavior of living things are to be explained go beyond anything contained in the general science of physical things. Accordingly, the upholding cause of the whole system of the universe is not just an unmoved nonmaterial cause of the continuance of the whole system in its physical aspect, but the upholding cause of a system which includes things some of which have life and knowledge, and which must accordingly be an upholding cause which possesses in a more eminent way, not just the power of causal agency, but life and knowledge, and whatever other properties are exhibited in a spread of analogous ways by things within the universe it sustains in existence.

However, granted that all these properties of causal agency, life, knowledge and so forth are possessed in ways not confined to any one form of material realization or indeed any kind of material realization at all, this still leaves us in darkness so far as our imagination and understanding are concerned as to the nature of this sustaining first cause of being and continuance.

Thus, a Gilsonian approach through considering the causation of what we perceive will leave us as deeply in darkness as to the nature of the first cause as any Balthasarian approach at the stage

33 In *Metaphysics* 1073b 1 – 2, Aristotle concludes that there must be some substance whose motion is first, as St. Thomas expounds in sections 2558 – 60 of *Lectio* 9 on Book Lambda in his *Commentary on the Metaphysics*, this part written at least three years after the relevant parts of the *Summa Theologiae*, and in 1074a 30 – 38, he shows that there is only one first heaven, cf. 2593 – 96 of *Lectio* 10.

before Balthasar introduces the notion of contingent existence as a free gift. The only thing the Gilsonian approach makes more clear at this stage is that the nature of the first cause excludes any evil or causation of evil—man at this stage of knowledge is not to be frightened of the first cause, even though he is not thereby given hope of any complete satisfaction, and not thereby given hope of any activity beyond this life.[34]

34 It is puzzling that von Balthasar should put such an emphasis on the need to strike free of the ways of thinking derived from Scotus, Suárez, Leibniz and Wolff, envisaging Heidegger as seeing the same need, and attributing these insights to Gustav Siewerth and yet should turn out to be still entrapped by them. This just shows that it must be Siewerth rather than Gilson on whom he was relying in his rejection of the whole way of thinking which sprang from Scotus and Suárez—even though it is said that von Balthasar once remarked that he regarded Gilson as the interpreter of St. Thomas on whom he relied. One can only infer that von Balthasar shows little sign of any perception of the full significance of Gilson's *L'etre et l' essence* in its 1948 edition, his *Being and Some Philosophers* of 1949 and 1952, his 1950 paper at the Thomistic Congress in Rome, or his 1952 paper "Les principes et les causes" with its distinction between causation and causality. All of von Balthasar's citations are from Siewerth's *Das Schicksal der Metaphysik von Thomas zu Heidegger* (Einsiedeln: Johannes Verlag, 1959). Von Balthasar sees a straight line between Duns Scotus's treatment of being as a univocal concept (Siewerth, 12–13, 16–21) and the thinking of Suárez (21, 23–25, 27–29), seeing Duns Scotus's approach as leading naturally to Ockham and modern empiricism, while seeing Suárez's influence as reflected in Spinoza and Descartes and thence to Leibniz, Kant, Fichte and Hegel. He attributes his own perception of the link between Scotus as the fount of the mistake concerned and Heidegger's rejection of the following tradition to Gustav Siewerth (17) and gives Siewerth as his authority for regarding Suárez's following Scotus in the conceptualization of being as the source of the root mistake at the foundation of modern metaphysics from Descartes to Hegel (25, 28). Von Balthasar refers to Gilson as an authority only on Duns Scotus and Scotus's disciple, François de Mayronnes (1288–1328) (17, 18, 19).

Von Balthasar regards the idea that being is a superconceptual mystery, a "One" which any conceptualization in any "metaphysics" within the sphere of *Nous*, as derived from Plotinus, whom he thinks of as an originating source and a Platonist only by disguise. And this makes von Balthasar think of Heidegger as having better attributed his idea of the "ontological difference" between the unconceptualizable "being" (*Sein*) and beings (existents, *Seiende*), to Plotinus than to the pre-Socratics. In the meantime, von Balthasar envisages the same

SECTION 4: THE PRINCIPLE THAT, IF THE *ESSENTIA* OF A THING IS DISTINCT FROM ITS *ESSE*, THE THING'S *ESSE* MUST BE CAUSED BY AN EXTERIOR AGENT: HOW ST. THOMAS USES IT, DEPARTING FROM ARISTOTLE

(a) HOW THE DOCTRINE THAT THERE IS A REAL DISTINCTION BETWEEN *ESSE* AND *ESSENTIA* IN EVERYTHING OTHER THAN GOD APPEARS IN ST. THOMAS

(i) AN ARGUMENT IN *DE ENTE ET ESSENTIA*

In St. Thomas's *De Ente et Essentia*, he is more occupied with the analysis of concepts than with proving such things as the existence of God. Nonetheless, it is curious that he offers there, in his earliest important work, an argument for God's existence of which, as an argument for God's existence, he makes no use to this purpose at any later time.

---

idea in Plotinus as the ultimate figure behind St. Thomas's distinction between *esse* as act of being and *essentia*. Here one can say that it is true that St. Thomas made much use of Proclus (the actual source of the compilation known as *Liber de Causis*) and his pupil the pseudo-Dionysius, on both of whom Plotinus had a large influence. It is as a result of this coincidence that von Balthasar could come to envisage Plotinus as the ultimate source behind both Heidegger's *Sein/Seiende* and St. Thomas's *esse/essentia* distinctions (*The Glory of the Lord*, V, 435). It is also as a result of this that von Balthasar can regard St. Thomas as still infected by Platonism, and in this very far from Gilson who enables one to see how St. Thomas understood the Platonic idioms he often used in a sense completely purged of Platonism.

One may remark that Heidegger's view that Scholasticism understands essence in terms of a being which is intelligible in itself, to which existence can ally itself or not, at will (or at God's will) as described by von Balthasar (*The Glory of the Lord*, V: 433) constitutes precisely the point at which Suárez falsified the interpretation of St. Thomas. As a result, if von Balthasar's interpretation of Heidegger is at this point correct, then the basis of Heidegger's rejection of the *esse/essentia* distinction as it occurs in St. Thomas himself is entirely ill-based, independently of whether or not the views of these philosophers on related matters are correct, and whatever the situation with other medieval philosophers. Whether von Balthasar understood St. Thomas's *esse/essentia* distinction any better than Heidegger is unclear.

It is very instructive to analyze the argument in this first occurrence, before considering the different use he makes of it in later writings.

> Everything that pertains to a thing, however, either is caused by the principles of its own nature, as risibility in man, or else comes from some extrinsic principle, as light in the air from the influence of the sun. Now, it cannot be that *esse* itself is caused by the very form or quiddity of the thing (I mean as by an efficient cause), because then the thing would be its own efficient cause, and the thing would produce itself in *esse* [i.e., in real existence], which is impossible. Therefore, everything the *esse* of which is other [*he doesn't distinguish being other logically from being other really, and his argument doesn't seem to depend on this, even if it ends up implying it;*] than its own nature has *esse* from another.
>
> And since everything that is through another is reduced to that which is through itself as to a first cause, there is something that is the cause of existing in all things in that this thing is *esse tantum* [*esse itself without anything added to it*]. Otherwise, we would have to go to infinity in causes, for everything that is not *esse tantum* has a cause of its *esse*, as said above. It is clear, therefore, that the intelligences are form and *esse* and have *esse* from the first being, which is *esse tantum*, and this is the first cause, which is God.
>
> "Everything that receives something from another is in potency with respect to what it receives, and that which is received in the thing is its act; therefore, a quiddity or form that is an intelligence is in potency with respect to the *esse* that it receives from God, and this received *esse* is received as its act. And thus there are found in the intelligences both potency and act although not matter and form, unless in some equivocal sense.... Furthermore, since, as said above, the quiddity of an intelligence is the intelligence itself, its quiddity or essence [*essentia*] is itself the very thing that exists, and its *esse* received from God is that by which it subsists in the nature of things; and because of this some people say that substances of this kind are composed of what is and that by which it is, or of what is and *esse*," as Boethius says [in *De Hebdomadibus*, PL 64, 1311 B-C].[35]

35 Thomas Aquinas, *On Being and Essence* (*De Ente et Essentia*), Ch. IV, translation by Robert T. Miller, 1997. https://sourcebooks.fordham.edu/basis/aquinas-esse.asp

In this passage, St. Thomas makes two assumptions: (1) that everything whose *esse* is other than its nature or essence must be caused by something (from which it follows that it must be caused by something else since it cannot be caused by itself), and (2) the second that one cannot go to infinity in causes of *esse*.

(ii) THE ARGUMENT OF *DE ENTE ET ESSENTIA* TURNED TO DIFFERENT USE IN *SUMMA THEOLOGIAE*

At first sight, the same argument recurs in *Summa Theologiae* I, q. 3, art. 4:

> [First,] whatever a thing has besides its *essentia* must be caused either by the constituent principles of that *essentia* (like a property that necessarily accompanies the species—as the faculty of laughing is proper to a man—and is caused by the constituent principles of the species), or by some exterior agent—as heat is caused in water by fire. Therefore, if the *esse* of a thing differs from its *essentia*, this *esse* must be caused either by some exterior agent or by its essential principles. Now it is impossible for a thing's *esse* to be caused by its essential constituent principles, for nothing can be the sufficient cause of its own *esse*, if its *esse* is caused. Therefore that thing, whose *esse* differs from its *essentia*, must have its *esse* caused by another. But this cannot be true of God; because we call God the first efficient cause. Therefore it is impossible that in God *esse* and *essentia* should be other than each other.[36]

However, what is presented here is not designed as a proof of the existence of God. Rather, a threefold classification is suggested of what is predicated of a thing (what it "has"), firstly, its *essentia*, secondly what is caused by the constituent principles of that *essentia* (e.g., the faculty of laughing in the case of a man), and thirdly, other things, typically contingent attributes (such as being wise). These last, if they have a cause, must be caused by an exterior agent. The text seems to assume that the second and third kinds of predicate must be caused.

36 Thomas Aquinas, *ST* I.3.4, modified translation of the Fathers of the English Dominican Province, 1920. Dominican English Translation.

As to what is predicated non-attributively of a thing, such as the thing's *esse*, this cannot be caused by the constituent principles of its *essentia*, because this would involve circularity. He then takes it as already established in q. 2, art. 3, that God has no cause [is "the first efficient cause"], and from this concludes that God's *essentia* must be identical to his *esse*. He seems to presume that otherwise God's *essentia* would be prior to his *esse*, and some exterior agent would have had to cause this *essentia* to be instantiated. Thus his argument here seems to depend on the idea found in the second argument he offers in *Summa Theologiae* I, q. 3, art. 4, namely that, if a thing's *essentia* is prior to its *esse*, this prior *essentia* stands in a relation to the thing's *esse* comparable to that between a potentiality and actuality, as when a thing's form exists in the mind of an artist before having real existence in the thing itself.

Throughout he is arguing in a manner which does not distinguish '"Fness" is predicated of X' from '"X's Fness" is predicated of X,' granted that X already exists (or of not distinguishing 'X has Fness' from 'X has X's Fness,' so long as X exists).

(iii) ST. THOMAS ENDS BY MAKING THE ARGUMENT OF *DE ENTE ET ESSENTIA* DEPEND ON THE PRINCIPLE OF THE PRIORITY OF ACTUALITY TO POTENTIALITY

In the same article of *Summa Theologiae* I, q. 3, art. 4, in his second argument to the same conclusion he says this:

> Secondly, *esse* is that which makes every form or nature actual; for goodness and humanity are spoken of as actual, only because they are spoken of as existing. Therefore *esse* must be compared to *essentia, if the latter is a distinct reality* [*quae est aliud ab ipso*, where the neuter *aliud* implies that a *res* rather than a person is being spoken of], as actuality to potentiality. Therefore, since in God nothing is potential, as shown above [art. 1], it follows that *essentia* is not another thing in Him from His *esse*. Therefore His *essentia* is His *esse*.[37]

37 Thomas Aquinas, *ST* I.3.4.

Here he is arguing that if in God *essentia* were distinct from His *esse* as a distinct thing, then it would have to be prior to it in the way a potentiality is often presupposed by an actuality or in the way they are sometimes dependent on each other (as for St. Thomas the matter and form of a thing are generally mutually dependent).

This way of reasoning might seem to us odd, inasmuch as, for there to be any such thing as "the essence (or nature) of God," it would seem that God had to exist, since the earlier argument was correct in insisting that essence presupposes existence, since unless X exists X's essence cannot exist, so that existence cannot be result or consequence of essence. Nothing can have its existence explained as "in virtue of its nature" or "by its nature."

However, the point of this remark is to mark a distinction between created things or things whose existence is contingent and God. Whereas the *esse* (in the sense of *actus essendi*) of any subsistent thing is as such an actuality, *actus* or *energeia*, by contrast, the *essentia* of that subsistent thing is not as such an *energeia*.

Now, in St. Thomas's view, there is no logical room for God not to exist (it is because of this that there is no room for him to have a cause of existence). This is, in his conception, because, in the case of God, God's *esse* and his *essentia*, although to be distinguished formally according to the different way in which we speak of them, are in no way distinct realities. Although in our manner of speaking, God's *essentia* is what he is, and contrasts formally or according to our mode of speech with his being or existing, that is with his *esse* as an actuality or *actus*, nonetheless, in the case of God, his *essentia* has a logically different character from the *essentia* of any created or contingently existing thing, inasmuch as there is no way it could fail to be actual—by contrast with creatures which are of such a nature as to "cry aloud that they were made" (St. Augustine, *Confessions*, XI, 4). Moreover, whereas in the case of created beings we are inclined to think of their natures as something like states, capacities or dispositions realized or actualized in activities and passions taking place at or over different moments, stages or periods within the period of their existence, since God is an atemporal being, there will be no distinction in him between a state, capacity or disposition and its actualization, e.g., between having in memory and actually remembering. Therefore,

God's nature or *essentia* is not something static relative to which his existing, living, understanding or loving are active. It should therefore not be counter-intuitive to say that God is his life or his being alive, his understanding, his loving, etc., although again in the statements we make we must take care to respect the formal distinctions which arise from the differences between concrete and abstract expressions.

St. Thomas is not a Platonist. For him, God is not an abstract object, with a timelessness analogous to that of the numbers, but the living God who acts in history, so that in regard to him the most appropriate forms of expression are what we call the concrete ones. What is special in the case of God, is that, although we speak of his *essentia*, his life, etc. using abstract expressions, these are, in fact, the more misleading forms of expression—it is because God's nature or essence is in this sense logically a "particular," and not distinct from God himself, that it is possible for creatures to have an intellectual vision of God.[38]

38 [Editor's note: the following note was ambiguously marked off from the main text by David. Since it digresses from the line of thought in the text, we place it here.] By contrast, in St. Thomas's view, even in the case of angels, both the angel and its *essentia* receive existence, rather than having it in their own right or underivatively, so that there is a real distinction between their *essentia* and their *esse*, and not just a distinction in our way of speaking about them, and *a fortiori* the same is true in the case of lesser creatures.

In a way, St. Thomas is suffering from problems which arise from Aristotle's application of the principle that matter is the principle of individuation to immaterial substances, such as the intelligences which move the lower spheres, or in St. Thomas's worldview the angels, so that he has to say that each angel is identical to its essence (*Summa Theologiae* I, q. 3, art. 3). Yet, after saying that each angel is identical to its essence, he has to insist that the angel is still composite because composed of its *essentia* and its *esse*, so that (*Summa Theologiae* I, q. 3, art. 7) it has to have a cause because things in themselves different cannot unite unless something causes them to unite, "because in every composite there must be potentiality and actuality,... since either one of the parts actuates another or all the parts are potential to the whole,... and because nothing composite can be predicated of any of its parts [as being an angel can be predicated of the angel himself]"—and, because of all this, although an angel is a unity it is not supremely one, since its substance is in a way compound (see *Summa Theologiae* I, q. 11, art. 4, and reply to objection 3).

The fact that St. Thomas is not comfortable with this way of thinking about the angels appears in *Summa Theologiae* I, q. 47, art. 2, where he gives it as a reason for the being only one angel of any angelic species, that in God's

It is because any created or really contingent thing is of such a character that it might not have existed and might cease to exist that its *essentia* or nature cannot be *as such* actual or *as such* an actuality. It is in this sense that St. Thomas holds the view that in every creature the relation of a created thing's *esse* to its essence is comparable to the relation of actuality to potentiality, inasmuch as its essence could have lacked actuality and could cease to have actuality, actuality being something it has only contingently or dependently.[39]

It is for this reason that he considers his First Way of proving God's existence the most fundamental, namely because, in his view, it establishes that in God there is no potentiality at all, there being no logical room for God not to exist, whereas creatures have such a nature as to show that their existence has a real contingency. But this absence of room for God not to exist is not something the human intellect can know *a priori*, not a matter of the statement that God does not exist being contrary to an extended predicate logic, not the matter of something which a divine understanding of human concepts would realize, but something known to us only *a posteriori*, from the need that created things have for a cause of their existence and continuance, and the impossibility that there be an infinite series of causes of causes of this existence and continuance. For there is no way in which such a series can have a terminus unless there is something in regard to which there is no room for its non-existence.

---

wisdom there would be no point in creating more than one of each species "as the wisdom of God is the cause of the distinction of things, so the same wisdom is the cause of their inequality ... And as the matter is on account of the form, material distinction exists for the sake of formal distinction. Hence, we see that in incorruptible things there is only one individual of each species, forasmuch as the species is sufficiently preserved in the one individual. Whereas in things generated and corruptible there are many individuals of one species for the sake of the preservation of the species."

39 Suárez seems to regard God alone as pure actuality, because he alone exists *per essentiam*, and he says that he himself is attracted by an argument of Giles of Rome whereby a creature's power is limited to drawing a pre-existing potentiality into actuality because it is itself composed of potentiality and actuality, although he says that Duns Scotus scorns Giles's argument. Suárez likes it because he thinks that a thing's ways of acting imitate other ways of being. See Francisco Suárez, *Metaphysical Disputations 20–22*, Disputation 21, Section 3, §. 44, p. 53.

We must now examine how it is that this conception that the relation of a created thing's *esse* to its essence, so that it is composed of them (together with its accidents), is comparable to the relation of actuality to potentiality, arises, not from any rejection of Aristotle's view that the Universe is without temporal beginning or end, but from his rejection of Aristotle's view that the Universe *could not have* a beginning or end. In addition, as we have already seen, in each creature there is a distinction between its essential *esse* according to its *essentia*, and its accidental *esse* according to its non-necessary qualities and activities, super-added to its essential *esse*, whereas in God, there is no distinction between his essential *esse* according to his *essentia*, and any accidental *esse* according to his qualities and activities, since he has no accidental *esse*.

(b) THE IDEA OF A REAL DISTINCTION BETWEEN A THING'S *ESSE* AND ITS *ESSENTIA* AS FOREIGN TO ARISTOTLE

St. Thomas is quite clear that this conception of there being a real distinction between a thing's *esse* and its *essentia* as distinct "parts" of its "composition," and of these as related in a way somehow comparable to the relation of actuality and potentiality is completely absent from Aristotle.

In parts of his *Commentary on the Metaphysics*, St. Thomas finds that Aristotle recognizes that the ideas of potentiality and actuality, applied first in connection with cases of change in place, quantity and quality, can and must be extended by analogy, the cases to which it can be extended having a certain relation or proportion to each other and being discovered inductively. However, the extension which Aristotle makes is only to the case of change in substantial nature, as when a log is burnt to ashes, or a seed grows into a plant, and he never conceives of some substance coming to be out of nothing, rather than out of some other bodily substance (*Metaphysics*, Theta, 6—8, and St. Thomas's commentary on these chapters). That Aristotle limits the extension of the application of these notions to this is because he has arguments that when something comes to be there must always be a state preceding a thing's coming to be and something making it come to be when it does, and in any case there must be a period preceding the moment when it came to be, since for him it is in the nature of moments to be dividing-points within a period, and not merely starting points or end points (*Physics*, VIII, 1–2). Likewise, there is no trace of any further extension of the notion of potentiality in *Metaphysics*, Delta, 12, as is apparent in St. Thomas's discussion of this chapter.

Again, even before this, when he is discussing Aristotle's treatment of 'being' in *Metaphysics*, Gamma, 2, 1003b 22–33, in sections 548–61 of *Lectio* 2, he takes up a position opposed to that of Avicenna who held that existence (and also unity) are things added to substance logically somewhat as accidents in the secondary categories are "added to" substance (553–58). On the contrary, St. Thomas insists that 'even though a thing's existence (*esse rei*) is other (*aliud*) than its essence (*essentia*), it should not be understood as something added to its essence after the manner of an accident, but something constituted, as it were (*quasi*), by the principles of the essence (*essentia*). Hence the term being (*nomen ens*) which is applied to a thing by reason of its existence (*esse*), signifies the same thing as the term (*nomen*, e.g., man) which is applied to it by reason of its essence (e.g., humanity)' (558).[40]

How then does St. Thomas come to envisage the relation of a created thing's *esse* to its essence as distinct "parts" of its "composition" as comparable to the relation of actuality to potentiality?

(c) HOW THE ARGUMENT TO GOD AS THE PRIMARY UNMOVED MOVER HAS A DIFFERENT SIGNIFICANCE FOR ST. THOMAS THAN FOR ARISTOTLE

To understand the contrast between Aristotle and St. Thomas, it is useful to go back to considering the overall shape of Aristotle's argument about the existence and nature of the primary first mover.

In *Physics* VIII, 1–2, Aristotle starts off with his arguments that there is an absurdity in supposing that time had a beginning, and the rest of *Physics* VIII can be considered as an enquiry into what could

40 One may note that the whole design of *Metaphysics*, Zeta, Chapter 6, is to explain the way in which (e.g.) man or humanity is in some way not distinct from the individual man of whom "man" is predicated or to which humanity is attributed, in such a way as to prevent any "third man" argument from arising.

guarantee that time, and with it physical process, should have no beginning or end, evidently supposing that there must be something which thus guarantees this unending existence of the universe. He considers the hypothesis that the universe might have no beginning or end in this way by means of some things passing away and every time other things coming to be, while whenever things pass away other things come to be, the whole process continuing endlessly into the future besides having gone on endlessly in the past. And he rejects this hypothesis on the ground that this would make the continuance of the universe accidental (*Physics*, VIII, 6), a universe of which as physical he regards spatial motion as the essential feature. Since he also regards any kind of change or motion which involves a succession of changes, even a succession of spatial motions, as having the same consequence, he concludes that the only way in which the universe can continue unendingly is through the causation of an unending circular motion, maintained by the mover of whatever circular motion is primary. In *Physics*, VIII, 10, he concludes that this first mover must be without magnitude or parts, exercising its force for an unending time. In *Metaphysics*, Lambda, he takes us further and argues that such an unmoved mover must be a being of a simple nature, a pure actuality and containing no potentiality for physical movement or change of any kind, and that any such must be unvarying in its action in moving the sphere which it moves. It will be an intellectual and living being, and as without potentiality entirely immaterial. The heavenly bodies are moved by such a mover or movers not in a physical manner, but in each case by being the object of desire, the heavenly bodies being living beings moved by desire. These features of Aristotle's account remain independently of the state of ancient and medieval cosmology.

This cosmology led Aristotle to introduce various complexities into the account he offers in Lambda. Because there are seven moving heavenly bodies as well as the sphere of the fixed stars and because several spheres are involved in the explanation of the movement of each heavenly body, there are, in Aristotle's view, many physically unmoving and unmovable movers. These move the heavenly bodies. But amongst the many unmovable movers, one is primary, namely the one which moves the outermost sphere (identified by Aristotle with the sphere containing the fixed stars, but a ninth sphere above the sphere of the fixed stars in the later astronomical theory referred to by

St. Thomas in his commentary on *Metaphysics*, Lambda, *Lectio* 9, n. 2558). Accordingly, he has to introduce the analogy of a commander giving unity to the order of an army in order to explain the unity of the universe, presumably the desires of the lesser unmoved movers being subordinated to the desire of the superior movers.

But we must grasp how it is that these complexities are irrelevant to the shape of Aristotle's underlying argument.

Firstly, his argument that the unmoved movers must be pure actualities which contain no potentiality relies upon the principle that actuality has to precede the realization of any potentiality. Secondly, his conception of the primary unmoved movers arises directly from his supposition that he has to give an account of what guarantees the unending motion of the outermost sphere—obviously presuming that there must be something that does this. He has put himself in the situation that his dialectic will not be satisfied unless it reaches to something which is necessarily imperishable or unending in itself, i.e., in such a way that there is no room for it to be caused.

However, St. Thomas questions Aristotle's view that the universe is necessarily without beginning or end. He thinks that this cannot be demonstrated (also arguing that one cannot demonstrate that it had a beginning).

Thus, in many places, e.g., in *Summa Contra Gentiles*, II.36, *Summa Theologiae* I, q. 46, arts. 1 and 2, and his commentary on *Physics*, VIII, 1–2, in *Lectio* 2, nn. 986–90, he argues that Aristotle's arguments that the universe is "eternal" (*aidion*), i.e., everlasting or perpetual in the sense of being unending or without beginning or end, fail to demonstrate this. Now, once this is conceded, then there ceases to be any necessity either in the universe's existing at all or in its continuing to exist, and at any time it is possible for it to cease to exist, leaving no remainder. Further, it would seem that it would be possible for the universe to come into existence, with there having been no previous time. For, if at any time in the history of the universe, it does not cease to exist, the relation between that time and its history after that time seem to be analogous to the relation between the time of the actual beginning of the universe and its actual history thereafter.

In the rest of my discussion, I take the reasons which St. Thomas gives for rejecting Aristotle's arguments to be quite valid. Accordingly, there is no sound a priori or philosophical reason for judging the universe to be without beginning or end (as well as, equally, in St. Thomas's view, no good philosophical or a priori reason for judging the contrary view). Therefore, it is logically possible that the universe had a beginning (which implies that there would have been no time before it began), and no absolute impossibility in its having had a cause of existing.

As a result of this, Aristotle's insistence that there must be a cause of the maintenance of physical motion, or of a system of physical motions or changes, in such a way as to make their constancies reliable, has more consequences for St. Thomas than for Aristotle. They can agree in the conclusion that this cause can only be something itself unmoving and unchanging, simple, without parts or magnitude, and so immaterial and in a modern sense 'non-physical'. They agree that it is without any capacity for change in place, size, quality or substantial nature. But whereas for Aristotle this is sufficient to constitute it as existing in pure actuality, necessarily imperishable or unending in itself, i.e., in such a way that there is no room for it to be caused, and so to guarantee the maintenance of physical motion or the system of physical motions or changes with its constancies, for St. Thomas more is required for this cause to be as such a pure actuality.

For Aristotle the question of the immaterial cause of the constancy of motion in the universe (immune to change, imperishable or necessary by nature) coming into existence or going out of existence cannot arise because the unendingness of time is a logical truth. By contrast, for St. Thomas, for a thing to be just immaterial, immune to change, imperishable and necessary by nature provides no logical guarantee that it had no beginning in time, that it has no cause of existence or that its existence will have no end. For it to exist in a nature making it immune to change or perishing from natural causes and in this sense, so far as the world of natural causes is concerned "necessary," might be the result of the whole order of natural causes itself having a prior cause. In that case, the thing might have a necessity of nature, or immunity both from change and from perishing through natural causes (causes from within the natural world operating according to nature) which arises from being caused to exist (and therefore to exist in this nature), being given existence in this nature by this prior cause, so having a derived necessity. It is only something necessary in itself, in itself such as to have an underived necessity of existence, necessary in such a way that there is no room for it to be caused, which can be capable of causally guaranteeing the maintenance of physical motion in its constancy, or causally guaranteeing the maintenance of a system of physical motions or changes with its constancies.

Therefore, for St. Thomas the first mover, that is the first cause of changes, that is of the actualizations of things that might not have been, must be the first cause not just of the primary movement of some already actual moving thing through which other changing things are changed, but the first cause of the existence of the ongoing system of things which move or change which we experience. For in an ongoing system of things which move or change whose nature contains nothing within itself to cause it to cease to continue, but also nothing guaranteeing unendingness, i.e., nothing which excludes its having come to be or its ceasing to be from some external or underlying cause such as might be the cause of its existence in the nature it has. For this, some cause is needed in the case of which there is no room for it not to exist, and this will be something whose essence is itself as such actual.

(d) WHAT WOULD BE THE EFFECT OF THE INSIGHTS OF MODERN SCIENCE UPON SUCH A MODIFIED ARISTOTELIAN ARGUMENT?

The insights of modern science have no effect, positive or negative, on the force of the Aristotelian argument modified in the light of St. Thomas's objections, except to allow the removal of some complications introduced by Aristotle.

Today we do not share Aristotle's conception that the constancies of the universe of things in various states of motion and change which we experience are the result of the reliable continuance of the outermost sphere in endless uniform circular motion. However, we still consider the universe to be of a such a nature that the things within it continue to behave in reliable constancy, but explain this in a different way, e.g., in terms of the conservation of matter or matter/energy (or, if not matter or matter/energy, then whatever else the "substance" of the world consists of), and the nature of this matter, matter/energy or whatever is such that momentum also is conserved.

Thus, still today, like Aristotle, we conceive the universe as something which is never in *stasis*, but always in motion or change. However, today, unlike Aristotle, we conceive the universe as having a beginning in time at least in the sense that we can identify a "start-time," such that to speak of times before that is to speak unscientifically so that such "times" are as St. Thomas would say "imaginary," the stuff of storytellers' fiction, not of science. Yet at that start-time, the universe was in a state of maximal motion or change, constituted as a thing whose nature is to be in a condition of continuing change, and to be in change as long as it exists. As it changes, at any stage its previous condition and existence in that condition passes away or becomes past, and at that stage the future does not yet exist. Whereas the past is settled and fixed, by contrast, because the future does not yet exist, it is open, remaining to be determined so far as it is determined by the activity of the natures at work in the universe, which do not so far as we have reason to think completely determine it, so that what eventuates or how things "fall out," e.g., which radium atoms decay, and what a particular person chooses, can only be known to us from nature itself after the event from the event itself, that is a posteriori.

In sum, the universe of moving things is a unity in the sense of being a single organized system developing according to one set of principles, although not a unity in the sense of having all its parts coexistent at once.[41] The conception of the unity of the universe offered to us in modern physics does not depend upon some ill-understood ordering between the wills of some large number (fifty-seven is the number Aristotle suggests) of unmoved movers within the framework set by the primary unmoved mover, but leaves room philosophically for only one cause of the universe of matter-energy. Such a causing of the existence of the universe would be an operation of giving being

41 More precisely, if we presume that relativity theory is valid, we should say that, as the universe develops and changes, things become increasingly differentiated within it, and what is absolutely past and what is absolutely future can only be judged relative to the viewpoint of particular participants in particular interactions at a particular juncture. At such a juncture, there will be some things which are absolutely past relative to that juncture, and some things which are absolutely future, but which other things are past is a matter in regard to which different participants in the interaction concerned should form different judgements. Accordingly, it is not even a unity in the sense of having a single continuous line of history, even though it began from one original start-situation or juncture.

to whatever the universe consists of, an operation which would be continued as long as the universe continued to exist. That is, if we call such an operation "creation," creation would not be an action taking place solely at the moment of the universe's coming into existence, but one which would need to be continued in the upholding of the universe in existence.

SECTION 5: ST. THOMAS'S ACTUAL ARGUMENT IN THE FIVE WAYS, AND THE KEY IMPORTANCE OF THE PRINCIPLE THAT WHATEVER IS POTENTIAL IN ANY WAY DEPENDS UPON SOMETHING ACTUAL

(a) A FRESH LOOK AT THE FIRST WAY

(i) THE RELATIONSHIP BETWEEN THE FIRST THREE WAYS

In the *Summa Theologiae* I, q. 2, art. 3, St. Thomas tells us that the existence of God can be proved in five ways. The relation of the first three ways is often misunderstood. The modern reader often misunderstands the relation between the First Way and the Second Way in which it is suggested that proof is to be achieved. This modern reader supposes that the First Way is an argument from our experience that some things are in movement and thinks of movement as being a matter of a things moving from one place to another, and not from an experience of efficient causation. This reader then goes on to envisage the Second Way as a separate argument from our experience of efficient causation. However, this way of understanding the relationship of the two arguments is quite wrong.

In both the *Summa contra Gentiles* and the *Summa Theologiae*, it appears clear that St. Thomas uses the verb *movere* solely as a transitive verb. That is, in its the passive form, *moveri*, St. Thomas always means "to be moved," and never gives the verb the intransitive sense "to move" so common in English, even though that use does occur in Latin of the period as well as earlier. In saying this, I follow James Weishepl and John Wippel.[42] Further, the verb which, for simplicity's

42 John F. Wippel, *The Metaphysical Thought of Thomas Aquinas* (Washington, DC: The Catholic University of America Press, 2000), 414 – 15, and n45, with the chief witnesses cited there, viz. James A. Weisheipl, "The Principle *Omne quod movetur ab alio movetur* in Medieval Physics" in James A. Weisheipl,

sake, we translate as if it referred only to being changed in place in fact refers indifferently to being changed in place, being changed in size and being changed in quality.

Accordingly, the First Way is an argument from our experience that some things are changed either by something else or in some way by themselves, that is it is an argument from our experience of change as having an efficient cause, and a consideration of the implications of this. By contrast, the Second Way involves a more particular consideration of what is involved in an ordered series of efficient causes operating in bringing about an effect.

One can now answer the question why he regards the argument to God as first mover of other things, i.e., causer of change, as the most manifest of the proofs he offers—rather than beginning with an argument to God as first cause in general, first cause of just anything. The answer is plain, namely that he thought it was evident to the senses that things are moved or changed, i.e., caused to move or change, but not evident that all things have a beginning.

And, whereas Aristotle's question was as to what could guarantee the everlasting occurrence of movement, St. Thomas's is asking us to take any individual instance of a thing being changed and to consider the causes of that instance of something being changed. Had the individual instance been the universe itself, he would have been exploring the causes of the universe not being in *stasis* but in constant movement, but not the cause of the universe's existing at all. But in the First Way, that is not what he is asking about.

In the Third Way, St. Thomas does turn to consider the universe as a whole, arguing that nothing can be the guarantee of the continuance of the universe as a system of things in motion which is not a cause of existence as such, and not just of motion or change, and that such a cause must have necessity of existence rooted in itself, not as something derived from its being given a imperishable nature by something else.

Nature and Motion in the Middle Ages, ed. William E. Carroll (Washington, DC: The Catholic University of America Press, 1985), 74–97; Joseph Owens, *St. Thomas Aquinas on the Existence of God*, ed. J. Catan (Albany: SUNY Press,1980). In *Summa Contra Gentiles*, c. 13, third para., what is evident to the senses being assumed to be not just the Sun's moving, but its being moved, something assumed by all the ancients to involve some deity as a mover.

However, in his consideration of the impossibility of an infinite series of causes of the relevant kind, he adds nothing in considering the Second Way which was already implicit when he considered the First, and his presumption that an infinite regress in causes is impossible in the Third Way derives from what he has already said about such infinite regresses earlier.

(ii) THE KEY ROLE OF "INTUITIVE INDUCTION" IN ST. THOMAS AND ITS IMPORTANCE IN ANY SCIENCE

The First Way is therefore not so much an argument from our experience that things move as an argument from our experience that things are moved, that is of one thing being moved or changed either by something else or by itself, as St. Thomas thought that an animal might be moved by one part of itself, viz., its soul. Now, when a thing is moved, it has to pass from a condition of a certain kind to another condition of the same kind, that is, in Aristotle's conception from one quality, size, or place to another. Further, supposing the second condition is that of being actually of the quality, size or place A, then it has to pass from being potentially A, to being actually A, but nothing can cause such a development unless it is in actual existence. And, by considering the situation with the phenomenon of movement, St. Thomas thinks that we can see that it must be true as a general principle that only something in actual existence can cause such a shift from being only potentially but not actually in a condition to being actually in this condition. He thinks that we can make this generalization by means of what William Kneale called "intuitive induction."[43]

What Kneale called "intuitive induction" is exceedingly important in human thinking. For instance, we think of the different colors as contraries, e.g., so that if something is red, it cannot be blue at the same time. We commonly consider that, presented with examples of a thing that are red along with something else which is blue, we can "see" that nothing could be both red and blue, in this case advancing from a single case to a universal generalization. Of course, if we

43 William Kneale, *Probability and Induction* (Oxford: Oxford University Press, 1949), 30–37.

consider the matter carefully, we realize that such a generalization can only apply to things seen in normal light, and looking at their services, and we realize that we could perfectly easily have a thin flat object which was colored red on one side and blue on the other—and we must in any case be speaking about the same point or local area of a service so as to exclude the problem of things which are striped with red and blue stripes, as well as to exclude supposing that our generalization is intended to apply to things which are only doubtfully red or blue, because close to the boundary between the maroon and the purple.

Or again, presented with two red marbles and then a further two red marbles, we can not only count and observe that we now have four red marbles but by considering that nothing here upon the redness or upon its having been marbles which were presented to our view, but only upon the things presented being discrete from one an another, we naturally move in our thinking to saying that "we can see that two discrete things taken together with a distinct further two discrete things will always constitute four discrete things"—something informally expressed by saying that two and two are four. Of course, given some decorations and the apparatus of predicate logic with identity we might consider that we could prove this, and similarly given suitable axioms and definitions within set theory, we might offer a proof of a different kind. But even from just a single experience, we can legitimately pass by "intuitive induction" to the general statement.

It is true that in support of conclusions said to be reached by "induction," Aristotle, and also St. Thomas, often offer a list of types of case. So it is in this case. In the *Summa Contra Gentiles*, I, c.13, at one point St. Thomas refers to Aristotle as proving that everything that is moved is moved by another. He then himself reviews causes of being moved, considering first things which are moved by accident and/or by violence, then things such as animals which are moved by a part of themselves, then things such as heavy and light bodies which are said to be moved by nature, and which are actually moved sometimes secondarily by the cause which removes obstacles to natural movement and always underlyingly by what generates them or makes them heavy or light and such like. But neither he nor Aristotle ever offer a demonstration that such an enumeration of cases is complete.

Rather, always, the review of cases serves the function of dealing with objections to the general proposition proposed,[44] not of removing the "intuitive" element from the judgement under consideration.

The full development of a science has always depended upon two things, the development and clarification of theoretical ideas, and the use of observation and experiment to test hypotheses. The modern tradition from Francis Bacon, Hume and their successors such as Popper in the analytic tradition has emphasized only the second, which has for the most part given biology (so far as it depends on the idea of the "survival of the fittest"), psychology and sociology their title to be counted as sciences in the new modern sense of the word.

However, this emphasis ignores the importance of the development of theoretical ideas, in geometry and optics, in the combination of Eudoxus's account of proportions[45] with Euclid's distinction between a line and a point as a cut in a line gives rise to the presumption that any such cut in something with continuous measure will itself identify a measure or quantity, the presumption which underlies the belief in the existence of limits to converging series relied upon in the differential and integral calculus from the time of Newton and Leibniz to today, the differentiation of the concepts of mass, momentum and energy in Newton, and the development of the concepts underlying electromagnetic theory of Faraday and Clerk-Maxwell, the key advances in the conceptual development of functional anatomy, the development of genetic ideas in connection with biology, the progressive development which began with the way the quantum theory made the periodic table intelligible, and so forth. Aristotle's more open conception of induction left far more room for understanding this first kind of development, in which fundamental concepts (with the generalizations associated with them) arise by a reflection upon things presented in experience, which

44 This is often Aristotle's procedure, of considering the phenomena, the *empeiria*, or *endoxa* (common opinions or seemings), and, when some of these do not cohere with the general picture which the rest suggest, offering an explanation of the temptation to reach a mistaken judgement.

45 The importance of Eudoxus is made plain in William Kneale and Martha Kneale, *The Development of Logic* (Oxford: Oxford University Press, 1962), 391, 403, 662, cf. p. 379 on the relation between Eudoxus (408 – 355 BC) and the later Euclid (325 – 265 BC).

precedes any far-reaching and useful application of the Popper's hypothetico-deductive method. For both Aristotle and St. Thomas, "induction" (*epagoge*) was a very wide and informal notion whose place was in the explanation of how we get knowledge (including how we achieve the abstraction of concepts from a spread of its instances), rather than in giving account of our warrant for belief or even for claiming knowledge.[46] This gave them a place much closer to that of how the advance of real knowledge whether in philosophy or science actually proceeds than that of those who regard epistemology as primary and allow their thought to be shaped by the epistemology of Descartes and the empiricism of Locke and Hume.

In effect, St. Thomas was exploring a set of theoretical ideas which we likewise gain by reflecting on experience but lying at a deeper level than those I have just instanced. It was his task to give greater precision and development to the ideas of Aristotle, in exploring these underlying concepts: first, of substance as the primary subject of concrete modes of speech, and the various types of predicate ancillary to it; second, of causation and agency, potentiality and actuality, differentiating states and 'acts,' and recognizing the relations between causal order and order in the succession of acts; and, third, within the context of the world of movement through space the differentiation amongst 'acts' between those thought of as happening at a time ("acts" or, in Vendler, "achievements") those persisting over a time, both those with no necessary terminus (in Vendler, "activities") and those with an inbuilt terminus ("processes," or, in Ryle, "tasks," in Kenny, "performances" and in Vendler, "accomplishments").

With the first three of the Five Ways, it is quite explicit that we have a relation of being a per se efficient cause of something which

46 Cf. John Haldane, "Insight, Inference, and Intellection," *Proceedings of the American Catholic Philosophical Association* 73 (1999): 31 – 43, especially pp. 31, 36 – 43; with Martha Nussbaum, "Saving Aristotle's Appearances," *Language and Logos: Studies in Ancient Greek Philosophy Presented to G. E. L. Owen*, ed. Malcolm Schofield and Martha Craven Nussbaum (Cambridge, UK: Cambridge University Press, 1982), 262 – 94; and G. E. L. Owen, "*Tithenai ta phainomena*," *Aristote et les Problemes de Methode*, ed. S. Mansion (Louvain: Editions Nauwelaerts, 1961), reprinted in G. E. L. Owen, *Logic, Science, and Dialectic: Collected Papers*, ed. Martha Nussbaum (Ithaca, NY: Cornell, 1987), 83 – 103.

is such that in regard to subsistent things, whenever one of them is a per se efficient cause of something, the two things are always distinct, and such that any series of such causes related to each other successively in this way must always have a first member, α, which is of such a kind that it is impossible that anything be a per se cause of this thing, α.

Intuitive induction is of key importance in establishing two general principles:

> (1) What the empirically given cases from which he begins immediately show him that anything which is being changed can only be changed so as to be actually at the goal of its change by something actually at that goal in the relevant respect. But his later argument shows that he considers this as exhibiting the more general principle that whatever is in potentiality in any way depends upon the causal action of something actual to be brought into actuality. In considering the simplicity of God, he thinks of created things as not as such, or as we might say in their own right, having existence or being (*esse*), so that their *esse* is something they receive. Thus, by an extension of Aristotle's use of analogy in thinking about potentiality, the relation of their *esse* as their *actus essendi* to their *essentia*, nature or *quidditas* (what they are) is comparable to the actualization of a potentiality.
>
> With the empirically given cases he has in mind, he thinks of this being changed by the action of something actual in terms of the changing thing receiving something from something else, e.g., hotness from something else which is hot in a greater degree, or knowledge of geometry from someone who knows more geometry, a way of thinking which also opens the way to his Fourth Way, the argument whose successful application to the case of God depends on the idea that the first cause of anything's having a positive property not dependent on matter must causally depend on something which has this property in the highest degree.
>
> (2) Any series of causes terminating in an effect P which are related to each other in such a way that each is the per se efficient cause of its successor in the series must always have a first member, , which is of such a kind that it is impossible that anything be a per se cause of this thing, α.

(iii) THE SHAPE OF THE FIRST WAY AND THE TREATMENT OF INFINITE REGRESSES IN CAUSATION

The text of St. Thomas in presenting his Five Ways is striking for its obviously summary character, clearly intended to identify certain arguments, rather than to give a tight statement of any of them.

In connection with the First Way, he simply tells us that the first and most manifest way of proving the existence of God is from motion, announcing to us that it is certain and plainly apprehended by the senses that some things change. Yet whatever is changed is changed by something else.

Next, he proceeds to prove this first proposition. What is changing is in potentiality towards that which it is changing, and not yet at that goal. It can only be changed so as to be actually at the goal of its change by something actually at that goal in the relevant respect. It cannot be potentially at its goal and at the same time actually there, and therefore it cannot change itself, but can only be changed by something else.

Next, he proceeds to exclude an infinite regress, noting that what changes something else must be either itself being changed or unchanging. If it is itself being changed it must be being changed by something else, and so forth. However, there is no proceeding to infinity because there would be no first unchanging changer, and no subsequent changes, because the intermediate causes of change are only brought into action by the first unchanging changer setting the process going, as when a man uses a stick to move a stone, for if the hand does not move the stick, the stick will not move anything else. Hence one is bound to arrive at some first changer which is not changed by anything else.

In response to the objection that an infinite series is perfectly possible, he makes it perfectly clear that a series without beginning or end of human fathers is quite possible (*Summa Theologiae*, I, q. 46, art. 2 ad 7). Presumably, this is because, if a father begets a son, the action of the father in begetting the son is quite independent of whether the son has heirs, and the action of the son in begetting a grandson to his father involves no participation on the part of the father at all, so that the second depends on the first only in this, that if the first action had not taken place the son would not have existed. He describes this as a case of proceeding to infinity accidentally, it being accidental at each stage whether the later action follows, this being because the son has the capacity to generate in virtue of being a man, not in virtue of being a son, and therefore generates as man, not as son. But at the beginning of his discussion of this objection, he states that it is an infinite series of efficient causes that are per se required for a certain effect which is impossible. Therefore, in order to understand what it means to be the first cause within a series of causes in the relevant sense, we need to discover what exactly St. Thomas means by being per se required for an effect.

In regard to this, if we look for examples of first movers or changers in his other works, we meet with various examples. For instance, when he says that "It is obvious to sense that something is moved (*aliquid moveri*), for instance the sun" (*Summa Contra Gentiles*, I, c. 13 third para.), he is not taking it that what is obvious to sense is that the sun is in motion—or, as we say in English, that the sun is moving or is in motion, using the verb "move" as here an intransitive verb—but that what is obvious to sense is that the sun is moved by something (whether moved by itself or by something else). Here, he is going to argue that such a case has to be one of being moved by something else, and in fact whatever immediately moves the sun, the first cause of its moving of the sun he will prove to be God, it being through the sun that God governs the lesser moving stars in their orbits and in the respective kinds of influence they have on human affairs (*Commentary on the Metaphysics*, Book Lambda, *Lectio* 9, n. 2560) as well as in bringing about generation amongst living things in general including man. In other places he presents us with the examples of the axe being moved by the craftsman as an instrument to cut wood (*QD de Potentia*, q. 3, art. 7), of many different hammers being used by craftsmen in order to accomplish their respective tasks, and of many different men, perhaps an infinite number successively, being used by God as instruments to generate their respective sons (*Summa Theologiae*, I, q. 46, art.2 ad 7), and in this process man's generation of another man also depends on the sun (*QD de Potentia*, q. 3, art. 7, sed contra 3, and many other places). If we consider the most extended of the lines of causation considered by St. Thomas, it is that by which using the sun's proper action on the planets and on living things, the day of the month on which a child might be born might be caused by God through the sun's action on the moon, and in the conception of St. Thomas and his predecessors, the action of the sun on the other planets so as to influence, each in a different way, the affairs of men would be instantaneous, and the whole action of God through secondary causes simultaneous. It will be noticed that, in his conception and according to his arguments, the sun and planets are in no way involved in causing existence as such, but only in influencing movement.

Duns Scotus speaks of causes ordered essentially and per se, and expresses matters in this way in his final work, *De Primo Principio*, 3.11:

> The first difference is that in essentially ordered causes, the second depends upon the first *per se* in the act of causing. In accidentally ordered causes this is not the case, though the second may depend upon the first for its existence or in some other way.
>
> The second difference is that in essentially ordered causes the causality is of another *ratio* (logical character) and order, inasmuch as the superior [i.e., causally prior] is the more perfect, which is not the case with accidentally ordered causes. This second difference is a consequence of the first, since no cause in the exercise of its causality is essentially dependent upon a cause of the same *ratio* as itself, for in the causation of another one cause of a given *ratio* suffices.
>
> A third difference follows, namely, that all the causes ordered *per se* are required necessarily at once (*simul*) for the causing: for otherwise some causality *per se* would be wanting to the effect. In accidentally ordered causes this simultaneity is not required.[47]

In this passage, Duns Scotus seems to be making explicit exactly the presumptions which St. Thomas is making, but not stating, in his presentation of his First Way.[48]

47 John Duns Scotus. *A Treatise on God as First Principle*, trans. and ed. Allen B. Wolter (Chicago: Franciscan Herald Press, Forum Books, 1966), 46.

48 As I remarked in an earlier paper: "the First Way was intended to prove the impossibility of a per se series of movers, i.e., so that all the movers are of the same thing (compare *Summa Contra Gentiles* I, chap.13, §.14, and note how *Summa Contra Gentiles* I, chap.13, §§.13, 15–19 confirm that he understood the First and Second Ways in parallel ways, while §§. 21 ff. deal with a difficulty raised by Aristotle's *Physics*, VII)."

(iv) ST. THOMAS'S ARGUMENT THAT GOD MUST BE THE FIRST CAUSE OF ANY INDIVIDUAL MOVEMENT: THE ACTION OF GOD AS FIRST CAUSE AS A COROLLARY OF A REALISTIC VIEW OF SECONDARY CAUSATION

I said that St. Thomas is considering the causal roots of any individual change. From this, it is clear that some objections lose their apparent force.

Thus, for the purposes of St. Thomas's argument, some line needs to be drawn between cases of being changed which are the result of the action of another substance and cases of being changed which are to be ascribed to "nature" or described as "natural." For instance, when one billiard ball moves because hit by another, and then moves again because hit again, or when a thing becomes first one bit hotter because of confrontation with one hot thing, and then hotter still because of another encounter, this is a succession of things being changed or moved by an accidental series of causes, in reality a succession of cases of being moved by violence. Or again, in considering projectile movement, Aristotle and St. Thomas look to the air pushed along behind to explain the continued being pushed, whereas Newton considers its continued movement with constant velocity in the same way as Aristotle and St. Thomas view the natural movement of the heavy downwards and the light upwards, since for Newton the effect of the air is as it were an exercise of continuous violence slowing the projectile down. The difference is not fundamental but a matter of how different changes of place are to be classified, as to which are natural, and which require explanation in terms of the action of a cause of the same order, nature, or *ratio* as the thing being moved or not moved.

In reflecting on the questions arising here, we must avoid being sidetracked by the strangeness of the way in which Aristotle conceives the natural movement of the heavy downwards and the light upwards, if indeed in his at points highly compressed explanations he did hold the view St. Thomas ascribes to him in *Physics*, Book VIII, 4 and 7. For St. Thomas understands Aristotle to hold that when the heavy moves naturally downwards, what makes it move is what made it to be heavy at an earlier stage (*Lectio* 8, 1034 and 1035), which will be whatever made its matter denser at that stage which will depend on local motion (*Lectio* 14, 1089); this will presumably involve the local motion of the continuous subparts of the matter concerned, but however understood it is all part of Aristotle's attempt to represent every kind of natural change as depending at root on local motion. However, there is no evidence as to whether or not this was St. Thomas's own view, and as can be seen from the passage in *QD de Potentia* which I will now examine, his argument in the First Way in no way depends on this peculiar way of thinking of the natural movement of the light and the heavy.

I say this because of the general way in which St. Thomas thought about movement, which can be best appreciated by considering *de Potentia*, q. 3, art. 7 when St. Thomas is enquiring in what way God works in the operations of nature, without this working being a creating or an additional giving of being.

He begins by mentioning that a thing can be the cause of another's action as giving them their powers to act, and how in particular God gives natural things the forces whereby they are able to act, not just as generating them but as upholding them in existence, and secondarily and derivatively as a cause in the way that a remedy which preserves sight may be said to be cause of a man seeing.

However, he then goes on to say, more importantly for my discussion, thirdly, that nothing moves or acts of itself (except an unmoved mover) but needs to be moved to action, not just by preserving its active power, but by applying the thing's active power to the action as a man applies the sharpness of the knife to cutting by moving it to cut. Here St. Thomas continues:

> since the lower nature in acting does not act except through being moved because these lower bodies are both subject to and cause alteration, whereas the heavenly body causes alteration without being subject to alteration, and yet still does not cause movement unless it be itself moved, so we must eventually trace its movement back to God and so conclude as a consequence which follows necessarily that God causes the action of every natural thing by moving and applying its power to action."[49]

49 Thomas Aquinas, *Questions on the Power of God*, trans. English Dominican Fathers (Westminster, MD: The Newman Press, 1952, reprint of 1932), q. 3, a. 7.

He then seeks to reinforce this way of viewing things by remarking that:

> the second [or non-divine] cause by its own power cannot have any influence on the effect of the first cause although it is the instrument of the first cause in regard to that effect—because an instrument is in a way the cause of the principal cause's effect, not in virtue of its own form or power, but insofar as it shares somewhat in the power of the principal cause through being moved by it. It is thus that the axe is the cause of the craftsman's handiwork, not by its own form or power, but by the power of the craftsman who moves it so that it shares in his power. Because of this we can say fourthly that one thing causes the action of another in the way a principal agent causes the action of its instruments.[50]

He continues his argument in such a way as to indicate that the first cause must play a role in the generation of individuals, and more generally in every individual case of making things change or move. The same conception is succinctly presented in *Summa Theologiae*, I, q. 103, art. 6, and q. 105, art. 5.

Whereas in the causing of being, there can be no use of instruments because the act is beyond the power of natural things (independently of whether it is a matter of giving existence to things without their having any material or natural efficient cause, or of continuing the same action in preserving things in being), by contrast, in the case of the causation of change or movement, the situation is quite different. For, in creating temporal things with natures involving the possession of natural powers, God creates the means whereby he can accomplish things by the instrumentality of these natural things. Further, sometimes God accomplishes something by the instrumentality of one natural thing, while in other cases he does this through using an ordered series of such things to accomplish the effect. The examples he gives of this latter appear most clearly when he is thinking of how God influences human beings by the ministry of angels, or the behavior of material things, plants, animals, human beings, and societies sometimes through the voluntary actions of human beings and sometimes through the actions of subhuman things or systems of things.

50 Aquinas, *Questions on the Power of God*, q. 3, a. 7.

In any of these cases which he regards as ordinary, it is not as if God could accomplish things in the ordinary non-miraculous way except by the creaturely thing performing the action proper to it. On the contrary, "what God does in the natural thing to make it operate actually is a mere *intentio*, having a sort of incomplete *esse*, as colors are in the air or the force of the craftsman is in his instrument" (*Q.D. De Potentia*, q. 3, art. 7, reply to obj. 7)—colors are only fully actual in being seen as we look towards what gives light of that color, and for this they have to be in the intervening medium in some way but not in such a way that the medium is colored, and likewise for the instrument to exercise force on what it is applied to, it has to have force in it in some way, but not in such a way as to exercise force on its own. That is, he repudiates any conception of what God does in such cases as a distinct "physical premotion" in the way suggested by Banez in the sixteenth century along with his later Dominican following.

Moreover, the action is so little God's own action that its occurring by God's using the creature as his instrument does not mean that, if, in the order of created causes, it occurs contingently, either because it occurs by chance inasmuch as the physical thing leaves it undetermined, or because it occurs by through the operation of reason and will. Thus, he says "the will is said to have dominion over its own act, not to the exclusion of the first cause, but inasmuch as the first cause does not act in the will so as to determine it of necessity to one thing in the way the first cause determines nature; hence, the determination of the act remains in the power of the reason and will" (*De Potentia*, q. 3, art. 7, reply to obj. 13). Or, as he states it in *Summa Theologiae*, I-II., q. 10, art. 4, "As Dionysius says (*Div. Nom.* iv), it belongs to divine providence, not to destroy but to preserve the nature of things. Hence it moves all things in accordance with their conditions so that from necessary causes through the divine motion, effects follow of necessity, whereas, from contingent causes, effects follow contingently." And he explains the whole matter more fully in his *Commentary on Aristotle's On Interpretation, Lectio* 14, §§ 16—24,[51] making it clear how neither the involvement of God's knowledge nor his will makes contingent effects necessary.[52] The situation is as Brian

51 *Commentary on Aristotle's On Interpretation*, trans. Jean T. Oesterle (Milwaukee: Marquette University Press, 1962).

52 Aquinas views God's act of will in respect of creation as taking place at

Davies has made clear that, where secondary causes operate according to nature, they genuinely act according to their own powers which they have according to their nature, and God's primary causality modifies nothing in this, so that his involvement does not show itself empirically in any way at all—this is part of what is meant by St. Thomas when he speaks of God as governing all things *suaviter*.[53]

---

the time of what he wills, so that he grants a healing at the time of the healing, and there is point in praying for him to act before the opportunity of his healing arises but not after it is past. However, his knowledge of his act of will is not temporal but in his eternity.

53 In a letter of 12th June 2008, Brian Davies made these remarks to me, in the setting of a reference to a draft of a paper 'The Action of God' for a Festschrift for Anthony Kenny:

> Aquinas wants to say that God acts in every operation. He has to say that given his account of God as the source of the '*esse*' of things. For, obviously, a created acting thing is a 'created' acting thing, something of which the continuing to be and to change derive from God as making things to be in all their different ways of being. The question is whether this means that created causes are not genuine causes. Aquinas thinks they are genuine causes since we can provide well-documented causal stories when it comes to a lot of what goes on in the universe—stories which we can tell without any reference to God. As I understand him, God comes into the picture for Aquinas as the cause that accounts for the being of things, a cause that does not interfere with their way of being but, precisely, makes it to be.
>
> Someone may say that he has to be {an occasionalist} if he thinks that when acid burns my skin God is creatively causing the acid to burn my skin. But not so. {I think Davies reckons that God causes the acid to burn my skin, but not creatively.} If we have acid doing its stuff, then we have acid doing its stuff. But it is acid doing its stuff because that and what it is derive from God as the source of '*esse*,' a source which is not itself part of the created order. God makes the so acting cause to be [and I think Davies reckons that this includes causing it to be with the nature and powers implied by that nature and thereby to act according to this nature in virtue of these powers].
>
> ... I sometimes paraphrase Aquinas for students by telling them that, according to him, God does not make any difference to anything. That's a bit quick, but it goes with Aquinas's insistence that for God to cause something to be is not for God to modify it somehow. If that is so, then I do not see why God's causality should be thought of as

That St. Thomas should be right in the theological view he takes here is a consequence of the immediacy of the presence of God to every created thing in every aspect of its being as the one who alone gives being, and so is present as cause of being. We must avoid a deistic picture of the relation between God and the natural things whereby one event takes place in God's eternity and another event takes place in the world, the first causing the second, the deist treating God as external to the world—whereas it is in the character of the created things to be created, that is to have their existence only by God's action immediate to them, so that God (in his whole being, possessing his whole life in one act) is within them as the first spring or first *principium* of their very being and activity. This is parallel to the way in which we must avoid a dualistic picture of the relation between the human soul and the human body whereby in intentional action, certain events takes place in the soul, and a separate group of events take place in the world, the first set causing the second, the dualist treating the body as a subsistent thing independent of the soul, whereas, although the intellectual soul may survive the perishing of the body, the human body depends for its nature and full range of behavior upon the soul. (This does not mean that God is, as it were, the soul of the creature or the universe. The intellectual soul does not come into existence until it comes into existence with the body as one rational animal in the first stages of its development, and the coming into existence of any rational animal, intellectual soul included, depends on activities of the parent and many other contingencies, and the natural powers which differentiate it, the intellect with the will, have no natural exercise without the body, whereas God has no

---

a rival to the causality of any creature or any created nature. There would be rivalry were God part of the created order acting on things so as to modify them.

In going forward with this paper, I owe much to Brian Davies's encouragement, and also to his drawing my attention to the commentary by St. Thomas on Aristotle's *On Interpretation* (*'Peri Hermeneias'*) Book 1, where *Lectio* 14 comments on Aristotle's Chapter 9 (18b26 – 19a22).

[Editor's Note, see Brian Davies, "The Action of God," in *Mind, Method, and Morality: Essays in Honour of Anthony Kenny*, ed. John Cottingham and Peter Hacker (Oxford: Oxford University Press, 2010).]

beginning of existence and is in no way dependent on creation or any creature for his existence and freedom to exercise his powers.)

Let me explain this comparison at greater length.

In human bodily movement, what happens by intention and choice is not discrete from its being intended and chosen, and what matters for its being intentional is that the choice be according to the intention, not that the intention should have preexisted the choice (in some cases, people change their minds at the last moment, in each of these cases as it were choosing in the act itself). That is, it is not a matter of one subsistent thing (the intellectual soul) performing acts of intellect and will, and a separate subsistent thing (the material body of the person) executing a bodily movement with all the bodily changes involved subservient to this happening. For the material body of the person is not in St. Thomas's understanding a subsistent thing at all and does not itself execute any bodily movement. Rather than there being two actions, there is one action, viz., the human person's executing a bodily movement intentionally.

The time of the action of the person is the time of the bodily movement which he or she intends.[54] Likewise the time of God's action is the time of the effect in creation. Thus, if a miracle takes place, and God heals a man in a way which is beyond the powers of natural things, being brought about by God intentionally not using the exercise of powers of natural things as his means or instrument, God's intentional act of healing is at the same point of historical time as the event of the man's being healed, and it is not as if God's action took place only at a "time" specified as eternity. Here, God, as cause of the being of things at every time in history in his eternity (the whole of him present wherever and whenever he is present), at the particular time concerned makes the course of history different

54 This holds even though there may be detectible signs in the brain of the movement of the person towards action even before the person is conscious of having made up his mind. It is only the Cartesian presumption that everything that belongs to the mind or will is of which we are immediately fully conscious which makes it seem surprising that the advance from indecision as to which kind of soup one is going to buy towards decision to pick buy oxtail rather than mulligatawny should be instantaneous, any more than deeper movements towards choice (such as religious conversion or to propose marriage) are altogether conscious, let alone instantaneous, which makes this seem strange.

from what consideration of natural causes would lead one to expect by making a thing happen otherwise than by the instrumentality of natural things. In other cases, where miracles are not involved, he makes things happen by the instrumentality of natural things, but his causal action is still not as a different time.

The puzzle to us is as to how St. Thomas can regard cases of one creature's acting on another naturally as cases in which he is using creatures as instruments, and how he can envisage this way of viewing matters, not just as a matter of an insight given by revealed theology, but as one which is particularly obviously demonstrable philosophically. How do we make a connection between St. Thomas's way of thinking here and our thinking today?

Addressing the problem directly, if one billiard ball makes another move, it seems evident to us that what makes the first billiard ball makes the second move is either the fact that the first billiard ball was already in movement carried by the momentum (i.e., naturally) towards the second billiard ball or that something has directly shoved the first billiard ball practically already in contact with a second billiard ball, and in either case do not see the need for a further cause to be operative in the transaction. Or are we being simply blind? Here we should note what Duns Scotus says, namely that the prior (*superior*) cause in causes ordered per se exercises a causality of another *ratio* (logical character) and order from the causality exercised at the lower level, e.g., of a different logical character and order from the causality exercised by one billiard ball upon another (this latter being the kind of causality we find exercised in accidentally related series of causes).

Let us ask: if one billiard ball A hits another billiard ball B which is not fixed in place square on and they are situated on a flat horizontal frictionless surface, what determines what happens? Newton's answer was that momentum would be conserved so that the second billiard ball would have to move in such a way that $m_A v_{A1} = m_A v_{A2} + m_B v_{B2}$, where m_A and m_B are the masses of the respective billiard balls, and v_{A1} and v_{A2} are the velocities of A before and after impact and v_{B2} the velocity of B after impact, and energy was conserved. A would slow down and both billiard balls would continue in the direction that A was originally moving. Intuitively, the force, impetus or active power of A made B move, and the inertial reactive force of B would be what made A slow down. (I cannot use the word "force" in the Newtonian sense, as if the notion of a push offered a clear distinction between force and impetus. If the billiard balls had been perfectly hard and inelastic, an infinite deceleration of A and infinite acceleration of B would be involved, and the whole interaction inconceivable in Newtonian terms, and so some elasticity would have to be assumed, and a calculation of forces in the Newtonian sense would be problematic.)

The laws of conservation of momentum and of energy describe what would happen, not what made it happen. The question would seem to arise: what is the cause of these laws applying? The Newtonian answer would seem to be that it is in the nature of matter that momentum and energy should be conserved.

However, this does not answer the question of how one should give a realistic account of, e.g., the particular interaction which I considered in which certainly one thing acted upon another. Could one say that in upholding matter[55] with its nature in existence, God consequentially makes A exercise its active power in moving B, and makes B exercise its active power in slowing A down? In that case, this kind of underlying action by God will be a corollary of a realist view of physical things, i.e., the view that it is because things have the natures they have, the powers to act and susceptibilities to be acted upon, that they behave in the ways that they do, both when they interact with other things and when they are continuing without being interfered with by other things (as a result behaving in conformity to the conservation laws in the way that we observe). This realist view is the one to be contrasted with opposite views, e.g., ones which make the appearance that things behave in conformity to law a matter of the conceptual construction we put upon our experiences, or ones which make this apparent conformity to law a matter of the conventions we find it convenient to enforce in describing these experiences, or on of how our mind feels itself compelled to think about them, if this apparent conformity is not a matter of mere coincidence.

In sum, it is in this way that by causing things to move and change as they do that God "governs all things gently" (*suaviter*, that is in accord with their natures), so that it is by his will that, if effects happen by the action of causes which act by natural necessity in the way

55 At low velocities we can say "upholding matter," instead of, more accurately, "upholding matter/energy."

they do, the effects are caused necessarily (while, if effects happen by causes which act by the free exercise of reason and will, or which leave things open to chance or undetermined, then they are caused contingently).

Each movement or change, then, must have a first cause which has itself, by arguments we have already met with from Aristotle and of which St. Thomas's students would have been entirely aware, no capacity or susceptibility to be changed in itself in any respect at all by anything else whatsoever.

(v) THE DEPENDENCE OF HIS ARGUMENT ON COMPARING THE RELATION OF *ESSE* TO *ESSENTIA* TO THE RELATION OF POTENCY TO ACT

The question then arises as to how we can know that every movement has the same first cause. Unless this is shown, it is not evident that this first cause is "what all men understand to be God."

Now, if St. Thomas at this stage meant "a God," his argument here in the *Summa theologiae*, q. 2, would be heavily dependent upon his later argument in q. 11 where he establishes that there is only one God. However, the evidence provided by the very next question, q. 3, on God's simplicity makes it plain that in fact he is relying upon a deeper understanding of the principle that whatever is in potentiality in any way upon the causal action of something actual to be brought into actuality.

This begins to appear first in q. 3, art. 1, when he offers three arguments that God is not a bodily being ("a body"). Firstly, as first mover, God must be himself unmoved (which he understands as meaning "not of a nature to be capable of being moved"). Secondly, God cannot be bodily,

> because the first being must of necessity be in *actus*, and in no way in potentiality. For, although in any single thing that passes from being in *potentia* to being in *actus*, the *potentia* is prior to the *actus*; nevertheless, speaking absolutely (*simpliciter*), *actus* is prior to *potentia*; for whatever is in *potentia* can be brought out into *actus* only by some being in *actus*.[56]

56 Thomas Aquinas, *ST* I.3.1 (mod. trans. English Dominican Fathers). He

However, the issue only becomes fully explicit in q. 3, art. 4, in his second argument that in God there is no composition of the kind which is out of *essentia* and *esse*:

> because *esse* is the *actualitas* of every form or nature: for goodness or humanity are not signified as in *actus* unless we signify its *esse* [i.e., signify that they exist]. Therefore it must be that *esse* itself must be compared to an *essentia* which is *aliud* (something other) from itself as *actus* is compared to *potentia*. Therefore, since in God nothing exists potentially (*potentiale*), as shown above (q. 3, art. 1), it follows that in him *essentia* is not *aliud* from his *esse*.[57]

(b) ST. THOMAS'S CONSIDERATION OF THE OTHER FOUR WAYS AS ADDING VERY LITTLE TO OUR UNDERSTANDING OF WHY HE VIEWED THINGS AS NEEDING A CAUSE

In the Second Way, the intended argument is aimed solely to the impossibility of a per se series of causes, as when we can say that A causes B, that A causes C and that A causes D, and can also say that B causes C and that B causes D, as well as C causes D—his favorite example is of a man using his hand to move his staff in such a way as to cause a stone (in this case, the first cause is the man). Hence, when he says we experience an "order of efficient causes" and refers to "all efficient causes following in order," he is referring to per se series in which in this way all the causes are of the same thing (this is made plain by the parallel passage in Aquinas, *Summa Contra Gentiles* I, chap.13, §.33).

If we limit ourselves to considering secondary causes, it will always be some creature, e.g., the man who used his hand to move his staff in such a way as to cause a stone to move. But the implication of the First Way is that the causal action of each secondary cause in such series depends upon God's acting as the first per se cause within any such secondary causal action.

---

then has a third argument depending on the conclusion of the Fourth Way. This is an argument from some bodily beings being animate, and from not containing in themselves the general principle of animation, which as prior to their being animate must be higher than any body. But this argument is not my present concern.

57 Thomas Aquinas, *ST* I.3.1. [Editor's Note: This appears to be Braine's own rough translation.]

The most obvious difficulty here is that arising from in cases where human beings exercise free will.[58] In upholding the order of secondary causes, rather than intervening with a miracle, God causes that the will of the human being will have such effect as nature allows: in the normal case when the human being is not paralyzed, if the human being wills to stab another person, with a view to murder him, then if he aims at the right object and is not frustrated by the other person's movement, he will accomplish his act of stabbing the other person; if the man wills to stab another person, with a view to killing a tyrant as when Ehud killed Eglon, King of Moab (Judges 4), he will again accomplish this act. If the common interpretation is right, the first will be a case of a human action which God permits, and the second might be the same. But, in the second case, if God not only raised Ehud up to deliver Israel from Eglon, but also guided him in his choice of means, then it will be an act commanded (cf. *Summa Theologiae* I, q. 12). In this case of things done in obedience to a command, St. Thomas speaks of the person commanding them to be done as their cause, as when he explains in *Summa Theologiae* I-II., q. 79, art. 1 (showing that God is not the cause of evil), in the reply to objection 3:

> The effect which proceeds from the middle cause, according as it is subordinate to the first cause, is reduced to that first cause; but if it proceed from the middle cause, according as it goes outside the order of the first cause, it is not reduced to that first cause: thus if a servant do anything contrary to his master's orders, it is not ascribed to the master as though he were the cause thereof. In like manner sin, which the free-will commits against the commandment of God, is not attributed to God as being its cause.[59]

Although, in this passage St. Thomas is not concerned with causes in the order of nature, but with the cause in the sense of the person responsible, the primary *responsable*, the one primarily due for praise

58 There is a worthwhile discussion of this in Francisco Suárez, *Metaphysical Disputations 20–22*, Disputation 22, Section 4, §§. 10–39, pp. 222–37.

59 Thomas Aquinas, *ST* I–II.79.1 ad. 3, trans. English Dominican Fathers.

or blame for the effect concerned, the case does illustrate his believing that the relation of being a per se cause is a transitive relation.

The argument of the Second Way therefore adds nothing to the first, except that from the start it would allow for the consideration of causing something to come to be from nothing, a case in which as we have already seen he has additional powerful arguments to the effect that there could not be any intermediates at all, but still the Second Way does establish that even if there could be intermediates, there would still have to be a first cause "to which everyone gives a name God."

This argument, then, serves only to make explicit generalization from the case of causing the occurrence of change or movement to any case of causation whatsoever, even the causation of being (as distinct from the causation merely of coming to be).

As I have observed, the Third Way is the only one in which the possibility that no contingent things whatsoever should exist, and in which in this way the question is asked "why is there something contingent, rather than no such thing?," from which he proceeds to an argument that, if any contingent things (*possibilia*) exist, it must be caused by something necessary. He then argues that all things are necessary either have their necessity caused by something else or do not, but that we cannot proceed to infinity in a series of necessary thing whose necessity is caused by another, where efficient causes are concerned, as has been proved. Therefore, it is necessary to suppose that there is something which is necessary *per se* not having a cause of its necessity caused by something else, but which is itself the cause of other necessary things. Here again we have the explicit consideration of the causation of existence, but the existence concerned is of at least one contingent thing. Moreover, it is clear that when he speaks of things whose necessity is caused by another, he has in view things whose nature is such as to make them naturally imperishable, but whose existence is derivative from something else—i.e., he is treating Aristotle's range of unmoved movers whose operations are ordered by a commanding first unmoved mover, not as all without beginning or end or any contingency of existence, but as having a caused existence. In this way, he is more openly treating as genuinely possible hypotheses which Aristotle would not have considered genuinely possible.

Strangely, after the treatment in the first three ways, St. Thomas abandons all semblance of attempting to present rigorous argument, which tells us something about the character of the Five Ways as a whole, namely that it is designed more to identify lines of reasoning or proof than to develop them in a disciplined way.

In the Fourth Way, he argues that some things we discover (he means in experience) to be more good, more true, more noble and suchlike, and asserts that such comparative terms describe varying degrees of approximation to something which is greatest in the way concerned, strangely comparing this with things being hotter and hotter nearer the approach being maximally hot (he appears to conceive pure fire as maximally hot, as if alluding to Aristotle's exposition, rather than seriously regarding sensory heat as itself a perfection). He cites Aristotle as his authority for treating the truest things as the things which are maximum in being. And he asserts that in each case what is greatest in any such kind of way is the cause of everything else of which the same is predicated in a lesser degree, using fire as Aristotle's example from *Metaphysics*, Book 2 (Alpha Minor), 993b25. He concludes that there is something therefore which causes in all other things their *esse*, goodness and suchlike perfections, and this we call God.

In his statement of the Fourth Way, he goes to the extremes of lack of rigor in his statement of argument, adopting a Latin idiom in such a way as to avoid any such term as "attribute," "property," or even the one I have slipped in, namely, "predicate," and the one that he does let by, namely, kind (*genus*) he lets by only because it is used by Aristotle in this context in this informal way. The "argument" here presented seems to have no function except to make clear the strategy of his later argument in *Summa Theologiae*, I, q. 4, whereby God possesses all the perfections of creatures in a most eminent degree, at the same time alluding to Aristotle as offering the same argument, implicitly applying to the supreme of the unmoved movers.

The Fifth Way he tells us is based on the "governance of things" arising from what he regards as a fact, namely that we see that things which lack knowledge, such as natural bodies, operate according to an end, which appears from their always or nearly always acting in the same way and consequently to the best result, from which it is plain (he says) that it is not fortuitously but out of intention that they attain their end. He then explains that this must arise from their being directed by something with knowledge and intellect, as an arrow is shot to its mark by an archer. Therefore, he concludes, there is some intelligent being by which all natural things are ordered to an end, and this we call God.

Here again there is no attempt at elaboration or consideration of any difficulties or objections but solely, it would seem, the indication of an aspect of God's relation to the world which is vital to the presentation of his overall view in Part I of the *Summa Theologiae*, although it is only in qq. 103 – 19 that he turns to consider God's ways of governing the world, with themes which become especially vital in Part II of the *Summa Theologiae*.

This cursoriness of presentation provides some indication of the function of the Five Ways in relation to the rest of the *Summa*. The only reasons that slightly more attention is paid to the argument in the case of the First and Third Ways would seem to lie in their relevance firstly to the presentation of God as pure *actus*, without any non-active potentiality at all, and secondly to the character of God's necessity and his role in relation to the universe as a unity.

Moreover, it is remarked that in the Third Way, he is treating God as the cause of existence, not just of things which are in an ordinary way contingent, but of beings whose nature presents itself to our thinking as having some kind of necessity, for him primarily the angels or intelligences which move the spheres with the heavenly bodies, and for us primarily the universe, the unity of which we now know to be far more deeply set and to involve a far more intricate web of modes of integration than were ever conceived of in mediaeval times, and known with a far more certain and deeper level of certainty as a result of the advances of modern science.

However, even this context of the Third Way, he shows no real attempt at rigor in arguing that even what is necessary may need a cause. Yet elsewhere, he does provide some actual argument to prove this point, namely, in his reply to objection 2 in *Summa Theologiae*, I, q. 44, art. 1, where he remarks that some have said:

> that what is necessary has no cause (*Physics*, VIII). But this is manifestly false in the demonstrative sciences, where necessary principles are the causes of necessary conclusions. And therefore

> Aristotle says (*Metaphysics*, V, that is, *Delta*) that there are some necessary things which have a cause of their necessity. But the reason why an efficient cause is required is not merely because the effect is not necessary, but because the effect might not be if the cause were not. For this conditional proposition is true, whether the antecedent and consequent be possible or impossible.[60]

(c) EVIDENCE FROM ELSEWHERE IN ST. THOMAS'S TEXT AS TO HOW HE VIEWED THE QUESTION OF WHY THINGS NEED A CAUSE

In the *De Potentia*, q., III, art. 5, and the corresponding discussion in the *Summa*, at this point a more careful exposition than that of the *De Potentia*, St. Thomas gives a remarkably direct statement of Hume's objection to the idea that one can say *a priori* that any substance needs a cause, namely that any substance can be conceived by the intellect without our concept of the substance implying that if the substance exists it has a cause. The only differences between Hume's expression of the objection and St. Thomas's are firstly that St. Thomas states it in terms of what is possible to the intellect and Hume states it in the less satisfactory terms of imaginability and that Hume concerns himself only with the coming to be of a substance and St. Thomas in terms of its being, thereby covering both its coming to be and its continuing in existence.

In *De Potentia*, q. III, art. 5, he states as the first objection that:

> Since the cause is more powerful than its effect that which is possible to our intellect which takes its knowledge from things would seem yet more possible to nature. Now our intellect can understand a thing apart from understanding that it is from God, because a sufficient cause is not of the thing's nature, so the thing can be understood without it. Much more however can there be something *in rerum natura* that is not from God.[61]

His reply in *De Potentia* is as follows: "Although the first cause, which is God, does not enter into the essence of created things, yet *esse*, as it

60 Thomas Aquinas, *ST* I.44.1 ad. 2, trans. English Dominican Fathers.

61 Thomas Aquinas, *Questions on the Power of God*, q. III., a. 5, obj. 1, trans. English Dominican Fathers.

is in created things, cannot be understood except as derived from the divine being, even as a proper effect cannot be understood except as derived from its proper cause."[62]

In the *Summa*, I., q. 44, art. 1, obj. 1, the corresponding objection appears in the form:

> there is nothing to prevent a thing from being without that which does not belong to it essentially, as a man can be found without whiteness. But the relation of the thing caused to its cause does not appear to be essential to beings, for some beings can be understood without it; therefore they can exist without it; and therefore it is possible that some beings should not be created by God.[63]

It receives a similar reply:

> Though the relation to its cause is not part of the definition of a thing caused, still it follows, as a consequence, on what belongs to its *ratio*; because from the fact that a thing is an *ens* by participation, it follows that it is caused. Hence such a *ens* cannot be without being caused, just as man cannot be without having the faculty of laughing. But, since to be caused is not *de ratione entis simpliciter*, therefore is it possible for us to find a being uncaused.[64]

What is notable in St. Thomas's replies is the care with which he makes it clear that, although no mention of either God or his *esse* enters into the definition or *essentia* of a created thing, it nonetheless follows from the fact that the created thing is an *ens* by participation, i.e., shares this predicate with other things, that it is caused by something else.

What he really wishes to say is that the thing's having a cause is a condition of its existence, not of our thinking about it in the way that we do.

Yet this is obscured in the degree that he is careful in his exposition. For his more careful exposition has taken one back to the doctrine that

62 Thomas Aquinas, *Questions on the Power of God*, q. III., a. 5, ad 5, trans. English Dominican Fathers.

63 Thomas Aquinas, *ST* I. 44.1 obj. 1, trans. English Dominican Fathers.

64 Thomas Aquinas, *ST* I. 44.1 ad. 1, mod. trans. English Dominican Fathers.

if a substance shares the predicate being with other substances, this *esse* must have a cause. This appears to be justified in the strategy of St. Thomas's argument by the idea that if a substance shares *esse* with other substances, then there must be something else to its *essentia* which goes beyond from its *esse*, so that its *essentia* cannot be its *esse*, but be in a way prior to it requiring some exterior agent to give it actual *esse* (comparably to the way a *potentia* requires something actually existing in order to be brought to actual existence).

THE IMPLICATIONS OF MY DISCUSSION

My review of St. Thomas's arguments has confirmed that at no point does he draw upon the principle of sufficient reason in arguing for the existence of God, or what Gilson speaks of as a principle of causality, distinguishing causality from causation. And it is true that when the modern philosophers under the influence of the rationalists, Hume and Kant, speak of causality, they commonly conceive this in terms of our experiences conforming to law and in terms of the existence of natural laws, and, although several considerable philosophers such as R. G. Collingwood, H. L. A. Hart and Wilfred Sellars have given separate attention to the concept of cause in its own right, J. L. Mackie has made a polished attempt at the reduction of such ideas of causation as they put forward to a matter of conformity to law. Within the analytic tradition, this leaves principally various philosophers of science and Elizabeth Anscombe as the most conspicuous proponents of ideas of causation not fitting into this rationalist/Humean pattern.

It is also true that at no time in his treatment of God's existence does St. Thomas rely upon any idea that "being as such is intelligible." That "being as such is intelligible" is a consequence of God's nature and wisdom, inasmuch as whatever he creates has what positive characteristics it has in virtue of some likeness to him, and so far as there is a reason for everything it is because God does nothing and permits nothing without reason, or otherwise than with a view to the good.

However, the question will be asked in objection: what else is the principle that "any *potentia* requires the efficient causal action of something actually existing in order to be brought to actual existence" than "a principle of causality"?

However, St. Thomas does not think of this principle as analogous to the laws of logic such as the law of noncontradiction in the way represented in Garrigou-Lagrange. He never thinks of it as a principle of a sort to neglect which would be to abandon rationality, as if our primary aim in enquiry was rationality rather than truth. This would be rather like thinking our primary aim in action was not to seek the good but to act virtuously, or according to reason—or, as if in loving one's wife, one's primary aim should be to love the principle of marital fidelity, rather than to love (in the appropriate sense) one's wife.[65]

True, the senses alone without the exercise of understanding would not yield any such principle as that "any *potentia* requires the efficient causal action of something actually existing in order to be brought to actual existence" to our knowledge. But equally for him, in human beings the understanding is unable in this life to form judgements without the aid of the senses, and it is by "induction" from observed cases (not merely imagined ones) that the intellect is enabled to make such judgements, attaining to first principles a posteriori by reflection upon what is going on in particular instances, e.g., of this or that particular example of something in *potentia* being brought into *actus* as a result of the causal action of some exterior agent.

His approach may seem more adapted to so called 'commonsense,' to some philosophy of science, and to theology than to 'critical philosophy,' but I have attempted to describe what I have found.

At root, he has the insight that, since it is in the nature of any thing, that is of any real entity, or of the universe of such entities, to be not in stasis, but either in successive activity like the angels or also in continuous motion like natural things, therefore any such entity and the universe of such entities, requires a first cause of the activities which take it from one state to another. This first cause, God, is the first cause of the actions of these things when they act according to nature, actions in which they are the agents, and in which God's part is to make their natures and the powers implied by their natures effective, not to exercise these powers or perform these actions.

65 The word "love" is highly ambiguous. The love here spoken of is the unconditional and respectful kind of love which belongs to marriage, not the kind of love one might have for one of one's pieces of furniture, or the lust a man might feel for a woman one finds attractive.

God makes things' natures and the powers implied by them effective by sustaining the things in being, since a thing's nature is only sustained in being in the act of the thing's being sustained in being in that nature. And, since the giving of being and sustaining of things in being is something which only God can do, it is something of which God is not just the first cause but the immediate cause. To give a bodily thing being or sustain it in being in any unconditional way, and in such a way as to give it its stuff or substance, is within the power of God alone. For, as we have seen, within some range of conditions and presupposing the underlying existence and continuance of the stuff of the bodies of bodily things, a bodily thing may cause another thing to come to be and protect it from going out of existence from some limited range of natural causes—and, in the case of non-bodily things, such as the angels of which there is no stuff which enters into their constitution, no creature can play any part in its coming to be or preservation in being.

In sum, God does not have a hands-off position in regard to creation as if he issued a Command and then, standing off in his eternity, let this Command take effect as it were independently of his activity, but God creates and acts in creation as it were "hands-on"—not by using hands, but by being immediate to the things he creates in giving them being and vigor.

PART III

THEOLOGICAL PAPERS

CHAPTER 5

THE UNIQUENESS OF THE INCARNATION: WHY GOD ONCE BECAME MAN[1]

I. INTRODUCTION TO THE QUESTION

The aim of this essay is to make it clear why the doctrine of the Incarnation and its uniqueness is essential to Christianity and to make clear how important it is to the good of man and the universe that it be true.

The problem which this doctrine sets for modern man arises from the fact that it makes man, and with man also the earth, central to God's plan for the whole universe.

Now, this seems immediately to invite three objections. Firstly, it seems to represent a whole way of thinking which could only arise within a geo-centric framework. Secondly, even if it did not involve Earth-centeredness, it surely involves man-centeredness. And, thirdly, it makes the consummation

1 [Editor's note: The earliest version of this essay is dated to 2011, though Braine spoke of it for several years prior. I can find no evidence that it was ever published or that it was ever read publicly.]

of the history of the cosmos coincide with the consummation of human history. Together, these objections raise the suspicion that the incarnation is not so much about God becoming man as about man projecting himself as a god.

I shall deal with these objections in sections II and III, but first I wish to make plain:

(1) what the Incarnation is,
(2) why it is so essential that it be unique, and the importance of this uniqueness for the reasonability of Christianity,
(3) the ways in which this uniqueness is clear within the structure of Christian doctrine, and
(4) what the Incarnation achieves which nothing else could achieve.

I.1. THERE IS A DIFFERENCE BETWEEN GOD BEING INCARNATE AND GOD'S INDWELLING, THE ONE PRESUMED TO BE UNIQUE AND THE OTHER MULTIPLE

Christianity has traditionally made a distinction between God's incarnation and God's indwelling a person.

In the Christian conception, in God's incarnation Jesus of Nazareth, who was born of Mary, truly human, and who was crucified in Jerusalem under the Roman Governor Pontius Pilate, and who died on a cross, this man was divine, was the Son of God the Father, living one life for all eternity with his Father, and through whom everything in the past, present and future, is given existence and maintained in existence.

It is the Christian belief that the one person Jesus is divine, as Son and Wisdom of the Father from the beginning of time in creation, giving it and upholding it in existence, and with his Father and the Holy Spirit engaged from the first moment of its existence in its redemption. In this, even before and historically independently of his Incarnation, he was joined with his Father through the Holy Spirit in giving the grace of friendship and supernatural relationship together with gifts of the spirit apt for the fulfilment of redemption and for the later enrichment of the company of the Church.

Jesus, eternal Son of God, took on the vocation of the Messiah. For this, he was conceived and born of a Jewish woman, the Jews being the people long prepared by God to be the people of the Redeemer. And he was to be the redeemer not only of the Jews but also, by their vocation as well as his, of the whole human race—indeed it was because in God's plan Jesus was to be the redeemer of the whole human race that God formed the Jewish people to be, as it were, the womb of his Son, and have a vocation toward the whole human race. The word "Messiah" means the anointed [*christos*] of God; he is the shepherd and king of Israel and of all those to be associated with Israel as his people, appointed to save them all, and to bring the whole of creation into unity. In Christian understanding, he achieved this by his life, crucifixion, death, and resurrection.

By contrast, the indwelling of the Holy Spirit is conceived as an indwelling of God in human beings in such a way that they remain persons distinct from God, distinct from the Holy Spirit who indwells. This indwelling is in many men and women over all the ages but is conceived to arise in a fuller way after the victory of Christ through suffering and the sending out of the Church.

The Incarnation is presumed to be unique and to involve such a complete unity that it is the very same divine person who takes on human nature and is truly man. By contrast, the indwelling is not unique but the source of spiritual diversity among human kind, the divine spirit indwelling many human persons while these persons remain distinct from each other and from the divine spirit itself.

I.2. IT IS ESSENTIAL TO CHRISTIAN BELIEF, NOT ONLY THAT THE INCARNATION WAS IN FACT UNIQUE, BUT THAT IT HAD TO BE

In recent times some Christians have questioned whether the Incarnation has to be unique, indeed even whether it is, in fact, unique. I shall discuss the inspiration for this questioning and show why I think these reasons are wrongheaded, blind to some of the most general features of the universe, in Section II.

In my own view, it would be contrary to God's wisdom for the Incarnation to have occurred more than once. Either it occurred just once, or it did not occur at all. The reasons for saying this can be stated quite simply, and I shall state them immediately below. But, further than this, one should realize that if one regards the Incarnation as something that happened more than once then one sets up a different religion from historical Christianity. For it is integral to historical Christianity that it had the same perspective on history as Judaism. Both of them conceive the history of the whole universe as unitary—they consider physics in the context of a history, instead of conceiving of history in the context of some background of a nonhistorical physics. Or, to put the point in a different way, they conceive the history of the cosmos and the history of man to be one and the same history. The book of Genesis presents the history of man as beginning with God's making the physical universe in a way that led to the animals and man. Similarly, St. John's Gospel begins with Jesus's life together with God his Father and with his role in creation before speaking of his being made flesh,—of his "coming to his own and not being accepted by them." Thus, Christian belief envisages the Incarnation as rooted in the history of the cosmos as a whole—as something essentially unique so that everything before this unique incarnation is envisaged as leading up to it or depending for its full meaning and completion upon it. And everything after this unique incarnation is seen as flowing from it, or as having the possibilities open to it altered and enlarged. The clarity with which this perspective is evident in the New Testament as a whole will be made plain in Section IV.

And in Section V, I shall indicate briefly from Christian history how quickly departures from this firm insistence on the uniqueness of the Incarnation, for instance in Origen, rapidly became associated with wilder variations on Christian belief, e.g., occultism and an interest in supra-physical beings with many different kinds of "body."

Of course, this view of history, shared by Judaism and Zoroastrianism, and inherited by Christianity and Islam, involves an acceptance of the reality of time—and therefore with this a rejection of any system of physical law and explanation which puts time on an explanatory par with other dimensions. But I do not intend to discuss these particular philosophical aspects of what is involved in the Christian conception of history in this essay—the reality of time is after all a view which Christians share with the rationalist believers in Progress who come from the Enlightenment, Marxists, and the commonsense of the man on the street.

I have two reasons for considering it contrary to God's wisdom for the Incarnation to occur more than once.

Firstly, being incarnate means being bodily, and the living body is the human way in which one human person presents himself to be known by others. It does not make sense to suppose two human bodies of Christ in Heaven, and for Christ to be risen and glorified means that by his ascension he has given Heaven, as where God is present as personally known, a bodily dimension—although, as St Paul says, we know not with what manner of body human beings are glorified in Heaven.[2]

Secondly, becoming incarnate is not just a matter of taking on a nature, so as to be listed amongst individuals with human nature, as in the Aristotelian view in which it is only an historical accident that two individual men are never, over all the ages, qualitatively identical. Rather it is a matter of taking on a human life and biography integrated in the tapestry which includes other such unfolding biographies, in accord with the idea expressed in the Apocalypse of John that each person has a unique name or character special to himself. This is incompatible with two places in world history.

In my own view the matter is so clear and important as to be an appropriate object of a definition by the whole Church, indeed if rightly explained very appropriate to this before the second millennium.

I.3. THIS QUESTION HAS APOLOGETIC IMPORTANCE

We need to recognize the importance of the question of whether God could be incarnate more than once. Most obviously it is important for apologetics—allowing us to explain that the reason why we must not put all sages on the same level is that, once granted that the Incarnation could only happen once, the effective result of putting Jesus, Buddha, and a few others on the same level is to make them all cases only of an indwelling of the divine spirit in a human being, and

2 I would add that if any other personal beings have things appropriately called bodies, then these also are that by which a personal bodily being by its very nature makes itself known by other personal beings. So, the argument above would still work if for the word "human" we substituted the word "person."

to therefore deny that an incarnation (that is, a man or woman's being God, rather than just being indwelt by God) ever happened.

To many people, there seems to be a wild folly in supposing that an event located in one region and one period, arising within the context of a particular animal species, as yet local to the earth and seemingly liable to be just as ephemeral as other earthly species, could have significance for the whole of this cosmos—considering the whole vastness of the universe over space and time.

I say all this because, although theoretically it is possible for there to be many different kinds of intellectual creature, even different kinds in different worlds, nonetheless, I insist that, whether there be one or many kinds of intellectual creature, the Incarnation remains an event of a kind which could only happen once. It is this which removes this appearance of folly in belief in the Incarnation.

It used to be said, "How odd of God to choose the Jews!"[3], and so, in a parallel way, in regard to the Incarnation, wherever it happened in the whole wide cosmos, the people there would say, "How odd of God to make it happen here!"—but if it was to happen at all (so that all the great good could come to the whole universe), it had to happen somewhere, and so there had to be a place where people would say, "How odd of God to make it happen here!"

Yet there would be no point in this insistence that in Jesus Christ God was incarnate, and did not just, while remaining a distinct person, indwell, unless two things were true: firstly that the gift of Himself involved in incarnation was essentially greater than the gift involved in indwelling; and secondly that God's becoming incarnate made possible a fulfilment for man and the universe essentially greater than any fulfilment possible if God was present only by indwelling and not by incarnation.

The practical effect of insisting that all great "gurus" are on a par or in an essentially parallel position to each other, so that all can be thought of as examples of indwelling, realizations of the effects of divine action within the human soul, but not themselves incarnations of God is to deny that any such incarnation ever occurred. So, the importance of insisting on the Incarnation depends on the two

3 I am told this went on "—yet not so odd as those who choose a Jewish God but spurn the Jews."

conditions named being fulfilled. It is only the realization that the Incarnation is so great a matter, so infinitely surpassing an indwelling by God within isolated souls, and so great in its consequences which makes this emphasis intelligible.

Thus, the picture is that within the context of a historical development rooted in one place and time something different and greater than any indwelling occurs, something of such a kind that it can only happen once. And because it can only happen once at a particular place and time it gives singular prominence to this place and time.

The presumption is that if the incarnation was to happen at all it could only happen once in the whole universe, and we must show that such an act would benefit not just the human race but with it the whole universe.

We can *say* that the Incarnation is an event which does more than free this little race on this little earth from sin, but brings them into the possibility of a fulfilment greater than there would have been even had sin never arisen. We can say that this is firstly because it makes possible the gift of the Holy Spirit, and with it, supernatural love and the vision of God. And we can go beyond this to assert that, secondly, by the action of the Holy Spirit, it brings this human race together with the whole universe in the completion of a symphony of struggle and triumph into full solidarity, integration, and fulfilment.

II. NEW WAYS IN WHICH THE QUESTION OF THE UNIQUENESS OF THE INCARNATION HAS BECOME CONSPICUOUS

II.1. CHRISTIANS HAVE ALWAYS HELD THAT THE INCARNATION IS IN FACT UNIQUE

However, in earlier times all human beings were presumed to be of one stock, descended from one primordial Adam and Eve. Stories of different kinds of fairy beings were mostly dismissed as mere fables or else accounts of appearances of pure spirits. Since the natural place of the element earth was the center of the earth, it was believed that there was no corruptible matter in the spheres above the earth, the spheres towards which fire naturally rose, so that the idea of other bodies like the earth associated with the planets or stars did not arise. Therefore, unsurprisingly, little attention was paid to the question as to whether it is impossible for God to be Incarnate more than once, or whether it was merely fitting.

Now in considering statements about what is possible for God we should distinguish between what is possible for God under one aspect of how we consider God and what is possible for God under another aspect.

It is against this background that we should consider such statements of Thomas Aquinas as, for example, that it was possible for the Son of God to have taken on more than one human nature at different times and places, or that it was possible for a different Person of the Trinity to have become incarnate. We must be wary of such statements of possibility in answer to what seems rather academic questions.[4]

In the case of his saying that it is possible for a person of the Trinity other than the Son to have become incarnate, Aquinas does not make it clear in respect to what aspect of God's being this is said to be possible. For it would appear that if the Father or the Spirit had become incarnate, then the prayer of the incarnate divine person would not have been the prayer of the Son to the Father, and the manner by which man's sin was atoned for would not have had the same relation to incorporation into the mystical body of the Son of God and the Son of God's headship of the Church as St. Thomas portrays. The point is that the impossibility arises not from the nature of the persons of the Trinity considered in themselves, but in the character and shape of the salvation God wills for created intellectual beings.

Likewise, although there is no impossibility in the Son being incarnate more than once from the side of the nature of the Son, there is an impossibility which arises from the nature of human persons to be in relationships of communion with one another.

It is not a matter of what stories the adventurous human imagination can put together in conceiving human beings in roles quite unlike

4 Elsewhere he has arguments against the possibility that a created thing might have an infinite series of causes each acting independently of its predecessors, but elsewhere it appears that he thinks that the power to give existence from nothing or to sustain things in existence cannot be deputized, so that there can be no intermediaries, not even one, between God and creation. That is, he does sometimes deal with supposed possibilities which are in his considered view merely academic.

any related to history, prehistory, or the rest of the universe, such as are met with in modern science fiction. Rather it is a matter of what purpose any Incarnation of a divine person might have in the real world. In the real world, to be a man is to be part of a biological stock, with a certain position within the ancestry and descent of members of that stock; it is to be in a position in which other men and women have come before the divine person's becoming a man. If his becoming a man is to open some real possibility of communication with those he lives amongst and who follow him, there will need to be some preparation of the people living in the context into which he is born in order they may have the capacity to grow into some appreciation of meaning of his being divine. After his becoming a man, he will forever after have other men and women as his contemporaries as a man, supposing that a person's human existence does not end at death. He, the divine person, will then have a following within human history, and the possibility of a relation with a human dimension with every other man and woman whose existence continues, including those who preceded his becoming a man.

It is a matter of how a divine person becoming a man can have a role fitting with the divine wisdom for the development of mankind and the development of the whole universe. For although, according to the logic of human concepts, it might be logically possible for the Incarnation of a divine person as a man to happen more than once, this does not mean that it fits with any possible divine wisdom for the development of mankind and the universe.

II.2. THE QUESTION IS IMPORTANT IN RELATION TO A COMPARISON OF CHRISTIANITY WITH OTHER RELIGIONS

Moreover, in the light of what I said earlier, the question gains a new importance.

For it is given a conspicuous extra importance because of the modern non-Christian tendency to put "great gurus" on a par, as if there could be one Christ or one divine incarnation for each culture (there is a Hindu tendency to think this way), as if each culture was a distinct "world." And it is nowadays taken to be a natural extension of this to suppose divine incarnations in each planet or planetary system, if there should be intellectual living bodily beings in these systems. I note that C. S. Lewis would have rejected this idea—What Maleldil does once, he does not do twice. For Lewis, if in any world there is a fall, then the situation will indeed be remedied by God, but in each place in a different way, exhibiting God's freshness and originality.[5] But such a view does not fit with the modern desire to regard all or most of the great religions of the world as essentially the same.

Syncretism regarding the greatest religious teachers and integration of their varied teachings is characteristic of Baha'i faith. According to some interpretations of Buddhism, such as that found in Thailand and in Tibet, different persons are spoken of as incarnations of the Buddha-spirit or of the Dharma, as when successive Dalai Lama's are spoken of as incarnations of Buddha. It is not clear whether these represent misinterpretations of the religious doctrines concerned. In fact, they seem far from the oldest traditions of Gautama Buddha as represented in the Pali canon surviving in a no longer spoken Sinhalese language. This in turn gives weight to the idea that historically Buddha made no claim to divinity.

However, views parallel to the Baha'i are found much earlier in Hinduism. For instance, in its many avatars—commonly translated as "incarnations," but perhaps more aptly translated "manifestations"—of the Divine Vishnu, of which the best known are Rama and Krishna. Vishnu under the form of Krishna may be spoken of as Restorer and Renewer, returning many times in order to reactivate the light in each new context, the stories about his childhood portray him as a prankster—as a playful god. Later, after taking eight princely wives, he is said to have rescued 16,100 imprisoned women, and then married them all on the same day in order to restore them to their former dignity.

Nevertheless, within Hinduism there is a certain externality of the God to the human form assumed, by contrast with the sameness of person insisted upon by Christianity.

5 This view would not fit with the argument of Anselm's *Cur Deus Homo?* but is allowed for in the writings of St. Thomas and others later than him whereby, although the suffering and death of one who was both God and man was the most fitting means whereby we might be saved and brought to full fellow-sonship with him and share in the vision of God, it was not absolutely necessary if the end were only the freeing from sin.

But, as we have seen, this suggests the question as to whether there is any real distinction between what is being called an incarnation of a Divine person and being indwelt by the Holy Spirit. Logically the distinction is plain, namely that in the case of an incarnation the person concerned is identically the same person as the Divine person of whom he is an incarnation, whereas in the case of indwelling the created person is distinct from the Divine person indwelling him. Yet the contemporary blurring of the two notions of incarnation and indwelling, associated with a reluctance to apply logic to statements about God, makes it unsurprising that people should begin to put, for example, Buddha alongside Jesus as specially indwelt human beings with special roles towards particular cultures.

Thus, putting Jesus on a level with other "gurus" has the tendency to raise the question of whether God was ever incarnate at all.

II.3. THE QUESTION IS IMPORTANT IN RELATION TO A GENERAL PHILOSOPHICAL CONCEPTION OF THE UNIVERSE.

Let us put this question in a wider perspective.

To modern man, conceiving of the Incarnation as really one of any number of indwellings is of course much easier. It fits with the modern tendency to want to regard all religions as identical in their essential content. It also fits with a dualistic way of thinking about souls and the way they come to exist in the universe. For there is a tendency amongst those who reject materialism to think of conscious experience, intelligence, emotion and will as interacting with suitable material vehicles as these arise within material nature, or else as a psychological by-product of material processes arising wherever such a material vehicle evolves. In these ways of thinking, the material universe is conceived of as having a physically determined history, and soul's figure as extra features arising in an adventitiously parallel history or series of separate histories of their own. In a parody of this view, the materialist might see believers in the soul as thinking of souls as a kind of spiritual floss floating on the surface of an otherwise material universe. Within such souls, God might indwell and such divine indwellings might be supposed to arise in many times and places, near and distant, and unrelated to each other—as unrelated to each other as one incarnation of Vishnu is unrelated to another. Within such a conception, each would be directed towards some separate localized subgroup of personal bodily beings or lesser animals, each group with its own history, the persons or animals concerned interrelating with each other within a localized framework within space and time. In this way of viewing things, there will be no one integrated spiritual history of the spiritual universe, let alone one integrated history of the whole universe, material, biological and spiritual.

II.4. THE QUESTION IS IMPORTANT IN RELATION TO THE REALITY OF TIME AND OF TEMPORAL SEQUENCE IN THE HISTORY OF MANKIND, EARTHLY LIFE, AND THE UNIVERSE.

By contrast, the idea of a unique Incarnation set within a unitary history of the universe conceived of in a Jewish way sets matters in a quite different light. It involves an integration of the history of the physical with the history of the spiritual.

In the Jewish/Christian/Muslim way of viewing history, God in his creating of things is not limited by any considerations of economy. He gives rise to the galaxies and to successive generations of stars and other kinds of celestial objects in an abundance arising simply from his pleasure; and the same is true at the biological level.

Yet the successive types of thing arise in a certain sequence with a certain direction. The order measured by thermodynamics, we are told, always decreases, but this is not the same kind of order as the kinds assessed by geneticists, biologists and linguists: the word "order" is used analogously, according to different criteria. Therefore, we can quite properly envisage the natural universe as a unity with a history of which one of the most characteristic features is a propensity for wholes to emerge exhibiting steadily advancing kinds and degrees of order. Moreover, in the later stages of this development we find further, that the sorts of increase in these kinds of order within bodily creatures are sorts of increase which are integral to a successive progression from the merely material, through successive forms of life and increasing levels of consciousness and intelligence, to the fully self-conscious and intellectual.

We must not be deceived by considerations of scale and vastness at the physical level.[6] What goes on in plant and animal life depends on material processes which depend on the operation of whatever principles govern quarks (and their components, if they have components), protons, neutrons, electrons and the like, atoms, ions and molecules, i.e., the same principles which govern what proceeds in the galaxies and within them the sun and other stars and lesser celestial bodies. However, the order exhibited in a gene considered in relation to its role in biological organisms, the order exhibited in the behavior of colonies of insects, the order exhibited in the eye of an insect, the order exhibited in the brain and nervous system of behavior of man are none of them types of order of the same kind as that exhibited in the universe as a whole, in the sun or in any other celestial body, or indeed in any other entity traditionally considered "material." Now, it is perfectly possible to envisage these kinds of order as successively each more significant—of more value and wonder—than what preceded it (if what preceded it is considered alone and without reference to its potentiality or tendency to underly these higher types of order). Within the physical universe, an increase in order of one of these latter kinds of order always involves a decrease of order (increase of entropy) of the purely physical or thermodynamic kind of order.

We can go beyond this. The order of linguistic behavior considered as the vehicle for the expression of understanding and of rational thought, in so far as it makes it possible for an organism localized in space and time to reflect on, enquire into, and gain a knowledge and understanding of the whole universe might seem greater than all the preceding kinds of order inasmuch as it includes a reflection of all these preceding kinds of order in their mutual relations. This is a knowledge and understanding which we have seen in recent times reach ever greater depths, somewhat as if reality was like an onion, so that at each stage of enquiry when we might seem to have penetrated to the deepest level we are liable to find ourselves able, as it were, to

6 Cf. E. L. Mascall, *Existence and Analogy*, Libra Books (London: Darton, Longman & Todd, 1966) Preface, xii-xiii.

peel off another skin and discover a deeper level, and then to find that even this is within reach of our capacity to enquire and understand—with the result that we can say that there seems no particular reason to suppose that this capacity is subject to systematic restriction at any stage. In this way, the order exhibited by human knowledge and understanding seems to exceed any of the kinds of order which materially precede it.

Further, what we see in the universe is something of roughly the following sort.[7] After a succession of earlier stages, we find kinds of stars arising which are capable of manufacturing the heavier elements, and then these stars bursting into supernovas from which lesser stars and systems of planets containing such heavier metals arise by condensation. Within this process, involving very many stages, we notice at every stage an aptitude of smaller constituents to aggregate into wholes, and commonly into wholes whose behavior is governed by laws not suggested by the laws governing the behavior of their parts, inclining one to say that the whole is greater than the sum of its parts. It was this which led nineteenth century thinkers to speak of "emergent wholes." Thus we note an aggregation of particles into the nuclei of atoms, the aggregation of atoms into molecules and this according to increasingly complex patterns, the aggregation of molecules into bacterial cells and the nuclei of plant and animal cells, the formation of plant and animal cells by the setting of such nuclei in the context of appropriate cytoplasm, the aggregation of cells to form the different types of tissue required by the structures of the various types of living organism, these organisms aggregate to societies, these organisms develop in complexity in ways geared to steadily richer forms of activity and, coordinate with this increasing richness of types of activity, we find different forms and levels at which these organisms are integrated together into societies. Therefore, as well as the order seen at each level, we can recognize also as one of the most evident of the "phenomena" to be recognized the order between these levels and its character as involving a steady increase in the intensity of the kinds of integration involved. This enables us to see the whole universe as

7 This paragraph reflects the argument of Teilhard de Chardin in *The Phenomenon of Man*.

having the character of looking as if it was designed to give rise to embodied intellect, so that in this way the universe or evolution can be said to "have become conscious of itself."[8]

This then should be our perspective on the universe. This perspective will envisage the heavens in their wonder and the microcosm in its wonder as presenting to the mind reflections of the abyss of the mystery of God. But within this setting this perspective will give peculiar pre-eminence to reflective knowledge and understanding as more significant for the richness of their mode of being than any amount of physical vastness. And it will envisage the whole universe, if directed towards anything, then directed towards the existence of beings possessed of such knowledge and understanding—involving this phenomenon of "evolution become conscious of itself." And it will see this capacity of the embodied intellect to reflect on its relation to other things in the universe, their character and their system of relations with each other as carrying with it the capacity of this intellect to reflect on the relationship between the things in the universe and God as their cause.

This still leaves the possibility of envisaging the separate development of intellect and personhood in many different places and times within the natural universe and the resulting societies remaining forever separate from one another. But the same principle whereby smaller units at each level tend to aggregate into larger wholes, might suggest the possibility of all these societies being brought together in relation to one another, so that in this way the unity of the universe should be, as it were, rounded off.

Now, it is here that the significance of the Incarnation with its uniqueness lies. For Christianity envisages that all things will be brought into completion through Christ, all things being brought into "his body, the fulness of him who fills all in all" (Eph 1:23). How far we can get a positive grasp of what is here being spoken of remains to be seen. This is what I will attempt the beginnings of in Section V below.

8 This echoes the way in which St. Augustine envisages that everything in the universe in a metaphorical sense declares "God made us," but only man can give this thought judgement and voice.

III. REPLIES TO OBJECTIONS

OBJECTION 1: THIS WHOLE WAY OF THINKING AROSE FROM AND COULD ONLY ARISE WITHIN A GEOCENTRIC FRAMEWORK—NO! NOT SO!

This placing of Jesus, the Jew from Nazareth, and with him the Jews and the human race at the center of cosmic history is often thought of as rooted in a presumption that the earth is at the center of the universe, with everything else revolving around it.

To this I reply that such a charge involves first a simple confusion between earth-centeredness and man-centeredness, and second an added and worse confusion between being at the center physically and being noble in nature.

In ancient thought, in fact, the earth was considered very small and the element earth of which it was principally made up was the most humble element, giving the earth the most ignominious nature. We should realize that regarding matters otherwise would have seemed as foolish to the ancient Greeks and to educated Medievals as it seems to us. Eratosthenes and several others used a number of different empirical methods for assessing the diameter of the earth and most of them agreed on the figure of 400,000 stades (probably about 7,300 miles), and there would have seemed nothing untoward in this to the Phoenecian sailors who circumnavigated Africa, the Greeks and Romans who traded in pepper with South India and by 200 AD had reached the coast of Vietnam, or the Norse who reached north of Norway to the White Sea as well as west to Greenland, Newfoundland, and perhaps further south. The fact that the earth was large and not flat was not just a datum to anyone who accepted Ptolemy's geography, but obvious to any serious sailor.

Posidonius guessed that the Sun was 19,000 earth diameters away. While this was a bit of an overestimate, roughly the distance of Mars from the sun, he did render the sun's diameter vastly larger than the earth's, a view reflected in Epicurus.[9] Everyone reckoned Mars,

9 Presumably they realized that it was only because of the huge size of the sun that the moon close to us cast so small a shadow, the moon's closeness and smaller size being why the Earth's shadow commonly embraces the whole Moon in eclipses.

Jupiter, and Saturn more distant than the sun, and the sphere of the stars vastly more distant again. And earth was the basest element ever seeking to sink to the lowest place, the center of the earth, while fire was the noblest ever seeking to move upwards, planets and stars being yet more nobly constituted of incorruptible fire and moved by perfect intelligences.[10]

As such the sun was the most noble of natural things, the source of a light which is of so spiritual a nature as to produce no physical change in the air which it passes through or in the bodies it encountered. As source of light, the sun was the preferred image of what gives light to the intellect, whether the form of the Good or God. The elements were first fire, the most noble, seeking the noblest place which was upwards, and then air, water, and earth, successively less noble and ever seeking more lowly places, with earth the most ignominious of all. The earth itself was composed of mixtures of all four elements, while the celestial bodies above were composed of fire or in a yet more noble way. Nothing physical moved the celestial bodies in their spheres, no attraction to a higher or a lower place, but rather intellectual desire since they were conceived of as intelligent beings.

For the Greeks the only thing which gave man a nobility and distinction lacking to other mundane things was intellect, this alone perhaps divine, and this alone a possible root of immortality. For Jew and Christian the fact that reflective power gives rise not only to knowledge but also to the power of choice was also particularly significant, and not just a mark of weakness and contingency. In sum, nature was considered to give pride of place to the Sun rather than to the earth or man, and in general to God and the angels rather than to any natural creature.

For Jew and Christian, the angels as in the immediate presence of God and expressions of his glory immeasurably surpassed any intelligences supposedly moving the heavenly bodies. This left human beings, with their bodies composed of the most ignominious matter, earth and water, and thereby eminently corruptible, and with modes of knowledge dependent on sense-perception and therefore in the situation of being in Aquinas' words "the least amongst intellectual

10 Incorruptible because not involved in transmutations among things composed of fire, air, water and earth as material elements.

substances"—although (so far as he knew) the only rational beings to exist within the corruptible universe. That such a pygmy in this pygmy world should have cosmic significance was therefore almost as much folly to the ancients and to medieval thinkers as to us.

OBJECTION 2: EVEN IF THE ROOT OF JEWISH/CHRISTIAN/MUSLIM THOUGHT DOES NOT INVOLVE EARTH-CENTEREDNESS, IT DOES INVOLVE MAN-CENTEREDNESS—NO! NOT SO!

Before responding to this objection, I should comment that even though in the past belief in the Incarnation gave a key place to man in the whole universe, the present roots of man-centeredness are quite different.

Philosophically, even before the skepticism represented in Montaigne had received Descartes' response, making epistemology prior to metaphysics, there had been a subtle development of secularism. For Augustine and Aquinas God is immediate to each thing, upholding it in existence, but in Duns Scotus it begins to appear that the natural causes of things are adequate to explain the being and continuance of things, not just their coming to be. And in the same Duns Scotus we have the beginnings of an ethical theory in which the rightness of an act depends primarily upon an act of will, either of God, expressed in divine command, or the command of a human will, a development completed in Suárez, infallibly reproduced in Hobbes and Hume. All this was the root of the secularism increasingly prevalent from 1700 onward.

The first effect of this secularism is to remove God from the center of the human perspective in thinking about the world and his action. It leaves a space that many great physicists and some environmentalists are content to leave unfilled, but which nevertheless presents a constant temptation to substitute man for God.

If we wish to find the main philosophical root of man-centeredness in modern times we should find it first in the arguments of Locke and Kant, limiting the sphere of genuine human knowledge to the earth-centered sensible world, and second in the way Hegel was developed by Feuerbach in his making man substitute for God and, proceeding from this, by Marx's giving priority of importance to *praxis* or action, rather than pure thought. These developments have come to dwarf religious presentations or often to reshape and distort them. The combination of subjectivism or conventionalism in regard to the theoretical or "ultimate" matters of fact with subjectivism or conventionalism in regard to the ethical has produced a man-centered perspective on all the world's affairs, allowing the development of an emphasis on worldly human good to dominate planning, to the detriment of the environment, to the detriment of the spiritual, and to the detriment of the individual's sense of meaning or direction.

By contrast, it is a complete mistake to think that the doctrine of a unique Incarnation depends on a geocentric world view or that it has been the main source of the vigor of geocentrism over the last three centuries. And it is false to suppose even that it peculiarly generates a man-centered world view. On the contrary, the Incarnation makes God the center. Indeed, the fact of God's being central and his immediacy to each thing to which he gives existence and upholds is the root of the wonder, respect and care which we feel towards non-human creation, the root of our sense of obligation to these things, and of the feeling of guilt we have when we violate this obligation.

Of course, one must qualify this assessment. Although belief in the Incarnation did not and does not depend on a world view centering on the earth and on man, nonetheless Jews and Christians tended to deny the existence of other bodily persons other than man, for example, elves, gnomes, banshees, and so on, conceiving belief in these as mere popular superstition, or else reckoning them to be fallen angels or demons presenting themselves under some appearance. The idea that each star might be like the Sun or even have other planets associated with them did not arise in their general picture. And within the context of such a perspective it was quite rational to suppose that there was only one race or stock of intellectual animal being, namely man. Yet, just because of this, the highlighting of the human race, envisaged as a single stock, can be represented as a recognition not of some locality or particularized group as such, but only of intellect—man being conceived of as the only intellectual bodily being in existence.

However, this way of dealing with the objection is superficial, overlooking a more general underlying problem.

The issue as to whether the Incarnation has relevance only to one race or stock arises independently of the possibility of life on other planets or of there being some truth in some of the popular superstitions we commonly dismiss. For it arises the moment one addresses the dispute as to whether or not human beings are literally from one ancestral father and mother.

The tendency in the past for Christians to assume such singleness of ancestry has stemmed not just from literalism in the understanding of Genesis, but from a sense of the given community of man (given, and not just the product of an optional voluntary contract or consent) and from the idea that the redeeming of man by Jesus's dying for him depended on the solidarity he had with them as being of one stock (cf. Hebrews 2:16–18, although the text does not imply necessity, but only appropriateness). In his 1951 Encyclical *Humani Generis*, Pius XII was very careful: he did not say that polygenism is false but only that it is difficult to see how it is compatible with the doctrine of original sin, at the same time also forbidding it to be taught.

Yet empirical science leaves the question of the origins of man on Earth open.

Just as it is only by a number of discrete mutations in the organization of its hardware that a computer becomes open to the application and use of certain programs, so it will be only by some crucial final mutation that the human body becomes an apt bearer of properly human capacity, perhaps best evinced in human linguistic capacity. Such a mutation will always constitute a radical discontinuity, inasmuch as a change which (physically described) seems minor may nonetheless provide a radical structural change in the basis of behavior. The Artificial Intelligence theorist will, therefore, if he follows reason, have no less absolute reason for insisting on discontinuity than the person who believes that only the rational soul is immortal.

In the situation of present empirical science, there is some tendency to think of mutations as sometimes arising in more than one individual in a community, but there is also a genetic argument for the single maternity of the whole human race (an argument from the measure of homogeneity in mitochondrial DNA), and alongside it a genetic argument for the single paternity of the whole human race (an argument from the measure of homogeneity in the DNA of the XY chromosome). In general, the question of polygenism is empirically open—the question, that is, of the human species taking its origin from numerous distinct stocks with a variety of distinct male and/or female ancestors capable of fertile intercourse with offspring also fertile, whether within one community or tribe or within already scattered groups, the resulting stocks interbreeding perhaps slowly, perhaps quickly; or of the human species taking its origin from one original pair. Up to the present, there have been no grounds for regarding such questions as closed, unless theological. As a result, perhaps as a backlash against unreasoned theological prejudice, the popular scientific tendency has been to presume polygenism and to be surprised when any empirical argument has arisen against it. No theologian or scientist supposes the story of Adam and Eve to be transmitted to us by historical tradition, so it has the status only of either a myth or a reconstruction, or on a pious view a divinely led reconstruction.[11]

Thus, independently of the question of whether there be unrelated races of bodily animal beings on other planets or in different parts of this earth, the question as to whether there has to be a distinct Incarnation of God for each distinct intelligent animal stock, or only one Incarnation in one particular stock availing to bring salvation to all stocks, whether on earth alone or spread over many worlds, is not a new question generated by modern speculations about life on other planets, but a question already presented by the framework of modern biological and anthropological speculation. It is thus a question preexisting any questions about other planets, a question arising whenever there are conceived to be other radically different and separate stocks or races of intellectual bodily creature on earth, forming separate self-sufficient political communities. If this question were also raised in regard to stranger beings, for example, different kinds of realistically conceived fairy peoples, this would not have made it a new question.

Thus raised is as to whether the Incarnation was simply or primarily for the sake of the salvation of those of the same stock as Jesus, i.e., the Jews and other peoples, perhaps all men, ancestrally related to them, or whether it had also some wider and deeper context

11 The theory that the early chapters of Genesis were communicated by direct divine speech to the compositors of Genesis, rather than by God's inspiring human authors through his guidance of their heart and mind to write in the terms they did, is a modern novelty among theologians, arising within Evangelical Protestantism.

and purpose. For, if it did have some such wider and deeper context and purpose, then this might give it a role not just in regard to man but also in regard to any other species or genera of intellectual being, including any such beings on planets other than the earth.

The difference between educated premodern views and modern views is that our predecessors mostly conceived humanly habitable land to be concentrated together, surrounded by seas within and beyond which all sorts of strange dangers and forms of life and existence might be located—Dante adopted the literary device of locating the pit of Hell and the mount of Purgatory at the antipodes of Jerusalem. Met out of context, as beyond the seas, rather than as attached to the Cathay which was part of the human occupied Euro-Afro-Asian land mass, alien types of human being have been in danger of being regarded as much an alien to human kind as elves, fairies or moon-dwellers. The Spanish and Portuguese, for their part, never had any doubt as to the human character of the peoples they met. Northern European attitudes, except for the Dutch in the East Indies, accorded some theoretical respect towards Indians and others in the Far East, although less to the "Indians" of the Americas. But whereas Southern Europeans and French were willing to accept and marry inculturated Africans, even south of the Sahara, Northern Europeans showed no trace of even this degree of respect for sub-Saharan Africans, feeling especial contempt for those referred to as "Kaffirs" and for the Australian aborigines, these latter commonly regarded as sub-human and hunted to death.

Thus, the problem as to how intellectual beings on other supposed planets might be saved or brought into relation to Christ is in no way specially different from the problem as to how a person in some outlandish part of the earth whether in 1000 BC or in AD1000 could be saved, as these might have been viewed in earlier times. From the point of view of human inter-communication relevant to salvation, peoples in distant lands and civilizations might seem to live or have lived as much in different "worlds" as any imagined beings from other stars or planets.

The Catholic and Orthodox traditions have always conceived the just of the Old Testament, whether outside the Jewish covenant[12] or

12 Christian tradition suggests that there will be countless unnamed figures, while being aware of those explicitly named in Hebrew scripture, e.g.,

inside it, to have received grace in anticipation of the Incarnation and to be amongst those who would enter into the salvation of Christ. The innocents massacred in Bethlehem have been conceived as holy and as martyrs, even though without any adult knowledge of Christ. And Aquinas conceives salvation as within the reach of every adult, even if through the mediation of an angel. Such ways of thinking as these leave it unproblematic that beings from other planets should be taken up in the same salvation or fulfilment.

In sum, there has long been the question as to whether unity in the salvation or fulfilment brought by Christ depends on unity of stock—so that it is only because we have solidarity with the sin of Adam that we have access to Christ's salvation. But this would already be a question even if the idea of personal bodily beings on other planets had never been raised: it has long been a question of dispute whether the question of whether the human race originated in a single pair was of theological importance. So, the question as to whether there are personal beings on other planets brings in no new issue.

Therefore, the question remains why a unique Incarnation should be the condition of the existence of any possibility of such salvation or fulfilment—the possibility of salvation for any personal being whether of human stock or not.

Therefore, I ask whether the Incarnation of God as man did have any such wider and deeper context and purpose. If it had this in regard to man, then it might have it in such a way as to be relevant to all other intellectual beings. Section V explains how this is indeed the case.

OBJECTION 3: IT MAKES THE CONSUMMATION OF THE HISTORY OF THE COSMOS COINCIDE WITH THE CONSUMMATION OF HUMAN HISTORY

Suppose that our argument succeeds, and that it is made sufficiently plain that the Incarnation of God in one stock has the effect of opening out a fulfilment, in filial relationship to God, not just to those with common ancestry with Jesus, but to all other intelligent beings—except when they have declared a definitive "No!" to friendship with

Abel, Enoch, Noah, Melchizedek, Jethro, Balaam, Job, and Danel (according to Danielou, an ancient Canaanite king) referred to in Ezekiel 14:14, and 14:20.

God in the interests of being entirely self-directed and maximally self-sufficient.

Then a further problem still arises: should one indeed consider the whole physical universe as set in the context of a unitary history, rather than various histories as in the context of the physical universe?—and will this unitary history be one which makes the consummation of the history of the cosmos coincide with the consummation of human history? Then indeed geocentrism will be back with us with a vengeance!

Nonetheless, if the perspective proposed in the creeds be true, then it remains that Christianity involves that the consummation of the history of the universe be coincident with or at the very least centered and dependent on the consummation of human history. This is very difficult for modern, "secular" man to stomach.

Yet, this is, of course, the usual human perspective anyway. It has been quite typical for Man to accord an unexplained centrality to "the history of the proletariat" or of "the march of human progress." One can be rather surprised at the optimistic presumption involved in the progressivism of the Enlightenment whether as expressed in liberal optimism, in Marxism, or in various forms of racism or eugenics. Perhaps, paradoxically, all of these have their ultimate roots in Biblical eschatology—having the status, as it were, of modern deistic or atheistic heresies—the same historical directedness, except to a paradise only on earth, but somehow without God.

We learn from Scripture that "no-one will know the day or the hour." That is, there will be no way of reading the timing of the end of the universe from our knowledge of cosmology any more than from the tendencies in human history. We are to expect a Parousia, a completion of all things in the second coming of Christ, a coming in glory—raising the dead and judging both living and dead, and constituting "a new heaven and new earth," inaugurating the kingdom of God, the new Jerusalem, the Holy City described in the last two chapters of the Apocalypse. No doubt, it will then be evident in retrospect how all things have been made ready for it, and all things led up to it. But, if indeed "no-one will know the day or the hour," then there will be no way of knowing this beforehand—as St. Paul and Barth insisted, as against the German National Socialists and many others under the influence of Hegel.

The whole Cosmos will indeed have been prepared, but we will not now be able to see what it is being prepared for or how it is being prepared for it. Astronomy and biology will be as useless as human affairs for the purposes of calculating the time. It will be useless to speculate that the universe will come to an end or to this or that kind of physical climax—useless to calculate when the condition of the sun will make life on earth untenable, or when this or that other crisis will arise. The future is not yet; it does not yet exist and its existence at each stage depends on God's action in upholding things in existence. Indeed, it is because it does not exist that its possibilities may not yet be all determined let alone knowable—all depends not only upon man's freedom, but upon God's.

IV. THE CLARITY OF SCRIPTURE: THE CENTRALITY OF THE INCARNATION TO UNIFIED COSMIC HISTORY

The Scriptures portray Jesus, God from God, through whom all things were made, conceived in the womb of the Virgin Mary, crucified and dying, rising again to glory to be recognized even in his humanity as Lord of Lords, whose name is above every name, as having a cosmic role even in this humanity.

This perspective is most obvious in St. John's Gospel. In this, he joins the author of Genesis in making history include physics, rather than considering physics as fundamental, history overlying it as various series of incidents accidentally arising on its surface or as a side effect. Genesis begins by telling us that "In the beginning God created the heavens and the earth" and the Gospel begins by telling us "In the beginning was the Word, and the Word was with God, and the Word was God. He was in the beginning with God; all things were made through him, and without him was not anything made that was made."

And the same perspective appears, not only in the Book of Revelation, but also extendedly in St. Paul, envisaging the Incarnation as central to the consummation not just of man but of the whole universe. Thus, in Colossians 1:15–20, St. Paul says:

> [Jesus] is the image of the invisible God, the first-born of all creation, for in him all things were created, in heaven and on earth,

> visible and invisible, whether thrones or dominions or principalities or authorities—all things were created through him and for him. He is before all things, and in him all things hold together. He is the head of the body, the church; he is the beginning, the first-born from the dead, that in everything he might be preeminent. For in him all the fullness of God was pleased to dwell, and through him to reconcile to himself all things, whether on earth or in heaven, making peace by the blood of his cross.

And we can take this together with the fuller Ephesians 1:3–10, 15–22:

> [God and Father of our Lord Jesus Christ] ... destined us in love to be his sons through Jesus Christ, according to the purpose of his will.... For he has made known to us in all wisdom and insight the mystery of his will, according to his purpose which he set forth in Christ as a plan for the fulness of time, to unite all things in him, things in heaven and things on earth ... according to the working of his great might which he accomplished in Christ when he raised him from the dead and made him sit at his right hand in the heavenly places, far above all rule and authority and power and domination, and above every name that is named, not only in this age but also in that which is to come, and he has put all things under his feet and has made him the head over all things for the church, which is his body, the fulness of him who fills all in all.

One of the key features of Old Testament theology is the idea of the unity of creation and of God as Lord, not just of Israel, but of all peoples, and not just of all peoples but of all the worlds and beings in them, creating and sustaining all things in existence—for he loves all that exists since if he had not, he would not have made it. How, if he did not will it, could a thing persist, how could it be conserved if not called forth by him? (cf. Wisdom 11:25–12:1). This perspective appears in Genesis 1, repeatedly in the prophets, especially Isaiah, repeatedly in the Psalms and all through the main Wisdom Literature, notably Job, Proverbs, and Daniel.[13] To the New Testament reader, it is

13 Jewish tradition groups Daniel with the Writings, of which the wisdom literature and Psalms are the principal components, rather than with the Prophets.

first conspicuously announced in the prologue in St John's Gospel in deliberate echo of Genesis, then in the passages of St Paul which I have already cited, and again in Hebrews and in the Book of Revelation. In all these cases it is made clear that the history to which the Incarnation is central is not just the history of man but the history of the universe. All the Gospels, St. Paul, II Peter, and the Book of Revelation present the consummation of human history as coinciding with the consummation of cosmic history in the epoch begun in the initial creation, to be succeeded in the arrival of a "new heaven and earth."

V. THE REASON WHY THE INCARNATION WAS NECESSARY FOR THE FULL SALVATION GOD INTENDED

V.1. GETTING TO THE ROOT OF THE MATTER

The key to understanding the necessary uniqueness of the Incarnation lies in getting a proper insight into the difference between God's being incarnate and God's merely indwelling.

What we need to do is understand the full significance of Jesus's Divine Sonship having two modes of realization. Thus, this sonship has its original and primary realization within the furnace of the life of God independently of creation and all time, the furnace which immediately present to each thing gives it existence and sustains it in existence and has done this for each thing since the beginning of time.

But the Incarnation has the significance that besides this, Jesus's sonship also has another realization, its realization in human nature which was something not just static but as he grew involved the progressive opening out of every possibility of this human nature to express and answer to the divine nature, a progression consummated in his glorification in his resurrection and ascension. We have to give emphasis to the Ascension because when we speak of the Resurrection, we are directing our attention only to the complete restoration of man so as to be restored in body and freed from all the weaknesses of the body. But there is more to be spoken of: this we are speaking of when we speak of the Ascension, for then we are putting the accent on the raising of humanity to the glory and vision of God, so that by the Ascension humanity is raised, as it were, to the measure of the ecstatic and unlimited love and immediate vision which this requires.

The word "son" can be used as a metaphor to refer to many different degrees of intimacy in kind of relationship. The significance of the Incarnation is that by taking on a created nature, Christ raised the meaning of the word "son" as applied to created personal beings to a maximum, to a level measured to his own creaturely expression of his own sonship, so that we as human beings stand as brothers and sisters, friends and companions of the ever living, risen Jesus, thereby taken up into a sharing in his life with God. Thus, when Jesus in his own humanity prayed "Abba, Father," he set the measure of what it means for angel or man to say "Abba, Father."

God's intending the Incarnation in his original act of creation is what gave existence to this maximally heightened kind of sonship. The Incarnation is what constituted this role of being a son, giving it an existence which otherwise it would never have had. For man who is an historical being, Jesus's becoming man pioneered this role, created a hope, an inheritance of which otherwise man would never have had—and, being by nature a social being, no man could enter into this role in its fullness until Jesus himself had done so in his humanity.

Let me explain the matter more fully.

V.1.(a) THE MEANING OF THE TERMS "FATHER" AND "SON" IN REGARD TO THE RELATIONSHIP OF GOD AND MAN

I think it will help if I develop the explanation of this in what may seem a rather speculative way, before coming back to see its entirely Scriptural and traditional character. Belief is a precondition of understanding—but once a glimmer of understanding is attained, it may help in the exposition of belief.

We are, I believe, apt to be misled by the ease with which we and others seem able to use the terms "son" and "father" in regard to the relationship between man and God—misled into supposing that they are used clearly and unambiguously in this context. We meet, indeed, in the Old Testament various uses of the phrases "son of God" and "sons of God" as well as the sentence quoted by Jesus "ye are gods," and we have the reference in Luke to "Adam, son of God," and numerous Old Testament references to God as father, sometimes father of Israel. "Out of Egypt have I called my son," "I will be to him a father, and he to me a son," are but two of a multitude of instances.

But what is implied in the use of these terms "father" and "son"? Evidently, the primary things might seem to be the implication of loving care in God, and of the appropriateness of willing duty in man. And this loving care may be for those who are yet immature, not yet ready for their full inheritance. But, whenever the term "son" is used, there seems to be some implication that either the present relationship, or the fulfilment or inheritance it is oriented towards, includes more than is implied, for instance, in the relation of servant to lord, more even than in the relation of friend to friend. There is implied some likeness of sons to father, and some likeness making possible some sharing as it were in one family life, or in a relationship in which the son has or may inherit something of his father's kind of life, place, standing or status.

However, thinking a priori without bringing in revelation, there seems no reason why there might not be many degrees of likeness, many degrees of sharing and reciprocity, many levels of supernatural or grace-dependent relationship or friendship between man and God. In the case of all of these levels, a metaphor of "sonship" might not seem inappropriate—but in this picture there would not be any single well-defined role, or level of intimacy picked out by this metaphorical use of the word "son." And just as, if we think of the natural numbers 1, 2, 3, 4, 5, and so on, there is no greatest natural number amongst them, and we can always find a bigger one, so also, it might seem to us that there were no maximum in kinds of sonship.

But, in that case all knowledge of God would be (we might anticipate) in a way indirect, in that man could never attain to a stage of knowing God by vision, in the manner God knows Himself. And (we might further anticipate) all love of God would be as it were controlled or limited, men pleasing God and showing themselves as friends and sons by preferring God's will to all other ends in their deliberate choices, but never seized or enraptured by God, so as to have God as the central pre-occupation of their attention or their heart and desire. In such a context, although there would be no limit to growth in this indirect knowledge, and in this controlled or deliberate love, and no maximum in the receiving of grace to make it possible, still it would remain that there would never be any knowledge or any love or any grace which was in any way at all proportioned to God's infinity. As even very large numbers fall short of infinity by as much as very small numbers, so also in this case. And, so long as there is no kind of sharing in God's mode of knowledge, or in God's mode of love, i.e., no kind of sharing in God's kind of life, then still we might say, that the distance remains infinite in a way incompatible with friendship or any kind of companionship. And in such case, the metaphor of sonship would lack definite or uniquely determined sense and be in no way forced upon us—and indeed would seem strained and remote.

There will be, then, a clear and well-defined role and kind of relationship picked out by the word "son," only if a change of mode of relationship is possible from limited and controlled to uncontrolled ecstatic love, from indirect and conceptual to direct knowledge or vision. But it is not in the least clear to unaided reason that any such change and elevation of the mode of man's relationship with a God is possible for man. We are aware, reading such writers as St. John of the Cross, following in a long tradition beginning with St. Paul in Corinthians, that human faculties must become in some way passive in more intimate unions with God. But there is a question as to how, in the beatific vision spoken of in I Corinthians 13 and Revelation 22, these faculties could continue to operate at all in any way—yet if they do not operate, our act is not involved, and in that case, there seems no sense in saying that we are involved at all. If our love and knowledge are not there, then there is no vision, no love, on our part, and therefore none of this sharing in the Divine Life which is spoken of.

V.1.(b) THE SIGNIFICANCE OF JESUS MADE MAN BEING SON OF GOD

Now, let us return to consider the Incarnation and the role of the work of Jesus in the flesh directly.

For I wish to suggest to you that the role of "son of God" ("son by adoption and grace"), of which Christians speak, as a role open to men, is not a role which could exist at all for man apart from Jesus's bringing it into existence. God the Father had to be known by some man as natural Father, as Father in virtue of the very identity of the man concerned, in virtue of who he was, before any man could know Him as Father by gift and adoption. Precursors of Jesus, both ones in the Old Testament and others, are sons in a proper sense only in virtue of the promise of an inheritance not yet entered into, in virtue of an enablement for an actuality not yet actualized. Jesus is, I would suggest, the pioneer of actual human filial love for God the Father as Father, pioneer of the actual exercise of the full human filiality I am speaking about. The role of a "son" capable of entering humanly in a human manner, with human faculties, into the Divine Life, participating in God's kind of love and knowledge, is a role created, brought into existence, only through this pioneering of Jesus. And the gift of the Spirit which Jesus gives when he is glorified is the Spirit of sonship which moves us to cry "Abba, Father," giving us knowledge of our own sonship—the Spirit in virtue of which, just as Jesus, while loving the Father ecstatically unrestrictedly before all things, yet continued all the while doing the Father's work in and for the world, so we are made able also to continue the Father's work in the world, sharing his priorities and His love of the world, all the while growing in an uncontrolled fire of love for Him before all things.

Let me restate the matter and develop it in four points.

(1) Apart from the Incarnation, and apart from relationship to Jesus as God incarnate, there could be no maximum in the manner in which man received grace, also there could be no receiving of grace however great in any man whatsoever which allowed any friendship, companionship or sharing accommodated to God's infinity. There would be no sonship in the full sense Christians envisage, only various grades of diminished relationship, different in kind from this—only a giving of the spirit by measure, to a few and in a restricted respect, as in Numbers 11:16–30, not "without measure" as through Jesus (Jn 3:34).

However, it would be nonsense to say that this man Jesus was the eternal Son of God, if His filial love and knowledge did not have a human realization and expression, if he did not humanly know His Father as Father, and thence know Himself as Son, in the full sense of the words "father" and "son," implying the capacity to share in the same mode of love and knowledge and life. Therefore, in Jesus there arrived a created capacity for love and knowledge which, while not equal to God's infinity, was somehow proportioned to it in such a way as to allow a perfect expression of his divine sonship in his humanity; and God could not will or bring about the Incarnation without willing and bringing about this. The uncontrolled or ecstatic love which is a condition for, and of a piece with the Beatific Vision, and which is in us a gift depending on Jesus, was native to Jesus.

It is not that Jesus, in virtue of his identity, was possessed of a rather large quantity of grace and rather high degree of perfection (granted that there is no maximum in these things), but that he was possessed of a different mode of grace and perfection—or, if you prefer to put it this way, a different mode of relationship—from any that might have been possible apart from the Incarnation.

(2) God could not give this mode of relationship to Jesus without thereby opening the possibility of it to other men. Emile Mersch explains that God could not divinize Jesus's humanity, without therein also divinizing His sociality, this being integral to His humanity. We could put the matter in this way: God could not establish or hold this man, Jesus, in filial relation to Himself, without thereby opening the possibility to other men to be Jesus's brothers. By becoming man once and making the Spirit of Sonship present in one man, he thereby opens the possibility to all. The situation of a human son of God needed to be created and constituted; this was achieved in Jesus; but once created, it could not be limited, for it is in the created nature or state of man as such that men are brothers in spiritual community with one another, so that to choose to become Incarnate, to become one man alongside others, could not but carry with it the opening of sonship of God to all. Smuggle the Spirit of Sonship into mankind in one man, and thereby it is established as accessible for all. But it has to be established as intrinsic and native to one, before it can be received by gift by others. Yet once present in one, it is fecund for all.

(3) The fecundity of Jesus's humanity, whereby he could communicate the Spirit of sonship to all, waits until His human faculties have been raised to be able to participate in a human manner in all the gracious workings of God, waits therefore until the restrictions on human consciousness associated with the present condition of our human life have been shorn away, waits therefore until His glorification or Ascension following the Resurrection. Thus, as I remarked before, I see the Ascension as primarily the completion of the unfolding of what was naturally involved in the Incarnation—the Incarnation implied an unfolding in which Jesus would in His human faculties, firstly be able to love

His Father with the uncontrolled love proper to a Son, and then growing out of this to participate humanly ever more extensively and in the end perfectly in all the gracious works of the Father. This unfolding is consummated after Jesus's death, when in being glorified, he became able to impart to others what he had in Himself as man as well as coming to participate humanly in the knowledge and willing of the whole of creation.

(4) Jesus knew of His own Sonship in knowing His Father as Father, but we (I would suggest) know of our sonship only in knowing the Father as primarily the Father of Jesus, but thereby as also Father of us, alongside Jesus. Our Sonship, our capacity for uncontrolled love, and ultimately for direct knowledge, our capacity to retain our human faculties within the context of rapture and vision, and even somehow to exercise them within this context, so that it is we who are loving and knowing, absolutely depends (I would suggest) on a continued relationship with Jesus in his humanity, that is, on a relationship with Jesus who lives in us as the ground of the working of the Spirit in us; the Jesus who is the Object of our love, whom we address in prayer, receive in Communion, has to be realized as human as well as divine; His being in reality, and not merely in imagination or supposition, actively present, not just in his divinity but also as man, present alongside us as our companion in the love, worship and knowledge of the Father, is indispensable to the possibility of our loving and knowing God in the uncontrolled and direct way I spoke of, to the possibility of our being sons whose inheritance is an entering into, a sharing of, the Divine Life, in the sense I spoke of.

Thus, my suggestion is that it was because, in the very act of creating anything, God intended to be incarnate that in the very act of creation he set what it would mean for a created being to be by adoption and grace a son of God. To essentially bodily beings such as man, set within an essentially physical or body-including universe and social by nature, and therefore in an essentially historical and time-bound setting, this means being in a setting which the full gift of the Holy Spirit and possibility of unmeasured love and immediate vision of God waits upon the historical death and glorification of Jesus, God made man, thereby initiating a humanly social company of human sons of God.

V.2. THE CONSISTENCY OF THE COSMIC PERSPECTIVE: THE ANGELS

The passages from St Paul which I cited earlier imply a cosmic perspective, extending to the whole universe and embracing even the angels, a perspective evident also in other passages to which I alluded earlier. This breadth of perspective might be questioned by some, appealing to Hebrews 2:10–18:

> As it was his purpose to bring a great many of his sons into glory, it was appropriate that God, for whom eveything exists and through whom everything exists, should make perfect, through suffering, the leader who would take them to their salvation. For the one who sanctifies, and the ones who are sanctified, are of the same stock; that is why he openly calls them *brothers* in the text *I shall announce your name to my brothers, praise you in full assembly*; or the text: *In him I hope* ; or the text: *Here I am with the children whom God has given me.*
>
> Since all the *children* share the same blood and flesh, he too shared equally in it, so that by his death he could take away all the power of the devil, who had power over death, and set free all those who had been held in slavery all their lives by the fear of death. For it was not the angels that he took to himself; he took to himself *descent from Abraham*. It was essential that he should in this way become completely like his brothers so that he could be a compassionate and trustworthy high priest of God's religion, able to atone for human sins. That is, because he has himself been through temptation he is able to help others who are tempted. (Jerusalem Bible, Heb 2).

Or, in the corresponding RSV translation of the key verses 14–18:

> Since therefore the children share in flesh and blood, he himself likewise partook of the same nature, that through death he might destroy him who has the power of death, that is, the devil, and deliver all those who through fear of death were subject to lifelong bondage. For surely it is not with angels that he is concerned but with the descendants of Abraham. Therefore he had to be made like his brethren in every respect, so that he might become a merciful

> and faithful high priest in the service of God, to make expiation for the sins of the people. For because he himself has suffered and been tempted, he is able to help those who are tempted.

However, there is no real problem introduced by this passage and the frequently recurring thought that the most evident reason for the Incarnation was to save man, undoing the results of sin. In the Christian conception, the original plan of creation included not only the aspects or stages of the unfolding history of the natural universe, each in itself good, indicated in Genesis 1, but also that there should be company, companionship, communion between God and his creatures. God desired that creatures should enter into his glory.

God is in himself self-sufficient, not needing to create anything. For he would not have been alone even if there had been no creation, since he includes perfect community within himself, of Father with Son, and of Father and Son with the Holy Spirit—no relationship such as Father with Son, or any other duo, being complete in itself without a completion, a fruit, an expression of its non-enclosed nature *qua* personal relationship.

Yet, there is no envy in God, no jealousy making him wish to limit the enjoyment of his fullness to himself, no jealousy inhibiting him from creation, and no sense of economy in the variety of ways in which his wonder might be reflected and echoed in creation. And we are to understand that from the first he intended that there should be intellectual creatures, "persons." Intellect embraces not only theoretical or contemplative (imitating the Latin, "speculative") knowledge but also appreciation and enjoyment of the good, above all the highest good, other persons and love of them. Such persons, we must see, should be in company with him. So, in Jewish understanding, especially from the time of the exile, a special feature of the glory of God was that he lives surrounded by a company of angels, the seven archangels corresponding with the seven branches of the candlestick before the altar of God, their very presence thus symbolized an expression of the glory of God.

The angels are described as "sons" of God. And they live, not in a separate world or paradise of their own, but in the very presence of God, in Christian understanding "seeing" God. And this was from the very beginning of time, not waiting for the Incarnation to take place.

How then does the rapture of the angels, their being truly "sons" of God, depend on the Incarnation? Because the possibility of any creature being a "son" of God, of enjoying such intimacy with God so as to be brought within the ambit of his glory and to enjoy the sight of him, depended on its creation being from the very first set within a general plan which included that God the Son, divine by nature, should at some time take on creaturely nature. The meaning of what it is and always was to be a "son" of God, and what it depends and depended on—how it is that created persons can hold company with God—was made plain and effected by God himself taking on some personal creaturely nature.

But why did God take on human nature, rather than for instance some angelic nature?

For this we can give three reasons.

Firstly, and most evidently, God took on human nature in order to save man from the effects of sin, man having been created so weak and changeable as to be capable not only of falling from grace only by the assistance of some self-deception, but also as to be capable with the help of grace of a willing repentance. It is commonly supposed, however, that the angels with clearer vision have no such weakness and changeability of will.

Secondly, it would seem more fitting to take on human nature because it is social, conceived and born into a family so that all human beings are in a sense siblings. A human's roots include not only his human forebears but the whole of nature from which he springs and with which he remains in community. And, in this, the human condition is especially apt to reflect the character of God as containing relationship within himself and the whole plan of God to form not just a set of individuals but a company of persons in relationship.

However, we can follow the indications of Scripture and the idea commonly expressed by the Fathers that, although they are not bodily creatures, not parts of the physical universe, nonetheless the angels were not created before or separately from the physical universe, but at the same time having the role of ministers to us.[14] As it says in

14 Aquinas conceived even the angels as created in relation with the world, and as having a succession of acts though not at dividing points in our continuous time (*S.Th.* Ia, Q. 61, art. 3, and Q. 62, art. 5, reply 2, cf. art. 9, reply 3).

Genesis 1:1, "In the beginning, God created heaven and earth"—not first heaven and then earth. And all explicit references to angels in the Old Testament seem to have to do with some ministering to mankind, and the same is true in the Gospels and Acts. It also fits with St. Paul's conception of the whole of creation being subject to futility (Romans 8) awaiting the revelation of the sons of God and of creation as a whole only being brought to completion in Christ, the fullness of all in all.

VI. ILLUSTRATIONS OF THE WAYS IN WHICH THE IDEA OF MULTIPLE INCARNATION HAS BEEN PERCEIVED AS ALIEN TO CHRISTIANITY: THE SIGNIFICANCE OF THE REJECTION OF ORIGEN

The importance of the intrinsically unique character of the Incarnation is borne out in the history of discussion after the first century.

Origen held the view that in order that Christ might save "the spiritual hosts of wickedness in the heavenly places ... we should not fear to allow that something similar [parallel to the crucifixion] also happens there [in the heavenly places] and will happen in the ages to come until the end of the whole world." In his *Commentary on the Gospel of John* (1, 34), Origen tells us 'the Savior became "all things to all" that he might either "gain all" (cf. 1 Cor 9:22) or make them perfect: he became a human being to the humans and an angel to the angels' and (19, 1) refers to Christ as "him, who is also angel, and the rest of the powers," and in his homilies on Genesis at 8, 8 says that "among the angels he will also be found as an angel." Jerome thus seems to be right to attribute to Origen the view that Christ not only became a man to save human kind but also became a daemon to save daemons (cf Origen, *Commentary on the Gospel of John*, 1, 34)—a view Jerome emphatically rejects.

This rejection was formalized by the bishops gathered together for the Second Council of Constantinople in 553.[15] The anathemas thus directed against those regarded as followers of Origen include many elements indicating groups imbued with Gnostic ideas with some evidence of occultism, which considering the strange features of modern superstition, begin to seem more relevant to our day than

15 Grillmeier, A., *Christ in Christian Tradition*, Vol. 2, Part 2, 402–10.

they have been for many centuries. However, the seventh anathema does directly relate to what Origen actually held, and is the one most directly relevant to our present concerns, and runs as follows:

> If anyone says that *nous* [Christ] is said to exist in the form of God and before all the ages was united to the God-Logos and at the end of the ages emptied itself into what is human and showed mercy, as they say, on those who in multiformed ways had fallen out of the *henade* [a supposed original unity in which all intelligences were gathered together in nakedness pre-existing their different forms of body] and with the intention of leading them up, came to all and assumed the form of various bodies and acquired their names, by becoming all things to all (cf. 1 Cor. 9:22), to the angels an angel, to the powers a power, and to the other orders and types of rational beings he was changed to each in the appropriate manner and thus participated in us similarly in flesh and blood (cf. Heb. 2:14) and became for human beings a human being, and whoever does not confess that the God-Logos emptied himself and became a human being, let him be anathema.[16]

There are many issues wrapped up together here. The so-called Origenists viewed all created intellectual beings as pre-existing any bodies, and so as united in an original nakedness, then, having been redeemed, returning to unity in this original kind of nakedness. In considering the logical significance of the statement of the bishops, we have to realize that they would have had no definite views as to whether or not all or some supernatural or preternatural beings had bodies.[17] The bishops of the council might quite naturally have thought, in accord with St. Paul's way of thinking in I Corinthians, that there are many kinds of bodies which we do not know of, and they may have supposed that some different kinds of angel had different kinds

16 Grillmeier, 405.

17 They would not have been tied to St. Thomas's view that angels had no matter (a view rejected by Duns Scotus) or to its Aristotelian corollary that each angel is of a different species, although they are still grouped in genera. And when early Christian writers speak of daemons, they commonly have in mind bodily beings, treating satyrs and fauns as examples (Augustine, *De Civ. Dei xv*, cf. Aquinas, *S. Th.* Ia Q. 51, Art. 3 ad 6, cf. Q. 52, art 3 obj. 3 and ad 3).

of body, although presumably not of corruptible flesh and blood.[18] What is clear in these anathemas is firstly the bishops' rejection of any idea of created beings with bodies pre-existing these bodies, and secondly of the idea of a being created bodily having a fulfillment without a body—in particular they were rejecting the idea that in the final consummation human beings would be without bodies. (They also rejected the subordinationist view that *nous* or Christ had a mediatorial role in creating bodies in which God the Father had no intrinsic part.) The whole decree has the implication that God the Word took on created nature, once, and once only, not many times in different worlds or different bodies for different kinds of being.

Historically, the notion of a many times repeated incarnation of God, for the sake of each different stock and each different nature, was associated with dualism, many different kinds of spirit preexisting many different kinds of body, and this type of dualism (often associated with astrology) was often in ancient times associated with the occult cultivation of relationships with such spirits. It was also presumed that the same spirits which had been at the beginning without bodies, and had sinned while in the body, would be in the end after redemption again restored to a supposed original unity or community in the spirit world, the body in the natural universe having no place in the final end of all things.

Other confusions can enter in. For instance, when Hindus think of Rama and Krishna as "incarnations" of Vishnu, these are only two out of a supposed twenty-four, and these include supposed incarnations in some lower animal natures, fish and the like. If one reflects on this, it seems likely that some of them have an Apollinarian conception of incarnation, namely, a conception in which the God who is incarnate substitutes for the human or other soul. By contrast, Christian tradition has considered it vital that Jesus had a human soul, mind, and will.

Western theological opinion has been that, while God is immediately present in each and every thing as immediate cause of being, upholding it in existence, a divine person can only be incarnate in an intellectual (rational, *logistikon*) creaturely nature. That is, the divine person is thus one *hypostasis* (Aristotelian first substance[19])

18 Duns Scotus held that the angels were composed of form and matter.

19 Cf. Thomas Aquinas, *S. Th.* Ia, Q. 29, Art. 2.

in two natures, divine and creaturely, or as Latin theology says, presuming the limitation to intellectual creaturely natures, one person in two natures, by God's choice the creaturely nature being human rather than any other.

The willingness to envisage multiple incarnations of the same person, whether the person be simply human as in applications of the law of *karma* in Hindu understanding or more complexly understood as in Tibetan and some other Buddhism, or divine as in Christianity and as with the supposed multiple incarnations of Vishnu in Hindu belief, is always dependent on a divorce between the person and his or her multiple embodiments and associated earthly biographies. It goes with a substitution of the notion of the reincarnation of a human soul, incarnated many times in a human or animal body, for the Christian conception of a single biography of the human person, once and once only to be resurrected, his or her resurrection state being a continuation or further growth from one single already established earlier biography.

The Incarnation, therefore, happened once. This does not, however, restrict its consequences, but works in the exact opposite direction. It is precisely its singularity which renders it so unfathomably fruitful, which gives it the scope to redeem not just mankind, but the cosmos itself.

CHAPTER 6

THE INCARNATION AND MAN'S SALVATION[1]

For what purpose did God become incarnate? The Nicene Creed declares that it was "for us men and for the sake of our salvation" that Jesus, God from God, begotten before all ages, became man.

Why was the Incarnation thus necessary to the achievement of this purpose of our salvation, or how was it for our sakes? Or, if it was not strictly necessary but only suitable, fitting, and conducive to this purpose, still the question remains as to how it was thus suitable, fitting, and conducive?

In recent times, some theologians have suggested that there is no theory of the Atonement which explains why the Incarnation should have been necessary to human salvation or even peculiarly suitable as a means to it—suggesting that man's being freed from sin and brought to life in communion

1 [Editor's note: The earliest version of this essay is dated to 2007. Braine continued to develop it into 2014. I can find no evidence that it was ever published or that it was publicly read in anything near its current form.]

with God could just as well have been accomplished without God's having become incarnate. These same theologians tend to view the doctrine of the Incarnation as insupportable in the light of modern biblical criticism except as a construction of the Church's later thinking, and even as inherently paradoxical and logically contradictory.[2] In the view of these theologians, since the doctrine is of no use in explaining the Atonement or man's salvation, then in view of the supposed difficulties arising from biblical criticism and from logic, the doctrine appears to be an incubus which theology would be better without.

Such is the background of our present discussion. We have to rediscover the way in which the Incarnation is indeed necessary or conducive to man's salvation.

1. TWO APPROACHES: THE INCARNATION AS THE HISTORICAL CONDITION OF SALVATION, OR ONLY AS ITS MORAL CONDITION

We need to begin by distinguishing two ways, not necessarily exclusive of each other, in which the incarnation, life, death, resurrection, and ascension of Jesus have been thought to make it possible for other men to come to share in the Divine Life.

1.(a) THE NEW TESTAMENT PRESENTATION OF THE INCARNATION AS THE HISTORICAL CONDITION OF OUR SALVATION

In the first place, the New Testament clearly represents to us what I will call an historical or causal connection of Jesus's incarnation, death, and ascension with men's salvation.

Three things are involved in this New Testament presentation of the matter.

(i) There is some fuller gift of the Spirit, given at Pentecost, prophesied by Joel, which belongs to the end-time of the world inaugurated by the completion of Jesus's work in his death, resurrection, and ascension, and which was not given to men until this work was completed.

2 Conspicuous among such thinkers was Maurice Wiles in his *The Remaking of Christian Doctrine* (London: SCM, 1974).

(ii) Further, it was not accidental that this gift was not given to men before the completion of Jesus's work. Rather, this gift absolutely could not be given before that time, before Jesus had not only died, but also risen and ascended to glory. Thus St. John says (16:7) "Unless I go, the Comforter will not come to you; but if I go, I will send him to you." And St. Paul says: "It was said that he would: when he ascended to the height, ... he gave gifts to men ... The one who rose higher than all the heavens to fill all the Universe is none other than the one who descended [right down to the lower regions of the earth]" (Eph 4:8,9). And one may recall that before this time, St. John's Gospel tells us that Jesus himself did not baptize (Jn 4:2).

There is nothing new in the idea that the Holy Spirit resided by grace in human beings before Jesus's becoming incarnate but was given in a fuller way at Pentecost. Thus, Pope Leo XIII tells us that it is certain that the Holy Spirit resided by grace in the just who lived before Christ, instancing the prophets and from St Luke's Gospel Zechariah, John the Baptist, Simeon, and Anna. The self-communication of the Holy Spirit at Pentecost was not such that "then for the first time he would have begun to dwell in the saints, but that he was poured on them more abundantly; crowning, not beginning his gifts; not commencing a new work but giving more abundantly" in the words of Leo the Great.[3]

(iii) Finally, it is not just that that the completion of Jesus's works is an external and moral condition for God the Father to give this gift of the Spirit, as it were, independently of Jesus's human involvement. Rather, it is precisely from Jesus in his glorified humanity, with his Father, that we receive this gift of the Spirit (as St. John has it "living water flows from his belly [innards]": that is, he implies that the Spirit flows from Jesus's humanity, that it flows in virtue of his death). Jesus lives in us, in such a sense that the Spirit within us is, as it were, his breathing or breath in and through us; and the Jesus who lives and breathes in us is not Jesus in his Divinity alone, since Jesus no longer exists in his Divinity alone, but Jesus as he has remained since his conception in the womb, complete man as well as perfect God—the risen, living, continuingly human, Jesus.

3 Leo the Great, *Sermon 77*, as quoted by Leo XIII in *Divinum Illud* (1897).

We should not think of the Ascension as the closing off of an episode in the existence of the eternal Son of God, an episode of which his conception in the womb of Mary was the beginning, an episode during which he had been able to complete certain tasks on earth, including the making of a supreme sacrifice, achieving certain moral and legal purposes, but an episode now over. Rather the taking on of human life for Jesus was something with a beginning but without an end: he remains everlastingly unendingly man in company with us.

Further, we should see a process of growth from childhood to adulthood in Jesus, a process in which his human faculties were brought from an undeveloped infant state to a state of mature humanity, and to envisage an increasing participation of Jesus in a human manner in his Father's work in the world. Everlastingly, Jesus participates in a divine manner in his Father's work, even before the Incarnation. But does he participate in a human manner? Is his humanity involved in these works of the Father? Surely, we are told that in his earthly existence, it was not just that the lowliness of the condition he took on consisted in his becoming man, but that this lowliness consisted in taking on humanity in a serf-like condition, willingly not drawing upon his Vision of the Father to gain knowledge or consolation inappropriate to this condition and his ministry and so with the restricted human consciousness, liability to privation, dependence on others, and openness to death at the hands of others, that go with that condition. And I take it that the significance of the Ascension or glorification of Jesus is that in it, Jesus's humanity attained a freedom from restriction appropriate to who he was, a capacity to participate not just in a divine manner, but in a human manner in all the gracious works of the Father.

If Jesus's humanity is not in this sense raised to God but remains always in a separate lower sphere of action, then the Incarnation (God's choice to live a human life) is partial and grudging in its unfolding. *For this reason, the Ascension was the completion of the unfolding of what was implicit in the Incarnation*: the Incarnation means that the proper state of Jesus in his humanity is of the state which the disciples temporarily glimpsed at the Transfiguration, but (as St. Paul says) he did not cling to this state, but accepted the condition of a slave (he did not call upon the legions of angels when his betrayal took place, but accepted death).

So, whatever essentially depends on the Ascension can be properly described as springing from the Incarnation. The Incarnation is not a merely physical event celebrated at the feasts of Jesus's conception and birth, the Annunciation and Christmas, but something of which the principal feasts are Easter and the Ascension when what was hidden came to light and took on the powers natural to it, including the power to give the fuller, Pentecostal, gift of the Spirit. This, then, is what is most prominent in the New Testament: an historical or causal dependence of our receiving of grace upon the Incarnation and upon the unfolding of what the Incarnation implied.

You might ask why does the giving of this fuller gift of the Spirit have to be a giving by Jesus in his humanity? Why could not the Father, the eternal Son with him, give it before, even before the Incarnation? Why is it that men are only able to receive it in company with Jesus in his humanity, only able to receive it when they arrive in some real connection: not only with God as such, but with Jesus human as well as divine? These are the key questions.

1.(b) THE CONCEPTION OF UNIVERSALLY AVAILABLE "SANCTIFYING GRACE" BEFORE THE INCARNATION

It is evident that men received some gift of grace, some gift involving the Holy Spirit, before the Ascension, and indeed before the time of Jesus's conception. This grace made men able to love God, to respond to him, to be in friendship with him; a grace such that, if a man died in it, then such a man would be able to enter into the full salvation opened for men by Jesus, would be able to receive the fuller gift and powers of the Spirit that belong to salvation. And there are many New Testament passages envisaging the Old Testament saints, prophets and kings, as waiting until the coming of Christ before being able to enter into that salvation of which they had had only a distant glimpse—entering in, indeed, to "the assembly of the firstborn citizens of heaven" with "the spirits of just men made perfect," which the Epistle to the Hebrews envisages as having been brought into existence through Christ's blood.

Let us call this underlying enabling grace "basic grace": in Roman Catholic writing it appears most commonly as "sanctifying grace," and in Protestant writing as "saving grace" inasmuch as those who die in it are destined for salvation or "justifying grace" inasmuch as by it human beings are made at root right with God.

Now, this basic grace, is commonly said to have been given to men in anticipation of the merits of Christ. It is a grace implying union with the Paschal Mystery, dependent upon it. The fact that in God's counsel and foreknowledge it was decided and certain that Jesus would become incarnate and would accomplish what he did accomplish made it positively fitting for God to give grace. I say positively fitting because the notion of merit is stronger than that of atonement—satisfaction and redemption suggest the removal of causes of unfittingness, whereas merit suggests deserts positively calling forth or requiring the gifts concerned, and it is Jesus's merits which we are here concerned with. But both ideas, merit and atonement, appear to relinquish the idea of an historical and causal dependence of grace-giving upon the work of Jesus, in favor of a moral or legal connection whereby Jesus's work makes grace-giving possible by somehow rendering it fitting.

Now, it is not difficult to see how these two types of connection between Jesus's work and our salvation fit together. There is an underlying basic grace which Jesus's work makes fitting, and which enables men, makes them ready to receive later on the fuller gift of the Spirit which depends historically and causally on Jesus's work and upon involvement in his humanity—enables them to enter into the full salvation which is God's desire for man, but in many cases only after a long delay, waiting until the time of Jesus's Incarnation and glorification, and waiting until after their natural deaths.

1.(c) THE FALSE IDEA OF THE INCARNATION AND PASSION AS ONLY MORAL CONDITIONS OF SALVATION

However, it has been common in giving an account of what Jesus's work achieved to take the second type of connection, the moral and legal, as what is fundamental and almost to ignore the first type of connection, the historical and causal, except so far as it might be explicable quasi-naturalistically in terms of the psychological impact upon individual men of their knowledge of Jesus's life and example.

Thus, there has been a tendency to deny or ignore any distinction between what I call basic or enabling grace and the full gift of the Spirit which I call Pentecostal or end-time grace; and to try and make the essential part of what was objectively achieved by the Incarnation and its sequel something independent of history, consisting only in this moral or legal element. Instead of thinking of the risen and glorified Jesus as the one who gives the Spirit, and instead of thinking of the Eucharist (because of this continued presence and activity) as more than just a memorial meal, there has been a tendency to think of the key and only indispensable part of his redeeming work as consisting in the removal of a moral or legal obstacle to the giving of the Spirit. Instead of thinking of Jesus within us animating us with his Spirit, so that we like him may cry "Abba, Father," so that union with Jesus and possession of the Holy Spirit are one and the same thing, we are led instead to think of Jesus as some man or person external to us with whom we have no connection, except insofar as the Spirit who was in Jesus as he had previously been in the Old Testament Prophets is now also in us; and to think of Jesus's work as relevant only to the removing of a moral or legal obstacle to this giving of the Spirit.

One can speculate upon how it happened that this flagrantly unscriptural account of what Jesus's work achieved become so predominant. Perhaps it resulted partly from a tendency not to ask straightforwardly "What positive end did the Incarnation achieve for us?"—to which the answer might be "that we should be made sons of God, imbued with the Holy Spirit" or "that we should have abundant and eternal life" or "the kingdom of God" or something like this—but instead to ask "What evils within creation rendered the Incarnation and Crucifixion either necessary or at least most suitable?"

But in fact the good achieved for us by the Incarnation and Crucifixion is greater than the mere remedying of various evils, greater than the mere restoration of man to the state he would have been in had these evils never arisen.[4] And God in fact remedied these evils and freed us from sin by opening up to us a way to a higher gift than the one which sin had robbed us of. It is wrong to suppose that the positive answers to the question "What was the Incarnation for?"

4 Thus, Aquinas gives five reasons why suffering and death of Christ were the most suitable way for us to be redeemed from sin, although in his view not absolutely necessary, five reasons each going beyond the mere fact of the remedying of these evils (*S. Th.* III, Q. 46, Art. 3) as we shall see in our discussion below.

contain no more than the negative ones. The preoccupation of the Scriptures with sin in describing God's ends is less exclusive than that of some theologians: eternal life is more than just the failure to perish everlastingly.

Whatever the explanation of this tendency in theological thinking, its harmfulness is very apparent.

(i) It pushes us back to a purely legalistic conception of the atonement, and of the satisfaction achieved by Jesus for men's sins, a conception whereby Jesus's death and passion have no other function except providing satisfaction for sin, so that it seems as if God is exacting cost, pain and suffering for their own sake. This is strange. Normally when we pay debts, we give people money; we give them something that by its nature is of some use to them, not something that has no function in itself at all. However, if Jesus dies on the cross not only in order to satisfy for sins, but also to achieve the end of so identifying himself with the human lot that he can communicate the Divine Life even to the most miserable of his fellow men, then the costliness of the means required means that the act atones for sin, removes any cheapness or mere condoning of evil, without this atonement having been the sole indispensable purpose of the act.

(ii) It pushes us back to an individualistic view of salvation wherein any connection with other men, even with Jesus, is solely moral or legal, with no real relation at the human level being required—as if the only thing that mattered was that Jesus died and not that he is now alive and that we are now in a present human relation to him.

(iii) It makes us think of atonement, expiation, and satisfaction primarily as legal requirements, resulting from a contingent non-necessary decree of God, rather than as arising from intrinsic needs of man. It is not just that it makes the atonement into something merely moral and legal. The situation is worse.

The problem can be stated more starkly, it might seem irreverently, like this: This view makes the atonement look as if it were just words on paper: indeed, how can we say that God became man in order for men to share his life, if he was perfectly capable of giving man a share in his life without this, if he never even had to make the legal requirement that his incarnation then enabled him to waive? Such a way of thinking seems to introduce a circular arbitrariness in the actions of God

Now, this is of course a caricature of the true situation. The decree of God requiring satisfaction is contingent and non-necessary in the sense that God did not need to give grace to human beings, putting them in supernatural friendship with himself. However, granted that God did do this, the good will of God to restore this friendship required what is called satisfaction.

Therefore, in order to see what form this satisfaction needed to take, let us first examine the form it did take, and only then turn again to consider why it was necessary that it should take that form. As Luke asserted, it was 'necessary that the Christ should suffer these things and enter into his glory' (Luke 24:26), necessary that is in order for him to fulfil his vocation as Christ to redeem man. Accordingly, we should first see if we can understand the historical and causal connection of the Incarnation with our salvation, and only then examine whether the moral, fittingness aspect falls into place.

2: THE NATURE OF THE FULLER GIFT OF THE SPIRIT, WHICH CAN ONLY BE GIVEN AFTER THE INCARNATION AND PASSION

What, then, is this fuller gift of the Holy Spirit, this end-time or Pentecostal grace, which Jesus before his passion and death was unable to give to us, and which, after he has been raised in his humanity in the Ascension to glory, he became able to give to us? What is this gift which can be poured out by the risen Jesus, and received by us from him, but which we cannot receive except through his humanity, and cannot receive from him until this humanity has suffered and been brought to glory?

I have only two reasonable answers.

The first is that the end-time gift of the Spirit is that gift of the Spirit which constitutes the Church, marked as she is by that rich interlocking diversity of charisms and workings of the Spirit which make her analogous to a body, the Body of Christ.

And, in a way, this answer is right—but one needs to ask, "What is it about the Church which requires such a special gift of the Spirit?" It cannot be merely the various elements of what is involved in the restoration of human faculties, both to their right use and to the attainment of their goal in their use, the goals of truth and virtue, in thought, word, deed and in the whole communal, social life of man.

All this and even the integrated ensemble of them, indeed flow appropriately from the Incarnation made effective through the Ascension, but neither the parts nor the whole, specified only in this way seem absolutely to require the Incarnation as an historical pre-condition. Indeed, in a fragmentary way, some of the same restorative workings of God are found in the Old Testament and elsewhere prior to the Incarnation, just as also that basic enabling grace which I referred to earlier was present prior to the Incarnation—perhaps and indeed depending upon the fact of the Incarnation legally or for its moral fittingness, but not depending upon it historically or causally.

Rather what makes the constituting of the New Israel, the Church, depend historically and causally upon the work of Jesus in his humanity must be some other more fundamental aspect of the Church, underlying these aspects of restoration, fulfillment, and their communal character. And it must be something which has to do with the special relation to God the Father, and to Jesus in his humanity as its Lord, which constitutes the Church, and from which its other aspects flow, as marks, signs, or effects.

So, this brings me to the second suggestion which needs to be considered as to why the Pentecostal or full gift of the Spirit waits upon the Incarnation and Ascension, namely that it is only after these events that human beings can become in a full sense sons and daughters of God. The Holy Spirit is the Spirit of sonship whereby we are made able alongside Jesus, to pray "Abba, Father."

3: THE PURPOSE OF CHRIST'S SUFFERING AND DEATH

Why did the Messiah have to suffer and die before he could be exalted (Lk 24:26), before he could communicate and impart the Spirit (which he had native to himself) to others?

3.(a) GENERAL PERSPECTIVE UPON THE QUESTION

Granted deprivation as our actual human situation, a situation of physical, psychological, moral, and physical disorders, how could Jesus possibly communicate his Spirit of sonship to us, render us able to participate with our actual, historical and so wounded faculties in knowing and loving the Father, if he had made himself a man of a different ilk, in a different state? God does not work by magic, transforming us independently of our will, but through drawing us to himself, making himself at the same time Object and Ground of our relation with him. There would seem to be some dishonesty or pretense, just as if the Incarnation might just as well have happened in another world, or in a theatre as a mere performance, if God had become man in another state than ours, as if to redeem us independently of the human fitness of our response to his act.

Let us put the matter in another even more metaphorical way. If Jesus is to carry the world with him to God, so that he is as it were carrying its weight, it is not enough that he just passes through the world: he needs to mesh with it. If he had begun and ended his earthly life in such a style as to fail to make man in his present state and condition able to respond in faith, hope and love, in such a style as to fail to make this response as it were natural and congruous for man in this enfeebled disordered state, then there would have been no meshing of such a kind as would enable him to carry the world with him to God, or (to remove some of the metaphors) of such a kind as to enable him to communicate his Spirit and his relationship with the Father to us. The meshing does not consist in the actuality of our response, but in that which Jesus did which is fit to rouse our response, the fact that this response is appropriate being a sign of the honesty and seriousness of the meshing.

Thus, Jesus, the eternal Son, did not merely become a man: he became a man in our condition, the condition of a slave, subject to all our trials and temptations, and to the liability to wounds and injuries inflicted by others, choosing to be in our lowly condition in order that, when exalted, he should be able to communicate his Spirit and his life with his Father even to us in our confused and disordered state. Indeed, scripture and tradition put it more strongly: he so accepted, identified himself with, involved himself with our lowly condition that he needed to suffer and die, not only for our sakes so that, when exalted, he should be able to communicate and impart all that was his to us, but also even for his own sake, in order to come to his glory; he had, as it were, put himself in a situation beyond a point of no return, so that there was no way in which his humanity itself could come to glory, except through death; so, he is said by his death to have merited, not only our, but even his own glory, and his passion is said to be necessary, not only for our deliverance, but even in order to enter his own glory.[5]

It has been said that in virtue of his being divine even the least suffering of Jesus would have had an infinite significance and sufficed to atone, satisfy, or expiate for the sins of the whole human race. Now, academically speaking, this suggestion, traceable in Anselm and Duns Scotus, seems to be correct. That is, if such suffering were undertaken for the sake of love of mankind, and had been inflicted by the sinful acts of other men, then, if we recall who Jesus was, and therefore consider the enormity and abomination constituted by any such infliction of suffering upon him, then I think that we can see that indeed, *if expiation and legal satisfaction had been all that were needed*, then even such a small suffering would have sufficed.

But what was aimed at was not just the paying off of a debt, or the removal of an obstacle to men's serving God, but the positive drawing of men to God, the bringing of men into a state of willing obedience to God, to conversion from sin by acts of love. But it was also the bringing of men into a higher state than this, a state in which they had the Spirit of sonship which would enable them to enter into the uncontrolled love and vision within the Divine Life itself. And it is this, not expiation or satisfaction alone which made Jesus's death necessary. For, as Aquinas tells us, "Christ by his Passion not only freed man from sin, but also merited justifying grace and the glory of bliss."[6] By his Passion Christ not only undid the effects of Adam's sin, but also brought man into the new setting of co-sonship of the Father, the love-formed faith orientated towards the loving vision of God.

What place, then, do the notions of "satisfaction for sin," "paying the debt, incurred by man as a result of his sin" and so forth, have in an understanding of the work of Jesus? How are they to be understood, and why are they still so central to Christian understanding? What is the interconnection between the historical and causal role of Jesus's work, and its moral or legal role?

5 Thomas Aquinas, *Summa Theologica*: III, Q. 49, Art. 6; Luke 24.26—cf. *S. Th.* III, Q. 46, Art. 1, Reply.

6 Thomas Aquinas, *S. Th.* III, Q. 46, Art. 3, in the Reply.

3.(b) THE SPIRITUAL COMMUNITY OF THE HUMAN RACE

In order to explain this, I need as a preliminary to make some remarks about the spiritual community of the human race as a whole.

It is absolutely key to understanding human nature and the human situation to realize that human beings have been created and constituted by God as social and communal beings. We are very familiar with the dependence of children on their parents, and of the interdependence of men, upon one another in general. But it needs to be insisted that God has made the human race interdependent in respect to grace as well as in respect to natural things. God does not push grace upon man without man's consent or desire but raises up the consent and desire in preparation for giving grace. And the consent and desire of others, expressed in prayer, for example, or in the consent and desire of parents bringing their children to baptism, opens the way to grace. Besides the public history, knowable to historians, there is also a secret history of mutual interdependences between men in respect to grace. No one receives grace without the implicit consent or willingness of some others somewhere; and no one receives grace without himself or herself thereby implicitly consenting to others receiving grace. Whoever were to reject this implication, and to prefer that others should not receive grace, as if to close the company of those to receive grace, would kill the life of grace in himself or herself. Whoever acts thus against the spiritual community of mankind, *ipso facto* alienates himself or herself from grace and from God.

The underlying and unrepealed primordial and permanent intention of God is that those who share human nature, simply in virtue of membership of the human race, should be members of one spiritual community, capable of affecting each other by refusing the evil, for good. The way given to us to understand this is that there was once primaevally in principle the possibility open for the human race of no man sinning or turning away from God, and of all men being from their very conception in a state pleasing to God, capable of unimpeded growth in a supernatural relationship of friendship and reciprocity with God. As a result, membership of the community of the human race would, as it were, have had an instant, immediate and universal fecundity in respect of grace, a fecundity transmitted at the same time as life itself, at conception. This is portrayed in Genesis 1 and 2. The effect of some man's having sinned is to destroy this universal fecundity—to deprive this fact, the fact of being spiritually (not merely materially and biologically) members of one another, of the efficacy for supernatural good originally belonging to it.

At this stage we have to envisage two possibilities.

Firstly, there was the possibility that God could have gone entirely back upon the plan of men being spiritually members of one another; could have made it that membership in the human race did not as such carry with it any orientations or dispositions either towards grace, or away from it. As a result, men would not be held back by other men's sins, but at the expense of the gift of community. If God had chosen this way, he would have offered grace to individuals independently of whether or not He had offered it to anyone else. In this hypothetical situation, the human race as a whole would have been radically ungraced, all ultimate inner disposition towards grace or sense of the need for grace being removed. God of his free graciousness might, if he pleased, grace each individual separately, but the total picture would be wholly individualistic, of human individuals extracted from their context each to a relation with God which might just as well have been solitary.

Secondly, there was the possibility actually realized, namely that God should not go back upon his plan that man should be intrinsically communal, not only in respect to natural things, but also in respect to spiritual things; and that, although the basic grace enabling man to come to a state pleasing to God could no longer be transmitted with life itself in the very act of generation, nonetheless a new way should be found whereby man might attain this grace in spiritual community with other men; and that, in anticipation of the work of Jesus, already, in all places and times even before Jesus's coming, God should maintain the power of men's spiritual community for good and not allow all its effects to be evil, for instance still inspiring men to pray for grace for themselves and for others.

We make a mistake when we regard the human race individualistically, and unsurprisingly this makes nonsense of any doctrine of original sin. What is it to be in the state of original sin? It is (a) to be without grace (the basic saving or enabling grace referred to earlier), due to a fault not one's own, owing to a fault of which one is guiltless, and (b) still to be in the situation in which in God's eyes grace ought to be present, although actually absent, and therefore (c) still to be within the scope of the underlying standing determination of God to give grace to the human race. These are the primary aspects of "original sin," although in a longer discussion other consequent aspects would also require mention.

After these preliminary remarks about the spiritual community between Jesus and all men living, even those who are turned away from, let me make a second set of preliminary remarks—this time about satisfaction, expiation, or atonement. We will then be able to draw together the various threads into a unified picture of what is required for man's salvation.

3.(c) DISTINGUISHING TWO ASPECTS OF THE ECONOMY OF GRACE.

In considering what is required for man's salvation, one must distinguish two interrelated questions:

(i) What made it fitting for God to give grace either to individuals or to the whole human race, and, sin having arisen, what makes it again fitting?

(ii) Once a person is in a state of grace, "a member of Christ," what atones for the sins of that person?

Let us address the second question first. Aquinas explains "The head and members [of the Church] are as one mystical person; and therefore Christ's satisfaction belongs to all the faithful as being his members," and that this also fits with the pattern whereby in virtue of a relationship of charity between two persons what one does can atone or "satisfy" for the offence of the other.[7] The headship of Christ is key to Aquinas' understanding of how Christ atones for our sins.[8]

7 Thomas Aquinas, *S. Th.* III, Q. 48, Art. 2, Obj. 1. He adds that in this way atonement differs from contrition and confession: one person can atone for another, even though they cannot be contrite or confess for another.

8 At the very beginning of his explanation of how Christ's Passion achieves its effects, Aquinas explains (*S. Th.* III, Q. 48, Art. 1, corp.) "As stated earlier (Q. 7, arts. 1 and 9, Q. 8, arts. 1 and 5), grace was bestowed upon Christ, not only as an individual, but also as he is the head of the Church so that it might overflow into his members; and therefore, Christ's works are referred to himself and to

He explains, "For since he is our head, then, by the Passion which he endured from love and obedience, he delivered us as his members from our sins, as by the price of his Passion: in the same way as if a man by the good industry of his hands were to redeem himself from a sin committed with his feet. For, just as the natural body is one, though made up of diverse members, so the whole Church, Christ's mystical body, is reckoned as one person with its head, which is Christ."[9] In this way, the merits of Christ suffice to atone for all the sins of those brought into charity, into union with him.

Both Leo and Aquinas make a comparison with medicine: Jesus does not free all men from death, but he provides medicine which, if they avail themselves of it, is able to free them from death; he prepares a medicine by means of which all sicknesses can be cured, that is all sins past, present or to come—but it is a medicine which needs to be applied to each person for their personal sins to be forgiven.[10] St. Thomas tell us "Christ's Passion works its effect in those to whom it is applied through faith and charity and the sacraments of faith' and 'Christ's satisfaction works its effect in us inasmuch as we are incorporated with him as the members with their head," this membership requiring conformity with the head by "receiving the spirit of adoption of sons."[11]

Thus, within Aquinas' summary of the Fathers explanations of Christ's Passion, the way in which it achieved its effects and what these effects are, the whole possibility of Christ's Passion satisfying for men's sins—or, in traditional figures, of his bringing about our salvation "by merit," "by atonement," "by sacrifice," and "by redemption," and of his freeing us from sin, delivering us from the power of the devil, freeing us from the debt of punishment, reconciling us with God and opening the gate of heaven to us—is made to turn

---

his members in the same way as the works of any other man in a state of grace are referred to himself. But it is evident that whosoever suffers for justice's sake, being in a state of grace, merits his salvation thereby, according to Matthew 5:10: 'Blessed are they that suffer persecution for justice's sake.' Consequently, Christ by his Passion merited salvation not only for himself, but likewise for his members."

9 Thomas Aquinas, *S. Th.* III, Q. 49, art. 2, Reply.

10 Thomas Aquinas, *S. Th.* III, Q. 1, Art. 5; *S. Th.* III, Q. 49, Art. 1, ad 3–4.

11 Thomas Aquinas, *S. Th.* III, Q. 49, Art. 3, ad 1, 3.

on our being brought into solidarity with him as members of a body of which he is the head.[12]

We raised two questions, to the first was what made the giving of grace (especially after sin) fitting, and the second was how it was that Christ satisfied for the sins of those who have received grace, that is, who have entered into communion with God by being brought into solidarity with Christ. So far Aquinas' discussion seems to throw light only on the second question.

But now, standing back from the discussion, we can see that it was always God's purpose that man should be in communion with him, and man was made in such a way that this was fitting. After sin, God's underlying original purpose had to be realized without violation of the basic nature of man, and so without prejudice to his dignity and solidarity as an intrinsically social being. Therefore, what was required for suitability was not just the negative thing of deliverance from sin, but firstly that the way of this deliverance should be such that man is moved to it by his will in accord with the proper patterns of human motivation, and most particularly moved to it by love;[13] secondly, that the way of this deliverance should encompass the whole of the fuller salvation intended by God, i.e., extending to the life of glory;[14] thirdly, that it should be by man himself, Jesus in the flesh, that satisfaction should be made and the devil should be overcome, and as we have seen, this satisfaction only applies to men in virtue of an intimate union between them and Christ as comembers of one human social body.[15] In these ways, respect for human dignity and solidarity are taken up within the framework of a larger salvation than was promised in man's creation.

What makes the giving of grace to sinners fitting is the possibility for it to be done in a way appropriate to human nature—with man's full consent and co-operation, in accord with his dignity, without any withdrawal of the essential gifts constitutive of man's special character

12 Thomas Aquinas, *S. Th.* III, Q. 46 – 49.

13 Thomas Aquinas, *S. Th.* III, Q. 46, Art. 3, Reply, first, second and fourth reasons given, and Q. 49, Art. 1, Reply, the first way mentioned.

14 Thomas Aquinas, *S. Th.* III, Q. 46, Art. 3, Reply, third reason given, and Q. 49, Art. 5.

15 Thomas Aquinas, *S. Th.* III, Q. 46, Art. 3, Reply, fifth reason given, and Q. 49, Art. 2.

in creation, notably his solidarity, man with man, and his bodiliness—and in such a way that the good achieved in this salvation was fuller than the good lost by sin.

3.(d) THE BARRIERS TO THE GIVING OF GRACE WHICH HAVE TO BE OVERCOME

Now, let us draw the threads together, let us ask: what are the barriers to God giving that basic grace, which establishes man in a path which, if he does not depart from it, will bring him to salvation?

The barriers are of two kinds: First, men's hardness of heart, reluctance to repent, attachment to lesser goods, culpable ignorance and such like could raise a barrier. This kind of barrier is reduced or removed through a combination of preliminary graces, as when the heart of man is softened by reading the Scriptures, hearing the word preached, or by realizing the folly, shortsightedness, or emptiness of his plans or priorities.

The second barrier is more imposing. It could be simply unfitting for God to give grace to such sinners as man has become. To this I reply, it would be unfitting for God to do anything which made his total plan for man's salvation violate or set aside human nature, anything which made it incongruous with the way God in his wisdom and foreknowledge had created man.

And I suggest that something incongruous with human nature would result:

(a) if God set aside as outside the scope of restoration or redemption, the concreteness, physicality, bodiliness, and historicality of man. To put the point dramatically, nothing is ultimately to be left in the hands of the devil, no genus of thing, no aspect of man, is ultimately to be turned aside from its right use, or from the attainment of its end, be it truth, or virtue, or beauty, in that use. Nothing, neither mind, nor voice, or marriage and the faculties it involves, nor human social organization and relations, nor art, nor anything else can be abandoned without something incongruous with human nature occurring.

(b) if God were to set aside the spiritual community of the human race, on earth and in heaven, treating men individualistically.

(c) if men's love of God were marred by some need for them to condone or ignore the evil which they had committed, as if to pretend it had never happened.

How are these things avoided in the Christian dispensation? Let me take them in reverse order, beginning with (c).

It is in consideration of this that the aspect of atonement, expiation, propitiation, and satisfaction has traditionally come to the fore. Man's salvation consists in the communal sharing in the Divine Life which only that fuller gift of the Spirit of sonship which came at Pentecost makes possible, the gift that can only be communicated to men through Jesus's glorified humanity. Those who receive grace before Jesus's work is complete wait in hope for its completion before they can receive this salvation. None can receive it except through coming into community with Jesus, and in community with him not according to his divinity alone, but in his humanity, which through his resurrection and glorification becomes accessible to them. Now, if I know my salvation is made possible only as a result of Jesus's passion and death, chosen by him in order that, once exalted, he should be able to communicate to us, then there is evidently no condoning or ignoring of evil involved—for I am knit together with Jesus only through grace and charity, and know my salvation as achieved only through his sufferings, the sufferings of him who has made himself friend and brother for my sake, and as I grow in love and intimacy I grow to care for his sufferings as much as if they were mine, for this is what love and friendship brings. If Jesus had been of another ilk, raised above our condition, then I might have reckoned his sufferings to be objectively regrettable facts about the world, but not felt them, or been involved in them with my will because they would not be my business: but Jesus made himself perfectly one ilk with us, and so I cannot but value at, wonder at, sorrow at, feel, Jesus's suffering on my behalf, my emotions being important here only as elements in or reflections of the real involvement of my heart or will. So, nothing is condoned.

The giving of grace, then, involves no condonation, because the state of salvation towards which it is orientated involves no condonation: men know themselves as being in that state only at the cost of Jesus's death. God requires that sin be not condoned, not in virtue of some arbitrary decree of his good pleasure, setting forth independently of any good for man that the wages of sin is death, but solely because it is an intrinsic need of man, if he is to enter salvation honestly, that there should be no pretense that he has not sinned, no mere ignoring or condoning of evil. The justice of God is not an external decree, but a merciful respect for this condition of man's truth and honesty: and this merciful care which God has for man is costly to God himself in his Son.

Secondly, responding to the question (b) above, the Christian dispensation preserves perfect respect for the spiritual community of mankind, and indeed depends upon it. Instead of removing that community, and opening some path of individualistic salvation to men, God chooses to make our non-solitariness in salvation essential; community with Jesus in his humanity carries with it community with the human race; and the fecundity of human sociality, for good and not just for evil, is not removed, but infinitely enhanced. Grace given before Jesus's becoming man makes sense; it is not unfitting, is not without a goal consistent with man's nature, because it is all orientated towards a salvation which depends on, indeed consists in, a community with Jesus.

Thirdly, responding to the question (a) above, the Christian dispensation preserves perfect respect for man's bodiliness, and the bodily spatio-temporality of his social and historical existence. Jesus lives an earthly life; he heals; his resurrection is historical. The men who follow him, the Church, the people he brings into existence, are an historical concrete embodiment, wherein representatively, on behalf of all mankind, by grace, man cooperates with God in the work of bringing every faculty and aspect of man's nature to its right use and order. In the power and Spirit of the resurrection, nothing is left in the ultimate power of the devil, nothing in final futility.

So, to summarize, my picture is this: God frees man from sin, not just by restoring him to the state he would have been in if he had not sinned, a state of friendship with God but not a state of fellowship with Jesus the Son of God, but by the costly opening up to us of a way to a higher state. Thus, it is that "God became man, to share human life with us, and even to share with us our poor condition of human life, in order that men should be able to come to share the Divine Life." And this, the receiving of the Spirit of sonship, whereby, through community with the risen, now forever human, Jesus our Lord, we are able to love God uncontrolledly, uninhibitedly, and ultimately to know him directly as in vision.

And, all this is done in such a way as to achieve all the lesser ends which men's salvation requires: first, the establishment in man of the power to restore all things, even natural and historical things; second, the maintenance of man's spiritual community with man, and of its power for good, and the giving to it of a new fecundity; and, third, the satisfaction for sin, whereby nothing is done cheaply, condoningly, pretendingly, contrary to what man's truth and honesty require. All these needs of man's nature were provided for as it were incidentally by the manner in which the first and higher end was achieved.

CHAPTER 7

AN INTEGRAL DOCTRINE OF THE INCARNATION AGAINST DUPUIS'S RELIGIOUS PLURALISM[1]

In his book *Toward a Christian Theology of Religious Pluralism*, Jacques Dupuis gives a review of the Fathers' understanding of the Church, a sensitive account of vestiges of a sense of the Trinitarian shape of man's relation to the divine to be traced within Islamic, Hindu and Buddhist tradition, and an analysis of John Paul II's relevant teachings. However, his essential position is implicit in Rahner and Schillebeeckx, and is open to certain key criticisms.

Firstly, the notion of cosmic covenant drawn from the Fathers as restated by Danielou is obviously in need of clarification and a consideration of the natural developments required for consistency, such as I attempt, drawing upon de Lubac, in Section 1. Once such development is supplied Dupuis can be seen to have interpreted Danielou rather woodenly and his criticisms fall to the ground.

1 [Editor's note: The earliest version of this essay is dated to 2007. Braine continued to develop it into 2014. I can find no evidence that it was ever published or that it was publicly read in anything near its current form.]

Secondly, after treating the concept of the Church in the Fathers in a very non-legalistic way, he treats the same concept in the mediaeval Roman Church as if it were conceived strictly legalistically. In this, he sets aside innumerable arguments and dicta of the best mediaeval dogmatic theologians (as opposed to canon lawyers). Further, in treating both mediaeval and modern authors, he proceeds as if "Church" were a univocal concept rather than a concept with many different uses all of which are interdependent. In particular, he neglects the need for continuity between the mystical body of Christ as it exists on earth and the mystical body of Christ (still a body) as consummated in heaven. These are the topics of Section 2.

Thirdly, as Section 3 shows, he neglects the ways in which consistency in manner of speech was particularly insisted upon by the Fathers of the early Church, especially in the early Councils.

Fourthly, as I argue in Section 4, he adopts the strategy of emptying the notion of 'person' of any connotations of intellect or will in its application to the divine Persons, and in this and other ways destroys the doctrine of the Incarnation, by removing divine intellect and will from Jesus. I attempt to show how the realization that terms like "know" and "will" are applied analogically, not univocally, when we apply them to God, enables one without imprecision or deception to combine insistence on giving full content to the word "person" as applied to the Persons of the Trinity, in particular Jesus the Son, with equal insistence on Jesus's perfect humanity.

In Section 5, I give a summary of my conclusions.

SECTION 1: THE IDEA OF A COSMIC COVENANT

1.(a) THE CONCEPT OF "HISTORY"

In order to understand Danielou's conception of a *cosmic covenant,* one has to make distinctions in regard to history. Firstly, one has to take up the distinction introduced by Cullmann between sacred or salvation history and profane history.

By profane history is meant any accurate account of what actually occurred—what some people call "empirical history." By sacred history one means an account of history as geared to a consummation in which God becomes intimate to his creation in new ways so that it can become aware of his presence and work, enter into relation with him and attain the salvation which he has prepared.

As this sacred history is told in the Old Testament, the purpose is to give an account true to the general shape of the central line of development in these workings of God and faithful in the general picture or account it gives of the key figures in the different stages of the unfolding of God's purposes, in this process using what documents and traditions were available at the different stages of compilation, without the aim of accuracy in the empirical sense. These workings have so many aspects as to require that the teaching and history concerned be presented in many different ways. Sometimes this is in laws and a sacrificial system whose meaning only became clear in stages (in Christian understanding it finally became clear in Jesus), sometimes in biographies embedded in larger books, sometimes in the teachings of certain prophets and prophetic schools, and sometimes in the development of what is called the 'wisdom literature'. All is presented in the setting of some continuity from the beginnings of God's workings with the Jews, up until the key developments in New Testament times.

The different character of the New Testament arises from the insistence that the accounts derive from eyewitnesses or those close to them. This is compatible with liberties in writing history analogous to those taken by Thucydides together with some of the symbols and conventions adopted in Jewish historical writing (e.g., in describing what defies description: for instance, God's making his presence known is typically represented in terms of a cloud shielding man from God's glory), as well as different side-purposes of their authors (e.g., St. Matthew reorganizing the materials at his disposal for his catechetical purpose).

In both the sacred and the profane cases, the word "history" can be used in two senses. Thus, in each case one can use the word history so that the start of history is the beginning of the universe and in another sense so that "history" began at some date between 6000 and 1700 BC.

Thus, one can talk of a history of the universe, regarding this as embracing the history of the whole system and the earth, and the development of the earth's whole structure and the inter-related geological, atmospheric, and biological developments, culminating in the emergence of man. Within the unfolding of this history of man, there comes a point at which knowledge derived from archaeology is constructively assisted by reference to written and oral tradition. It is at this point that the work of the historian in the ordinary sense begins, and this constitutes the second sense in which the expression "profane history" is used.

In a parallel way one can speak of sacred history as beginning from the time of God's creation of the universe. This history proceeds in stages each of which has value in itself but also yet greater value in relation to the later stages it makes possible. Its first consummation is in the creation of an intellectual animal, man, in the "image and likeness of God." As being in the image and likeness of God, this intellectual animal was in friendship with God, and therefore in technical terms possessed of sanctifying grace, but possessed of this grace in such a way as to have the freedom to set it aside. Irenaeus conceived this as unfolding in two stages, one, a covenant with Adam, and the second a covenant with Noah. Both of these covenants were universal and underline all later covenants.

However, while sometimes speaking of sacred history in this way (p. 28, *The Lord of History*), Danielou can also speak of these things as belonging to the pre-history of salvation, adopting another use of these expressions "sacred" or "salvation" history in which this history only begins with Abraham. One can see two reasons for this. Firstly, whereas Adam and Noah figure in the Jewish and Christian picture as representatives of mankind, Abraham identified as a Hebrew figures as representative and founder of the Jewish people, this people being in some way focal for God's plans for all mankind. Secondly, this Abraham, identified as a Hebrew by being son of Terah, brings the traditions of a call by and the worship of Yahweh, of the duty of faith and obedience, of the replacement of human sacrifice, of the rite of male circumcision binding Jews together and of promise to this people, into connection with the public face of history, i.e., with profane history.

1.(b) THE NOTIONS OF THE SUPERNATURAL AND OF SANCTIFYING GRACE

The best modern exposition of the notion of the supernatural is provided by Henri De Lubac. He suggests that we completely separate the philosophical treatment of the idea of a thing's "nature" from any theological idea of the natural.

In the most straightforward philosophical sense, there are many things which belong to human nature, and which are presumed not to belong to, for example, the nature of rabbits. For instance, philosophically, it belongs to the nature of man to have a highly structured language, culture within which language has an indispensable role, along with religion, humor and such like, besides the features he shares with other animals. Each thing has its nature whether or not we can express it in language—the proton, the hydrogen molecule, the virus, the amoeba, the oak tree, the star, the angel, and even God. The action of any of these things according to their nature and within their natural power is natural in the philosophical sense. What is not natural for such things is, for instance, to be born with only one leg. When such anomolies are bodily and psychologically intimate to the thing, as in these case of taste, they are described as unnatural. In the relations between different things, many are natural because the coordinate fulfilment of the natures of the things involved is natural in this chief philosophical sense of the word.

This brings us to the theological view of the words "supernatural" and "natural." Here it is the notion of the supernatural which is primary and that which is "natural" is simply that which is not supernatural. Accordingly, if we bring the philosophical and theological views of the term together, we shall say that it is part of man's nature in the philosophical sense to have a desire for God. But this natural (in the philosophical sense of "natural") desire for God is itself supernatural in the theological sense.

The book of Genesis tells that when God first created man, he created him in his own image and likeness. Thus, it is part of man's nature, as he comes from the hand of the creator, to be created with the supernatural desire (*desiderium, appetitus*, orientation) for God. I am putting here De Lubac's conception of how things stand. In this he is, I believe, faithful to St. Thomas. Neither have any time for the notion that man's nature could have its ultimate satisfaction other than in God—as if man could find fulfillment in some natural supreme end, not dependent on grace or Revelation, for example, in the "integral human fulfilment" spoken of by John Finnis, along with Grisez and Boyle.

De Lubac's conception of how it belongs to human nature to exist with a supernatural appetite or orientation towards God is very like Karl Rahner's notion of man as, in his empirical existence from his first beginnings on earth, living within a supernatural "existential," or as he also says within a supernatural "horizon." The key difference between De Lubac and Rahner would seem to be that, while both see the goal as Jesus Christ and union with him and, within that union, union also with the Father and the Holy Spirit, Rahner sees non-Christian religions as having a greater role as paths towards this goal than De Lubac. Danielou has the same view as De Lubac; both of them deny that other religions can have parallel roles to that of Judaism in preparing the way for a person's becoming a Christian, and, more vitally, both deny any parallelism between the role of other religions and the role of historical Christianity in preparing the way for eschatological union with Jesus Christ.

In De Lubac's conception, the word "supernatural" covers everything which derives from God's will to adopt man. This is marked in two stages, well explained by the Eastern tradition. When Genesis says that man was made in the image and likeness of God, one has to understand that the likeness was something he lost in sin, so that his being in the image of God connotes the capacity for understanding, the freedom and inbuilt desire for God, constituting a constant call to find God, while the likeness connotes the being like God which comes when by his grace we respond to this call in love, so as to become genuinely like him. In a parallel way, St. Thomas distinguishes different senses in which man can be in the image of God, so that this is only properly said of those in a state of sanctifying grace, a life which is completed in glory. And the early Karl Rahner treats Aquinas' account of the conditions of the life of glory as specifying the conditions of the life of grace which is rewarded in glory,[2] the whole thing, grace as well as glory, being the supernatural work of God, taken as a whole not merited by us but in God's gift by Christ's merits.

This will to adopt man is the will that all men become brothers of Jesus, taken up within the divine life so as to have a share in this life.

2 Karl Rahner, "Some implications of the scholastic concept of uncreated grace," 319–46, Vol. I, *Theological Investigations* (a paper reprinted and revised 1954, from an original in 1948–9). His argument does not depend on his idea of the knower's knowledge as a modality of the knower's being present to itself, rather than an energeia of the thing known, which seems to have been the original meaning of the Hegelian phrase he uses (misconstruing it in the same way as he did in *Spirit in the World*, 1936).

This sharing does not mean becoming themselves divine, uncreated and preexisting their conception, but means having the grace of having supernatural love in virtue of God's presence in the soul.

This presence and response in God-enabled love makes those who cleave to Christ ready, after Christ's passion and sending of the Holy Spirit, immediately to enter the community of the new-born; this is the community of those whom the Spirit makes able to pray "Abba, Father," adopted sons of the Father of whom Jesus is the son by nature, and who by the presence and indwelling of this Holy Spirit thereby have the Father and Son (the breathers of this Spirit) also abiding in the soul. But, for those who received this grace and died before Christ's passion and the sending of the Spirit, it made them orientated and set to enter this community at once as soon as Christ's work was accomplished (the "It is accomplished" spoken on the cross, Jn 19:30), having waited "to enter in with us" (Heb 11:16 and 29–30). According to tradition, they were brought out from *Sheol* following Christ's death (Mt 27:52–53) and descent into Hell (Hades, i.e., *Sheol*, not Gehenna, even bringing out some who had disobeyed, I Pt 3:19–20), so that Hebrews 12:23 can speak of the "assembly of the first born ... and the spirits of just men are made perfect" as a group already existing.

To sum up, this grace (in the Eastern way of speaking, the grace involving "the likeness to God," and not just being in "the image of God"), enables all who have it to live a kind of life which—persevered in and brought to maturity—will be completed in coming to enjoy the vision of God within the context of a perfected friendship with Jesus and all his brothers. The way to this is by the actions of the Holy Spirit breathed into us by Jesus and thereby firstly incorporating us into his mystical body, and secondly giving this body its diversity, so that the whole human race is as it were an orchestra within which each player has a different role, as it were integrating the richest polyphony within one symphonic scheme.

As several of the Fathers said, "God became man in order that man should be divinized." That is, Jesus, who is the *Logos* or Wisdom of God, by nature Son of God from eternity—from the beginning of time joined with the Father first in the work of creating and preserving things in existence, and then in the work of redeeming things and by the Spirit sanctifying them—this Jesus became man in order that the

Holy Spirit might transform human beings into the likeness of himself and transform them so that each has their own unique character and role in his mystical body. In one action the Holy Spirit makes us able to pray "Abba, Father" by making us members of Jesus's mystical body.

The notions of "member" (which always means member of a body), "incorporation" (which means being made member in a body), and "mystical body" are all coordinate with one another. "Mystical body" in modern times has come to mean "social body" knit together by one indwelling spiritual principle, in the case of the body of Christ, this principle being the Holy Spirit.

1.(c) THE IDEA OF AN INTERMEDIATE STAGE

To have sanctifying grace is to be indwelt by the Holy Spirit in such a way as to be either already a member of the mystical body of Christ, or in a state destining one to this.

I make this distinction because there is no sense in which human beings could be described as incorporated into Christ until Jesus, eternal Son of the Father, had actually become man, finished his work of redemption by his death on the cross and been glorified so as to make a place for human beings within the divine life. Until that time there was no position as adopted sons alongside the natural Son to pray "Abba, Father," no possibility of the extension of the baptismal gift of the Holy Spirit, a gift not given in John's baptism, from Christ to his brother human beings, and no body of Christ, no mystical body for human beings to be incorporated into.

For this reason while all the holy men and women before the time at which Jesus's work was accomplished from the beginning of man's history to Mary and John the Baptist, along (one may presume) with many of other races and cultures, received sanctifying grace, in Mary in the fullest way possible, without yet being able to attain the destiny promised to them, but having to wait until Christ had been glorified and had thereby opened a place for man in the immediate presence of God, only then, as the Epistle to the Hebrews expresses it, able to "enter in with us" (Heb 11: 38—40, cf. 12: 22—24). (It may be that those who even after have no knowledge of the gospel, or visible connection with the Church in its historical life, are in the same position of being in a state of sanctifying grace, but like those before Christ in a position of waiting.) The existence of this intermediate stage is discussed by Dupuis (pp. 76–77) with reference to the different explanations given by Saldanha, Durrwell, and Congar, and what I am insisting upon with Congar is that the grace given in those times before Jesus's conception already embraced the grace for salvation which Christians receive. This means that it was already the sanctifying grace which grounds the virtues of faith, hope and charity involved in supernatural friendship with God, the state of friendship dying in which man can in no way fail of the same salvation as is promised to the persevering followers of Christ.

What I have said departs in one respect from what Danielou and De Lubac appear to say. They often appear to deny the possession of sanctifying grace by any figures before the Incarnation. Yet the general context of Scripture and of their other writings (e.g., Danielou's *Holy Pagans*) make it incredible that they should have held this.

What is clear is that both of these authors see man's ultimate hope as only fulfilled in Jesus's redeeming work, his glorification, and his then, with the Father, sending the Holy Spirit—the Holy Spirit making it possible (a) for man to share in the divine life and (b) for the riches of the diverse human community to be brought within the ambit of this sharing. The community is diversified in a way which combines man's natural gifts with a new kind of working of the same spirit.

I have departed from the apparent teaching of these authors because my view not only fits with the teaching of the Fathers, but also fits with the teaching of Scripture which presents man as created in supernatural friendship with God and many individual Old Testament figures as restored to such friendship and justified by faith (i.e., trust). I see no sense in the notion of a supernatural friendship with God which is not the relationship referred to by Aquinas as charity, like justifying faith a theological virtue depending upon the presence of sanctifying grace. However, it is equally clear from New Testament scripture that Jesus's redeeming work made possible, not just the giving of sanctifying grace by anticipation before even Jesus's conception, but also beyond this after Jesus's Ascension a richer indwelling by the Holy Spirit bringing richer gifts and a richer fulfilment, a richer fulfilment not available before but thereafter available to all who preceded.

1.(d) THE UNIVERSAL COVENANT OR COVENANTS BEFORE ABRAHAM

In what is portrayed in Genesis 1 – 11, man is created in the image and likeness of God, this has always been interpreted as meaning that he was created in a state of supernatural friendship with God, that is, in a state of sanctifying grace.

It should be noted that in Genesis 1 the term "man" (*adam*) is used generically, that is without distinction of sex. The same is true of the beginning of Chapter 2 where it is also used without distinction between individuals. Man is a person in friendship with God, in sanctifying grace, and this is a deeper fact about him than his being one of many, an individual. I do not mean that anything is being taught about empirical history as if there had been in existence a single man before there was any wife, family, or community, but only that personhood is deeper than our individuality. He only becomes spoken of as one human being distinct from another after his being given a companion, Eve, i.e., a relationship to other human beings, in particular the one to be his wife.

For man to be created a person he has to be created in a state of freedom in which he has a choice whether to act in accord with this friendship with God or prefer other things to it. And it is in the situation of being individuals that human beings are portrayed as preferring something else to friendship with God, namely the possibility of becoming as gods. It is after this that full extent of God's love begins to be revealed. He makes a promise to Adam and Eve that even though they must leave Paradise, find that work now involved toil, and be subject to death, nonetheless his good will and his intention of redemption remained. His good will is shown in his giving them the possibility of continence (symbolized by clothes) and his blessing them with children, and then successively renewing friendship with these children—even showing mercy in forbidding automatic capital punishment for murder. When natural disaster overcomes mankind, he makes a further covenant with Noah, a covenant never to allow mankind to be destroyed by natural disaster for the rest of history. In the text mankind is also given permission to eat animals, but with the proviso that some respect be given to the value of their lives. As to the Tower of Babel story, Danielou suggests the interpretation that because of human over-ambition, God allows an already existing multiplicity of human languages to become an occasion of lack of mutual understanding, sympathy and cooperation.[3] This, with some adjustments to the detail, is Danielou's picture of what was involved in what he calls the cosmic covenant, treating all things as a unity.

Certainly, Danielou regards part of what the covenant was founded on as the knowledge of God and his relationship to the world, and of man and what is good for man, which is natural in the philosophical sense of being accessible to philosophy without the assistance of any supernaturally given knowledge. However, he intends this covenant to be that portrayed in Genesis 1 — 11, and this unmistakably involves supernatural friendship with God. Philosophy shows God as being underlying efficient cause of the being of whatever has being, besides being many other things, but does not reach to revealing him as Father or, in the words of Pope John Paul II in *Sign of Contradiction*, as a loving Heart, and having concern with individuals. Yet this is clearly a part of the picture which comes across in the early chapters of Genesis. These chapters are not intended as an empirical history but are intended to show the character of God's background relationship with man. And these features are key parts of this.

1.(e) OTHER RELIGIONS: FIRST OBSERVATIONS

Danielou sees human religions in their differing forms as developments within the context of the cosmic covenant he has portrayed. Danielou sees them as in large part arising out of man's natural desire for God. The results of man's searchings often lead to a deepening in his understanding of God and the way to God, but are sometimes corrupted by other elements. As an instance of the latter, he might think of human sacrifice, and the giving of one's sexuality to God in temple prostitution, as well as more general moral deviations as examples of such corruption. However, he would tend to see all such developments, when good, as preparatory to the Judeo-Christian tradition, rather than as parallel to it.

3 This view of Origen, that the punishment of the over-ambition of Babel lay in a new lack of mutual understanding and that diversity of language already existed beforehand, is the one Danielou proposes (*Lord of History*).

However, the increasingly unanimous teaching of the Church seems to be that grace is liable to be at work within all religions, even so as sometimes to bring human beings into friendship with God, friendship implying the dynamic interrelation involved in sanctifying grace. In such development, the wise men and religious teachers of other religions, and some of their rites, may play a positive role. We find this perspective expressed in some of the remarks of Vatican II. Since then, Pope John Paul II has spoken of recognizing the work of the Holy Spirit in the prayer, "firm belief," and activities of other religions, associating the people of goodwill concerned in whose hearts grace is active invisibly, the Paschal Mystery being involved with grace (*Dominum et Vivificantem*, 1986). This should be understood as explaining how all the work of God in his redeeming and sanctifying activity before the passion of Christ was done in anticipation of the work and passion of Christ, his meriting gifts for man, but not so as to involve separate activities either of the not yet incarnate Logos or of the Holy Spirit before the passion of Christ (I note this in accord with the traditional insistence on the same point, repeated in the 2001 Notification in regard to this work of Dupuis).

Since then, in *Redemptoris Missio* (1990) John Paul II stresses "Christ's one universal mediation" but also recognizes the possibility in the order of salvation of "participated forms of mediation" but which "acquire meaning and value only from Christ's own mediation and cannot be understood as parallel or complementary to his." This should be understood in the light of his remarks, in 1994 in *Tertio Millennio Adveniente*, when he insisted again that Jesus did not speak in the name of God like the prophets, but as God himself, and speaks of Christianity and the incarnate Word as the fulfillment of the yearning present in all human religions—their sole and definitive completion.

The underlying conception is that although the rites, teaching and teachers may have some subsidiary mediatorial role, this is not parallel to that of Christ. Further these religions are not *in themselves* salvific, meaning that they do not *as such* envisage the goal of our becoming adopted sons of God, alongside Jesus, who is the Son by nature.

SECTION 2: THE CHURCH

2.(a) THE ROLE OF THE HISTORICAL CHURCH

God became man in Jesus, born of Mary, accomplished our redemption and was glorified, all with the purpose that he continuing as man should open out a place for us as fellow men and brothers alongside himself joined together in relation to the Father.

Now, the purpose of all the preparation of the Jews before his coming, was not that he should just accomplish all this and go away, leaving the situation of mankind on earth otherwise unchanged. No! The significance of the preparations amongst the Jews was far greater.

Jesus could only achieve our salvation by becoming man because becoming man meant entering into solidarity with the whole of mankind, supernaturally as well as naturally: for God created man, not just each person supernaturally separate, but so as to make man supernaturally as well as naturally communal, supernaturally one family, one community each affected by the joys and burdens of every other. Accordingly, it could not be that God saw no value in human community, its growth in mutual enrichment. Nor could it be that there was no special significance in Jesus's work of redemption and glorification having eye witnesses, and in these eye witnesses passing on what they knew, in this intimate way to others, and with these others growing in the understanding of the significance of this witness.

Accordingly, the purpose of the preparation of the Jews was not just in order that Mary should be able to give a perfect consent to being the mother of the Son of God and a perfect consent to what was involved in his way of suffering as well as being able with Joseph to bring Jesus up and teach him the things of Jewish tradition so that he would have this knowledge in the ordinary human way—although supplemented by prophetic insights and knowledge coming from his intimacy with the Father.

No! The purpose of this preparation, of his having companions and eyewitnesses brought up in the same Jewish tradition, of Jesus's ministry and of his passion, resurrection and glorification, was to give to his Church a visible, concrete realization here on earth destined to continue and grow.

Part of the meaning of God's making man in his own image and likeness is that he wanted there to be some part of the natural creation which would respond to him, as it were representatively on behalf of the whole of creation. His constituting the natural creation and the way living things develop are two things which themselves show the value he places on the things of nature, on bodiliness, on organic relation and on community. Now in creating man in his own image and likeness, he created him, not just bodily, but also as communal, in both natural and supernatural respects. Accordingly what God wants to save is not just individual souls. Rather he wants human beings to be saved *as human beings* that is in their intellect and thinking and in their imagination and arts, in their dancing and singing, in their music, art and architecture, all these being brought together in their expression of love in worship and liturgy. And he also wants them to exercise their intelligence and imaginativeness in seeing what love of neighbor involves, and in understanding, wonder, and enjoyment of the whole of natural creation The riches, intellectual, imaginative and artistic, and the other aspects of culture, originating in each separate culture should be brought in, in order to enrich all, and what goes on in the history of the Church should be in earnest and a kind of beginning of its being brought to perfection in the Church as she is in Heaven, what St. Paul refers to as our Mother, the Jerusalem to come. This will not be a place where all bodiliness is to be done away, but in which we shall be raised in bodies of a kind whose principle of life and continuance we cannot imagine.

Born in the setting of Jewish tradition and custom, the development of Christian understanding and custom has never needed "inculturation" into Judaism—and this rooting has meant that Christianity has always had the possibility of some enrichment from developments in Jewish thought, to some extent Muslim thought and practice, and to some extent those of the Sufis and Zoroastrian tradition and more distantly the Sikhs, since each of these last three have some kind of family relationship with Judaism and Christianity, which makes applying the notion of inculturation to them awkward.

The first processes of genuine inculturation are quite distinct from these. The processes of the inculturation of faith into Greek thought forms and customs and into Latin ones began at a very early stage. At the same early stage, it was inculturated into the Syriac and Egyptian world. The inheritance of this inculturation in Africa is seen amongst the Copts.

The effects of inculturation into the Germanic and Celtic worlds have been more subtle. The Celts appear to have derived some artistic and other traditions from the East (from the Syriac world of present-day Syria and Iraq and from Egypt). These doubtless mixed with some Anglo-Saxon features from Britain, permeated the Anglo-Saxon missions to Germany. The Celts developed a system of penitential rules of which it is obscure whether they represent something existing earlier in Celtic culture or whether they were spontaneous developments of a rather legalistic kind inspired by monastic ideas and Latin influence. It is certainly from Ireland that they seem to have spread through the rest of Europe.

We think of Greek and Latin elements in the Church's life as something universal within churches of western root. But in this we ignore the universality of other influences. For example, it seems that all western forms of chant over the first fifteen centuries of the Church's life may have had a Syriac root, going back as far as A.D. 200.

The Church also penetrated the Slavonic world. In Poland this took a distinctively western Catholic form, while further south and east it took a form originating with Greek liturgy and custom. The Greek liturgy lacks the economy of words of Latin-rooted liturgies, having taken on a marvelously expansive rich lyrical style. The East also makes greater use of the litany forms being capable of use inside the liturgy, and its hymns inside and outside the liturgy sometimes exhibit a kind of timeless weather-beaten, long suffering peasant faithfulness. We can meet these not only in Greece and the former Yugoslavia but throughout the Christian regions of the former Russian Empire. In Russia, the spirit of patience came to form a spirituality and atmosphere of a character not found so strongly anywhere else in Christendom. This was perhaps born of a life of long endurance under the Tzars and has given the churches of the former imperial Russia, the Russian, Ukrainian, and Georgian, the capacity in which Christian faith has survived so strongly since 1917, despite extreme persecution.

The other distinctive feature of Eastern Christianity is the importance of icons and the development of distinctive and ever purer style in iconography. The production of an icon is conceived of as something requiring preparation, prayer and fasting. And the role of icons in the life of prayer is quite different from that of a religious painting in the west. In the west a painting may be useful for teaching purposes or as a reminder of something relevant to worship but is not itself the vehicle of worship. The nearest parallels to an icon in the western Church would seem to be the crucifix, relics and perhaps religious statues when set in a religious place or shrine and or turned to special use in processions and other ceremonies. All such things, including icons, come under the heading of what in western theology are classified as sacramentals, not objects of worship but in some way focuses or vehicles of worship.

What the Church now needs to see is parallels to the above-mentioned fruitful examples of inculturation, parallels developing within African, Indian, Chinese, and Japanese settings. All these things here have been long delayed because of the geographical ghetto into which the Church was confined by the military force of Islam. It was only in the second half of the 1400s that the redevelopment of sea techniques made it possible for Europeans to circumnavigate Africa, rendering the east readily accessible in a way which it had not been since before 700.

However, the carrying through of this missionary process was subverted by rival preoccupations within Europe itself. The most obvious of these was the Protestant Reformation, but more important were the exigencies of dealing with the intellectual developments in natural science, first physical and then biological, so often envisaged as implying determinism and physical materialism. At the same time the development in Europe and the U.S.A., fortified by trade and the steadily increasing power of western weaponry, followed by the development of capitalism and with it the doctrine of free trade, meant that the underlying tendency of western approaches to other peoples and civilizations was towards domination and exploitation. This was accompanied by contempt.

Moreover, as a result, even developments good in themselves, such as the rich development of western music from 1500 onwards, and along with it the developments in the other arts, painting and sculpture, whether along realistic, classical, romantic, or other more modern lines depending on new treatments of light, sound and space, together with a sense of continuous advance in the sciences and technology, yet further increased western conceit, and fortified the western preconception that other peoples and races were primitive, static or barbaric. All this constituted an enormous obstacle to the advance of Christian mission, each such advance increasingly seeming to the other peoples like an imposition—part of the imperial or colonial western package. It is only slowly during the latter part of the twentieth century that Christians have begun to become able again to pursue their mission with the spirit of learners like Ricci in China and Nobili in India, and increasingly to do it as indigenous members of the peoples concerned, born and bred within the cultures themselves.

Accordingly, the process of bringing the riches from this great multiplicity of non-European cultures and modes of thought into the Church, so as to enrich it, has a long way to go. This does not mean a process in which Christianity loses its distinctive character. Just as in the encounter with Greek culture and thought involved a Hebraicization of Greek ways, rather than a Hellenization of Jewish ways of thinking, so it should be whenever inculturation takes place. Just as Greeks, Romans, Celtic, and Germanic peoples and then the Slavs came to experience Christianity as something at home amongst them, not alien, so it should be in these modern cases of inculturation. Inculturation means this use of the customs and thought-forms of the other peoples in such a way that Christianity can be experienced as something not foreign or alien, and yet at the same time in such a way that these thought-forms and some aspects of practice become able to be shared by the whole of the Church.

Accordingly, the role of the historical church and its mission will not be complete until all these developments have taken place. And since the Church is a less temporary phenomenon than any particular political or economic system, such as imperialism or laissez faire capitalism, the completion of this mission will give time for the rescue of those elements of key value in other cultures which seem presently under threat of burial by western capitalistic materialism.

2.(b) TENSIONS BETWEEN CHRISTIANITY AND OTHER RELIGIONS

The recognition of the good points, the strengths of positive value, of other religions should not make us think of the extension of the Christian Churches and the Christian teaching as simply a form of imperialism. Many of the politically correct of Western society clearly echo values inspired by Christianity and Judaism when they object to female circumcision, to women being treated as property and deprived of all rights, who object to torture, to punishment disproportionate to the seriousness of the offence, to capital punishment, to racialism, genocide, and slavery. What Danielou says is no more an example of imperialism than the insistence on these politically correct values and the application of this insistence to thinking about human rights in China, Tibet, Burma, and elsewhere in other countries where capitalism finds such insistence inconvenient.

Danielou is aware and expounds in a positive way the riches of each of Christianity's main rivals and how key elements of these riches would be desirable to see in the Christian Church. But he also sees the negative features which impede the coming together in unity. The strengths of community and family and the strength of the extended family and society mean any Muslim who converts to Christianity is in danger of death and of becoming a complete outcast. Parallel though lesser penalties attend conversion from Judaism.

In the case of Islam, its militarism and systems of law have enforced the zealotry and militaristic aspect of Zionism in an extreme form, so that even non-Muslims who are not converts have often been in danger of death by war and by application of the law.

The Indian tradition is supposed to exemplify tolerance, but this tolerance is like the tolerance claimed by western secularism. It forbids many of the practices of those that do not share the basis of this tolerance.

The French forbid Muslim women from wearing scarves in school, the Indians dislike any baptism and any Christian preaching with a view to conversion, the Americans forbid the exhibition of any religious symbols apart from the American flag in publicly funded schools or University classrooms.

The evils in this secularism as politically embodied, can be dramatized by considering the example of Bavaria in the Second World War. Bavaria differs from most of the other *länder* of Germany in being almost homogeneously Catholic in tradition in modern times. It was also distinctive in that Hitler, out of prudence, possibly considering the loyalties of the army, found that it was the only part of Germany in which he could not enforce his rule that all crosses or crucifixes should be removed from classrooms and replaced with a portrait of himself.

This symbolized the continuance within the state of the Catholicism which Hitler had failed to control, the only organized public group within the state not subject to him, and the tradition which after Judaism he abominated most. Bavaria presents an example of how insistence on religious symbols can be a valid way in circumstances in which forces opposed to dictatorship can defend freedom. One can compare this resistance to Gandhi's bringing India to a standstill by declaring a day of fasting after the massacre of Amritsar.

By contrast, the Protestant churches as public bodies despite the witness of some individuals were, along with the unions, in large part as putty in Hitler's hands, except for the Confessing Church which refused to enter in to the activities of Hitler's new creation, the National Democratic Church—indeed under the leadership of Dietrich Bonhoeffer refusing any co-operation with Hitler from 1936 onwards. The underground resistance group organized round the international lawyer Von Moltke along with Bonhoeffer is known to us chiefly not for the witness and works of many diplomats, admirals, members of the Wehrmacht and others but for Von Stauffenburg's failed assassination attempt.

Both dictatorship and secular democracy achieve political correctness through the news, media, and education, or by reducing the influence of the parent, giving dominance to the peer group and the school. In Britain, an example of this secularism is the illegality of religious radio channels in a context of which it is increasingly rare for representatives authorized by particular churches to be given adequate time for a proper exposition of their position, a liberty likewise impaired in the case of Sikhs, Muslims and other traditions. Yet in this field as in others all that is required is protection from distortions arising from the overdominance of any one source or type of source of capital support.

Danielou's view is that on first encounter with any new culture Christianity has, from the first, met with opposition. The Greeks displayed philosophical contempt and religious opposition, culminating in the attempt by the emperor Julian the Apostate to outlaw Christianity.

In the relation to Roman culture, the situation was worse. Not only was there conscientious objection to worshipping Roman eagles but also some conscientious objection to war itself. There was opposition to incest, divorce, and polygamy and also an opposition to infanticide, abortion, and contraception. In Christian and Jewish eyes, the Romans were worse than the Greeks. The Greeks were pagans seeking to impose the worship of pagan Gods, the Roman were the same, but they were also the most barbaric people ever to flourish in Europe until modern times. Their method of killing by crucifixion was more cruel than most any invented by Greeks or other European peoples.

Danielou's line of approach makes one anticipate that there will normally be tensions in Christianity meeting with any culture, Chinese, Indian, Japanese, African, American Indian. In each case the appropriate approach is that recommended by St. Gregory the Great, of destroying as little as possible in the cultural aspects of the life of converts, rather turning it to Christian use or social benefit, only abolishing what is obviously or after careful study incompatible with Christianity. This careful study is very well exemplified by the Jesuit approaches seen in the late 1500s and 1600s. It is also exemplified by the approach of Jesuits and Dominicans amongst the original Americans and approaches such as those of the White Fathers in Africa.

I mention these cultural tensions arising in the encounter of Christianity with non-European peoples, but it would be false to suppose that the cultural struggles of Christianity ceased in Europe with the general conversion of the Greeks, Latins, Celts, Germanic, Scandinavian, and Slavonic peoples. For example, throughout the period 1000 – 1500 there were struggles between the Church and the feudal baronage throughout Europe, forbidding tournaments, seeking gradually to eliminate trial by ordeal or by combat, and punishment by mutilation or by death.

The Church also developed the doctrine of the just war, more and more limiting the occasions on which war was morally justified. As to tyrannical regimes, St. Thomas tells us that it is the tyrant rather than the subjects who is seditious. St. Thomas's theory on monarchy is analogous to the concept represented in Anglo-Saxon and later English legal theory before Henry VIII, and in African chieftainship. The king ruled in a way consistent with the views of his wise men or council, and although that succession was normally hereditary this was subject to the agreement of the general good sense of the council.

The idea of absolute monarchy derives from Roman law and arises whenever some series of rulers come to think of themselves as having the same status as a Roman Emperor, ruling according to the principle that the Emperor's word is law. Henry VIII applied this idea in practice and might be considered to have initiated the theory of an absolute sovereignty of the King in Parliament in the 1530s. The French kings largely ruled as if absolute sovereigns, from Louis XI up to the time Louis XVI called the Estates-General, although it was not the theory of the French constitution. The first two Stuarts to reign in England held the theory of the Divine right of Kings, a right which James insisted extended to the settlement of matters of religious doctrine, his successor, Charles I, losing his head in consequence. The Russian Tsars perfectly exemplified the Roman theory from the end of 1400s until 1917. Prussian rulers inclined to the theory and Hitler exercised it. The Russian dictators so abused the Soviet constitution as to enable Lenin, Stalin, Brezhnev and Andropov to act largely in the manner of the Tsars.

One of the constant difficulties of the Church has been firstly struggling with emperors and kings who conceive of their authority in this way, and secondly the influence of this notion of authority on canon law and its treatment of the authority of the Pope and the Bishops. We can see an example of how absolutist ideas of authority formed from Roman Law distorted many arguments about the infallibility of Popes and Councils and added a legalistic note to some theologians' conceptions not only of the authority but of the meaning of the things they decreed. The war of the Church with absolutist ideas of monarchy has been followed by wars of the Church against all other absolutist conceptions of human sovereignty and absolutist conceptions of property—ideas also rooted in Roman Law.

2.(c) THE NATURE OF THE CHURCH

In the traditional Christian view, Christianity constitutes the fulfillment of all that is good in other human religions, constituting their consummation so that all the workings of grace to be found within these religions are thus enabled to achieve their destiny and purpose in this completion.

Man is essentially a unity of mind and body. Hence firstly the workings of grace are not separable into purely inner and purely outer bits in this life, and even in this life have social and communal aspects. Secondly, all that belongs to the workings of grace, perfecting and going beyond nature in this life, in personal life with the mutual enrichment of one person by another, and in society and community, is to be completed in the general resurrection in which imagination, bodiliness, society, and mutual communication are brought to perfection in a transfigured way in keeping with consummation in grace and glory. These things are the reasons for the importance of the idea of the Church as the Mystical Body of Christ. There has to be a continuity between the Mystical Body in this life and the Mystical Body in Heaven. This is therefore also the reason why the Church in her teachings has been so reluctant to separate the notion of the Kingdom of God from the notion of the Church.

The Church in her teachings has been reluctant to use the word 'Church' in one simple way. For it is essential that the community of those in grace from the beginning of history onwards, the community of those who persevere in this grace, the community to whom first began to be committed the public revelation of God's purposes (continuing even now in modern Judaism), this community extended by the universal promulgation of the Gospel, this community as at particular times joined in one communion with the see of Rome, this community considered as it exists as a community joined by prayer on earth, in purgatory and in heaven, and finally the church as it will exist consummated in its final new beginning at the end of history—that all these—should be interdependent as realities, not just that the uses of the word "Church" of each of them should be interrelated.

The Church has been spoken of as extending back to include, in some way, all the just who have responded to God in his invitation to friendship since the beginning of man's history. The Fathers, conspicuously Augustine, speak of the Church from Abel and Melchizedek, and many have envisaged Adam as repenting and therefore as the first of those whom Jesus would lead out from *Hades* (*sheol*, not *Gehenna*), in his "descent into Hell" as the misleading English translation has it, after his crucifixion, taking them with him into glory.[4] Such figures as Abel and Melchizedek have a role in sacred

4 The justice and acceptance by God of Abel is attested by Scripture whereas while Scripture portrays the mercy and positiveness of God's dispensations towards Adam, Eve and Seth with his descendants, and even

history because in the Jewish and Christian conception, whether such figures be mythical or legendary in origin, the story being told is part of the beginning of the history of the universe and the world, a beginning of whose shape the early chapters of Genesis give a truthful portrayal, leading on to the history of Israel and afterwards that of the Christian Church, moving towards a goal.

The active redeeming mission of the Church since the apostles is directed towards joining in the active redeeming mission of Christ, having as its goal the redemption of the whole of man, not just his soul—the whole man involving his bodiliness and sociality as well as the intellect and imagination. It is mad to suppose that there is value in this redemption of the whole man and then do nothing about it as if the supposed inner self was all that mattered. This Church is therefore visible and concrete, not just a "spiritual" in the sense of an "immaterial" reality—indeed, the word "spiritual" in the New Testament does not signify "immaterial" but "having the Holy Spirit as the principle of its life."

Kant says that the thing of ultimate value is the good will, whereas for Aristotle, virtue and moral goodness were things which involved education by the training provided by the practice of doing good things for the right reasons and developing the emotions appropriate to such a combination of action and right reason—satisfaction or pleasure being the bloom on the face of such practice. Therefore, the norm includes good action and excludes wrong action, for without action the will has no complete expression. For a person to have good will but to be unable to act even by praying is a rare condition characteristic mainly of people deeply disabled. Such disability is amongst the things to be done away in the general resurrection.

Death is characteristic of our present state, a fact mainly ignored by modern Western man as if by some kind of subconscious repression rather than being treated as something obvious as in the poorer parts of the world. Accordingly, Western man has a preference for Eastern religion because of its seeking only some illusory, inward liberation. He inclines to a dualist view of man according to which what matters

---

his forebearingness in respect of Cain and his descendants, the reasoning that would make us believe that Adam and Eve repented is less direct, depending on considerations of fittingness and coherence.

spiritually is only the soul. He may spend his energies having disguised the fact of death from himself, entirely on the material things of life, exhausting himself in the pursuit of money, sexual happiness and wasting his playtime on things no better than soap operas. This he thinks of as liberty. As all these things lie to hand in the rich west, he does not feel in need of liberation. When the exercise of this worthless liberty ends, he is content that his death should be invisible, and all he asks for is that it be made painless.

Most Africans, most Latin Americans, most Slavs, and Chinese conceive life differently. For them liberation from poverty is vital, but they are having imposed on them a Western form of life quite alien to them, even while they are still interested in the imagination and the spiritual. For them, salvation as traditionally conceived by Christians in which human beings are still in community and communication with each other and in which the faculties involving the body and the imagination, although transformed, remain even at the transformed bodily level, retains its value and meaning as an object of hope.

Here my main criticism of Dupuis is that he does not give respect to the unity of man, culture, body, and spirit. True, he does notice that in this life other religious traditions involve religious rites and, in this way, involve the exterior as well as the interior. This is part of his argument that if people of other religions can receive grace, this must have some connection with their religious tradition which is something outward, but this is part of a separate argument that, if grace comes to individuals outside the historical context of Judeo-Christian tradition, then this must involve a grace-bearing role in the religion which the individual concerned practices. But it is as if the resurrection was unnecessary. The way that religious traditions and practices enter into Eastern religion as means of teaching and passing on the religion concerned is after all secondary. What primarily matters to any religion is, in his view, interiority alone as the essential channel of grace—God acting and our coming nearer to God by our exploring inwards in account of detached introspective movement accordingly in his account, although there may be historical figures (Buddha, etc) who serve in a certain way as saving figures and although the practices may have a role which makes them occasions of grace, nonetheless, history and the body have no intrinsic value, and these Eastern religions do not themselves believe either in grace or in the value of the body. Rejecting the idea of personal diversity, these Indian rooted religions reject the notion of resurrection which implies a single separate biography of each person who has died, rejecting this notion of resurrection in favor of that of reincarnation, and think of the cycle of repeated reincarnation as something to be escaped, as if the body was given us as a kind of punishment or in order to provide the opportunity of training in detachment and lacks any value in itself.

Dupuis thinks that Jewish, Christian, and Muslim traditions are distinctive because of the importance they set on history as a channel of grace; a fact especially true of Christianity and the *Logos* being incarnate in Jesus of Nazareth. But he scarcely ever mentions the humanity or bodiliness of Christ after the Resurrection. He speaks of "the glorified humanity of Jesus Christ as the universal channel of grace through his resurrection from the dead and, therefore, of the consummation through it of the indwelling Spirit"[5] but his footnote shows his main interest in this as non-eschatological. We find that the transformation of Jesus by his resurrection and glorification makes him "transhistorical."[6] And yet, he seems to have no interest in the general resurrection, which he never mentions.

I shall draw attention to this emphasis on interior and neglect or disparagement of the bodily and historical later. It is the first root of the relatively low place he gives the Church.

As to the Church, whereas the Fathers and the New Testament think of the Church as an edifice like Solomon's temple with riches from every nation and culture, he thinks of the Church as a limited, temporary organization with visible and identifiable boundaries. He recognizes that elements from different cultures do enter into the permanent structure of the visible Church but regards this as quite unimportant except as a corollary of the symmetry of dialogue—equally elements of Christianity enter into other religions, for example, ideas from the Gospels entered into the thinking of many Hindu thinkers. This is the second root of the relatively low place he gives the Church.

The early Fathers, notably St. Cyprian and St. Augustine, taught that "outside the Church there is no salvation." This teaching, often

5 Jacques Dupuis, *Towards a Christian Theology of Religious Pluralism* (Maryknoll, NY: Orbis Books, 1997), 77.

6 Dupuis, *Religious Pluralism*, 297.

repeated in the intervening period, appears in the teaching of Popes and Councils from Innocent III (1208), the Fourth Lateran Council (1215) and the Council of Florence (1439 – 42). There is a tendency of modern liberal theologians to take this as an arch-example of a case of error in the teaching of Popes and Councils. However, when they argue this, they ignore contemporary evidence as to how the word "Church" was understood in the periods concerned—it had the full variety of use which I sketched earlier.

The sense of statements can be understood in reference to their context of utterance, the general presumptions evident in the tradition and its interpretation by the theologians of the time and place.

Only a few statements are stated with the precision of the scientist or the mathematician and expected to be understood context free once their key terms are understood. A sentence in Newton's *Principia* means the same as it did when it was written and the same applies with such statements as Euclid's theorem that prime numbers are unending. And only a small subset of theological statements are similar. Such context independent precision may be intended, for example, in the case of the definitions and anathemas of the first six General Councils concerning the Trinity and the Incarnation—but these constitute special cases, cases of the sort which arise in the context of heresy and doctrinal controversy, but which are not characteristic of statements of things not under dispute.

I remarked earlier on how conceptions of the authority of Popes and Councils were distorted by legal absolutist ideas derived from Roman Law. In an earlier conception, the pope's word was not supposed to be unchangeable on every point, like the law of the Medes and Persians. Rather, the tradition normally saw it as something put forward in the context of discussion with the bishops and wise advisors and drawing on earlier theological opinion, especially that of the Church Fathers.

The statements of Popes and Councils vary in character. If one considers the saying that there is no salvation outside the church, found in many of the Fathers and several of the medieval councils, as well as in modern teaching, then one will find that none of these groups thought of the Church as if it was an earthly, social organization like a denomination. When they made such a statement it was assumed that there would be found many people of every nation amongst those who were saved, who were united to the Church without knowing by any normal means of the existence of Jesus as man or the Apostles or the later church, and even some who rejected Christian teaching. St. Thomas and Dante follow a sermon doubtfully ascribed to Gregory the Great in placing even the pagan Emperor Trajan, one of the chief early persecutors of Christians, in heaven.

Just as when the Devil tempts us, it is not like an inner voice speaking to us but just a slightly uncharacteristic shifting of desire in the direction the Devil wants, so if an angel speaks to us or enlightens us, it may not be an actual voice but an insight that occurs so that something presents itself in a fresh light that we had not appreciated before. We see how it fits with our thinking and gives us a greater sense of understanding. An angel drawing us towards good again may simply increase our attraction towards that good thing because we are brought to see how it fits our inclinations in a way we had not understood before. So, when St. Thomas speaks of every adult having the opportunity of salvation even if it be by the revelation of an angel, the angel may act in this invisible way so that we suddenly see that embracing faith is a leap into the light, not the dark, and see some act or vocation as helping a fulfilment of our lives and opportunity to worship God and serve our neighbor. St. Thomas's insistence is that every adult has the opportunity of salvation and therefore the opportunity of being joined to the Church. St. Thomas plainly did not think that this conception had been excluded by the traditional dictum that there is no salvation outside the Church.

SECTION 3: THE IMPORTANCE OF DISTINGUISHING BETWEEN PARADOX AND STRICT CONTRADICTION

3.(a) THE DIFFERENCE BETWEEN THE NOTIONS OF CONTRADICTION AND PARADOX

It has become popular in modern times to emphasize the way Christian faith involves paradoxes. There is a tendency in some Protestantism to represent faith not as a leap into the light, enlarging our understanding, but as a leap into the dark. In this context Tertullian is often quoted: "I believe, because it is absurd."

In accord with this way of thinking, Dupuis seems to be attracted to what he takes to be the Indian approach of saying yes to both halves of a contradiction (*et-et*), as opposed to insistence on the acceptance of either the one or the other, but not both (*aut-aut*).[7] However, one cannot run the two horses together. One cannot rely on the normal logicians' rejection of contradiction in one's own theological argumentation on the one hand, while at the same time insisting on the acceptability of antinomy, on the other. Traditional Christian doctrine has held that Jesus Christ is one divine person in two natures, a perfect divine nature and perfect human nature. The idea of one person (existing in or exercising two natures is paradoxical, but not contradictory. Likewise, the idea of God as one being with one nature existing in three persons is similarly paradoxical without being contradictory.

3.(b) HOW THE FATHERS AVOIDED CONTRADICTION IN THE DOCTRINE OF THE TRINITY

The Fathers of the fourth century are particularly careful to avoid contradiction. It is because of this that, having accepted the term *ousia* to signify the being or essence of God, they sought for a different term for the persons of the Godhead, adopting the term *hypostasis* to apply to the persons (explained by Aquinas as meaning, in the logical sense, the primary subject, as what is neither predicated of nor present in something else). Augustine says since God is one something and three somethings, one has to be able to answer the questions, "one what?", and "three whats?" Since Latin writers for many centuries had already used *substantia* as the translation of *ousia*, one had to find another word to use in place of the word *hypostasis*, choosing the Latin *persona*, since otherwise one will have a strict contradiction for example God would be one being and three beings at the same time.

The Fathers were aware that words could have different meanings and sometimes change their meaning. When a heretic initiates a heresy it is always his use of certain words in certain ways which are condemned. When an important local council condemned the use of the expression "one *ousia*" in regard to God in the late 200s, their purpose was to exclude the idea that God was unitary in such a way that the Father, Son and Holy Spirit were only different aspects, roles,

7 Jacques Dupuis, *Towards a Christian Theology of Religious Pluralism* (Maryknoll, NY: Orbis Books, 1997), 198–200.

or ways of being experienced of one being, an idea expressed by speaking of them as three *prosopa* or *personae*. These latter words were thought inadequate because their original meaning had been to refer to the mask worn over the face or head of an actor in a play in classical times in order to signify what part he was playing, so that the actor (the real person, in the modern sense) underneath might be the same in many different roles. We frequently get a symptom of this approach when God the Father is said to be the "creator," God the Son, the "redeemer" and the Holy Spirit the "sanctifier," whereas in truth all three activities are the work of one and all. We meet it again when we are told that God the Father is the one to be revealed, God the Son the revelation of the Father, and God the Holy Spirit he who makes them known. All these are forms of what was condemned as Sabellianism. The distinctions between the members of the Trinity must be more radical than that of being different aspects or roles of the same thing.

Yet it still had to be insisted that Jesus and the Holy Spirit were of the same divinity as the Father—as against the Son being subordinate to the Father, as the heretic Arius taught. This has to be insisted upon because if God the Father sent a mere created deputy to live with human beings and be crucified, and not someone of the same *ousia*, being or essence with himself, then we cannot see the Father as having so loved the world as to send his only son in order that all men should be saved—so that, as it were, the heart of God the Father throbs with the heart of the Son. Sending a mere first creature, even a first creature through whom the angels and other things were made, is no better than sending a mere servant or prophet to die on the cross and save all mankind. Accordingly, Athanasius by the force of his argument got the Council of Nicaea (325) to decree that Jesus was born before all ages out of the *ousia* or being of the Father, *homoousion* with the Father. The Sun for the ancients was of its very nature both light in itself and the source of light in such a way that without light coming from it, it would not exist; hence, inspired by analogy with this, the Creed of Nicaea also describes Jesus as God out of God, Light out of Light. So strong an assertion of unity must be balanced by an insistence on the threeness. This came to be expressed by the First Council of Constantinople (318) in the terms of the Father, the Son and the Holy Spirit being each a distinct *hypostasis*.

Just as a strong assertion of unity, "one *ousia*," had required complementing by a strong assertion of threeness, three *hypostases*, so now this new strong assertion of threeness itself needed qualification. As a result, the Cappadocian Fathers began to explain the identity of the three *hypostases*, Father, Son, and Spirit, in terms of their relationships to each other. So, the Father *is* by being ungenerated, at once the source without source (*arche*), while the Son *is* by being generated by the Father, and the Spirit *is* by his being breathed out by the Father through the Son. They use this to explain their referring to the members of the Trinity as ways of being (*tropoi huparkseos*) a phrase they use only very occasionally. At the same time the Greeks also began occasionally to use the word *prosopon* in apposition with *hypostasis*, a word whose original meaning was, as we have seen associated with different roles or parts in the same dramatic play. This makes it less surprising that Latin speakers should have adopted the word *persona* which had the same previous meaning as *prosopon*, as a translation of *hypostasis*.

3.(c) THE ATTEMPT OF THE FATHERS TO AVOID CONTRADICTION IN SPEAKING OF THE INCARNATION

Once it had been made so clear that Jesus was a divine person or *hypostasis*, it became vital to make sure that this did not prejudice his full and true humanity. Arius had rejected Jesus's divinity making him instead a first creature above all the angels, not a man. From much earlier times, the view had survived that Jesus was so special that he could not have died on the Cross in reality, but only in appearance. This view survived and was held by Mohammed (who believed in the Ascension of Christ without believing in his death). Apollinaris taught that in Jesus the divine person took the place of the human mind and will, so that Jesus had only a human body, a view condemned by the First Council of Constantinople (381). Nestorius of Constantinople was reckoned to think it impossible that the same person should be both divine and human, and therefore to hold that Jesus consisted of two persons, Mary being the mother of the human person dying on the Cross, resurrected, and ascended, but the divine person being neither born of Mary, nor dying, and therefore not resurrected and not needing ascension. He held that there was some unity, more intimate than that exemplified by the Spirit's indwelling in a human being, but still without an identity of person. This view was roundly condemned by the Church Council of Ephesus (431) under the leadership of Cyril of Alexandria, insisting on the unity of *hypostasis* or person.

However, Cyril's ways of speaking introduced a new complication in that he held that Jesus was one *phusis*, a word usually translated into Latin by the word *natura*. Cyril himself did not have the least trace of desire to diminish the genuineness of Jesus's humanity or, as one would say in English, human nature. On the contrary, of the better-known Fathers up to his time, he is perhaps the most eloquent of all in his insistence of this—most especially eloquent in his expositions of the text of the Epistle the Hebrews which includes the passage "tried (= tempted) at all points like unto us, except without sin." The trouble was that at that time the word *phusis* like the word *natura* had more than one meaning. For Cyril it meant a reality in such a way that to say that Jesus had two *phuseis* would be to deny that he was one reality. This use corresponds to the use found in English of the 1500 and 1600s whereby the angels are referred to as "those most excellent natures," using the word "nature" to signify the thing with a certain distinctive kind of character rather than just the kind of character concerned; in the same way, even now we use the word "Nature" to refer to the universe. But the more common use in both Latin and English is to use the word *natura* or nature to refer to what distinguishes one kind of thing from other kinds of thing—it is that of which one would wish to give what Aristotle calls the definition of a thing as opposed to giving the meaning of a name.

However, in 449, Dioscouros of Alexandria went further than Ephesus and, calling a council himself, got this council to condemn the saying that Jesus had two natures or two *phuseis*. All this was done without Rome indicating concord or being represented at all, features of all three previous councils claiming to be general. At Ephesus, Rome had come to the support of Alexandria against Constantinople, insisting on the unity of Jesus's person, but now Rome came rapidly to the support of Constantinople and secured a new General Council at Chalcedon (451) which insisted that Christ had two natures, not condemning Cyril but condemning Dioscouros and other defenders of the one nature formula.

Every time a general council issues a defining pronouncement in the manner of Nicaea, Constantinople, Ephesus and now Chalcedon, in order to determine a controversy, it has to fix upon some particular use of certain key words in order to express the sense it wishes to convey—setting aside other perfectly innocent uses of the same words. It is as a result of this that both the Catholic and Eastern Orthodox church in commissions have separately agreed that the present-day Coptic Church although still using the formula "one *phusis*," holds the true doctrine and is not heretical, although in schism.

What this illustrates is that contradiction only arises when the person asserting and the person denying something, in the same form of words, are using their words in such a way that what is being said of the subject is denied in the same sense, in the same respect, and in respect of it at the same time, as Aristotle makes clear.

Let what Aristotle says suffice. If contradictory statements can both be true then neither of them means anything, and whosoever asserts either might as well remain silent. Statements are not realities but the expressions of judgements about reality. It is pairs of statements which can be contradictory to one another, and it is pairs of statements which sometimes, while not contradictory present a paradox, for example, when electrons are described both in terms of waves and as particles, or when we say that God is eternal but still make tensed statements about him.

Neither contradictions nor paradoxes are mysteries. The mystery is the reality about which we find ourselves having to make paradoxical statements, but still without contradiction.

SECTION 4: SOME RECENT TREATMENTS OF THE NOTION OF PERSON AND THEIR PURPOSE IN REGARD TO THE PERSON OF JESUS CHRIST

4.(a) PRELIMINARY REFLECTIONS

The attempt to remove modern content from the word "person" as used in theology is particularly motivated by the desire to represent all religions as directed towards the same object, "the real," "the ultimate" or "the absolute."

This strategy is a very strange one in the light of the origin of the modern use of the word "person," since this use is derived from theology, and it is only from theology that it passed on into philosophy and ordinary discourse. We have seen in Section 3 how the word "person" passed from meaning an actor's mask to meaning the reality—the intellectual, reflecting and choosing subject behind the mask—something in itself deeper than a temporary appearance or a face taken on. It is only with the doctrine of the Trinity that this word came to take on this deeper meaning. This meant that the models for the relationship between persons were derived from the doctrine of the Trinity, firstly from the relation of Jesus as Son to his divine Father, and secondly our relation as adopted sons to the same Father, brothers to Jesus and to one another. The conception of the Holy Spirit as a person is particularly clear in the body of St. Matthew's Gospel, even before it appears in the baptismal formula with which St. Matthew concludes his Gospel. It is equally clear in the writings of St. Luke, both in his Gospel and in the Book of Acts, and again equally clear in St. John's Gospel. And as new hymns and liturgies appeared from the fourth century, we find the Holy Spirit increasingly praised and invoked.

One of Augustine's analogies suggested that the Father, in his act of understanding conceives the Word and is moved by this understanding and conception to his act of loving, from which issues the Holy Spirit (which as a result, was often referred to as "Love"). This analogy has been open to a misunderstanding whereby the Holy Spirit, rather than being personal in character, is more analogous to the loving mutual relationship between the Father and Son. However, St. Thomas escapes this difficulty by thinking of the act of loving as always having an object, its goal or fruit. Here, he seems to conceive the character of *amor* (love) as found in possessing or enjoying as needing to be understood partly by analogy with its character as seen in seeking or desiring. The object of *amor* or love when already possessed and enjoyed is what would have been its goal if initially not possessed but only desired. But for a person the perfect object of love is also a person, and therefore the Holy Spirit is indeed a person.

As we have seen, at the very same moment that the Fathers introduced this way of using the word "person" in regard to the Father,

Son, and Holy Spirit, they also introduced the explanation of what it is for each of the persons to be who they are in terms of their relationships. We normally think of relationships as abstract things like slavery, which are accidental properties of their subjects, which is something else (e.g., the slave is a human being in himself, and not essentially a slave at all). However, for the ancients it was usually the concrete terms like "master" and "slave," which were thought of as relational terms, and the word "slavery" only came into the picture secondarily. Accordingly, when it is said that in the Trinity "*Persona est relatio*," what is meant is that the relationships marked by the words "Father," "Son," "Spirit" are not accidental but essential terms: e.g., what it is for the Son to be is for him to be generated by the Father, and so forth. The *esse* of the persons is the *esse* of the relevant relation. This relational character which we find in the persons of the Trinity, expressed by the Greeks in their explanations of such expressions as "three ways of being" and "three *prosopa*," was thus further developed by Augustine, by Richard of St. Victor in the 12th century, and St. Thomas Aquinas in the 13th century.

The situation of human beings is somewhat different: just as they begin as embryos and fetuses and only later exhibit the things which make us call them human beings, things like intellect, reason, freedom of choice, hope and despair, so they begin as individuals, and only in stages develop successively richer kinds of relationship reaching to personal relationships, from the most superficial to the fullest kind. So man is a person from the beginning, but what makes this title legitimate is only seen as fully personal relationships emerge, and in Aquinas' conception it is only given its full justification when we enter into a relationship with God through sanctifying grace.

The same doctrine appears among the Eastern Fathers and the Eastern Church in the form I described earlier: when Genesis says that man was made in the image and likeness of God, one has to understand that the likeness was something he lost in sin, so that his being in the image of God connotes the capacity for understanding, the freedom and inbuilt desire for God, constituting a constant call to find God, while the likeness connotes the being like God which comes when by his grace we respond to this call in love, so as to become genuinely like him as we might say in modern idiom "like him in character."

In these ways we see that the basic elements of the modern conception of person, namely knowledge, will, emotion and a capacity for personal relationship, derive from these developments in the thinking of the Church. It is therefore strange when modern theologians try to make out that God as such, and the persons of the Trinity, can be thought of just as well or better in impersonal terms as in personal ones.

4.(b) THE REAL, THE ULTIMATE, AND THE ABSOLUTE

Dupuis is one of those who explore the possibility of treating God impersonally, following on Hick and others in referring to God in such terms as the Real, the Ultimate, the Absolute. But it is never made clear why one should think that these expressions refer to anything at all. As these appear in Hick, one is reminded of the various forms of ontological argument to God's existence and their lack of force as arguments.

However, one of the general features of all Indian religion is a sense of the transitoriness and fragility of everything in the world. It is relative "unreality" in the sense of "contingency" and "transitoriness" rather than in the sense of "illusion" or "appearance" which Shankara (A.D. 799 – 833) seems to mean by "*maya*." And Indian ideas of the "Absolute" are rooted more in this cosmological background and a desire to escape from the relative non-significance of the transitory and the cycle of reincarnation than in anything resembling Western idealism.

In any case, Hick constitutes a strange bedfellow for Dupuis. Hick's conception of religious experience had its roots in the somewhat empiricist, Anglo-Saxon "evangelical" idea of a personal "experience of Jesus" or "personal knowing Jesus." He conceives such "evangelical" experiences as being fundamentally the same in different religions, although described in differing terms. In considering other religions, he is remaining within this western conception of "experience" (whether it be labelled idealist, empiricist, sentimentalist or romantic). Such preoccupation with "religious experience" and "religious feeling," things from which Carmelite and Benedictine spirituality as well as Indian tradition seek detachment, seems more at home in the modern west with its romanticism or sentimentalism and concern with subjective feeling than in either Catholicism or Indian tradition, whether Hindu or Buddhist. And the idea that something in common to such experience and feeling might constitute the heart of different religions as if it was their essence, against this background appears simply far-fetched.

The desire to escape from the relative non-significance of the transitory and come to stability in the absolute is something which gives the Christian the sense of deep community of spirit with other religions. Hindu and Buddhist spirituality seem to show the same deep rejection of secularism and they tend to be envisaged oversimply by Christians as in search for unity with God as the Absolute. It is here that the deep tensions between prophetic tradition, Jewish, Zoroastrian, Christian, and Muslim, on the one hand, and the traditions rooted in India, on the other, seem to arise: the fact that the search for stability in something absolute is expressed in radically different terms in the different traditions. The Indian idea that the individual by detachment may somehow learn to direct his attention inwards thereby ultimately bringing himself to stability in a unity with his true inner self, the Atman, or in Buddhism in the state of Nirvana, neither of which explanations have any obviously theistic form.

This formulation of the idea of detachment in terms of directing one's attention inwards has been one source of western misunderstanding of eastern teaching, namely a tendency to think of it as affording a certain kind of introspection, something particularly characteristic of western thinking since Descartes, whether dualist or empiricist, and also of romantic tradition, as well as being the predominant feature underlying twentieth century subjectivism.

The end aimed at by such detachment is ambiguous. Hick and Dupuis speak of it in terms of salvation and liberation. This ambiguity invites the common western misuse of eastern forms of asceticism, namely their use as a kind of therapy for the frenetic capitalist soul. For instance, in one particular Hindu system, the beginner begins by an established pattern of attentive breathing, focusing on each part of his body, each sensation, each bodily pain or pleasure without craving or fear. These meditation periods in one are said to bring about a great easing of the spirit as well as freedom from many muscular pains and tensions. This is the sort of motivation one tends to find in the West's look to the East.

The West is also tempted because of the absence in Buddhism of any theistic form of explanation for the end attained. This has made eastern religion seem particularly suited to the atheist and anti-metaphysical stance of western man, and, with the prevalence of a strange presumption that the devotee will attain the end, unity with the Atman or Nirvana, in this life, a convenient reason for unconcern with the prospect of one's own death, making it possible to turn a blind eye towards the awkward metaphysics of reincarnation.

The strength of the Indian tendency to think of human individuality as something to be escaped and the apparent lack of a compensating notion of the person make it difficult for a Christian to be certain that the Hindu or Buddhist traditions are addressed toward any reality at all as their goal. Both offer systems of meditation which bring a calm and serenity, but this does not itself imply any real object. However, such secular minded dismissal seems inappropriate if one considers the fact that Brahman who is not divided from Vishnu and Shiva is conceived of as the ground of all things, the transitory and material as well as the inner, and the way that much Buddhism seems to presuppose an order likewise governing both the world and what is involved in the escape from it into Nirvana. There are three problems. Firstly, there is the problem as to how to understand the cosmological perspective or aspect of Hinduism or of Buddhism. Secondly, there is the problem of how to interpret what is said about the inner or the self or the Atman in the case of Hinduism or else of how to understand the direction or goal of the way of detachment in the case of either religion. Thirdly, there is the problem of the relation of the concrete individual disciple to any of these things—the problem of individuality, a logical problem which seems hidden amidst obscurities in the notion of what detachment is from.

Indeed, the logical problem last mentioned constitutes but the tip of an iceberg. To the secular modern westerner, to whom knowledge of Christian or other prophetic tradition is more a matter of rumor and hearsay than of study or reflection, the resurrection spoken of by Jew or Zoroastrian, Christian or Muslim, is just a variant on reincarnation. But in reality, there is a gulf set between the two ideas. For Hindu or Buddhist, the cycle of reincarnation is something to be escaped, and reincarnation seems to involve somehow moral and ontological continuity without any psychological aspect.

By contrast, the idea of resurrection belongs with traditions which regard man as before all else bodily and communal so that a person's resurrection is a key part of his restoration and the completeness of human fulfillment, subsidiary to love of God and the ultimate fruition of this love in vision of God, but joined to it so that what loves and enjoys the presence of God is a complete human being in consummated concert with his fellow human beings, not some deprived human being, deprived of the bodily faculties and of the need for human community; and in this setting a person's resurrection is part of the completion of his biography and not lacking a psychological aspect. As I have said, it is wrong to posit two distinct ways to God, the one "interior," characteristically eastern, and the other "exterior" associated with the prophetic religions. It is especially wrong to consider interiority alone as what primarily matters to any religion and, as Dupuis holds, as alone the essential channel of grace. For the "interior" which matters is essentially personal, and therefore is a matter which has to do with the whole person in nature and disposition, the whole person as an historical, bodily and communal being—and it is this being whole and restored which will ultimately stand before God. As it is said in the Creed, God created all things, visible and invisible, and the prophetic traditions and, above all, Christian teaching insists that all, visible as well as invisible, will be brought to glory together.

However, it does not seem that the Hindu way of thinking is closed to just one line of interpretation or that the different strands are fully separable, and some of these suggest a strongly theistic and strongly personalistic interpretation.

In a way Sikh tradition, so clearly a form of monotheism fathered in a setting of prophetic tradition, suggests the possibility of a theism strongly impregnated with Hindu tradition. And the Syro-Malabar Church found and still enjoys an Indian mode of cultural existence which embodied a precious ancient Christian tradition, one that tragically the Portuguese found quite alien and so the object of their destructive aggression. However, neither of these seem to provide clear cases of inculturation at the religious level.

It therefore seems to be the possible vocation of some modern Western religious, Benedictines and Dominicans, partly helped by Carmelite spirituality, to achieve a deeper penetration of the meaning of eastern traditions at a religious and not just cultural level, approaching this vocation with the kind of generosity of spirit with which Ricci and Nobili sought to penetrate and participate in Confucian and Brahmin teaching and practice. It is not easy to see how else truth in the theology of religious pluralism is to be obtained apart from such an approach. It is only Christians inspired by such Christian religious orders that might have solid hope of making the required discernments. For, not only as they exist in the East, but even more in the variety of forms in which they have been exported to the West, superficially similar teachings may prove profoundly different at a deeper level.

However, Dupuis' project does not seem to lie along this line, and his attempt to make some unity between East and West consist in sameness in their ultimate ideas of salvation or liberation appears to be a particularly artificial piece of rationalization. And, although in his discussions he brings to light much richness from the traditions he discusses, his finding of the doctrine of the Trinity in other religions is another piece of rationalization, in this case depending on a betrayal of key aspects of Christian teaching.

4.(c) THE SUBVERSION OF THE NOTION OF "PERSON" AS APPLIED TO THE TRINITY, AND THE RESPONSE AVAILABLE IN TRADITION

The beginnings of some recent trends can be found in Rahner even before Vatican II. In the first volume of his *Theological Investigations* (1954), he asserts that there must be a human "I-center" or human center of consciousness distinct from the divine person of the Son, the *Logos*. This position when thought through, is essentially Nestorian. It implies, for instance, that the Jesus who prayed in the garden of Gethsemane, quite evidently speaking and feeling from this human I-center was distinct from the Son of God, and the same would apply in every other act of Jesus's saying something, supposing he was conscious of what he said, in which he used the personal pronoun for the first person, for example: "My God, my God, why hast thou forsaken me?" And "Unto you I commend my spirit" as well as "I thirst."

Certainly, Jesus had human knowledge and awareness and had a human will, but to follow the councils and say that the 'I' which was subject of this knowledge, awareness, and will was the Son of God, the *Logos* himself, is not to deny this.

Rahner here treats the expression "I-center" as if it were an identifying description with meaning, in the case of Jesus, "the person who was born of Mary, came to live in Nazareth and died on the Cross, the Cross being inscribed 'Jesus of Nazareth, King of the Jews.'" But it is a serious, logical mistake to treat the meaning of the pronoun "I" in this way, a fact of which Wittgenstein was peculiarly aware.[8] We are not necessarily aware in any particular present act of consciousness, even incidentally, of where we used to live and how we shall die. This is the logical origin of the modern distinction between the subject and object of knowledge. It is conspicuous in Descartes and Kant and the source of Hume's remark that there is no impression from which the idea of the self derives, and of Berkeley's insistence that we do not have ideas but only notions of spirit.

Rahner's way of thinking here is related to what Dupuis regards as the confusion between the theological concept of person and the modern conception of "personality, or consciousness" regarding the expression "human personality" and "human consciousness" as synonymous.

In this he seems entirely mistaken. In the general modern use of the word "personality," personality is something a person has, not what a person is. It tends to mean his character, especially, in those respects in which it is unusual or eccentric. In modern slang we can say, "He is a personality now," and by this we mean that he is well-known in the public mind because of his display of an exceptional or eccentric character. It is true that in speaking of struggles between persons, we can make remarks like "It was a struggle between two strong personalities," but by this we mean that it was a struggle between the persons of strong, or forceful and contrasting characters. If we speak of "split-personalities" we do not imply the presence of two persons within one human being, but one of several kinds of disorder in the consciousness of some particular human being.

As to consciousness, a human being has human consciousness, but is not identical with this consciousness—after all, he or she still exists when asleep and not dreaming.

The teaching of the first six Ecumenical Councils is that Jesus was one divine person possessing both a divine mind, knowledge, and understanding and a human mind, knowledge, and understanding, both a divine will and a human will, and with divine acts and with

8 Its most recent Anglo-Saxon treatment is by G. E. M. Anscombe in *Collected Papers, Vol. II: Metaphysics and the Philosophy of Mind* (Cambridge: Cambridge University Press, 1981), 21–36; cf. *Vol I*: 112–33.

human acts. Dupuis might readily have raised a difficulty, not in regard to the doctrine of the Incarnation, but in regard to the Trinity. He could have asked how it is possible for there to be in God one single divine act of self-understanding, one single divine act of self-love, both identical in the reality and identical also with God's one act of living and being, and yet at the same time for there to be acts of understanding and love in each person of which that person is the subject knowing and loving. To this two different answers can be returned. First, one might respond that the matter is a mystery of which we can achieve no understanding. Second, we might surmise that, if one distinguishes two kinds of human knowledge, the first in which the knowing subject stands over against or considers the object as if external, and the second in which the knowing subject is inseparable from the object known in the act of knowing, then the second is the nearest human life offers to us to a model of relationships within the Trinity.

Dupuis' arguments, in which he appeals to Rahner's later writings, depend on emptying the concept of *hypostasis* or "person" as applied to the Persons of the Trinity of any connotation of intellect or will, leaving only the idea of primary logical subject.[9] In this, he makes a very misleading appeal to Augustine. Augustine did not mean or say that the later church quite arbitrarily coined the word "person" to translate the expression *hypostasis*. On the contrary, Augustine implies no such complete arbitrariness in the choice of the word "person," as if it did not matter whether or what this word had meant earlier. On the contrary, the word *prosopon*, of which "person" is the natural translation, had already been used by the Greeks after 381 in apposition to the word *hypostasis*, and even in their older uses the word had implied personhood in the modern sense of the part being acted by the actor distinguished by the mask he was wearing, although not the personhood of the mask itself. Accordingly, the use of either word had the unavoidable connotation of personhood as something including intellect and will.

There is in principle no logical difficulty in the same person having both divine knowledge and understanding of all things, and human knowledge and understanding in a human manner of a hugely

9 Dupuis, *Religious Pluralism*, 264–66.

narrower range of things, some things in ways natural to human beings as such, some by gifts like prophecy and some through divinely given penetration in a human manner of God's vision of himself. This is because the way these words "knowledge" and "understanding" are applied to God is not to be understood in the same way as they are applied to human knowledge and understanding. This should be clear from any study of Aquinas' treatment of analogy and the way of thinking underlying it. In Aquinas' conception there is no single definition of how any pair of the following know or understand things, the angels, human beings, or the animals less than man. Therefore, a *fortiori,* nor could there be any shared definition of knowledge and understanding between God and the angels or God and man. The same applies to his active power, life, and love—the way these things are to be explained or understood in the case of God and angels, God and man, or man and angels can none of them be given one definition—none can be explained in terms of one set of implications or one set of criteria of application. The way Jesus exercised his divine knowledge and understanding was the direct, non-linguistic way in which his Father exercised it—such divine knowledge and understanding possessed and exercised in a divine manner would be as such absolutely incapable of entering into his human consciousness.

That which he knew in his divine way of knowing he did not thereby know humanly at all. The ways Jesus acquired and exercised his human knowledge and understanding were the ways human beings acquire and exercise it. Normally, they acquire and exercise it (if not immature, deprived, or diseased) in some ordinary empirical way, gaining it by observation or teaching. Other times, some human beings receive prophetic knowledge. In Christian belief, all human beings who attain to heaven enjoy a different mode of knowledge in the Beatific Vision, primarily knowledge of God, but also particular knowledge God gives them through this Vision, for example, the knowledge which moves them to pray for us.

Now, according to Catholic theological understanding, what the saints who enjoy the Beatific Vision know through it is measured by their love of God (charity) so that within that measure they humanly know what they desire to know; accordingly, since Jesus's human love (charity) of the Father was infinite, he knew humanly through the Beatific Vision which he had in virtue of his union with the Father whatever he desired to know, but what he desired to know (what, we might say, he was willing to ask the Father to show him) was limited by his self-emptying ("kenotic") love of man and concurrence with the will of his Father to empty himself in order to be like us in our deprived sin-limited slavish state. It is in this way that he could truly say of the end of history that "But that day and hour no one knows, not even the angels of heaven, nor the Son, but the Father only" (Mt 24:36), because by his and the Father's will he did not desire to be unlike us, and unlike any other creature, in knowing this. Indeed, the only things of which Scripture suggests that he had prophetic or Beatific human knowledge beyond his contemporaries are things pertaining either to his mission and the general intent of the Old Testament Scriptures or to the circle of his disciples and those he had special encounter with, such as the Samaritan woman at the well and the woman with a hemorrhage who sought healing by touching his garments anonymously in the crowd (it seems that he was not to be deceived).

Acceptance of the idea that the persons of the Trinity possess divine knowledge with all the omniscience and completeness of understanding which this entails in no way undermines our recognition of the limitations of Jesus's human knowledge.

It is quite wrong to suppose that the assertion that he possessed divine knowledge distinctly from his human knowledge makes the assertion of the divinity of Jesus's person into an empty logical trick. We wrongly suppose that in order to avoid any such trick, we have to psychologize his divinity and his divine mode of knowledge in some way, as if our faith depended on making the unimaginable imaginable.

However, a crude analogy may help. When a person plays a violin, he remains distinct from the violin so that strictly speaking, however expressive the sound of the violin may be, it is not the sound of the person himself, since he has not become the violin however expressively he is using it. By contrast, what is involved in the Incarnation is analogous to the person's becoming the violin. Accordingly, what is required is, not the transformation of the person into an already existing violin/man because there is no such preexisting or separately existing distinct violin/man, but the violin/man's constituting in its every aspect and activity in very truth and actuality the sound/expression of the divine person.

By this, I mean the following. The humility of the embryo and infant; his love and subservience to Mary and Joseph; his love and respect for other human beings and indeed for the whole world and everything in it; the work of his ministry and the love and subservience in this and in his whole earthly life to his Father, and in all this the *kenosis* consummated in his death on the cross; and his growth first in grace and then in glory to carry our humanity fully to his Father to enjoy in his and our humanity a sharing in the divine life: all these are the expression, the word, the sounding (as when we speak of the sounding of a violin) within the creation, not of a mere holy man but of the very Son of God, the Word or Wisdom of the Father. All these are embodiment or realization within creation of the Son who was with the Father before and independently of creation, through whom everything created is created, everything sustained in existence that is sustained in existence, whose activity in creation began in the very act of creating and has continued immediately upholding in existence everything up to now. As the Scythians sung it is not a mere holy man who suffered on the cross, but "one of the Trinity has died." And this person had divine intellect and this intellect was and is expressed in all these things.

In this, the divine intellect and will were not psychologized, as if the divinity which is in principle unimaginable could be made imaginable. Rather the human intellect and will, emotions, memory, and imagination, everything of soul with everything of body in Jesus was divinized, made the very embodiment, *phusis*, realization within creation of the eternal Son. Thereby the whole of creation was brought with the Son into the personal presence of the Father, human beings person-to-person, not just with one another but to the Father. God became man, took on solidarity with man as man with fellow man, in order that man should be able to enter into solidarity with God through the gifts of grace and glory.

As to how the nonmathematical infinite (referred to by Dupuis following Schillebeeckx as the "universal") can be expressed in the particular, the problem is not assisted by enlarging the mathematical number of such particulars, but only by supposing that we lack comprehension of Jesus's humanity. This answer is in good accord with St. Thomas's reply to the fourth objection to his thesis that whatever God does he could always have done better (logically there can be no best of all possible worlds, any more than there can be any greatest natural number or any maximum in complexity), when he concedes that God could not make Christ's humanity better, could not increase the happiness of the Blessed who enjoy the vision of himself, and could not improve the situation of the Virgin Mary inasmuch as she was mother of God.[10] It also accords with Eastern Orthodox teaching that there is a certain (nonmathematical) infinity in each human person because he is made in the image and likeness of God.

Once his subversion of the traditional meaning of the word "person" as applied to the persons of the Trinity has been refuted, and the traditional conception restored, Dupuis is left in no position to claim that the only existence, consciousness, or will exercised by the Son-of-God-made-man-in-Jesus-of-Nazareth was human existence, consciousness, and will.

Dupuis has the picture that Jesus, Son of God, the *Logos*, before his conception had no personal existence in any modern sense so that the only personal existence he had after his conception was human existence. This leads Dupuis into remarks such as "Christology of the God-man is an abstraction,"[11] and, referring to the preexistence of Jesus before the Incarnation as "Preexistence is not existence in a fictitious time before time," writing as if Mary's conception of Jesus was the beginning of time. He attempts to salvage the Incarnation by following this latter remark by the explanation "However, the fact remains that the incarnation of the Son of God involves, in a very real way, the becoming-human-in-history of the Word, who, independently of this becoming, exists eternally in the mystery of God." He concludes these thoughts by saying "Such is the real sense conveyed through the symbolic language of incarnation."[12]

The idea that the language of the incarnation is symbolic is misleading. It is a mistake to think that when we speak of bodies being *in* places, we are speaking literally but that when we speak of events as being *in* time we are speaking metaphorically, and that other metaphorical uses are involved when we speak of a particular pain as being *in* the leg and another *in* the abdomen and a third *in* the

10 Thomas Aquinas, *S.Th.* Ia, Q. 25, Art. 6.

11 Dupuis, *Religious Pluralism*, 205.

12 Dupuis, 296.

head. Certainly, the use of the word "in" in these cases is not symbolic. Aquinas would have said that these uses of the word "in" are analogous. Similarly, we do not speak metaphorically when we speak of life as being *in* the body or of an electrical charge as establishing a field which is *in* the places where the electrical charge can exercise its electrical influence. Likewise, we do not speak metaphorically when we say that God, as cause of their being, is present *in* all the things whose being he causes. Nor therefore, when it is said in the Creed that Jesus was made man and "became *in* the flesh," are we speaking metaphorically. Nor in any of these cases are we using the word "in" symbolically.

Dupuis quotes Schnackenburg, appealing to his remark that "Johannine Christology is not modelled on a set pattern of mythological speculation about a redeemer descending from heaven and returning there again" in his support.[13] But Dupuis is misconstruing Schnackemburg's meaning. The latter is not denying the preexistence of Jesus, a preexistence reasserted by St. John when he quotes Jesus as saying, "Before Abraham was, I am" (Jn 8:58). His purpose is rather that of repudiating the idea that St. John is copying the idea common to much speculation in some of the mystery religions of the time, drawing on pagan ideas, involving a previously absent heavenly being coming from outside (descending from heaven) to redeem man and after this returning to where it was before. This kind of speculation presents a false picture of St. John's thought. He does not think of the Word or Logos as coming from elsewhere in order to be made flesh but as already present everywhere. The contrast between the earthly and the heavenly in St. John is allied by him with the contrast between the bread which perishes and the bread which endures unto eternal life, between the water which one has to keep coming back to fetch more of and the living water which is to the one that drinks it a spring of water welling up to eternal life, and between the kingships of this world and the kingship which is not of this world. The contrast is not between that which is drawn down here and that which is celestial with or beyond the stars but between that whose principle is transitory and that whose principle is eternal. What makes life eternal is the indwelling Spirit which brings Jesus and his Father to abide in the person concerned. It is the use of words "up" and "down"

13 Dupuis, 296.

which are metaphorical and sometimes associated with symbols (e.g., the cloud associated with God's glory into which Jesus ascended in order to signify his withdrawal from presence to our earthly senses), not the use of "in." When Jesus withdrew from the visible presence of the disciples, it was not to become absent but to become by the Holy Spirit present in a new way, abiding within them. And, when he withdraws from the presence of his disciples, he remains man eternally in glory, and he remains man in order that he should remain our brother, and in order that we should be made able to join him in glory.

SECTION 5: SUMMARY OF CONCLUSIONS IN RESPECT OF DUPUIS

(1) Dupuis is aiming at a position in which the relations between the different religions is only one of dialogue, so that if a person is converted, it is by his spontaneous movement, and in no way the fruit of preaching or other missionary work directed towards conversion.

He regards the doctrine that all have the possibility of salvation, unless they persist in rejecting it, as going together with the idea that it is the norm (not just what usually happens, but what God has designed to happen because he thinks it good) that most of mankind come to salvation through some mediation and salvific power provided by their own religion. It goes together with thinking of mankind in Heaven at the end as united in the Kingdom of God, rather than in the Church.

This goes together with having come to limit the use of the word "Church" to the institutional Church as visible in its work in the world since the time of the Apostles.

(2) He neglects the aspect of this Apostolic visible Church whereby all the riches of other cultures are to come into it, and by an increase of understanding and a growing sharing in these riches, this Church is to come to embody and be the sign of a reversal here of the loss of understanding and sympathy symbolized in the story of the Tower of Babel.

In this way, the one organic body of the Church is to be the anticipation of the great orchestra in Heaven. Further, there is continuity between the visible organic Church of this period between the first Pentecost and the Last Day, and the heavenly

Church thereafter, as well as the discontinuities involved in its glorification, in its being joined with those who have gone before and in the general Resurrection.

If there is value in the human nature, the rational social animality, which the Son of God took on, then there is also value in bodiliness, in explicitness so far as it can be attained through art and verbal expression, in growth in the understanding expressed by the voice and realized in the mind, in sympathy, fellowship and community. But then there must also be value in these things being realized in the growth of the Church in this life, continued and perfected in the next.

The organic character of the Church in heaven is a completion of its organic character on earth. This neglect is partly the result of the neglect of his failure to recognize that the word "Church" is an analogous term.

(3) There is one point on which Danielou and De Lubac should have, and I think would have, made one important concession. I think that theology logically requires a position akin to that identified on page 76, the position whereby many are in the state of sanctifying grace but have to wait until Christ's Passion and Glorification to receive that fuller gift of the Holy Spirit which first came at that time, so that Jesus and his Father should abide in them, and they in Jesus. This fuller gift enables them 'to enter in with us' (Heb 11:39—40, cf. 12:22—23), and in this life is an anticipation of Heaven.

Yet again, if there is value in this fuller gift, then there is value in receiving it in this life. Therefore, this is the chief reason for the Church preaching in the hope of conversion—making this, and not dialogue alone, essential to its mission.

(4) Dupuis betrays the unity of man, soul, and body, by allowing two separate ways to God, one interior, the other historical. Any way to God or to salvation and liberation has to involve both, as different aspects of the same way. In allowing and even giving greater preeminence to the interior way, and in his treatment of other religions, his whole position comes slightly reminiscent of the aspect of Modernism described by Pius X in paragraphs 7 — 12 of his encyclical *Pascendi*.

This leads to the breakdown of his explanation of what he calls the "constitutive" character of Christ's work, depending on his being personally the Son of God as historically realized. He has not explained how the historical is necessary, if there are the two alternative ways described.

It also generates problems for the unitariness of his conception of salvation/liberation, which he struggles to present as one concept shared by all religions. He seems to confuse the general notion of happiness with the notion of the reality this happiness (our salvation/liberation) consists in, the salvation of life in the presence, love, and vision of God. This is a logical mistake analogous to confusing the notion of "common existence" with that of "Existence – Itself."[14]

It also explains the absence of attention to Jesus's Resurrection or to the general resurrection.

It also explains the near absence of any attention to the fact that the *Logos* remained man unto all eternity.

(5) Dupuis empties the term *hypostasis* of the implications of being a subject, which is neither predicated of a subject, nor present in a subject (in the way attributes or parts are present in a subject), and empties the term "person" both of these implications and of the implication of the possession of intellect and will. In this way he goes against the traditions embodied in the pre-Nicene Fathers and of the first six Ecumenical Councils, as well, as it may be strongly argued, against Scripture. The purpose of this is to allow him to deny that the Son of God, the *Logos*, has any personal existence in any sense acceptable to Church Tradition before 1960, except the personal human existence he has when incarnate in Jesus of Nazareth.

This denial of true personhood to either Son or Spirit as divine *hypostasis* is exhibited in the whole strategy of the argument of pages 264 – 79, centered on the discussion of the term "person" itself in pages 264 – 66. However, it most nearly becomes completely explicit on page 205 and pages 296 – 300.

(6) He allows the possibility in theology of direct and not merely verbal contradiction.[15] The language of the Indian passages cited on page 275 is reminiscent of some of the assertions of God's unknowability and the use of antinomies to be found amongst the Fathers of the Eastern Church—presenting paradox, but not

14 Thomas Aquinas, *S.C.G.*, I, c.26
15 For example, see Dupuis, *Religious Pluralism*, 198.

contradiction. However, the unknowability asserted by the Greek Fathers is not a matter of the impossibility of making true affirmative statements about God, rather a matter of God's incomprehensibility and unimaginability. In Section 3, we have already seen the anxiety of the Fathers, both Eastern and Western, to avoid contradiction—an anxiety very well exhibited in the unfolding of the disputes before and after the first six councils, and the formulations of these councils themselves. Always we have paradox and mystery, but never logical contradiction.

AFTERTHOUGHT: THE SCANDAL OF THE SMALL

Andrew Willard Jones, editor

Why would a highly successful academic philosopher spend a considerable about of time and effort on the problem of the Incarnation, on a distinctly theological problem? When I began the task of sorting through David's hundreds of unfinished essays, notes, and pieces of correspondence, looking for the "Incarnation Book" that he spoke of so frequently, this question was at the front of my mind. The answer grew in my understanding as I read. The answer is present in a somewhat formal and obscure way in the finished essays that are published above. It is more plain in the little notes and asides, the many false starts that he later discarded and never finished, the little autobiographical anecdotes sprinkled through his writings and correspondence. What became plain was that David was not a philosopher dabbling in theology. David was a philosopher whose philosophy sought its fulfillment in theology. David was driven to the Incarnation because the Incarnation was the conclusion to his philosophy because it was, in fact, where his philosophy started. It was its return to itself. Let me explain.

As we have all been taught, philosophy begins in wonder. From childhood, David was consumed by wonder, wonder at being, at the very experience of being in a world. He talks about being eight years old and delving into cosmology and evolutionary biology, an interest that led him to write a universal history of the cosmos, starting with the formation of the stars, as an eleven-year-old boy. From the beginning, this wonder had something to do with his at the time naïve religious convictions. As he studied the world, he also kept up a study of comparative religion. Even as a child he, perhaps intuitively, understood that his wonder at the universe had something to do with God.

This intuition was challenged when he went to university and encountered sophisticated skepticism. It is clear that this encounter disturbed him. But, if I might be so bold as to assert an interpretation, I would say that this religious skepticism disturbed him because it reduced the world itself to something simple, because it reduced the world to something no longer worthy of our wonder. In other words, the philosophy of the skeptics was the destruction of philosophy itself, the end of the joy David found in exploration of the cosmos through thought. David felt this as a tragedy.

From that first encounter with skeptics, there appears a missionary aspect to David's work. But this was not because of some sort of partisan theological conviction or some sort of prejudicial, ultimately prideful compassion. It was because he felt sorry for those who lived in a world devoid of wonder, a world without God was a world without philosophy. The Incarnation, the central dogma of Christianity, was the reintroduction of God into the world. The Incarnation was the most wonderous of all religious doctrines, across the world's religions, and it was the doctrine that restored wonder. Philosophy needed the Incarnation. This all needs a little explanation.

What David seems amazed with is our ability to wonder itself. Wonder flows out of our smallness in our greatness, out of the strangeness of being a little, finite, particular person who participates somehow in the universal. The insect is small, but it does not know that it is small. It is small only from the outside—only something bigger knows that the bug is little. Man is different. Only man is small on the inside, only man feels small, and this is because he participates in the infinite. He looks up and sees what's there. It is the tension between our particular existence and the rational nature of that existence, which reaches out to the universal, that makes wonder possible. Wonder is the experience of our bold turn toward the infinite. Our smallness is as integral to this experience as our greatness for it is the very gulf between the two that the word "wonder" captures.

We are seeing here already a move toward the relationship between theology and philosophy. It is not some sort of silly stacking or merely some methodological distinction based upon which data one uses in one's reasoning. Rather, philosophy begins in wonder and wonder is already a move into the theological. The smallness of philosophy is already a participation in the greatness of theology. Philosophy is already a handmaiden, but not within some sort of servile conception, but rather in the Marian form—the servant who will bear into the world her own master. The humility of the true philosopher is already an act of faith. To refuse this act of faith, to refuse this initial "leap into the light"—as David called it—is already to begin the rejection of philosophy itself.

The union of the small with the great. Here is wonder. But could we better begin in a description of the Incarnation? In the Incarnation, God not only comes down and assumes human nature, but in his resurrection and ascension, human nature goes up to become an integral and permanent aspect of the life of the Trinity. The second person *is* incarnate. It is essential for David that this happens only once because the once-ness of a man is a part of the smallness of a man. To become a man is to become a particular, finite man with a biography.

David understood that those who desire God to be incarnate multiple times are trying to avoid or mitigate this smallness. A single man is so limiting, so small, so particular. Wouldn't it be more fitting for the infinite God to appear more times, to more people, in more modes? As if through multiplying his incarnations, we could somehow close the gap between the finite and the infinite, somehow make the finite bigger, or the infinite smaller. This is to repeat the error of the skeptics in a different mode, to flatten the world and so to destroy the wonder of it all. The man Jesus is God. In order for God to be man he had to be *a* man because this is what men are. Part of what it means to become a man is to become small—to become one aware of one's smallness because a participant in the infinite, to become one capable of wonder. In Christ's perfect smallness and perfect greatness, Christ was the perfect manifestation of wonder, of philosophy, but a philosophy that was nothing other than divinity. Again, we find the profound connection between philosophy and theology, a connection that occurs only within the immeasurable gap between the two.

Multiple times in his writings, David evokes the Fourth Lateran Council's definition of the analogy of being, that no similarity between the creator and creature can be noted without a greater dissimilarity also being noted. The similarities, the smallness, are called out always against the backdrop of the ever-greater difference, the greatness. David understood that philosophy's movement within the smallness was founded on the greatness. This is why, I think, it wasn't so much modern man's lack of belief in hell that was so troubling to David as was his lack of belief in heaven, which can only be understood as an inability to find wonder at the world, an inability to situate our small participation in the true and the good within the ever-greater fullness of truth and goodness that lays always beyond. This is why for David the Incarnation must always be joined with the Ascension. It is not only the coming down, but the going back up that was crucial. Again, this is the basis of wonder.

I thought it might be a good idea to include as an epilogue to David's theological essays a talk that he once gave on his plan for a book on the Incarnation. I think it helps us understand his finished essays, even if we find ourselves disappointed that David was summoned home before the project was finished.

EPILOGUE

Faith as a leap into the light: explaining the Christian faith in the twenty-first century[1]

Jesus, Son of God, have mercy on us
The Lord has given me
a disciple's tongue.
So that I may know how to reply to the wearied
he provides me with speech.
Each morning he wakes me to hear,
to listen like a disciple.
My heart is stirred by a noble theme,
as I sing my ode to the king.
My tongue is the pen of a nimble scribe.

1 Although the occasion and date are not certain, this paper was most likely presented to the Aberdeen Theological Club. David's friend and editor of this volume, Tony Schmitz, read the paper, and David responded to questions. As far as we can tell, it was not otherwise presented or published.

THE AIM OF THE BOOK

I am engaged in writing a book explaining the doctrine of the Incarnation (the enfleshment of God), and how our minds and the minds of others today can be drawn to a rounded faith in Jesus as the Christ (our truly human leader and teacher) and Son of God—a faith to be received by us as disciples and followers of Jesus.

Discipleship means receiving what we are taught as given from the table of the master teacher, accepted as offered *Table d'Hôte*, because the host at the table is God himself guiding us into the way of Revealed truth. This is the opposite of approaching the teaching as if it was a series of opinions between which we could choose *á la carte*.

Jesus is the master teacher because he is the unique Son of God. This is something we could only know by revelation, a revelation coming from God, and through Jesus. And since it comes to us from him historically, it comes to us from him as truly human as well as truly divine, and must come by the teaching's being passed on through history, from his apostles and witnesses, through the understanding of the community initiated through them, and this community being guided by the Holy Spirit which comes through him.

Apart from patience in understanding the teaching which comes through this community and docility in this process, the docility of a believing disciple seeking understanding, what we believe would become a mere matter of opinions chosen *á la carte*.

Revelation is given in such a way that over time and through drawing on cultural influences of many different sources human understanding is to develop, but not in such a way as to change the essence of the teaching.

The purpose of this paper is to explain to you what I think is vital to the intellectual formation of Christians today.

Accordingly, it will be a bit like presenting you with a series of summaries of some different sections in the planned book, rather than presenting you with a whole argument.

I present you with an account of what things have to be contained in the book if it is to accomplish its purpose. What I would like is any suggestions as to the order in which I should present this material.

At every stage, I need to insist on the importance of Christianity being true and being presented as true—and this is how it presents itself.

Certainly, Christianity draws us through love drawing the heart—for what more could God do for us to draw our love than to become one of us, our fellow in being fully human, living with us and even dying a human death. He did all this in order for us that we should come to him and enjoy the divine life—God entering into solidarity with man in order that man should enter solidarity with God—God becoming man in order that man should be divinized.

However, Christianity can only do this if it is true, and must draw us as drawing us to the truth. Otherwise, we have only a story of God's love and how it was exercised in Jesus, *a very eloquent story, but still only a story.* If God does not even exist, or if Jesus was not in truth divine, then, although what Christians say makes a good story and a person might feel "Would that it were true." Still, if it is just a good story, it is of no use. Rather, it is vital that it be actually true.

It is therefore also vital that there should be adequate pointers to its truth. We can only be drawn to which is true if it draws the intellect, as well as the heart.

Every obstacle to believing Christianity to be true, is an obstacle to love as well as to faith. We must not be sidetracked.

For instance, it belongs to Christian belief that God is the Creator of all the things, seen and unseen, and this being creator is understood to be a matter not only of bringing things into existence, but also sustaining them in existence. In this way God is immediate to everything, given it being not from a distance but by immediate presence. It is this that matters about creation, not how God communicates this truth to us. Therefore, I shall treat the question of the role of the Old Testament, especially the beginning of Genesis, in the growth of this understanding, at a later stage, as part of a more general question as to how God teaches us.

We live in a culture which is quite alien to the Christian way of life. In addition, for most people every pointer towards the truth of Christianity has become obscured. It is also a culture in which people think that matters of religion are personal to the individual, none being able to claim that his or her opinion has a better standing than any other. The cultural norm is that we form our opinions from an *á la carte* menu of alternative opinions.

In this setting, it becomes puzzling that there should long remain many Christians at all!

I say that our culture is quite alien to the Christian way of life. This is true not only in our preoccupation with material goods and the things that depend on them—it has always been true that, when the word of the Gospel is sown, "much is sown amongst thorns, the worries of the world, the deceitfulness of riches, and other desires enter in and choke the word, and it becomes unfruitful." In the West, since the late 1500s, usury, living by means of lending money at interest, has grown into a culture of financial greed, as well as of aggression, war, and the pursuit of power, to dominate others economically, and this pursuit of domination extends to a much more efficient control over the opinions of others. We are here involved in a deep corruption at the social level, combining social and economic structures which strengthen the military-industrial complex, encourage wars and the structures which make peace dependent on military and economic pressures rather than concord of heart, and involve increasing greed and destruction in the treatment of nature, increasing the dominance of the state over education and the family.

The state has a role also in fortifying the things which more immediately affect the individual. But of recent times this role has in many ways been used to negative effect so as to distort what concerns the relationship between man and God, and man and man. Here I have in mind that today the preoccupation with sexual freedom, assuming steadily larger and larger proportions in our Western way of life since the 1920's, and especially since the 1960's, presents perhaps the largest non-intellectual obstacle to faith, affecting each individual's heart and mind directly.

People want to follow their own way from their teens onwards and even within marriage itself (that is if they do get married), and, unless they are disciples, an increasing alienation from Christian teaching about marriage and sex has been perhaps the biggest obstacle to listening to the rest of Christian teaching.

We have here a problem both of the will and the mind. Firstly, Christianity invites a way of life that people do not want. Secondly—and this is what is new—they do not accept the teaching given in this area because they see no reasons for it. They did not understand how it may be part of the framework of being able to keep God first in one life. This is, I think, primarily because it is taken altogether out of the context of a Christian understanding of the way of discipleship and of the goal of human life. If these things are also made more difficult by the pressures set by expectations of our family, the norm in one's peer group, one's other goals (career, a house, saving, etc.), and the pressures to have a large and expensive wedding—also the expense involved in conforming to what is required by law, e. g., by health and safety regulations, all on top of the greater expense of housing. It is not chiefly because of arguments about population limitation, but because of the standard of living desired, but people say things like "We cannot afford more than two children."

These things are also approached from within a rather protected Western setting, turning a blind eye on the wider context of the Westernized style of life and death wherever it has spread within different societies, and ignoring the conditions and concerns of those who are poorer in the world today.

Turning to deeper issues: it is often said that having lost a sense of God, Western man has lost a sense of sin. And, although some people are plagued by guilt arising from deep wrongs in their life, they have no feeling of offence against God.

But, far more important than this, Western man has lost a sense that religion matters—lost a realization that religion concerns what gives the greatest fullness to life, which is what "heaven" has to do with—indeed, for most, the word "heaven" has become almost empty of meaning.

Men and women have lost any appreciation of how, compared with life in God, which is the fruit of the life of discipleship, the suffering each person undergoes pales into relative insignificance. Yet, it is only a living faith that can help us keep a firm grasp of this—this living faith is not a matter of a sense of emotional consolation or reassurance, but of God's love for us helping us hold fast to hope in him in the midst of much human suffering.

A problem of a quite different kind is that many are very close to the Christian way in their care for others, their human virtue and generosity of spirit, and yet feel no need for Christianity for their being themselves moved to such care and generosity and see no such need for it in the case of others.

Again, the issue is of why religion matters—how it can make a difference to a life which is committed to self-giving anyway.

Here, there is a need for recognition that love of God gives fire, strength, and perseverance to love of neighbour, making it a work empowered by God, not just by human activism. And here in presenting Christianity, there is a great neglect in the presentation of examples. Everyone has heard of St Francis, a few others of Father Damien and Martin de Porres, or the multitude of others quite unknown.

However, while love of God should give fire to love of neighbor, we must also recognize that God did not become man in order to fortify virtue, but to bring us to himself.

This makes the fact that religion and in particular Christianity matter, a fact of urgency. It is a matter of urgency that people's lives should not be comparatively wasted.

There are many who are young and have gifts they may or may not know of, but whose lives may be largely wasted because they have lacked the fire that comes from God and through the Holy Spirit. But whatever age we are, we may yet be wasting the gifts God has given us in what time we have.

* * *

I come now to the paper and my outline of what I think is needed in my projected book. Much of the intellectual work that needs to be done in the service of faith is in the clearing away of difficulties.

However, what I am looking for first is a direct explanation of the Christian faith and dealing with difficulties will arise only incidentally. One's approach should *not* be to aim at *proving* the Christian faith. *Rather*, explaining the Christian faith should itself reveal the reason for believing it, and grasping why it commends itself to the mind in preference to other forms of religion.

In the course of this, one needs to make it explain how God is immediate to each thing as cause of its being, power, and exercise of activity, the furnace of energy which gives existence, life and vigor to whatever has them, intimate to what is innermost in each thing. One also has to explain how God's immediacy to the exercise of activity of each thing, his causal action and providence, does not eliminate either chance or free will. Further, God alone can give existence to things because he alone has existence in his own right—but this has to be explained in a coherent and nonmetaphorical way. But, once explained, it becomes clear that there is no sense in asking what caused God. Nobody in fact believes that the universe was caused by some lesser God, this lesser God by some higher God, and this by a yet higher God, and so on without a first in the series. But the reason why this suggestion is so absurd is that only what exists underivatively can give existence to anything.

There therefore cannot be any intermediates in the holding of things in existence. Hence God's immediacy or immanence is an immediate consequence of his transcendence. This will only be clear when the ideas of giving existence and God's having existence in his own right has been explained in a coherent and non-metaphorical way. These tasks are essential within faith even though they are philosophical tasks.

There is no way of approaching the faith that Jesus is divine without some understanding of what or who we mean by God. The Christian profession begins with "I believe in one *God, Father* Almighty, Creator of heaven and earth, of all things seen and unseen." The understanding of God as Father takes us beyond philosophy, and therefore I will consider God's Fatherhood when I go beyond philosophy to Faith itself and what we can only know because God has revealed, opening himself to us.

The first implication of God's being creator is that the physical universe has to be understood in the setting of an ever-unfolding development, and this temporal and causal perspective has priority over a purely physical one. Some suppose that the laws and nature of the physical universe are fundamental and see the unfolding history of the solar system, the earth, and life on earth as an accident within a wider setting of physical law and the physical universe. By contrast, this first article of the Christian Creed presents physical laws and nature as set within a cosmic history of which the history of the earth and life on earth is part.

This way of thinking has become familiar to us as we have got used to the Big Bang theory, and the working out of the stages in which our universe developed, and had earlier got used to modern conceptions of the geological and biological evolution of the earth.[2] But the ideas of

2 The Big Bang theory has not stopped physicists speculating on the possibility of the universe's history being cyclical or of its spawning over its whole history (cyclical or not) of other universes. Cyclical theories arise from the conjecture of unknowable quantum effects in proximity to the supposed

an expanding universe, then of its expansion from initial fireworks or a Big Bang theory was a novelty in the history of physics. From the time of Aristotle, Ptolemy, and Aquinas, a steady state view of the universe was dominant, and Einstein was only converted from it with extreme reluctance, a reluctance which persisted in the thinking of Fred Hoyle until his death in 2001. However, the proof of the presence of an almost perfectly uniform cosmic microwave background radiation (CMBR) in 1963 decided the question in favor of the Big Bang account, without any of the continuous creation surmised by Hoyle.

---

time of the Big Bang, my view on them was expressed in the following letter to Paul Davies:

> I was grateful for your reference in "The Mind of God" to Jaki's early discussion of cyclic theories and impressed by his later book "Science and Creation." But it does seem that people have a constant desire to revive cyclic theories, and so I have been looking into what is said about the ideas of Paul Steinhardt and Neil Turok. But there it seemed to me that Linde had some incisive criticism in 2002. And the verdict of Peter Woit of Colombia in 2007 on Turok's "Endless Universe," was that, although Turok's theory had not been disproved, nor had it been proved, and it depended upon equally unsupported assumptions derived from a certain form of string theory. As to Penrose's Nov 2010 ideas, as far as I can gather from reputable sources suggest that Penrose's supposed "circles of anomalously low variance in the cosmic microwave background (CMB)" are not statistically significant.
>
> Secondly, out of the consideration of "ambiguous locality" (such as Schrodinger's Cat suggested) has been the development of a theory of multiverses given life by Everett and Wallace as if the one universe in which we live throughout the time of its existence spawned an ever-increasing number of systems between which there is mutual ignorance (a simple consequence of increasing the number of spatial dimensions and making a few other suppositions which exclude "tunnels" between them). However, Penrose has argued that because of gravity no macroscopic or even middle-sized object can have such ambiguous locality. Therefore, it is a mistake to suppose that "ambiguous locality" such may occur on the small scale allow any universe of large mass, such as the actual universe to spawn.

Paul Davies's comment on the meaninglessness of the suppositions made about the state of affairs proximate to any big bang would be relevant to any discussion of other theories, including theories of multiverses.

One of the special features of St. Thomas's approach was to show from philosophy that the universe still had to be viewed as unfolding in time even if time had no beginning. And, because time is real, the universe would still need to be upheld in existence, receiving existence as a gift, even if there had been no beginning to this giving of existence by God. As Omar Khayyam put it: "The Moving Finger writes; and, having writ, moves on: nor all thy Piety nor Wit shall lure it back to cancel half a Line, nor all thy Tears wash out a Word of it" and this would still be true if the Moving Finger had been writing forever in the past.

This theological starting point, accepting that there are cases of one thing causing another to change, and therefore accepting the reality of temporal and causal order, were, we may recall, what St. Thomas regarded as the features of the world which made the existence of God philosophically the most manifest, not waiting upon revelation to be known.

This primary argument, from the existence of motion or change, was not in fact an argument from the existence of cases of things moving, but an argument from the existence of cases of things causing others to change or move. And his second argument, from the existence of causal order, reinforced the first. And these arguments take as their starting point, not the existence of the universe, but the conditions of any causal action at all.

In brief, for St. Thomas a realist view of causal action and a realist view of temporal order were data of experience, and reflection upon them generated a proof of God's existence—as a non-temporal first cause, meaning not a first cause in an accidental series of causes such as the series which includes Abraham begat Isaac, Isaac begat Jacob, Jacob begat Joseph, etc. Aquinas compared God to a blacksmith who can go on endlessly since when one hammer breaks, he can take another to continue his work, considerably getting through an infinity of hammers. So in his upholding the order of the world, God can use first one father and then another, in this case first Abraham, then Isaac, then Jacob and so forth, and there is no reason known to philosophy why Abraham should have a first ancestor—after all Aristotle was held to have thought that species were a constant of the universe, so that the need not have been any first human being.

THE IMMEDIACY OF GOD'S ACTIVE PRESENCE

From the theistic standpoint, the will of God as first cause gives each thing its existence, nature, and vigor in exercising this nature so that, not just the existence of created things but also their causal actions always depend upon this operation of God's primary causality.

That is, it is not just the universe that needs a first cause, but each individual action. It was in this way that Aquinas conceived God to be first cause. That is, even the individual causal actions of things in nature depend on his primary action for these things to operate at all, for it depends on him to give them existence and preserve it, and in preserving them in their nature and powers, he also supports them in the exercise of these powers. God is innermost to each thing, not only in its being or existence, but in its actions. God is the furnace which gives existence, continuance, and vigor to creatures, immediate to them in giving and sustaining them in being, and in their vigor of action.

It is important to approach things in this way, first considering what individual actions depend on before going on to consider what the existence of the universe depends on. For the universe is not an object, all of which exists at the same time—as it were a complex set in a fixed order. Rather the universe consists of the things which make it up, their actions (often undetermined), and each, from the point of view of any particular observer, has a past and a future, the future being open, and not fixed. When we speak of "the universe," we are speaking of an abstraction.

I said that it depends on God to give natural things existence and to preserve them, and in preserving them in their nature and powers, also to support them in the exercise of these powers. God, I said, is innermost to each thing, not only in its being or existence, but in its actions. But the effects of natural things exercising their natures arise from God's permission, not by his operation—but as we have seen they depend most intimately on him even when they arise by his permission, not determined by him. It is not that God operates directly in the cases where things are caused necessarily, and that permission is only involved in the case of things that happen by chance or by freewill.

Rather he has given each thing its own nature, sustaining its powers and in their exercise, in such a way that even when a thing acts by a necessity arising from its own created nature, the ultimate effects are still, examples of secondary causality, arising by permission not by direct divine operation. That is, although, in these examples of secondary causality, God genuinely "operates," supporting things in their exercise of their powers, this does not make them analogous to miracles—as when God does something which is beyond the natural powers of things, as in raising the dead, or as in accomplishing a healing with a suddenness that shows that it is not being achieved by reliance on the natural powers of things.

For God, the world is not static, but ever full of activity, its course ever unfolding, until it achieves some fulfilment. Thus, the Christian starting point envisages time as real, and as having a different status from the other dimensions. This is why St. Thomas's first argument is from the existence of motion.

It is not that every event is associated with certain coordinates, one of time and between three and ten of space, so that the dimension of time is as it were on a par with the dimensions of space, yielding a description of the world or space-time which is mathematically static. The universe could then be thought of as laid out before God with how things are spread out through time having no more significance than how things are spread out in space—the nearest image of this would be of the created world as in a state of everlasting *stasis*.

However, if the world was created, this must be a false picture. Instead, we must insist that time is real, and not only real, but has direction. What is earlier is capable of having causal effects which will come after it, but what is past is fixed and settled. By contrast, what is future does not yet exist and is therefore open. If the future remains at each juncture as yet to be fixed, then some of what happens may be wholly or in certain respects determined while some may be the issue of free will or matters of chance.

The unfolding history of the universe is indeed undetermined. For, if physical laws had been deterministic and all encompassing, then a description of one state of the universe as it stands at one time from the standpoint of one observer or succession of observers—it doesn't matter which observer—would disclose the identity of all other states at all other times for any other observer—the situation of the past and future being equivalent. This situation would be equivalent to one of *stasis*.

To this question about determinism, the quantum theory has supplied an answer: it shows that the future is not predetermined.

Therefore, chance and freewill do not have to be considered as fictions arising from the human mode of experiencing life, but integral to the way the history of the universe unfolds. We should further say that it is the openness and undeterminedness of the future which makes created nature an image of the divine freedom.

Because he, God, is act, actuality, activity (the Greek word is *energeia*) in himself, the best image of him is the one the temporal world provides, namely that of activity not of *stasis*—and only a world in which activity is undetermined can provide an image of God's being alive, as well as immediate in his presence to everything to which he gives being.

St. Thomas understands both his first two arguments as leading not just to the conclusion that there are examples of causal action, in which nothing causes itself, but to the further conclusion that there must be a first cause underlying such causal action or any series of causal actions leading up to that action. Either an action proceeds directly from a first cause, or else the action depends on a series of causes related *per se*—a series in which each action depends on the action of all its predecessors in the series acting together to achieve the effect.

Yet, in modern philosophy, nobody has the concept of a series of causes related *per se*. As a result, in modern times, arguments along Aquinas's lines are not understood because, especially since Hume, cause and effect are thought of as two events which are logically independent of one another, and between which there is absolutely no connection such as might be known *a priori*. For Aquinas, and later for Duns Scotus, these would be *accidentally related* causes.

By contrast to the modern view, in earlier times, and for Aquinas and Scotus, a cause was commonly thought of as an animate or inanimate thing which by the exercise of its active power brought about some new event in the world, and the new event would often be something which would only be specified by reference to the exercise of active power concerned, as when the weight of a heavy ball has the effect on the shape of a cushion of depressing it. Causal action and effect were not separate or logically independent.

In St. Thomas Aquinas's favorite example, a man by using his arm to exercise continued exercise of force upon a staff (a stick) might bring about the progressive movement of a stone—and perhaps if this example were amplified, then, God maintaining the existence of the mind, will, arm and its power to act, and permitting the man/will to act, the arm would be so used as,by means of the staff, to move the stone.

In Aquinas's conception there could easily be an infinite series of causes which are *accidentally related, that is in which the action of the previous causes are not internal to the action being considered*. Thus, he considers a series of causes of the same kind, each causing something to come to be, each a cause of the becoming of something, but not the cause of its being or existence as such, taking as an example a series of human fathers, Abraham begetting Isaac, Isaac begetting Jacob, Jacob begetting Joseph, and Joseph begetting Ephraim, and so forth. He compares God's role in this to that of a blacksmith able to use an unending series of hammers, so that when one wears out or becomes useless, he can take another. Firstly, God uses Abraham, then Isaac, then Jacob, then Joseph and so forth. Abraham's presence and action is not involved in Isaac's begetting Jacob, and this was not involved in Jacob's begetting Joseph. Abraham was dead when Isaac begot Jacob, and Isaac approaching death when Jacob's children were conceived.

All such cases are examples of what Thomas and others (e.g., later, Duns Scotus defines the notion) of *per se* causation in which the action of any cause later in the series is dependent on the contemporaneous action of every previous member of the series as a prior cause, that is the action of the previous members of the series is internal to the action of the last.

St. Thomas's argument to God's existence from the existence of causal order is often misunderstood. He says, "In the world of sense we find there is an order of efficient causes" and "from the nature of the efficient cause," and this is often assumed to be about efficient causes in the modern sense, namely accidentally related causes. However, on the contrary, Thomas is concerned with *per se* causes. That is, he is not arguing from our experience of series of accidentally related causes, but *from our experience of series of per se causes*, such as that of a stone being caused to move by means of man using a stick or staff.

We can see this from his argument: "in all efficient causes following in order, the first is the cause of the intermediate cause, and the intermediate is the cause of the ultimate cause, whether the intermediate cause be several, or only one. Now to take away the cause is to take away the effect. Therefore, if there be no first cause among efficient causes, there will be no ultimate, nor any intermediate cause."

This is exactly how a series of *per se* causes of an action or change works. But, if all the previous causes require a prior cause, and none has the power to cause in its own right without previous cause, then all the members of the series are of the same character, all dependent, all equally impotent in respect of initiating a movement. Yet, if the actions of the previous causes are needed *because their action is internal to the action or change whose explanation is being sought*, then nothing will happen because, *ex hypothesi*, none of them can initiate an effect independently. Therefore, the efficacy of any such series of *per se* causes depends on there being a first cause, prior to the supposed series of dependent causes, a prior cause which can cause in its own right without previous cause—a cause of a different kind from the intermediate causes, each of which was impotent, because incapable of initiating an effect without dependence on some prior cause.

As I said, for St. Thomas God is the furnace which gives existence, continuance, and vigor to creatures, immediate to them in giving and sustaining them in being. He alone possesses existence in his own right and underivatively, and there can be only one such being. And St. Thomas here follows in the tradition set by the prophets in the Old Testament and in the fathers of the Church.

That the world needs a cause, and indeed that any action causing change has to be by means of powers given by God, are things that St. Thomas thinks can be appreciated by reason.

Whenever Christians, Jews or Muslims argue that the universe must have a cause, and this is God, the response immediately comes "and why didn't God have to have a cause?" if the universe has to have a cause. And until one has grasped that God alone can give existence because he alone has existence in his own right, one fails to see why it is that there can be no distance between God and us in his sustaining us in existence, his action in sustaining us in existence is more immediate to us then the action of our throbbing hearts to our being sustained in existence. As St. Thomas says, "God is innermost to everything as cause of its being" (Q.VIII, Art. 1).

God alone can give existence or being and alone can continue this action in sustaining things in being. In St. Thomas's comparison, if the Sun ceased to give light, there would instantaneously be no light in the air or space intervening between the Sun and nothing would be lit up. It is not that they would gradually become dark but they would become dark instantaneously—for the purpose of his exposition he is contrasting radiation with other means of supplying energy. This striking analogy treats the Sun as if it had light in its own right in the way God has existence in his own right—only an analogy because the Sun does not have light in its own right since the Sun and its nature as creatures exist only derivatively—but parallel to the case of God's giving being in the lack of dependence on intermediates. The preservation of things by God is a continuation of that action whereby He gives existence, which action is without either motion or time; so also the preservation of light in the air is by the continual influence of the sun.

We have to distinguish between the fact that God exists (what is stated in the proposition "God exists") and his activity or act of existing. If we ask whether God exists, and give the affirmative answer that he does exist, then we have first the fact or truth that he does exist, and this is often what the expression God's existence or *esse* refers to. However, what matters for the present discussion is God's act of being or *actus essendi*, that is God's *esse* or existing as the reality, act, actuality, or activity which makes it true that God exists. God is one reality, one act, actuality, or activity (the Greek word is *energeia*), so that in his act of existing he lives, understands, knows, and loves. His acts of existing, of living, of understanding, of knowing, of loving, of willing, and of having active power, are not so many distinct acts, but one act, one activity, one actuality, in what is called his simplicity. (I follow St. Thomas's presentation.)

This act or activity of existing, of living, of understanding, of loving, this single simple reality, is what he understands in understanding himself, in no way something distinct from his essence or nature. The essence or nature of a thing is precisely what there is to be understood in understanding its being, or what it is, its nature as the principle of its activity.

Since creatures do not exist by necessity, their existence is the actualization of the potentiality that there should exist something of that nature or essence. By contrast, God's existence is not the actualization of a potentiality which might or might not have been actualized—if it had been, then there would have been something that caused him to exist, caused this potentiality to be actualized, rather than leaving it unactualized. But God's nature or essence is not abstract or a mere potentiality which could be actualized or not actualized, or actualized more than once, because it is identical with the single simple actuality which is his act or activity of existing, of living, of understanding, of loving.

Therefore, whenever it is asked "and why didn't God have to have a cause?," the answer lies in this identity of his activity of being and his essence—his essence consists, not in a potentiality which could be realized or not realized, or realized more than once, but in this already existing single simple reality. This is what is involved in "having existence in his own right."

Such is the furnace which gives and sustains existence and vigor in creation, immediate in his presence to everything to which he gives being and vigor. Yet, at the same time, in having existence in his own right he utterly transcends us in nature. But, as we noted earlier, because he is act, actuality, activity in himself, the best image of him is the one the temporal world provides, namely that of activity not *stasis*—and only a world in which activity is undetermined could provide an image of God's being a living actuality.

So, when St. Thomas defines what it is for God to be eternal it is his perfect possession of the whole of his limitless life all-in-one-act. It is not that he possesses his whole life in an instant, where an instant is a like a dividing point in a line without length, and within which nothing can take place. As St. Thomas says, God's present is not the now of time meaning this now which divides time. Rather, God's present is the now of an action.[3] For God's life is act, actuality, activity in himself, present everywhere in time and space giving being to temporal things, but not itself a temporal thing.

Because human beings are capable of reflection, both on their own existence and nature, and their situation in the universe, an animal

3 In this way, our human seeing of things moving is an act or activity—to see something moving is not to see it at one time first at one place, and then at a later time to see it as being at a different place, but in one act or activity to see it as moving over a stretch of space. In a yet clearer case, to have the thought "Heavens! The post has gone!," is not like sequentially thinking "Heavens!," "The post," " Has," "gone!"

among other animals, but also an intellectual being among other intellectual beings, and reflect on how they came to be and on the cause of the existence and continuance of the whole system of which they are part, they occupy a unique place in this system.

For as St. Augustine says everything by its existence expresses praise of God, its cause and the cause of all things, but it has no voice until the human beings can speak representatively for it. It is mad to suppose that God made the whole material and biological system of the world just to scrap it—rather its whole structure seems to be such as to make sense only if it makes possible the development of rational animals so that in the setting of this material and biological world rationality and spirituality should arise.[4] It would then seem mad to suppose that he made the whole material and biological system of the world just to extract this rational and spiritual element and then to scrap the rest.

Yet this is what some modern Christians have supposed—as if for them as to Plato and for some of his followers it is only the soul that matters, and the body not at all. So, to these Christians it does not matter whether or not Jesus tomb was empty, whether or not he did indeed eat and drink with his Apostles, whether or not Thomas could indeed put his finger into Jesus wounds in his hands and side, but mattered only that Jesus should have appeared or been experienced as alive in some way.

We see here a temporary triumph of philosophical idealism and romanticism—where what matters is only feelings and experiences, and these are thought of in Descartes' way as a species of *pensée*. The body has lost its importance in this way of thinking, and the whole Jewish, New Testament and Patristic way of thinking of human beings as essentially bodily and not just spiritual beings has been set aside.

Yet human beings are by nature psycho-physical beings and not pure spirits—and it was in order than such beings could exist that, in the perspective of Genesis Chapter 1, the whole of physical and biological creation was made. The problem "what is the human being"

4 Paul Davies, *The Goldilocks Enigma: Why Is the Universe Just Right for Life?* (London: Allen Lane, 2006; Penguin, 2007) in an extended discussion (pp. 260 – 92) coming to this conclusion.

raises questions which need to be considered at the philosophical level, just as the problems of "what is God" and even "is there a God?" constitute philosophical issues. This is important for the understanding of Christianity because Jesus is understood to be truly human as well as truly divine.

But philosophy has its limits. In Shakespeare's perspective, as we age, we reach the sixth and seventh stage:

The sixth age shifts

Into the lean and slippered pantaloon,

With spectacles on nose and pouch on side;

His youthful hose, well saved, a world too wide

For his shrunk shank; and his big manly voice,

Turning again toward childish treble, pipes

And whistles in his sound. Last scene of all,

That ends this strange eventful history,

Is second childishness and mere oblivion,

Sans teeth, sans eyes, sans taste, sans everything.

For in death, we are "sans everything"—which is why it is that we should live in hope of the resurrection, a restoration of complete human beings with all our faculties brought to fulfillment.

So far as philosophy can hint, it is only of a continuance of the human soul without capacity to exercise its faculties except by some preternatural or supernatural gift.

However, the Christian Creeds take us beyond anything philosophy might register. Firstly, these Creeds profess God, not just as Creator but also as Father, implying an intimate care for us, an opening out of the fullest friendship (there are many words translated "friend" in English, but what is concerned here is "being what is most dear," i.e., being *carus* in Latin. In these Creeds, we are taught and profess belief in God, not just as Creator but also as Father, and the meaning of this is to be understood in terms of God's being Father of the "one Lord Jesus Christ" of whom the Creed goes on to speak. For the Creed continues:

> and in one Lord Jesus Christ, the only-begotten Son of God, begotten of the Father before all worlds; God of God, Light of Light, true God of true God; begotten, not made, being of one substance with the Father, by whom all things were made, who, for us men for our salvation, came down from heaven, and was incarnate by the Holy Spirit of the virgin Mary, and was made man; and was crucified also for us under Pontius Pilate, suffered death and was buried, and on the third day rose again ..., and ascended into heaven, and is seated at the right hand of the Father.

Now pause. What is this, then, that one who is God from God, of one being with the God the Creator, should become man for our sake and for the sake of our salvation? We should observe that this second paragraph of the Creed gives an unforeseen content to the notion of God as Father. For this describing God as Father is not just a metaphor for his general relation to creation and to the personal beings within it, but primarily a reference to his relation to the one Lord Jesus Christ who is spoken of as his Son.

It is only at a second stage, in virtue of his Son's becoming man for the sake of our salvation, that he can become Father of those who are thereby brothers and sisters of his Son in virtue of his humanity. As Athanasius put it "God became man in order that man should be made divine," that is, as the second Epistle of Peter puts it, "should become partakers of divine nature, or in St. John's words "should have eternal life"[5] As it were, God entered into solidarity with us, sharing our nature and our frailty, in order that we should be able to enter into solidarity with him. This we are told is through the action of the Holy Spirit in giving us grace to become sons and daughters of God by adoption, more intimately brothers and sisters of Jesus.

All this about Jesus as Son from eternity, and about the Holy Spirit, and their part in our coming into relationship with God is entirely beyond philosophy, to be known by Revelation only. Perhaps, as I suggested, it is within the reach of philosophical reflection that cosmic history should be directed towards the emergence of creatures able to reflect upon themselves, the world and the cause of both of their existence and that of the world, whether in one or many different places in the universe. But it is quite a different matter that God should

5 Athanasius, *De Incarnatione* 54:3: *PG* 25, 192B quoted in CCC 460.

aim to relate to these creatures in such a way that he should be their Father and through the work of his Son and the Holy Spirit, that they should be able to share his own life—that the consummation of the life of creatures should be being taken up into the fire and light of the divine life.

We have to consider what salvation really is. It is not just being made freed from moral wrong and the sense of guilt from past moral wrong, so as to be at ease in human society and not in fear before God. Of course, salvation includes being made free from such sin, and more generally free from sin in the aspect of failing to love God with all our heart and mind, preferring other things to him and his will, especially by failing to love our neighbor as ourself. But salvation goes beyond this; it is not just the negative of being made free from sin, but the positive of sharing the divine life.

This theme of our becoming divinized, partakers of divine nature, having eternal life, recurs in all the Eastern Fathers, Gregory Nazianzen, Gregory of Nyssa and onwards, as well as in the Western patristic tradition. This is said while all the time insisting that this does not mean that human beings become God in his role in creation from the beginning, or in his infinity.

If Jesus were just a supernatural being intermediate between God and Man like the angels it would be impossible for him to communicate intimacy between God and Man, an intimacy whereby we are to share the divine life. In this intimacy we are all to be adopted sons and daughters alongside Jesus, who before he became truly man, was already Son of God, Word of the Father through whom all things were made and are kept in being. The Word took flesh (enfleshed) late in time in order to open out this possibility of our sharing the divine life. By using the theologically now technical term "incarnate" from the Latin *incarnatus*, we hide the connotation of stark carnality of the Latin *incarnatus* and the Greek *sarkōthenta*.

That is, it is quite a different matter that such creatures should enter into intimacy with God, even so as to be in a friendship with God, a friendship to be consummated by our entry into the divine life so as to enjoy the vision of God himself. For, in Christian belief, Jesus's Resurrection was not just a matter of his being restored to bodily life, but to this bodily life having a quite new character, seen in his ascension or being taken up into heaven, what John's Gospel and St.

Paul refer to as his glorification. This meant that by his Resurrection and Ascension he gave Heaven a human and bodily dimension, making it a place open to us to enter in. All these are matters quite outside the reach of philosophical knowledge.

Modern man thinks that religion does not matter, not because he has ceased to believe in Hell, but because he has lost any conception of what Heaven might be. As Dante expresses the idea of the beatific vision:

I saw, above the many thousand lamps,
a Sun that kindled each and every one
as ours lights up the sights we see above us,
and through that living light poured down
a shining substance. It blazed so bright
into my eyes that I could not sustain it.
O Beatrice, my sweet beloved guide!
To me she said: "What overwhelms you
is a force against which there is no defense.
Here is the Wisdom and the Power that repaired
the roads connecting Heaven and the earth
that had so long been yearned for and desired.

(Paradiso, Canto XXIII, vv. 28 – 39)

As Kierkegaard shows, no wondrousness of teaching, no miracles however great, no impact on history, no human demonstration of love could prove the Divinity of Christ, since there is here no argument from the finite to the infinite (cf. *Training in Christianity*, pp. 26 – 39).

These are matters which could only be known by God's own initiative in a free act of Revelation. In opening such friendship, God not only acts, for instance, becoming man, dying on a cross and rising again, opening the way to heaven, but also tells us what he has done and intends to do.

God then has created a world directed towards the emergence of reflective life in rational animals, but what pointers are there to his intending friendship with these animals? Friendship commonly implies some kind of equality. Therefore, how can we speak of friendship between human beings and God, since there is no equality between them?

In Christian understanding, this kind of relationship was made possible by God's becoming man, Jesus, son of the Father, taking on human nature, so as to be truly man as well as truly God, Son of God, begotten of his Father from eternity, and being the one through whom everything from the beginning was created and has been sustained in existence, and late in time made man, through the power of the Holy Spirit conceived and born of the virgin Mary. Thus, God entered into solidarity with human beings, like other human beings growing from the womb, being born, maturing and living a life subject to trials and injuries like other human beings, even to the extent of being judicially executed, in order that human beings might enter into solidarity with God.

In order to get some sense of how the Incarnation can achieve our redemption, we have to consider what goes on in human life. It is not the concern of this paper to find why God has allowed so much moral and natural evil to exist. However, the scale of such evil, at its center the evils related to the very facts of injury, disease, and death amongst all living things,[6] death in its universality, and a datum even in otherwise happy human lives, makes it plain that the aim of God in creating the world was not the natural happiness of man and women in this life.

Yet all this evil is but a little thing in comparison with mankind's being brought to enjoy God's immediate presence in eternal life. Whatever is good in creation and in human life owes this goodness to some likeness to God. Accordingly, there is no way in which human

6 It is traditional to ascribe the scale of this evil, affecting all living things where it is seen in evolutionary history in the part played by mass extinctions of species, to God's will to grant, not only human beings, but before them the angels freedom of will or *voluntas*, even so as to love their own autonomy in preference to friendship with God, and do this without having originally intended influence over the rest of creation reduced. It should be noted that St. Augustine's concept of *voluntas* was closer to that of love or holding dear (*carus*, the root from which the word *caritas* derives), and less narrow than that of *arbitrium*.

beings could come to eternal life unless they had been prepared for it by being brought to love God before all things. For unless we love God before all things and have not first fixed our love on something less than God, to be in God's presence would be to be burnt.[7]

Now, there is no way in which God could bring human beings to himself by acts of power, or by just creating them in a state of already loving God, or infusing love without any willingness or disposition or preparation on the side of man. For this human love for God has to be given willingly—it has to be an act of human *voluntas*.[8]

This then was the reason why God took on human flesh, became man not in a style or form reflective of his divinity, but as St. Paul says, in the form of a servant or slave, born in a manger, his first visitors being shepherds (indeed, even the royal style of earthly courts would be useless in reflecting his divinity—his most ceremonial act was entry into Jerusalem on a donkey).

He came in a hidden humble way, and as he was born, so he lived, not as one of the rich but as a carpenter, and then in his ministry in poverty as a person of no fixed abode, and by his mode of relationship with others, his love shown in healing the sick, his teaching, so that he could say when I am lifted up on the cross, I will draw all men unto myself. And it is only this way of living, and the love shown in dying for mankind, and its imitation by some of his followers that draws human beings to the love which makes eternal life possible for them.

It is vital to appreciate that for Jesus the son of God to be made man in the womb of the Virgin was not the beginning of an episode in Jesus's life which ended at the Ascension, but the beginning of the taking on of human nature for all time, so to be with us as man as well as God everlastingly. He is therefore ever present in the life of the world and in the lives of Christians in his continuing manhood.

7 In Western theological tradition, it is by the mercy of God that those who reject God are separated from this vision, to avoid thus being burnt. In Eastern Orthodox theology, it is said that to be in God's presence thus fixed on lesser things and thus to be burnt is the experience of Hell.

8 The mistake which John Rist seeks to identify is to think of the freedom that matters as something issuing from a prior *arbitrium* (*electio*), rather thinking of this election as the expression or fruit of a prior love. The problem emerges when St. Thomas describes *dilection* as implying, in addition to love, a choice [*electionem*] made beforehand (II-I, q. 26, art. 3, *in corp*).

And this is part of the significance of the Eucharist, that, in it, it is by his being personally present, body, blood, soul, and divinity, that he concretizes his presence to Christians, and makes the offering of the sacrifice of the cross really his own offering of himself each time the Liturgy of the Mass is celebrated, not repeated but made present in such a way that we should be invited to join in it offering ourselves with him. This is the root of the obligation to attend Mass and assist in it, entering into its spirit as much as we can.

Some people think of the life of prayer as a matter of private devotion, even though when we pray privately the whole company of heaven is present with us. But the Christian has the obligation not only of private devotion, but also (so far as he or she is able) of joining with the Church in the public Liturgy of the Mass, in which alone by the authority of Christ the priest makes Jesus present Body, Blood, Soul and Divinity in such a way that the Church can enter into his offering of himself. This is not something which the individual Christian can do in private. But it is something done on behalf of the Church, including ourselves and for all mankind, living and dead. By entering into the Mass, really and spiritually, or if we cannot receive at least spiritually, we are nourished with divine life. This concretizes Jesus's promise, "I will be with you always to the end of history." Whenever Jesus is present in his humanity, it is by the power of the Holy Spirit.

This is especially important in regard to what is called by different traditions, the Eucharist, the Divine Liturgy, the Mass. The word Eucharist means "the thanksgiving" which is the name given in the early Church to this central part of the Church's worship—this was in continuity with the Jewish synagogue tradition but transformed by what is presented to God in memorial, namely the death, Resurrection and glorification of Jesus the Son of God, body, blood, soul, and divinity. By it, the death which was offered for our salvation, "my body given for you," is presented in memorial with thanksgiving again to God. But it is only by the action of the Holy Spirit that he is indeed made present again, so that we might in community join again in this offering, and by this body be spiritually fed and nourished to strengthen and enliven us in continuing in the Christian life of love of God and love of neighbor. We can say our prayers privately, and whenever two or three are gathered together, Jesus is there in the midst of them. But it is in the public Eucharist that Jesus is present most concretely in a way which conforms to his being truly resurrected and alive in the body, although because glorified present to us, as it is said "body and blood, soul and Divinity," only in an indivisible way.

This concrete presence in the community of Christians is made possible by the action of ministers who have authority to consecrate bread and wine, first to transform them into the body and blood of Christ, making him present in his wholeness, body and blood, soul and divinity, so that glorified in Heaven he is present here in the Church in an invisible way, known only by faith. No self-choosing group of Christians can confer this authority, but only a commission derived from the Apostles—such was the tradition which Christians received in the same period that they received the New Testament. For they were not given the New Testament except through its recognition by the Church rooted in what the Apostles handed over or passed on (the "tradition of the Apostles"), and the same tradition envisages both teaching authority in the Church and authority to act in Christ's name in celebrating the Eucharist as passed on through a commission coming from the Apostles....

INDEX